AUGUSTINE TO FREUD

WHAT THEOLOGIANS & PSYCHOLOGISTS
TELL US ABOUT HUMAN NATURE
{ AND WHY IT MATTERS }

KENNETH BOA

BROADMAN
&HOLMAN
PUBLISHERS

NASHVILLE, TENNESSEE

0-8054-3146-2

Published by Broadman & Holman Publishers
Nashville, Tennessee

Dewey Decimal Classification: 253.5
Subject Heading: CHRISTIANITY—PSYCHOLOGY \
PASTORIAL PSYCHOLOGY

Unless otherwise noted, Scripture quotations are from the RSV, Revised Standard
Version of the Bible, copyrighted 1946, 1952, © 1971, 1973.

1 2 3 4 5 6 7 8 09 08 07 06 05 04

To the memory of my mother and father.

CONTENTS

INTRODUCTION

During construction of Emerson Hall at Harvard University, president Charles Eliot invited the renowned psychologist William James to suggest a suitable inscription for the stone lintel over the doors of the new home of the philosophy department.

After some reflection, James sent Eliot a line from the Greek philosopher Protagoras: "Man is the measure of all things."

James never heard back from Eliot, so his curiosity was piqued when he spotted artisans working on a scaffold hidden by a canvas. One morning, the scaffold and canvas were gone. The inscription? "What is man that you are mindful of him, the son of man that you care for him?"

Eliot had replaced James's suggestion with words from Psalm 8:4. Between these two lines lies the great distance between the God-centered and human-centered points of view. They are the distance between light and darkness, hope and despair, even life and death.

As members of the human family, all of us live with certain assumptions about our own nature—about what it is to be an embodied self in this world. These assumptions, often unarticulated or held uncritically, will have a profound influence on the course of our lives and destiny. People are inherently on a quest to satisfy what they perceive to be their fundamental needs, and this raises two questions: (1) What are these needs? (2) Where do we seek to fulfill them? To answer these questions, we will explore what six great theologians and eight great psychologists have said about human nature and human needs.

Concerning the first question, *Augustine to Freud* will compare theological and psychological accounts of human needs to identify areas of overlap (convergence) and areas of contrast (divergence). The three areas of convergence in the thought of the six theologians are the need for forgiveness and grace, the need for love and community, and the need for purpose and hope. In spite of significant areas of divergence among the eight personality theorists, an area of convergence is found in the observation that each of these psychologists has something to say about four basic areas of human needs: survival needs, identity needs, relational needs, and ideological needs. Despite the differences in presuppositions, vocabulary, and proposed solutions to the satisfaction of these needs, there is a correspondence between the theological models and the psychological models.

Concerning the second question, we will discover a significant divergence between the theological and psychological accounts. This is because the human quest for fulfillment relates to the issue of worldview: Where did we come from (origin)? Why are we here (purpose)? Where are we going (destiny)? The psychologists in this book largely embraced a naturalistic worldview, though some (Jung, Maslow, and Rogers) were moving toward a more monistic worldview late in their careers. By contrast, the theologians in this book affirmed a theistic worldview, though Tillich's understanding of God was unconventional. The answer to the question of where we seek to fulfill our fundamental needs is radically different for naturalists and theists. The former must look to the created order, while the latter look to the Creator.

In part 3 of this book, I will argue that it is through bonds of commitment to others that people become fully human and that the true source of unconditional commitment in self-giving love is not the organismic self-actualization tendency but the unconditional love, acceptance, and forgiveness of God. When people love God completely (above all other loves, and for himself, not for his gifts), they become capable of loving themselves correctly (seeing themselves as God sees them—forgiven, beloved of God, children of light) and loving others compassionately (with selfless *caritas*). The more clearly they discover that their needs for identity, love, and hope are met in Christ, the freer they are to love and serve others unconditionally. They are no longer bound to manipulate relationships in the quest for need fulfillment, since it is their Creator and Redeemer who satisfies their needs for security and significance.

The brief introductions to part 1 and part 2 explain why I selected the six theologians and the eight psychologists for this study. There I explain why these writers combine to provide good representative models of human nature from the theological and psychological perspectives.

The thesis of this book is developed in part 3, and it is that theology must be primary and prior to psychology, since naturalistic approaches to psychology unsuccessfully seek to explain away or ignore human needs for transcendence, significance, and moral certainty. I will argue that because the acute perceptions concerning human traits and behavior that are developed by the personality theorists are embedded in a reductionistic worldview, the solutions the psychologists offer are comparatively superficial. Emancipation from belief in the transcendent does not bring happiness; it brings either despair or denial of creatureliness. Without God, people are limited to finite meanings and substitute ends in a milieu of resignation, escapism, or futile attempts to create absolutes within a bounded condition. But the ineradicable longing for mystery, majesty, dignity, hope, and transcendent power cannot be found in the identities, relationships, and secular ideologies of the world. The yearning for ecstasy and awe remain and can only be satisfied in an unbounded personal context of faith, hope, and love. In the Christian vision, death is not extinction, but the birth canal into a larger world in which the whole person—body, soul, and spirit—will be transformed and completed in an unlimited future of unending felicity. Because of the image of God, humans manifest a transcendence within immanence which no earthbound source of identity, purpose, or hope can fully satisfy. As some of the psychologists observed, being is indeed more fundamental than doing; but one's sense of being, identity, and personhood must be defined by God and not the world.

Paul Tillich divided the interrelated anxieties of human existence into three categories: the anxiety of fate and death, the anxiety of meaningless and emptiness, and the anxiety of guilt. For the psychologists, these are fundamental problems that must be assuaged through treatment. For the theologians, these are consequences of the image of God that has been distorted through the fall. God uses this existential angst to draw us back to himself, since our hearts are restless until they find their rest in him.

A Brief Overview

This book is an adaptation of my D. Phil. (Doctor of Philosophy) thesis at The University of Oxford that was completed in 1994. In a future edition of this book, I wish to add references to secondary resources that have been published in the last few years. However, I want to stress that the conclusions in *Augustine to Freud* are based on the primary resources of the writings of the theologians and psychologists rather than the secondary resources.

The purpose of this book is to compare and contrast what selected theologians and psychologists have written about the nature of human needs in order to discover the extent to which the two accounts can be synthesized. This involves three convergence/divergence studies: six theologians, eight psychologists representing two basic models of personality theory, and the theological and psychological accounts of human needs that emerge from the first two studies.

Part 1 is concerned with theological accounts of human needs. This involves a study of what six significant figures in the continuing Christian tradition (Augustine, Aquinas, Edwards, Kierkegaard, Tillich, and Rahner) have written about the nature of human needs. After a critique of the theologians, this part concludes with a comparison and contrast of the theological models.

Part 2 develops psychological accounts of human needs by examining the work of eight psychologists who represent a conflict model (Freud, Erikson, Jung, and Rank) and a fulfillment model (Maslow, Rogers, Adler, and Fromm) of the personality. This is followed by a critique of the psychologists and a comparison and contrast of the psychological models.

Part 3 considers the metaphysical and moral assumptions held by the eight psychologists, psychological accounts of theism and theological accounts of nontheism, the role of human needs in the justification of religious belief, the problem of self-interest and self-love, and a contrast between immanent and transcendent solutions to human needs. The comparison and contrast of the theological and psychological models regarding human needs also touches on cognate areas like the question of goodness in human nature, the source of morality, the purpose of life, and the quest for meaning in view of the reality of death.

—Kenneth Boa
Easter, 2004

PART 1:
THEOLOGICAL ACCOUNTS
OF HUMAN NEEDS

Part 1 will look at what selected figures in the continuing Christian tradition (Augustine, Aquinas, Edwards, Kierkegaard, Tillich, and Rahner) have written about the nature of human needs. These theologians were chosen because of their anthropological insights and the profound influence they have exerted on Christian thought. They also represent a significant diversity of historical, theological, and philosophical perspectives. Augustine, Aquinas, and Rahner epitomize the seminal thinkers of the ancient, medieval, and modern Roman Catholic Church. Edwards, Kierkegaard, and Tillich illustrate different aspects of post-Reformation Protestant theology from the eighteenth to the twentieth century. Edwards represents a strongly Calvinistic perspective; Kierkegaard remained a Lutheran though he was a vehement critic of its institutionalism; and Tillich exemplifies twentieth-century Protestant liberalism.

Karl Barth was not included in this study because his theocentric theology, as a reaction against the anthropocentric theology of liberalism, led him to such a radical view of total depravity that he saw no point of contact between the grace of Christianity and the human need for God. Religion, as a quest for God, is a human artifact, whereas revelation creates the conditions of its own reception. Barth had limited interest in human needs apart from faith since he believed that aspirations of transcendence have little to do with the God who is absolutely free.

CHAPTER 1
THEOLOGICAL MODELS OF HUMAN NEEDS

Augustine

While Augustine is generally regarded from a theological and literary standpoint as the greatest of the Latin church fathers,[1] his teaching in some areas, particularly human sexuality and predestinarian theology, have disturbed many who have otherwise appreciated his genius. The bulk of his work was not written in a spirit of academic detachment but in response to practical concerns. In his *Confessions,* he used his own life as a case history to illustrate the nature of man, and this and other books "have remarkable affinities with the language of later mystics."[2] Augustine was more a personality than a system-maker,[3] and there is a considerable amount of discursiveness, change, and development in his extensive literary output. His early writings were strongly influenced by Neoplatonism, particularly through the *Enneads* of Plotinus, but this influence gradually subsided through Augustine's growing understanding of the Scriptures.[4] By 396 when he became sole bishop of Hippo, his views on most theological issues were largely developed, though his anthropology continued to be shaped in the following years because of his role in the Pelagian controversy.[5]

Augustine's nine-year immersion in Manichaean doctrine made it difficult, in the first years after his conversion, for him to develop a clear account of the soul's distinction from God. He had to repudiate the Manichaean claim of the unity of the soul with God, but in his early theory of man, he spoke in terms of the soul's "divinity." Bonner argues that Augustine did not use this term to imply that the soul was divine by nature but to characterize the grace of adoption into sonship with God through the merits of Christ.[6] However, O'Connell contends that after Augustine clarified his position on the soul's distinction from God, he repudiated any phrases that insinuated the divinity of the soul.[7]

With increasing clarity, Augustine accentuated the profound difference between the Creator and the created, but he was also concerned with the doctrine of the image of God in man. This theme, the "cornerstone of augustinian anthropology,"[8] is an underlying current that flows through his writings. **Augustine develops the polarity between the depths into which humanity has fallen through sin and the heights into which humanity can be raised by the redemptive grace of God. The possibilities of human life are immense, but the actual human condition of alienation from God renders these possibilities unattainable apart from divine grace.**[9] In his early thought, Augustine regarded the image of God as annihilated by Adamic sin, but he later came to the position that there is a vestigial image in man, the darkened and distorted remnant of the prefall image.[10] In *De Trinitate*, he portrays the psychological image of the Trinity in the inner man, consisting in self-memory, self-knowledge, and self-love.[11] This image provides the potential basis for remembering, knowing, and loving God when it is renewed and referred to God.[12] The image "lost righteousness and true holiness by sinning, through which that image became defaced and tarnished; and this it recovers when it is formed again and renewed."[13]

It is through the redemptive work of Christ that the deformed image of God in man is reformed and restored. "God's love in forgiveness re-creates His own image in the sinner," so that redemption is in fact a new creation, "restoring in sinful man the love toward God which he had lost."[14] **The life, death, and resurrection of the incarnate Christ is the basis for the reformation of the divine image; as man was created in Adam, so he must be recreated in Christ.** The Image of the Father became flesh, and in his kenosis and exaltation Christ has opened the way "that we may be refashioned after the image of God."[15] But this reformation does not take place all at once; there is an initial renewal, followed by a gradual process of renewal and a final renewal.[16] The Christian life is a movement toward conformity with the divine exemplar,[17] but it will not be perfect until the state of beatitude in the resurrection body. "When the resurrection of the body has taken place we shall be freed from our temporal condition, and shall enjoy eternal life in ineffable charity and with a constancy that knows no corruption."[18] "For the likeness of God will then be perfected in this image, when the sight of God shall be perfected."[19] The mature Augustine no longer viewed the body as "the ground of existential alienation" but affirmed the whole person, body and soul as a unity of activity, on the basis of his later understanding of the incarnation.[20] Augustine came to accept the Pauline eschatological tension between the present process and the future fulfillment.[21]

An important feature of Augustinian anthropology is his analysis of the sin that led to and derives from the distortion of the image of God in man. Even in his early writings, he maintained that "all sins are included in this one class, viz. turning away from things which are divine and truly abiding, and turning to things which are changeable and uncertain."[22] The soul sins when it has "abandoned the higher things and prefers to enjoy lower things."[23] As he put it in his *Confessions,* "My sin was this, that I looked for pleasure, beauty, and truth not in him but in myself and his other creatures, and the search led me instead to pain, confusion, and error."[24] Sin is the love and pursuit of the creature in place of the Creator; it is also a revolt against God and a refusal to accept one's status as a creature by making his own desires the center of his existence.[25] **"Not the being of the self, nor its desire to know and enjoy, are evil: its *preference* of its own being and of the knowledge and enjoyment of things temporal, to the one eternal Good, is what constitutes sin."[26]**

Since Augustine adopted Plotinus's doctrine that evil is a privation of right order in the created will,[27] he affirmed that "to the extent that man turns away from God, who is perfect being and goodness, he becomes less good and more evil."[28] Burnaby summarizes this position: "The pride of man is evil because it is the 'privation of good,' self-severance from the love of God: it is punishable because it is revolt against the universal Order."[29] The gift of free will was abused in the disobedience of Genesis 3 when man turned away from the source of his own being. After the fall, humanity lost the ability to please God; the bondage of sin reduced human freedom to choices between sins. The self-destructiveness of sin is due to a wound in the nature of those who oppose God's rule.[30] Those who receive God's grace are freed from their bondage to sin, but this liberation is only partial in this life.[31] By the gift of the Holy Spirit, they are able not to sin, but it will not be until their bodies are resurrected that they will be not able to sin. Thus, "the true freedom of the will that is to be attained in heaven will be different from—and even better than—the first freedom of the will that men possessed before the Fall."[32]

Because of fallen humanity's slavery to sin, the greatest human need is the grace of God whereby forgiveness and restoration from spiritual death are granted. "[T]he grace of God liberates man from the misery inflicted on sinners, because man was able to fall of his own accord, that is, by free will, but was not able to rise of his own accord."[33] Humanity is powerless to restore the distorted image; the gulf between the holy, transcendent God and sinful, contingent creatures cannot be bridged from the human side. Divine grace is necessary before a person can even begin to will to love God.[34]

> But mortals cannot live righteously and piously unless the will itself
> is liberated by the grace of God from the servitude to sin into which it
> has fallen, and is aided to overcome its vices. Unless this divine liber-
> ating gift preceded the good will, it would be the reward of its merits
> and would not be grace, which is grace precisely because it is freely
> given.[35]

Augustine's experience of the character of grace in 396 was reflected in the primary theme of his *Confessions*. It is not until people recognize their absolute dependence for their salvation upon the unmerited favor of God that the delusionary pride of self-effort is overcome.[36] This was the thrust of Augustine's anti-Pelagian writings: "The Pelagians are a new brand of heretics who assert the freedom of the will in such a way as to leave no room for the grace of God, since they say it is given to us according to our merits."[37] Without the direct intervention of God's grace, the natural man has no hope of redemption.[38]

The basis of redemption is the work of the incarnate Word; "the Word of God descend[ed] to man, so that man might in turn ascend to God."[39] **"I began to search**

for a means of gaining the strength I needed to enjoy you, but I could not find this means until I embraced the mediator between God and men, Jesus Christ. . . ."[40] Augustine's search was borne out of a need to know the truth, and this need was satisfied in his encounter with God in Christ. "[S]ince the chief good is recognized to be truth and is possessed when truth is possessed, and truth is wisdom, in wisdom let us discern the chief good and possess it and enjoy it."[41] Without the knowledge of the truth, Augustine could not attain the happiness he longed for.[42] This knowledge is preceded by a process of purgation of corporeal and sensual images; since the rational mind is the site of the image of God,[43] the mind must see and know itself so that one can "perceive his true nature as an image of God."[44] In this way, self-knowledge is a preparation for knowing God.

Miles observes: "It was Augustine who first brought to conscious realization and painstaking systematic articulation the task of reuniting soul and body, that is, of uniting consistent intellectual formulation with the deepest human longing."[45] As God is sought with both the mind and the heart, he gives the seeker a growing capacity for him:

> He whom we need to discover is concealed, in order to be sought after; and when found, is infinite, in order still to be the object of our search. . . . For He satisfies the seeker to the utmost of his capacity; and makes the finder still more capable, that he may seek to be filled anew, according to the growth of his ability to receive.[46]

"It is good for us that our reach should exceed our grasp, that enjoyment should never quench desire."[47] **It is essential that people become aware of their need for God and that more than anything else they long for him.** Burnaby argues that contra Nygren, Eros and Agape are not antithetic. "[I]f God has given Himself to men in Christ, it is because men need Him, and that consciousness of the need, so far from being an obstacle to acceptance of the gift, is its necessary condition."[48] Both the soul and the body are in need of being raised again, "For each of the two was dead; the body by weakness, the soul by iniquity."[49] Therefore, to the extent that people look to themselves, to others, and to the things of this world to satisfy their craving for joy and peace, to that degree they turn their eyes away from the true source of happiness.[50] The potentiality for human happiness can only be satisfied by the One who created it.[51]

> The simple truth is that the bond of a common nature makes all human beings one. Nevertheless, each individual in this community is driven by his passions to pursue his private purposes. Unfortunately, the objects of these purposes are such that no one person (let alone, the world community) can ever be wholly satisfied. The reason for this is that nothing but Absolute Being can satisfy human nature.[52]

When a person turns away from the unity of God, the "multitude of temporal forms" leads to a host of lesser needs:

> [F]or he pursues one thing after another, and nothing remains permanently with him. So what with his corn and wine and oil, his needs are so multiplied that he cannot find the one thing needful, a single and unchangeable nature, seeking which he would not err, and attaining which he would cease from grief and pain.[53]

In *The City of God,* Augustine gives an exposition of Marcus Varro's observation of four ends which men naturally pursue: sensory pleasure, calm or serenity, the combination of pleasure and serenity, and the primary demands of nature "which include, besides pleasure and calm, such needs of our body as wholeness, health, security, and such needs of our soul as man's innate spiritual powers, whether great or small."[54] While these needs are true of the city of man, the City of God looks beyond them to the supreme good of eternal life versus the supreme evil of eternal death, and says that "we should live rightly in order to obtain the one and avoid the other."[55]

> Those who think that the supreme good and evil are to be found in this life are mistaken. It makes no difference whether it is in the body or in the soul or both—or, specifically, in pleasure or virtue or in both—that they seek the supreme good. They seek in vain whether they look to serenity, to virtue, or to both; whether to pleasure plus serenity, or to virtue, or to all three; or to the satisfaction of our innate exigencies, or to virtue, or to both. It is in vain that men look for beatitude on earth or in human nature.[56]

Augustine personally illustrates the human longing for the eternal within the temporal order. He says: "There is a world of difference between the joy of hope that comes from faith and the shallow happiness that I was looking for. . . . I was greedy to enjoy what the world had to offer, though it only eluded me and wasted my strength."[57] Human life cannot be made happy and secure by what is on earth but only by the hope of heaven. **"It is because the philosophers will not believe in this beatitude which they cannot see that they go on trying to fabricate here below an utterly fraudulent felicity built on virtue filled with pride and bound to fail them in the end."**[58] It was this failure that spurred Augustine to look beyond earthly felicity to God: "As my misery grew worse and worse, you came the closer to me."[59] Each person must come into contact with the soul's deepest need and desire, "the unsatisfied longing of the homesick heart"[60] that is implanted in all humans as part of the image of God.

> Now what thou longest for, thou dost not yet see: howbeit by longing, thou art made capable, so that when that is come which thou

> mayest see, thou shalt be filled. . . . So God by deferring our hope, stretches our desire. . . . Let us desire therefore, my brethren, for we shall be filled. . . . This is our life, that by longing we should be exercised.[61]

It is necessary, then, to regard the beauties of creation as pointers to the Creator rather than ends in themselves.[62] We were made to love God and find our happiness in him: "You made us for yourself and our hearts find no peace until they rest in you."[63] Since God is the Supreme Good, he is to be loved for himself and for no other reward or object. "Happiness is to rejoice in you and for you and because of you. This is true happiness and there is no other. Those who think that there is another kind of happiness look for joy elsewhere, but theirs is not true joy."[64]

> The promised reward of virtue will be the best and the greatest of all possible prizes—the very Giver of virtue Himself. . . . God will be the source of every satisfaction, more than any heart can rightly crave, more than life and health, food and wealth, glory and honor, peace and every good. . . . He will be the consummation of all our desiring—the object of our unending vision, of our unlessening love, of our unwearying praise.[65]

> To whatsoever man attains, forthwith that to which he has attained becomes of little worth to him. Other things begin to be desired, other fond things are hoped for; and when they come, whatever they be, become of little worth. Hold fast then to God, for He can never be of little worth, since nothing is more beautiful than He. These things become of little esteem because they cannot endure, because they are not what He is. For nought, O soul, sufficeth thee, save He who created thee. Whatsoever else thou obtainest is worthless; for He alone can suffice thee Who made thee after His own image.[66]

Since "the real goal of our present life" is eternal life in the kingdom of God who is "the source of our happiness and the very end of all our aspirations," no other pleasure or desire is worthy of comparison.[67] The soul "clasps sorrow to itself" even when it clings to things of beauty if their beauty is outside God.[68] **People cannot avoid worship and service, whether of God or of worldly things. The service and love of God leads to freedom and blessedness; the service and love of the world through the lust of the flesh, the lust of the eyes, and the pride of life (1 John 2:16) leads to bondage and unhappiness.**[69] God is the only satisfying center of human life: "He who loves only what cannot be snatched from him is indubitably unconquerable, and is tortured by no envy."[70] Augustine acknowledges that knowing this is one thing, but applying it is another. There are always temptations for a follower of Christ to be drawn aside by a love of temporal things:

> [The enemy of our true happiness] sets his traps about me, baiting
> them with tributes of applause, in the hope that in my eagerness to lis-
> ten I may be caught off my guard. He wants me to divorce my joy from
> the truth and place it in man's duplicity. He wants me to enjoy being
> loved and feared by others, not for your sake, but in your place, so that
> in this way he may make me like himself and keep me to share with
> him, not the true fellowship of charity, but the bonds of common
> punishment.[71]

There is an ever-present danger of transferring one's hope from eternity to the
present. No one should hope for present blessings or the promise of worldly happiness and honor, because what God has promised is not of this life or this earth; he
has promised himself, and for the Christian, anything less is a misplaced hope.[72]
Drawing a distinction between use and enjoyment, Augustine warns against enjoying those things which ought to be used. Those who do so get "entangled in the love
of lower gratifications" because they substitute the eternal and unchangeable with
the temporal and mutable.[73] Instead, the things of the world should be used in such
a way as to lead to heavenly gain; "we are to love the things by which we are borne
only for the sake of that towards which we are borne."[74] **Since earthly happiness
does not compare with the beatitude of eternity, virtue makes the right use both
of the goods enjoyed and the misfortunes suffered on earth.**[75]

> The rational soul can therefore make a good use of even material and
> temporal felicity, if it does not give itself over to the creature, to the
> neglect of the Creator, but rather applies this felicity to the service of
> the Creator, of whose abounding liberality it has been bestowed.[76]

Augustine was not an advocate of a negative or ascetic mentality toward the
things of this world; temporal blessings can be profitable provided that they do not
lure the heart away from the higher calling of eternal blessings. "Use the world: let
not the world hold thee captive."[77] Christ's kingdom, the city of God, is not of this
world; the citizens of his kingdom are therefore pilgrims and sojourners on the
earth.[78] As pilgrims they groan and long for their true heavenly country, but the citizens of the earthly city are at home in the world because it is here that they seek to
be satisfied through the pursuit of pleasure, prestige, and power.[79]

The two cities are "two peoples whose nature is determined by the object of their
love."[80] A person is committed either to the love of God or the love of the world. The
former is moved by love (*caritas*), the latter by lust (*libido*), which Augustine
defines as "an appetite of the mind by which to eternal goods any temporal goods
whatever are preferred."[81] The soul becomes like what it loves: the history of the
human race is the history of the dialectic of the two wills and the two dominant
loves, one forming the city of Jerusalem, the other the city of Babylon.[82]

Through the gift of faith, one attains the knowledge necessary for the love of God; this love in turn prompts the freedom of obedience to God's commands.[83] The essence of these commands is for the believer to love God above all else and to love his neighbor as himself. The love of God is prerequisite to proper self-love, and the latter is necessary to the genuine love of others. **"It cannot be that he who loves God loves not himself; rather he alone knows how to love himself who loves God. Self-love can do no more than seek earnestly to enjoy the supreme and true Good. . . . Wholesome self-love is to love God more than self."**[84] Augustine recognizes that there is a natural self-love that requires no command, and he uses this form of love to build a rational case for the love of God.[85] Faith is necessary to transcend the gap between natural and perfected self-love.[86] The latter is "entirely coincident and coextensive with the love of God," since to love God is to pursue the Supreme Good, the supreme source of happiness: "When God is rightly worshipped, it is wholly to man's benefit, not to God's."[87] "The love wherewith a man truly loves himself is none other than the love of God. For he who loves himself in any other way is rather to be said to hate himself. . . ."[88] Notwithstanding, Augustine emphasizes that the true love of God does not seek the private interest of the self. To be preoccupied with the satisfaction of one's own need in the course of loving God is a selfishness that is ironically self-defeating because it focuses on the creature rather than the Supreme Good.[89] But when God is loved for his own sake, Christian duty does in fact serve self-interest in its fullest sense.[90]

The proper self-love that is based on the love of God is the condition for the right love of others.

> It is this Good which we are commanded to love with our whole heart, with our whole mind, and with all our strength. . . . To love one's own self is nothing but to wish to be happy, and the standard is union with God. When, therefore, a person who knows how to love himself is bidden to love his neighbor as himself, is he not, in effect, commanded to persuade others, as far as he can, to love God?[91]

For Augustine, the content of neighbor-love is evangelistic in that it seeks the highest good of others by leading them to find their blessedness in God.[92] The perfection of love in the community of the redeemed will reflect the *koinonia* of the godhead; "love can have no other purpose, as it can have no other source, but the mutual 'inherence' of persons, life in one another."[93] **The beatitude of heaven is not private but corporate; "community is the very principle of the *pax aeterna*."**[94] "God will be all in all in such a way, that, as God is love, love will bring it about that what is possessed by each will be common to all."[95]

Thomas Aquinas

The Thomistic synthesis of Aristotelian philosophy with Christian theology has exerted an enduring influence on Western Christendom as twentieth-century neo-Thomism attests. Like that of Aristotle, Aquinas's realist and concrete philosophy starts with the study of the principles of being made known by reflection on sensory experience of the existent world.[96] But his adoption of Aristotelianism was highly innovative and not merely a Christianized version of the philosopher. The framework of his thinking is derived from Aristotle's system, but Aquinas went beyond it (e.g., the Unmoved Mover versus the necessary Being of God the Creator) and wove a coherent fabric from a variety of other influences, including Neoplatonism, Augustine, Boethius, the early Christian fathers, and Scripture.[97] There are many non-Aristotelian elements in Aquinas's writings, such as the immortality of the soul and his moral theory, because the substance of his theology was essentially Augustinian.[98] He provided a metaphysical grounding to the teaching of Augustine; specifically, in his view of man as an incarnated intelligence, Aquinas filled "the Aristotelian bottle of matter and form with the life of the Augustinian wayfarer."[99]

Gilson observes: **"At the basis of [Aquinas's] philosophy, as at the basis of all Christian philosophy, there is a deep awareness of wretchedness and need for a comforter who can only be God."**[100]

> Natural reason tells man that he is subject to a higher being, on account of the defects which he perceives in himself, and in which he needs help and direction from someone above him: and whatever this superior being may be, it is known to all under the name of God.[101]

Since God is the end of humanity, it is essential to gain the truth concerning God that will rightly direct humanity toward that end. The problem is that the human intellect, though not radically distorted, is weakened in its present fallen condition. Because of the limits of natural reason, philosophy alone is not enough; metaphysics "points upwards and needs to be crowned by theology: otherwise man will not realise the end for which he was created and will not desire and strive towards that end."[102] **Through natural reason and the principle of analogy one can arrive at the existence of God as the First Cause and the Perfect Being, but this knowledge falls short of the essence and character of God. Human reason needs to be supplemented by the infusion of faith and the illumination of revelation, without which humanity will not be able to attain the knowledge of God for which it was created.**[103]

Thomas combined reason and revelation in his view of human psychology. He applied Aristotle's concept of form and matter to the relationship between the soul and the body and stressed the unity of human substance; the human being is a composite substance of body and soul.[104] "Soul copenetrates body to the very essence of its being; they give themselves to each other, and thus form one unit."[105] In this way, Aquinas's moderate realism steered a middle course between the idealism that minimizes the body and the materialism that limits knowledge to what can be seen and measured.[106]

Since the body with its vegetative, animal, and rational capabilities is the external condition of the soul, the human composite is determined by the soul's intellectual substance: "the intellect which is the principle of intellectual operation is the form of the human body."[107] While the human soul is an intellectual substance, it must also be the substantial form of an organic body so that, as an incarnated intelligence, it is enabled to exercise its sensory powers.[108] But it is the single human being, and not the body alone or the soul alone, who feels and thinks.[109]

Aquinas states that "the intellectual operation which we call the soul, is a principle both incorporeal and subsistent."[110]

> Not only is [man] like other composite substances in nature, one through the unity of his substantial principle, but this principle—the soul—also happens to be a spiritual substance in its own right. The full strangeness of man, therefore, consists in this, that, as a composite reality including an organic body within his being, he exists wholly and radically in and through a spiritual principle.[111]

Humans are creatures of both the corporeal and incorporeal worlds, and as such, they are related not only to animals but also to angels. As Chenu observes, Thomas's concept of man as a microcosm of the hierarchy of creation was influenced by the Neoplatonism of pseudo-Dionysius.[112] As a middle being, man is a mediator as well as a summation; in the hierarchy of being, the human mind functions as a mediator between the material and the spiritual.[113]

> Man is the king of the world. He is also its priest, through whom the world is blessed, consecrated, and elevated. His body is a compendium of all material things. When his body is controlled by his soul, and his soul united with God, it follows that man, as an intermediary, or priest, by his intellect, elevates matter into spiritual places by the union of the spirit of mankind with God.[114]

As a microcosm, man exhibits a descending hierarchical order from the rational level of intellect and will, to the animal level of sensations and passions, to the vegetative level of nutrition and growth.

> There exists . . . an operation of the soul which so far exceeds the corporeal nature that it is not even performed by any corporeal organ; and such is the operation of the *rational soul*. Below this, there is

another operation of the soul, which is indeed performed through a corporeal organ, but not through a corporeal quality, and this is the operation of the *sensitive soul*. . . . The lowest of the operations of the soul is that which is performed by a corporeal organ, and by virtue of a corporeal quality. . . . Such is the operation of the *vegetative soul*. . . . Now the powers of the soul are distinguished generically by their objects. For the higher a power is, the more universal is the object to which it extends.[115]

Thus, the object of the vegetative soul is its own body, while that of the sensitive soul extends to all sensible bodies. The object of the rational soul unfolds far beyond this to the realm of all being. But Aquinas stresses that these souls "are numerically one soul"; the human soul needs all three powers to be complete.[116] The soul, as form, has an essential tendency toward union with its matter, the body, and though it will be separated from the body between death and resurrection, it will not be complete until it is united with the resurrected body.[117] Kirk notes that **Thomas is "perhaps the first Christian philosopher to take the corporeal character of human existence calmly."[118] Humans are embodied souls: the soul "is not entombed in, but endowed with, a body."[119]**

Aquinas's concept of "desire" or "appetite" applies to the whole order of nature: along the entire hierarchy of being, all creatures tend towards the good. "Since goodness is that which all things desire, and since this has the aspect of an end, it is clear that goodness implies the aspect of an end."[120] The end of every imperfect form is its perfection; God is the anonymous object of all desire because it is only in him that entities find the completeness, harmony, and metaphysical unity for which they were created.[121]

> All things, by desiring their own perfection, desire God Himself, inasmuch as the perfections of all things are so many similitudes of the divine being. . . . And so of those things which desire God, some know Him as He is Himself, and this is proper to the rational creature; others know some participation of His goodness, and this belongs also to sensible knowledge; others have a natural desire without knowledge, as being directed to their ends by a higher intelligence.[122]

All things desire God because they have come from him, but he is not the ultimate end of all creatures in the same way; it is reserved for rational creatures to know and love him "as He is Himself."[123] The Thomistic concept of desire is not psychological but metaphysical. "[D]esire for him signified precisely that intelligible relation of a particular nature to its end; it is essentially a relation of finality."[124] Within the context of the metaphysical synthesis of Aquinas, desire is the transcendental relation of a creature to its final end.

Since man is a microcosm of the hierarchy of creation, his desires or appetites reflect this diversity. Humans share with inorganic beings and plants a natural appetite that is related to "the natural powers of the vegetative part, which are not subject to our will."[125] Above this is the animal or sensitive appetite: this form of desire is related to the life of the body with its corporeal needs and passions.

> The sensitive appetite is one generic power, and is called sensuality; but it is divided into two powers, which are species of the sensitive appetite—the irascible and the concupiscible. . . . There must needs be in the sensitive part two appetitive powers—one through which the soul is simply inclined to seek what is suitable, according to the senses, and to fly from what is hurtful, and this is called the concupiscible: and another, whereby an animal resists these attacks that hinder what is suitable, and inflict harm, and this is called the irascible.[126]

Just as the animal or sensitive appetite accompanies and supplements the animating activity of the body, so the higher intellectual or rational appetite accompanies and supplements the intellectual activity of the soul.[127]

> [T]he intellectual appetite is a distinct power from the sensitive appetite. For the appetitive power is a passive power, which is naturally moved by the thing apprehended. . . . What is apprehended by the intellect and what is apprehended by sense are generically different; consequently, the intellectual appetite is distinct from the sensitive.[128]

Thomas identified the will with the intellectual appetite and distinguished the interior determination of the will from the exterior determination of the sensitive appetite.

> [T]hings lacking knowledge entirely have natural appetite only. And things endowed with sensory knowledge have, in addition, sense appetite, under which irascible and concupiscible powers are included. But things possessed of intellectual knowledge also have an appetite proportionate to this knowledge, that is, will.[129]

The will or intellectual appetite is based upon abstract representation, while the sensitive appetite is based upon sense perception. The natural, sensitive, and intellectual appetites tend toward good, but the higher the appetite, the more general the good.[130]

The activity of the rational soul consists in the power of the intellect as well as the power of the will. Aquinas situated the passions (emotions) in the sensitive appetite of the organism ("passion is more properly in the act of the sensitive appetite, than in that of the intellectual appetite"), though he recognized the mutual influence of the sensory and intellectual natures.[131]

Just as the appetite tends towards the good, so the intellect tends toward the true.[132] In spite of this difference in object, the two faculties of will and intellect are interdependent.

The will and the intellect mutually include one another: for the intellect understands the will, and the will wills the intellect to understand. So then, among things directed to the object of the will, are comprised also those that belong to the intellect; and conversely. Whence in the order of things desirable, good stands as the universal, and the true as the particular; whereas in the order of intelligible things the converse is the case. From the fact, then, that the true is a kind of good, it follows that the good is prior in the order of things desirable; but not that it is prior absolutely.[133]

Sensible pleasure is experienced when an object capable of satisfying a need of the sensitive appetite is possessed. But humanity is composed of spirit as well as matter: corporeal pleasures are corruptible and inferior to the spiritual pleasures of the intellect.[134] It is the task of reason to determine the relative values of the pleasures of the body and of the mind and to recognize that lower ends in the hierarchy of value must be subordinated to higher ends. At the pinnacle of the hierarchy there must be a supreme end to which all other ends are properly subject.

The apprehension of the senses does not attain to the universal good, but to some particular good which is delightful. And consequently, according to the sensitive appetite which is in animals, operations are sought for the sake of delight. But the intellect apprehends the universal good, the attainment of which results in delight: wherefore its purpose is directed to good rather than to delight. . . . We should form our estimate of things not simply according to the order of the sensitive appetite, but rather according to the order of the intellectual appetite.[135]

The rational inclination or intellectual appetite is the agent of moral choice. In Aquinas's thinking, there is a harmony between the right and the good, since the duty of man is determined by his highest nature. The intellectual appetite tends toward the good, and happiness, its final end, is morally virtuous.[136]

Aquinas acknowledged the relative value of goods along the hierarchy ranging from the external goods of the body to the inner goods of the soul.[137] The basic needs of the body (e.g., food and drink) must be satisfied for the preservation and maintenance of the individual. External goods are necessary for the development of the intellectual, moral, and spiritual qualities of the personality, for maintaining a state in life, and for the realization of the duties of friendship and charity.[138] In addition to individual needs, Thomas also recognized communal needs.[139] But he subordinated all of these needs to the highest human need of spiritual beatitude.

Human activity is characterized by teleology; some things are willed as means to various ends, others are desired as ends in themselves. "[E]ach of the things produced through the will of an agent is directed to an end by the agent. For the proper object of the will is the good and the end. As a result, things which proceed from will must be directed to some end."[140] The end of a thing is its perfection, and its perfection is the good.

> [S]ince everything desires its own perfection, a man desires for his ultimate end, that which he desires as his perfect and crowning good. . . . It is therefore necessary for the last end so to fill man's appetite, that nothing is left besides it for man to desire. Which is not possible, if something else be required for his perfection.[141]

Thus, "the ultimate end is that beyond which the agent seeks nothing else"; since everything is directed toward good, God as the supreme good "must be the end of all things."[142] Though people often are not conscious of the last end, all other ends are subordinate to it and derived from it.[143]

Thomas clearly distinguished two ends of man appropriate to the orders of nature and the supernatural. The final end as considered by the philosopher is limited to the realm of natural causality, but for the theologian, the final end goes beyond the realm of nature to the vision of God.[144] Natural happiness is "imperfect and is had in this life"; beyond this earthly vocation is a supernatural vocation that is perfect and unattainable in this life.[145] The imperfect felicity of the natural end can be achieved through the exercise of human power and virtue, but the perfect beatitude of the supernatural end is not humanly realizable. "There is ever hovering on the horizon the Divine Magnet which attracts all, and if the finite seems satisfied with its immediate realisations, yet there is hidden hope, and a tendency that transcends such proximate results."[146] The aspiration of the final good of man as a spiritual being transcends natural faculties and can only be fulfilled by the grace of God.

Since human beings were created for a supernatural end, no natural end can fully satisfy their greatest need, that is, to know God. The knowledge of God gained through demonstration and even the knowledge of God gained through faith is not enough.[147] The will desires a beatitude that can only be found in the vision of God; "final Happiness consists in the vision of the Divine Essence, Which is the very essence of goodness."[148] Thus, "It is impossible for any created good to constitute man's happiness."[149] Only the universal good, which is found in God alone, can satisfy the deepest human desire. But while all people desire the last end as "the fulfillment of their perfection," they are not in agreement as to what constitutes this fulfillment.[150] Certainly more people seek it in wealth and pleasure than in the knowledge of God.

> Because bodily delights are more generally known, the name of pleasure has been appropriated to them. . . . The vehemence of desire for sensible delight arises from the fact that operations of the senses,

through being the principles of our knowledge, are more perceptible. And so it is that sensible pleasures are desired by the majority.[151]

Corporeal goods are unsatisfying surrogates for the universal good. St. Thomas argues that true felicity does not consist in the senses and the pleasures of the flesh, in honors, in human fame or glory, in natural or artificial wealth, in worldly power, or even in goods of the soul such as acts of moral virtue, prudence, or the operation of art.[152] "[T]he highest perfection of man cannot lie in a union with things inferior to himself, but, rather, in a union with some reality of a higher character, for the end is better than that which is for the sake of the end."[153] It is the love of God that draws human affections away from the multiplicity of temporal goods to the one source of true happiness.[154]

> Whatever is desirable in whatsoever beatitude, whether true or false, pre-exists wholly and in a more eminent degree in the divine beatitude. . . . As to earthly happiness, which consists in delight, riches, power, dignity, and fame, . . . [God] possesses joy in Himself and all things else for His delight; instead of riches He has that complete self-sufficiency, which is promised by riches; in place of power, He has omnipotence; for dignities, the government of all things; and in place of fame, He possesses the admiration of all creatures.[155]

Since God is the source of all good things, every human desire will be fulfilled in the divine vision. The intellectual desire will find its highest fulfillment through the vision of the First Truth; the desire to live in accord with reason and virtue will be fulfilled when reason is enlightened by the divine light so that it cannot divert from what is right; the desire for a high position of honor will be consummated when the blessed reign with Christ; the desire for popular renown will be met in the glory of heaven; the desires for wealth and the enjoyment of pleasures will be satisfied in the plenitude of the Father's house; and the desire for preservation will be fully satisfied "when the blessed attain perfect sempiternity and are safe from all harm."[156] **There is nothing wrong with these desires since they are God-given, but the pursuit of their corresponding goods must not become an end in itself. The improper use of these things can distract the mind from its inclination toward God.**

> [T]here are many impediments presented to man in the attaining of his end. For he is hindered by the weakness of his reason, which is easily drawn into error by which he is cut off from the right way of reaching his end. He is also hindered by the passions of his sensory nature, and by the feelings whereby he is attracted to sensible and lower things; and the more he attaches himself to these, the farther he is removed from his ultimate end, for these things are below man, whereas man's end is above him.[157]

The desires of the body and the soul must be controlled by reason, not for the purpose of eliminating them, but in order that, as instruments ministering to beatitude, they may serve rather than hinder the quest for man's final end. "[M]an must be so ordered by divine law that his lower powers may be subject to reason, and his body to his soul, and so that external things may subserve the needs of man."[158] Natural inclinations are "present in things from God," and therefore cannot be evil in themselves.[159] The use of food, sexual capacities, external possessions, and the possession of wealth are not illicit, "provided the order of reason be respected."[160] In fact, the contemplation of God presupposes a reasonable placation of a number of needs, including "soundness of body, . . . freedom from the disturbances of the passions— this is achieved through the moral virtues and prudence—and freedom from external disorders, to which the whole program of government in civil life is directed."[161] In the following text, Aquinas specifically endorses the needs for physical and social goods:

> For imperfect happiness, such as can be had in this life, external goods are necessary, not as belonging to the essence of happiness, but by serving as instruments to happiness, which consists in an operation of virtue. . . . For man needs in this life, the necessaries of the body, both for the operation of contemplative virtue, and for the operation of active virtue, for which latter he needs also many other things by means of which to perform its operations.

> On the other hand, such goods as these are nowise necessary for perfect Happiness, which consists in seeing God. . . . If we speak of the happiness of this life, the happy man needs friends, . . . not, indeed, to make use of them, since he suffices himself; nor to delight in them, since he possesses perfect delight in the operation of virtue; but for the purpose of a good operation, viz., that he may do good to them; that he may delight in seeing them do good; and again that he may be helped by them in his good work. For in order that man may do well, whether in the works of the active life, or in those of the contemplative life, he needs the fellowship of friends.

> But if we speak of perfect Happiness which will be in our heavenly Fatherland, the fellowship of friends is not essential to Happiness; since man has the entire fulness of his perfection in God. But the fellowship of friends conduces to the well-being of Happiness.[162]

There is some continuity between the natural and supernatural ends of earthly and heavenly beatitude. As Gilson comments, "The last end is not the negation of our human ends, rather it gathers them together sublimates and refines them, because human ends are but partial imitations of our last end and imperfect substitutes for it."[163] For humans, the perfect beatitude of heaven, like the imperfect happiness of earth, is that of a composite of soul and body.

All people, without exception, desire happiness, and this out of necessity. Just as the intellect cannot deny a proposition when it recognizes its necessary connection with first principles, so the will adheres of necessity to the general notion of happiness.

> For the general notion of happiness consists in the perfect good. . . . But since good is the object of the will, the perfect good of a man is that which entirely satisfies his will. Consequently to desire happiness is nothing else than to desire that one's will be satisfied. And this everyone desires.[164]

The "deep, insatiable need of uniting ourselves to that which is capable of perfecting us in every way and forever" exerts a constant pull on the will, and to this extent the will is determined.[165] But the will is free in regard to particular goods because these are not bound to beatitude by a necessary connection. **While humans are obliged to desire the last end, they are free to choose the means to the end.[166] This liberty in the choice of imperfect goods underlies Thomas's moral theory. Endowed with the power to choose and to act in accordance with particular ends or goods, people can order their steps toward the fulfillment or destruction of their own true interests.[167]** They necessarily desire the happiness that can only be found in the possession of God, but failing to see this connection, they often make choices that draw them away from the infinite good. In this way, they sin against God by rebelling against the deeper dynamism of their nature that points beyond itself to God as the true end of creation.[168] "The creature must seek the true final end or obtrude unrighteously its own puny self as its own end; it seeks the true metaphysical unity of things, or loses itself in the labyrinth of multiplicity."[169]

If men were granted the vision of the divine essence as the blessed will receive when they behold God, they would immediately recognize the necessary connection between true happiness and God; they would see him as the true source of satisfaction of all their needs and be drawn indefectibly to him.[170] But in this life they lack this clarity and need the grace of God to pursue him above all lesser goods.

Thomas affirmed the preeminence of the mind over the will and, unlike the Franciscans, located human perfection and beatitude more in the intellectual vision of God than in the love of God. The will with its desire cannot be the ultimate end because only the intellect can possess the object of desire.

> [I]t is impossible for the act of desiring to be the ultimate end. For it is by desire that the will tends toward what it does not yet possess, but this is contrary to the essential character of the ultimate end.—So, too, the act of loving cannot be the ultimate end. . . . The ultimate felicity

of man lies substantially in knowing God through his intellect, and not in an act of the will.[171]

As rational creatures, humans participate most fully in the image of God through their "proper operation of understanding Him."[172] Thus, the end of the intellectual creature is to understand God, the most perfect intelligible object. "St. Thomas cast his net upon the universe and carried off all things, transformed into life in the mind, towards the beatific vision."[173] **However, Aquinas's view of the supremacy of the mind over the will does not mean that he minimized the importance of the love of God. This love is the consequence of the intellectual vision of God, since in the beatitude of heaven, the mind and the will are complementary.**[174]

This final state of affairs is actually reversed in this life, however, because here on earth, the love of God is more perfect than the knowledge of God.[175] This is because the will tends to God directly, while the intellect knows God only analogically and mediately. But in the beatific vision, the mind has an immediate apprehension of the divine essence, and its intrinsic supremacy over the will is manifest.[176]

Thomas wrote in the context of an ongoing controversy carried over from the Greek fathers who emphasized the transcendence of the invisible God and the Latin fathers who argued that man's vocation was to see God.[177] He recognized that the created intellect, in and of itself, is incapable of beholding the substance of God; such an ideal of human knowledge in this life would be utopian.[178] Yet he also affirmed that there is a natural human desire for the knowledge of God. This raises the problem of how there can be a natural desire for that which is humanly unattainable. Somehow there must be a capacity to see God: if the created intellect could never see God, "it would either never attain to beatitude, or its beatitude would consist in something else beside God; which is opposed to faith."[179] The natural appetite of an intellectual substance cannot come to rest until it reaches its ultimate end, which is the essence of the First Cause.[180] The solution to this problem of desire is that there is a twofold potentiality in humans, the first being in accordance with their own operative capacity, and the second requiring for its realization the cooperation of an external agent.[181] This second potentiality is brought to fruition by divine grace, which elevates the human mind beyond the natural plane to the vision of God. This involves an immediate apprehension of the presence and activity of God rather than an indirect knowledge through the formation of concepts.

> [M]an's happiness, which is called life everlasting, consists in this divine vision, and we are said to attain it by God's grace alone, because such a vision exceeds all the capacity of a creature and it is not possible to reach it without divine assistance. . . . For such a noble vision, the created intellect must be elevated by means of an influx of divine goodness.[182]

In this way the natural light of the human intellect is "strengthened by the infusion of gratuitous light."[183] There may be different degrees of supernatural illumination, so that some see God more perfectly than others, but all who are granted the vision of God will see his substance.[184] This is made possible when God unites himself to the created intellect and becomes the intelligible form of the intellect. "[I]f the divine essence is seen, it must be done as His intellect sees the divine essence itself through itself, and in such a vision the divine essence must be both what is seen and that whereby it is seen."[185] It is through this vision that the created intellect participates in eternity. No one will ever tire of the beatific vision, and once having partaken, it is impossible to lose it.[186] Aquinas adds that the glorified body will not see the divine essence as an object of direct vision but only indirectly in the resurrected bodies of the blessed and, most of all, in the body of Christ. However, "the intellect will see God so clearly, that God will be perceived in things seen with the eye of the body, even as life is perceived in speech."[187]

The human need for divine grace extended even before the fall, since gratuitous power over and above nature is required in order to do supernatural good. But with the loss of the integrity of the pre-fall state, an additional work of sanctifying grace was needed to cause the love of God in man as well as faith and hope.[188] "[I]n the relations between God and humanity, the movement of descent of the divine plenitude into the depths of human nature is of greater import than the movement of ascent by which human nature is fulfilled and mounts toward God."[189]

Jonathan Edwards

In the last few decades, there has been a growing appreciation of the importance of Jonathan Edwards in the religious and intellectual history of America. He has been called "[t]he most original and acute thinker yet produced in America" and "the greatest philosopher-theologian yet to grace the American scene."[190] Three of his writings, *A Treatise Concerning Religious Affections*, *Freedom of the Will*, and *The Nature of True Virtue*, are recognized as great works in the psychology of religion, the philosophy of religion, and ethics, respectively.[191]

Edwards's entire literary output was shaped by his own religious experience. The themes of God's sovereignty, holiness, and grace on the one hand, and human sinfulness and need of redemption on the other, are the central motifs of Edwards's personal memoirs and appear constantly in the corpus of his works. **As a young man, he came to a profound awareness of his need to seek God's sovereign grace in salvation. His previous objections to the doctrines of divine sovereignty and election were suddenly overcome, and he embraced the conviction that God**

owes salvation to no one and may justly withhold pardon from anyone.[192] His memoirs stress the majesty and grace of God and his longing for greater knowledge of God and holiness. The external world of affairs held less importance for him than the realities of the kingdom of God. These sample entries illustrate the concerns that would motivate him for the rest of his life:

> My mind was greatly fixed on divine things; almost perpetually in
> the contemplation of them. . . . The heaven I desired was a heaven of
> holiness; to be with God, and to spend my eternity in divine love, and
> holy communion with Christ. My mind was very much taken up with
> contemplations on heaven, and the enjoyments there; and living there
> in perfect holiness, humility and love . . . solemnly vowed to take God
> for my whole portion and felicity, looking on nothing else as any part
> of my happiness. . . . Have this day fixed and established it, that Christ
> Jesus has promised me faithfully, that, if I will do what is my duty, and
> according to the best of my prudence in the matter, that my condition
> in this world shall be better for me than any other condition whatever,
> and more to my welfare to all eternity.[193]

Although Edwards wrote that he increasingly experienced God's grace and love, he also grew more aware of his own sinfulness, and this dual theme characterized his public ministry.[194]

Edwards drank deeply at the well of the older Puritan authors, and his writings clearly represent the Reformed tradition. He stated that "I should not take it at all amiss, to be called a Calvinist, for distinction's sake: though I utterly disclaim a dependence on Calvin."[195] He did not embrace Calvinistic theology out of a commitment to Puritanism, but because he judged its essence to be biblical. By the early eighteenth century, in fact, New England Puritanism had lost its earlier vitality.[196] But Edwards was optimistic about the future course of Christianity and saw the Awakenings of 1734–35 and 1740–42 in New England as forerunners of the fulfillment of the biblical prophecies concerning the end times.[197]

As a Reformed theologian, Edwards repeatedly emphasized the absolute sovereignty of God and salvation by sovereign grace alone.

> [God] will show mercy only on Christ's account, and that, according
> to his sovereign pleasure, on whom he pleases, when he pleases, and in
> what manner he pleases. You cannot bring him under obligation by
> your works; do what you will, he will not look on himself obliged. But
> if it be his pleasure, he can honourably show mercy through Christ to
> any sinner of you all, not one in this congregation excepted.[198]

Man is dependent upon God not only for redemption, but even for faith in the Redeemer.[199] Edwards defended the doctrine of election,[200] but insisted that divine sovereignty is not inconsistent with human responsibility. The burden of *Freedom of the Will* is a refutation of Arminianism's claim to the contrary. The Arminian teaching that the grace of God can be resisted by human will could easily pass over into Pelagianism, and beyond into deism or natural religion, "in which the ethical and the human gain complete ascendancy."[201] But Edwards argued that the liberty of self-determination is incompatible with divine sovereignty and that God's prescience requires predetermination. Since the will acts according to the dictates of a fallen human nature, man's moral faculties are indisposed to do spiritual good. On the other hand, Edwards believed that determinism is compatible with moral praise and blame.[202]

Edwards criticized both Arminianism and also the general trend in scholarship for the tendency to elevate human reason above divine revelation. They fail to take into account the inherent spiritual darkness of the human mind as a result of the fall.[203] Because of this darkness, reason is an insufficient substitute for revelation.[204] Still, Edwards held human reason in high esteem and saw it as a supplement to revelation. In his scientific and philosophical investigations, he avoided making a distinction between the secular and the spiritual.

The doctrine of original sin was important to Edwards, who "saw superficial views of the gravity of human corruption as the primary cause of the neglect of commitment to a *supernatural* redemption."[205] In his posthumously published book on original sin, he maintained that "all mankind are under the influence of a prevailing effectual tendency in their nature, to that sin and wickedness, which implies their utter and eternal ruin."[206] Because the mind has a natural propensity to evil rather than righteousness, a radical change of state is necessary to overcome the consequences of human depravity.[207] The image of God in man was defaced in the ruin of the fall, and the consequent state of spiritual death can only be overcome by the redemptive work of Christ. "The design of God was, to restore the soul of man to life and the divine image in conversion, to carry on the change in sanctification, and to perfect it in glory."[208] **Thus, the fundamental human need is a restored relationship with God which is brought about through repentance of sin and faith in Christ.** A profound consciousness of this need characterized the revivals of 1734–35 and 1740–42.[209] Edwards recognized that there was a wide variety in the manner of conversions, but he observed: "It is God's manner to make men sensible of their misery and unworthiness, before he appears in his mercy and love to them; particularly before he appears in his redeeming love and mercy to their souls."[210] In his sermons Edwards often exhorted his hearers to maintain a sense of conviction of sin, rebuked the foolishness of showing no concern for their condition before God, and warned them of the judgment upon those who die impenitent.[211] He stressed the urgency of the moment and urged them not to neglect present opportunity. People cannot obtain salvation without seeking it, and they should "seek the Lord while he may be found."[212]

Justifying faith is a "proper reception of Christ and his salvation, or a proper active union of the soul to Christ as a Saviour."[213] Justification entails freedom from the guilt of sin as well as the imputation of the righteousness of Christ. The conditions of justification are repentance and faith, and this involves complete dependence on the grace of God as opposed to human works.[214] But saving faith itself is a supernatural gift, and people are in need of the spiritual light that will enable them to sense "the divine excellency of the things revealed in the word of God, and a conviction of the truth and reality of them thence arising."[215] **Only the Spirit of God can convict people of their sin and bring them to a consciousness of their false security and need, and only the Spirit of God can bring them to the point of regeneration.**

> Truly gracious affections are produced by a supernatural, spiritual, and divine influence on the heart. . . . The influence of the Spirit of God, thus communicating himself and making the creature a partaker of the divine nature, is what I mean by truly gracious affections arising from spiritual and divine influence. . . . Natural men are represented in the sacred writings as having no spiritual light, no spiritual life, no spiritual being; and therefore regeneration is often compared to the opening of the eyes of the blind, to the raising of the dead, and to the work of creation. . . . Grace is the seed of glory in the heart, and therefore the earnest of the future inheritance.[216]

Thus, there is a need for a change in the condition of the human heart by the power of the Spirit of God that is as radical as the transformation from death to life.[217]

Unlike the Arminians who opposed the Awakening, Edwards and other Calvinistic ministers held that conversion cannot be determined by the human will. Those in the Reformed tradition also contended that a renewal in holiness is inseparable from conversion. The Arminians objected that this position undermines justification by faith alone, but Edwards responded in *A Treatise on Religious Affections* that the freeness of grace and the necessity of a holy practice are mutually consistent.[218] Holiness is love to God, and this love is the source of perseverance in Christian practice: "He that truly loves God, constantly seeks after God in the course of his life: seeks his grace, and acceptance, and glory."[219] Edwards affirmed the Reformed doctrine of the perseverance of the saints,[220] and from his perspective, a profession of conversion that is unaccompanied by holiness of practice does not mean that the individual concerned has lost salvation but that he has not yet obtained it.

Thus, in the aftermath of the Awakening, Edwards found it important to distinguish between genuine and deceptive religious manifestations, and to this end he wrote his work on *Religious Affections.*[221] This treatise begins with these words: "There is no question of greater importance to every individual of mankind than this: What are the distinguishing qualifications of those that are in favor with God, and entitled to his eternal rewards?"[222] Edwards had to deal with two extremes that surfaced after the revival. The first extreme was a skeptical attitude and opposition to experimental religion. In part this skepticism was a response to the opposite extreme of excess, disorder, and fanaticism. Edwards argued that the revival was indeed a work of the Spirit of God, but that it was hindered by "carnal enthusiasm" and commotion. He insisted that "[w]e should distinguish the good from the bad, and not judge of the whole by a part."[223] "As it has been, so it probably will be, whenever religion is greatly revived, till we have learned to distinguish between saving experience and affections, and those numerous fair shows and specious appearances by which they are counterfeited."[224]

Edwards admitted that his definition of the word *affections* as "the more vigorous and sensible exercises of the inclination and will of the soul" is imprecise,[225] particularly because it involves both volitional and emotional elements. **The affections are essentially conative in that they are the wellsprings of purposeful behaviour. Edwards affirmed that true religion consists in holy affections and "fervent exercises of the heart" and not in "weak and lifeless inclinations."[226]**

> And though there are different degrees of grace, and some Christians are but babes in Christ, in whom the exercise of the inclination and will towards divine and heavenly things is comparatively weak, yet every one who possesses the power of godliness in his soul, has his inclination and will exercised towards God and divine things with such strength and vigor, that those holy exercises prevail in him above all carnal and natural affections.[227]

Thus, Edwards criticized those who wished to discard religious affections; people need not only light in the understanding, but also warmth in the affections.[228] He encouraged the use of any scriptural means that would have a tendency to move the affections. On the other hand, he observed that religious affections can be deceiving and that their manifestations are not sufficient to enable one to discern between true and false conversions. Affections concerning religious things may be raised very high, they may stir the body, they may stimulate religious conversation, they may be attended by an appearance of love and joy, they may cause religious devotion and activity, they may create a sense of comfort and confidence, and they may procure the good opinion of spiritual leaders, but these phenomena do not prove either that the related affections are truly gracious or that they are not.[229] Instead, **"Truly**

gracious affections are founded on a love of divine things for their moral beauty or holiness."[230] The difference between real saints and the unregenerate is that the former are captivated by the moral perfections of God and have a divinely instilled spiritual taste for the beauty and holiness of God which they regard above all else as their chief good.[231] They are spiritually convinced of the supreme importance of divine things, and they renounce all dependence on their own righteousness.[232] Other characteristics of gracious affections are spiritual knowledge, a change of nature or disposition (allowances being made for natural temper), a meek, forgiving, and benevolent spirit, and a balanced proportion of the various affections.[233] But the clearest mark of the true Christian is the pursuit and practice of holiness. "Christian practice, or a holy life, is a great and distinguishing evidence of saving grace. But I may go further, and assert that it is the chief evidence of grace, both as it respects ourselves and others."[234] "Christian practice is that evidence which confirms every other indication of true godliness" including repentance, faith, love, humility, fear of God, hope, and joy.[235]

According to Edwards, divine things should be regarded as "transcendently excellent and amiable in their own nature; and not on account of any conceived relation they bear to ourselves, or to our own interest."[236] Edwards acknowledges that people are naturally inclined to those things that are most consistent with their interest, and he recognizes the place of human instincts, appetites, and aversions.[237] But self-love and self-interest should be subservient to the higher principle of love toward God. The difference between the joy of the hypocrite and the joy of the true saint is that for the former, the foundation of his joy is more in self than in God.[238] The saints rightly rejoice in the benefits that Christ provides on their behalf, but they should primarily rejoice in God for who he is in himself.[239]

People need to develop a spiritual taste, an appetite for the moral excellence and holiness of God. They should desire above all else the reality of communion with God.

> The saints desire the sincere milk of the word, not so much to testify the love of God towards them, as that they may grow thereby in holiness. Grace is the good man's treasure. Isa. 33:6. Godliness is the gain of which he is covetous. 1 Tim. 6:6.[240]

This is the wisdom of "treating things according to their true value," rather than setting the heart on inferior things.[241] The natural human tendency, however, is to value earthly enjoyments above heavenly happiness.

> [H]ow common is it among mankind, to have their affections much more exercised and engaged in other matters than in religion. As to those things which concern their worldly interests, the desires of men are eager, and their love warm and affectionate. In reference to these objects they

are much impressed, and very deeply concerned. They are much affected with grief at worldly losses, and much elated with joy at worldly prosperity. But how insensible and unmoved are most men about the great things of another world. How languid are their affections as to these things. How insensibly they can sit and hear of the infinite love of God in giving his dear Son to be offered up a sacrifice for the sins of men.[242]

The enjoyments of earth are good, but the Christian, as a pilgrim, should not rest in them. "We ought to possess, enjoy, and use them, with no other view but readily to quit them, whenever we are called to it, and to change them willingly and cheerfully for heaven."[243] In view of the brevity of earthly existence, worldly goods and temporal happiness should not detract Christians from their true calling. Instead, they should seek first the kingdom of God:

> Heaven is that place alone where our highest end, and highest good, is to be obtained. God hath made us for himself. . . . God is the highest good of the reasonable creature; and the enjoyment of him is the only happiness with which our souls can be satisfied.—To go to heaven, fully to enjoy God, is infinitely better than the most pleasant accommodations here. Fathers and mothers, husbands, wives, or children, or the company of earthly friends, are but shadows; but the enjoyment of God is the substance. These are but scattered beams; but God is the sun. These are but streams; but God is the fountain. These are but drops; but God is the ocean.—Therefore it becomes us to spend this life only as a journey towards heaven, as it becomes us to make the seeking of our highest end and proper good, the whole work of our lives; to which we should subordinate all other concerns of life. Why should we labour for, or set our hearts on, anything else, but that which is our proper end, and true happiness?[244]

Since earthly existence is transitory, people's true state of happiness or misery is determined by their condition in the eternal state. "Prosperity or adversity in the present state alters them but very little, because this state is of so short continuance."[245] "Happiness and rest are what all men pursue. But the things of the world, wherein most men seek it, can never afford it; they are labouring and spending themselves in vain."[246] All are in need of true happiness, but this cannot be found in the vanities of the world; God is "the only fountain of happiness."[247]

One who is really convinced of the truths of heaven and hell will be influenced by the things of religion above all things in the world. To venture on the report of the gospel is to prefer God before anything else in heaven and on earth, and to make God one's "supreme, governing, and ultimate end."[248] Edwards stresses that God's purpose in creation is in man's highest interest.

God acting for himself, or making himself his last end, and his acting for their sake, are not to be set in opposition; they are rather to be
considered as coinciding one with the other, and implied one in the
other. . . . God in seeking his glory, seeks the good of his creatures;
because the emanation of his glory . . . implies the communicated
excellency and happiness of his creatures.[249]

God and his glory are the objective ground of human happiness. His loving purpose in uniting men to himself through the redemptive work of Christ leads to their
highest good.

Christ, who is a divine person, by taking on him our nature, descends
from the infinite distance and height above us, and is brought nigh to
us; whereby we have advantage for the full enjoyment of him. And, on
the other hand, we, by being in Christ a divine person, do as it were
ascend up to God, through the infinite distance, and have hereby
advantage for the full enjoyment of him also.[250]

The joy of heaven will be the communal joy of the church, the bride of Christ.
The saints in heaven will jointly participate with Christ in his glory and blessedness,
and will delight in the vision of God.

The glorious excellencies and beauty of God will be what will for
ever entertain the minds of the saints, and the love of God will be their
everlasting feast. The redeemed will indeed enjoy other things: they
will enjoy the angels, and will enjoy one another: but that which
they shall enjoy in the angels, or each other, or in any thing else what-
soever that will yield them delight and happiness, will be what shall be
seen of God in them.[251]

Søren Kierkegaard

Kierkegaard's influence upon twentieth-century philosophers,
psychologists, and theologians continues to build momentum.
Martin Heidegger, Karl Jaspers, Jean-Paul Sartre, Ludwig
Binswanger, Rollo May, Karl Barth, Emil Brunner, Rudolph
Bultmann, Reinhold Niebuhr, and Paul Tillich are all indebted to
his work. The writings of Kierkegaard have been used in support
of divergent viewpoints, for example, both the theistic and nontheistic versions of existentialism. This is due, in part, to the
many facets of his personality as expressed in his writings (poet, psychologist,
humorist, tragic lover, iconoclast, philosophical critic, eccentric, passionately
earnest Christian),[252] and to his frequent use of indirect communication (pseudo-
nymns, irony, parables, anecdotes, metaphors, and other poetic devices).

An important theme that runs through a number of Kierkegaard's works is his criticism of the Hegelian system and his opposition to the prevalent attempt to integrate Hegelianism and Christianity. Although there are terminological correspondences between them, Kierkegaard was opposed to Hegelian philosophy throughout his writing career.[253] He attacked not only Hegel's rationalistic attempt to formulate a conceptual scheme by which all reality could be ordered but also his elevation of the state above the individual. In contrast to Hegel, Kierkegaard affirmed the worth of the individual as greater than that of the institutions.[254]

His own experience became paradigmatic of the development of the individual through four stages or spheres of existence that he called aesthetic, ethical, "religion A" ("religion in the sphere of immanence"), and "religion B" ("religion in the sphere of transcendence"). His aesthetic stage lasted until 1836, and after a brief transition through an ethical stage, he embarked on the religious stages. The entries in the first years of his *Journals and Papers* show a movement away from criticism toward contemplation of Christianity, and his conversion evidently took place in 1838.[255] Kierkegaard's books appeared after this date, but several of them reflect the viewpoint of the earlier stages. The situation is complicated by his use of pseudonymous "authors," and the degree to which these "authors" represent Kierkegaard's own position is debated. He broadly regarded the pseudonymous literature beginning with *Either/Or* as aesthetic in orientation, and after the transitional *Concluding Unscientific Postscript,* the bulk of his writings shifted to a religious orientation. Although Kierkegaard disassociated himself at the end of *Postscript* from the statements of his pseudonyms, he later claimed that he had always been a religious author, and that all of his writings were related to the problem of becoming a Christian.[256] Through the vehicle of indirect communication, Kierkegaard clothed his message in the pseudonymous writings in aesthetic language "to make the familiar (i.e., the claims of Christianity) unfamiliar, so that those who deceive themselves into thinking they are Christians might be reawakened to what Christianity is really all about."[257] The works written after 1848 were no longer indirect,[258] and his last writings were in fact a frontal attack upon established Christianity. But all of his writings, indirect and direct, were written from within the Christian community, and not as an outsider.[259] The unifying theme throughout this literature is how to become a Christian within Christendom.[260]

Kierkegaard's anthropology stresses both the immanent (psychosomatic) and the transcendent (spiritual) reality of the individual. **"[M]an is a synthesis of psyche and body that is constituted and sustained by spirit. . . . Man, then, is a synthesis of psyche and body, but he is also a synthesis of the temporal and the eternal."**[261] "A human being is a synthesis of the infinite and the finite, of the temporal and the eternal, of freedom and necessity."[262] As a composite being, the individual experiences a tension between the psychosomatic and spiritual dimensions. Anxiety is induced by a combined awareness of the possibility of freedom and one's inability to overcome the constraints necessary to attain authentic selfhood. "Anxiety is neither a category of necessity nor a category of freedom; it is entangled freedom, where freedom is not free in itself but entangled, not by necessity, but in itself."[263] **Anxiety or dread is proportionate to a person's conception of God; the more he is conscious of existing before God, the more he is aware of his unlikeness to God. Paradoxically, this painful awareness expands the self and requires divine assistance.** "Merely to obtain the knowledge that the God is unlike him, man needs the help of the God."[264] It is this "absolute qualitative difference between God and man" that constitutes the possibility of offense; sin, as such, must be against the infinite God.[265] Thus, Kierkegaard sees the consciousness of guilt as "the decisive expression for existential pathos in relation to an eternal happiness."[266]

Kierkegaard defines *sin* as "before God, or with the conception of God, in despair not to will to be oneself, or in despair to will to be oneself."[267] Human beings, by virtue of the imprint of the image of God, possess a temporal/eternal duality which becomes imbalanced when people either refuse to aspire towards the eternal ("in despair not to will to be oneself") or, amounting to the same thing, are content with the purely temporal ("in despair to will to be oneself"). Despair is "the sickness unto death."[268] Anxiety (or dread) is not the same as despair; despair arises from sin, an unwillingness to be oneself before God. Faith, the opposite of sin, means not only trust in God but also the state that "in relating itself to itself and in willing to be itself, the self rests transparently in the power that established it."[269] By an act of responsible freedom, the individual chooses to become himself by relating himself to God. In the dialectic of freedom, this qualitative leap enhances selfhood by uniting the temporal and the eternal in a higher *telos*. Thus, it is through the narrow way of the consciousness of sin that a person learns to enter into Christianity.[270]

Kierkegaard noted in his *Journals* that "the difference between a pagan and a Christian is not that the latter is without sin; the difference is how he regards his sin and how he is kept in the striving."[271] **The Christian acknowledges his sickness, whereas the pagan tries to overlook it. In the risk of faith, the former clings to grace, while the latter sinks in despair or hangs onto an unfounded optimism.**[272]

In his theory of the stages on life's way, Kierkegaard develops a phenomenology of human consciousness that traces this quest for authentic selfhood.[273] According to this psychology, the individual does not fully become a person until he has integrated each of the spheres of existence in the deepest religious sphere. Each stage or sphere has its own dialectic:

> If the individual is in himself undialectical and has his dialectic outside himself, then we have the aesthetic interpretation. If the individual

is dialectical in himself inwardly in self-assertion, hence in such a way that the ultimate basis is not dialectic in itself, inasmuch as the self which is at the basis is used to overcome and assert itself, then we have the ethical interpretation. If the individual is inwardly defined by self-annihilation before God, then we have religiousness A. If the individual is paradoxically dialectic, every vestige of original immanence being annihilated and all connection cut off, the individual being brought to the utmost verge of existence, then we have the paradoxical religiousness.[274]

The aesthetic stage, depicted by the writings of "A" in the first volume of *Either/Or* and by the descriptions of the ethicist's "young friend" ("A") in the second volume, is characterized by a romanticism that overlooks the eternal in the pursuit of the pleasures of the moment. This stage does not satisfy the deepest human longings, and its failure is manifested in despair. There is a dialectic to this despair: it can be buried within oneself and hidden from view, it can take the form of a defiant despair of eternity, or one can "despair in truth" by "choosing oneself in one's eternal validity."[275] It is in this third form of despair that the individual breaks loose from his bondage to the temporal.

In his *Postscript*, Kierkegaard summarizes the contrast between the aesthetic and ethical existence-spheres in the two parts of *Either/Or*:

> [I]n the first part, an imaginative inwardness which evokes the possibilities with intensified passion, with sufficient dialectical power to transform all into nothing in despair; in the second part, an ethical pathos, which with a quiet, incorruptible, and yet infinite passion of resolve embraces the modest ethical task, and edified thereby stands self-revealed before God and man.[276]

The ethical stage, depicted by Judge William in *Either/Or* and *Stages on Life's Way*, involves the pursuit of meaning in life through obedience to duty. It stresses the importance of choosing and the "baptism of the will which lifts up the choice into the ethical."[277] "Duty is only one" in the ethical sphere of existence: "to love truly with the inward movement of the heart."[278] The true ethicist seeks to translate duty from the external to the internal and idealizes conjugal love.[279]

The ethical is often accompanied by a vague religiousness, but it is a religion of immanence that lacks a consciousness of sin. The ethical is situated in the law of the general and is powerless before the fact of individual sin. A sense of guilt and a corresponding response of repentance and "infinite resignation" before God is the only way to transcend the ethical sphere.[280]

Kierkegaard describes two boundary zones that correspond to the aesthetic, the ethical, and the religious. Irony is the boundary between the aesthetic and the ethical. As Kierkegaard used it, irony is "necessity's iron law of negation, which cancels all human strivings and aspiration, causing them to add up to zero."[281] By contrast, humor, the boundary between the ethical and the religious, relates to divine freedom and is an awareness of the inability of human reason to grasp the contradictions between the temporal and the eternal. **"Humor is the insight that God is wholly other, and so if his truth is ever to break into the sphere of human endeavor, it will surely appear very different than our finite comprehension of what it ought to look like."[282] Humor, then, makes a person receptive to the paradoxical truth of the religious sphere.**

Religiousness A is the relation to an eternal happiness through the dialectic of inward transformation and existential pathos.[283] But this form of religion "can exist in paganism, and in Christianity it can be the religiousness of everyone who is not decisively Christian, whether he be baptized or no."[284] Kierkegaard's purpose was to "make it difficult to become a Christian," that is, to bring people from religiousness A into the true Christianity of religiousness B, which appropriates the "absolute paradox" of the incarnation as its object of faith.[285]

Although the religious stage dethrones the aesthetic and ethical stages, it does not repudiate them; rather it restores their concerns to legitimate roles within the overall province of the religious. Each sphere of existence leads to the next, and when a person enters into the deepest religious sphere, the aesthetic and the ethical spheres continue to exist, but directed by and dependent upon the religious.[286]

Kierkegaard was keenly aware of the need for the human heart to find satisfaction and overcome the sense of spiritual alienation. His whole theory of the stages illustrates this quest to discover the fullness of human existence. In the highest stage, this is realized in the subjectivity of the Christian life. Placing more stress on personal appropriation than on doctrinal assent, Kierkegaard encouraged inner experience and "infinite, personal, passionate interest in one's eternal happiness."[287] It is only through the inward emotions of the heart that a person is able to possess Christian truth. Kierkegaard did not seek to eliminate objectivity, but he wanted to prevent it from suppressing the spiritual dimension of life. In his rebuttal of speculative philosophy, he used reason to demonstrate the limits of reason, showing that the unaided human mind is incapable of grasping ultimate reality. He was not opposed to philosophy as such, but he held that it is a mistake to base one's eternal happiness upon a comprehensive system of objective knowledge. In the ethical-religious realm, action through the passion of choice is more important to the existing individual than objective reflection.[288]

In contrast to the disinterestedness of objective reflection, subjective reflection always involves introspection and engages the feelings of the individual.

[S]ubjectivity is truth; for an objective truth is like the eternity of abstract thought, extraneous to the movement of existence.

Abstract thought is disinterested, but for an existing individual, existence is the highest interest. An existing individual therefore has always a *telos*. . . .

The way of objective reflection makes the subject accidental, and thereby transforms existence into something indifferent, something vanishing. Away from the subject the objective way of reflection leads to the objective truth, and while the subject and his subjectivity become indifferent, the truth also becomes indifferent, and this indifference is precisely its objective validity; for all interest, like all decisiveness, is rooted in subjectivity.[289]

In the *Postscript,* Kierkegaard contends that Christianity is concerned with the development of the individual's subjectivity; "it is only in subjectivity that its truth exists, if it exists at all; objectively, Christianity has absolutely no existence."[290] Defining subjective truth, he states: "An objective uncertainty held fast in an appropriation-process of the most passionate inwardness is the truth, the highest truth attainable for an existing individual."[291]

History provides no objective certainty or proof but only probability and approximation, and this is a wholly inadequate basis for an eternal happiness.[292] Indeed, there is an objective historical element in Christianity, namely the incarnation, but the remaining historical detail is less important for faith.[293] Christ, the object of faith, cannot be objectively known from history; he can only be believed.[294]

Because of the absolute difference that distinguishes God and man, the idea that God entered time and history and existed in human form is the absolute paradox.[295] It is absurd that "the eternal truth has come into being in time, that God has come into being, has been born, has grown up, and so forth" and that there can be a historical point of departure for an eternal happiness.[296] **The true Christian is "nailed to the paradox of having based his eternal happiness upon the relation to something historical."[297] The Christian lays hold of the paradox by the inwardness of faith, which leads to the forgiveness of sins.[298] Thus, the absurd is the object of faith.**

Kierkegaard uses *faith* in a variety of ways, some of them corresponding to the aesthetic, ethical, and religious stages of existence.[299] He defines religious or existential faith as "the objective uncertainty due to the repulsion of the absurd held fast by the passion of inwardness."[300] This form of faith cannot be proved, substantiated, or cognitively grasped; it believes against the understanding.[301] Through encounter with the absolute paradox, "the true Christian adventure lets go of probability," and takes the passionate risk of choice in faith.[302] This is far from easy, since Christianity not only requires that the individual should existentially venture all, but also that he risk his thought, venturing to believe against the understanding.[303] Since on the Kierkegaardian account, subjectivity increases as objectivity decreases, prudentialism must give way to a faith that risks everything on that which has no objective warrant. In the absence of rational security, the transition to existential faith can only be accomplished by a leap, a decision of the will based on the needs of the heart.[304] One can never avoid the problem of doubt,[305] nor can one be neutral about Christ in view of his claims. A choice must be made: a person must respond to the paradox in faith or in offense.[306]

Because of the enormous qualitative difference between God and man and the effect of sin on the faculties of reason, emotion, and volition, it is virtually miraculous that a human can arrive at the faith of paradoxical religiousness. **"Faith itself is a miracle, and all that holds true of the Paradox also holds true of Faith."[307] Belief in the incarnation, the central doctrine of Christian affirmation, is an "eternal condition" given by divine grace in the "Moment" when one becomes conscious of the new birth.[308] But in Kierkegaard's thought, there is a dialectic of grace and free will, and this need for the grace of God to come to faith does not negate the reality of human choice.** In opposition to the doctrine of predestination, he stresses the freedom of the will; a person is responsible for his choices and capable of accepting or rejecting grace.[309]

Existential faith makes the believer contemporary with the absolute, and because of this, there are no second-hand disciples. "For in relation to the absolute there is only one tense: the present. For him who is not contemporary with the absolute— for him it has no existence."[310] The human soul is the meeting place of time and eternity, and through the gift of faith, a person becomes new while yet remaining himself. In this new birth or "repetition," the believer enters into the prolepsis of eternal life.[311] The expectation of faith is the victory that conquers the future. "Hope, by reaching out its spiritual arms, seizes eternity for the Christian believer, though not as an existential possession (for paradox forbids such possession), but as a passionate possibility instead."[312]

All needs are minor in comparison with the overriding human need for the grace of God, "the most precious of all good gifts."[313] Since "man's need of God constitutes his highest perfection," it is the saddest of all tragedies when a person passes through life without discovering that he needed God.[314] To become aware of this need, one must sink down into his own nothingness and "be completely persuaded that he can of himself do nothing, absolutely nothing."[315] This is far from easy, but it is the only way to view life "according to its perfection."[316] "Just as the self-knowledge which reveals one's own nothingness is the necessary condition for knowing God, so the knowledge of God is the condition for the sanctification of each human being in accordance with his specific end."[317] A person must recognize the futility of depending on his own resources before he can be conscious of his absolute need of him who is the Truth and the Life.[318] This will not happen in detachment or speculation, but in personal response to the light one has been given.

> Everybody living in Christendom has absolutely enough information about Christianity to be able to invoke and supplicate, to be able to turn prayerfully to Christ. If he does that with a sense of inward need, in honesty of heart, he will yet become a believer. If only it is quite definite before God that this man feels the need of believing, he will in due time get to know quite definitely what he is to believe.[319]

The greatest barrier to this process is a preoccupation with the manifold temporal needs that leads to a neglect of the single eternal need. When a person's heart is captivated by earthly riches and abundance and the desire to become something in the world, the idea of an eternal happiness is relegated to another item on a list of wanted goods.[320] On the aesthetic level, "it is quite in order to wish for wealth, good fortune, and the most beautiful of damsels; in short, to wish for anything that is subject to an aesthetic dialectic."[321] But this will not suffice on the ethical-religious level, where "purity of heart is to will one thing," that is, the eternal as the highest good.[322] If a person is unwilling to give up anything for this good, or if he wills this good for the sake of the reward of happiness, he is double minded: the single-minded person sees the good and the reward as one and the same.[323]

Kierkegaard does not say that the eternal eliminates the temporal but rather, that the eternal introduces a standard by which the temporal is to be judged. The believer "still lives in the finite, but he does not have his life in the finite."[324] When he is single-minded, he derives his values and strength from the eternal and uses them to control and order the temporal.[325] In this suspension of preoccupation with temporality, the believer learns to cling less to external things and to "care more and more for the things of the inner man, for the understanding with God."[326] He recognizes that when earthly goods are possessed, "they should be possessed as the unimportant; but the supreme good cannot and must not be possessed as the unimportant."[327] By nature, temporal possessions are lost temporally, but only the eternal can be gained eternally.

> Is not this then joyful, that wherever in temporal existence there is loss and the pain of loss, eternity is then at hand to offer the sufferer more than compensation? . . . To let go of the temporal in such a way that it is lost temporally, to lose only temporally the lost temporal possession, is a precise indication of the presence of the eternal in the loser, is the token that the eternal in him conquered.[328]

The fullness of existence, true freedom and significance, and the discovery of the real capacities of the self are found only in God, not in earthly utopias. The human synthesis of temporal and eternal is reflected in the existential movement toward the *summum bonum* through the aesthetic, ethical, and religious spheres.[329]

While the human heart can be satisfied with nothing less than the assurance of eternal happiness,[330] this is not evident in the individual's outward life, where

> the idea of an eternal happiness will not *profit* him at all, since the idea is not actually present to him until he has learned to despise the external and to forget the earthly mind's notion of what is profitable. Externally it cannot *harm* him to lack this conception; without it he may nevertheless very well attain to the dignity of husband, father, and champion rifle-shot, and if it is something such that he desires, the conception of an eternal happiness will only stand in his way. The essential existential pathos in relation to an eternal happiness is acquired at so great a cost that it must from the finite point of view be regarded as simple madness to purchase it, which view comes to expression often enough in life, and in a variety of ways.[331]

In spite of the cost, "the one thing needful" is the courage to discover and respond to one's need for eternal happiness.[332] When a person has an "infinite interest in his eternal happiness," he devotes himself absolutely to an absolute *telos,* and relatively to a relative *telos*: to reverse the elements in this teleology is both foolish and sinful.[333] But it is always a temptation, not only because of the immanence of the temporal order, but also because of the inward suffering the God-relationship entails.

> Thou canst perhaps by shrewdness avoid what it has pleased God once for all to unite with being a Christian, namely, suffering and adversity. Thou canst perhaps, by shrewdly evading this to thine own ruin, attain what God has eternally separated from being a Christian, namely, enjoyment and all earthly goods. Thou canst perhaps, befooled [*sic*] by thy shrewdness, be totally lost at last in the vain delusion that it is precisely the right path thou art on, because thou dost win the earthly—and then an eternity in which to repent![334]

There is an anguish in being a Christian, and "the degree of one's faith is proved only by the degree of one's willingness to suffer for one's faith."[335] But the believer's earthly suffering is only a transition to an eternal triumph.[336]

Kierkegaard's criticism of the compromise and worldliness of institutional Christianity reached a climax in his last years. He lamented the steady reduction in the price of what it is to be a Christian and the low forms of religiosity that were prevalent.[337] For him, action was more fundamental than knowledge, but the church had lost its practical vitality and had succumbed to a theoretical orientation. The *sola fide* position of Lutheranism had been abused to the point of disassociating obedience from faith. Kierkegaard was in agreement with Luther's position on salvation by faith through grace, but he contended that this had degenerated from a passion into a doctrine that diminished the vital power of faith.[338] **The need to rely on divine grace does not minimize the calling to bear one's cross and imitate Christ; indeed, grace and discipleship go hand in hand.**

> Christianity's requirement is: Thy life shall as strenuously as possible give expression to works—and then one thing more is required: that thou humble thyself and admit, "But none the less I am saved by grace." . . . [People] applied "grace" in such a way as to exempt them from works.[339]

The real Christian simplicity is to translate Christian thought into the action of obedience before God.[340] Unconditional obedience is the true manifestation of love for God: "the love which loves God is the bond of perfectness, which in perfect obedience makes man one with the God he loves."[341] A person is to love God because he needs him; this is not a matter of selfishness because this is "the only way in which a man can in truth love God."[342] In addition, self-love is the condition Christianity presupposes in order to command one to love his neighbor as himself.[343] But human love is ultimately grounded in the love of God, and the need to love and be loved is fundamental to the created order of human existence. "How deeply is the need for love grounded in man's being! . . . throughout all ages everyone who has thought more deeply about the nature of man, has . . . recognized in him this need for companionship."[344] Love, the most important condition of inwardness, comforts when all else fails, and persists when all else changes.[345]

> To defraud oneself of love is the most terrible deception of all. It is an eternal loss for which there is no compensation either here or in eternity. . . . For a man may perhaps succeed in getting along in the temporal existence without love; he may succeed perhaps in getting through time without discovering the self-deception; he may perhaps succeed—how terrible!—in continuing in his self-conceit, glorying in it; but in eternity he cannot do without love, and he cannot fail to discover that he has forfeited everything.[346]

Paul Tillich

By his own account, Paul Tillich was on the boundary line between theology and philosophy and between religion and culture. In the tradition of Schleiermacher, he attempted to construct a synthesis out of all the elements of theology and relate it to the cultural conditions of his time.[347] Decisive to the profound influence of his theology was his ability to diagnose the human situation and to interpret the Christian message in a way that would speak directly to contemporary questions and problems.

As a radical reinterpreter of the tenets of the Christian faith, Tillich sharply criticized American fundamentalism. But his view of the human situation also led him to criticize the form of liberal theology that stemmed from the optimistic humanism of the nineteenth century.[348] He admired the honest realism of the Freudian assessment of the unlimited libido in man and regarded this as an insightful account of the human predicament on the existential level.[349]

Tillich used the term *concupiscence* to denote the unlimited desire to draw the whole of reality into one's self. Concupiscence is a distorted form of libido and "refers to physical hunger as well as to sex, to knowledge as well as to power, to material wealth as well as to spiritual values."[350] This never-satisfied striving is symptomatic of the existential estrangement of man from the true source of his essence. "Every individual, since he is separated from the whole, desires reunion with the whole. His 'poverty' makes him seek for abundance."[351] When libido is united with love in any of its forms, it is directed toward another being with whom it wants to be united. But it is distorted into concupiscence through the temptation to become centered in oneself, futilely attempting to draw the universe into one's particular existence.[352] **"Biblical realism knows both that libido belongs to man's created goodness and that it is distorted and ambiguous in the state of man's estrangement."**[353]

Because of this estrangement, the human condition is characterized by ontic, spiritual, and moral anxiety:

> Nonbeing threatens man's ontic self-affirmation, relatively in terms of fate, absolutely in terms of death. It threatens man's spiritual self-affirmation, relatively in terms of emptiness, absolutely in terms of meaninglessness. It threatens man's moral self-affirmation, relatively in terms of guilt, absolutely in terms of condemnation.[354]

The first of these three forms of existential anxiety relates to the awareness of one's own finitude. This awareness of oneself as a finite mixture of being and nonbeing produces a deep anxiety. "All creatures are driven by anxiety; for finitude and anxiety are the same."[355] Faced with the anticipation of their own death, people need the courage to affirm existence in spite of this threat.[356] The second type of anxiety relates to the problem of the meaning of life, which is central in Tillich's thought. The loss of a spiritual center that provides ultimate meaning leads finally to the anxiety of total doubt.[357] The third type of anxiety, that of guilt and condemnation, is produced by the ambiguity between good and evil that permeates human actions.[358]

All three types of anxiety are woven together and contribute to the experience of despair or hopelessness. Tillich observes, however, that most people are relatively successful in avoiding the extreme situations that lead to despair, since "all human life can be interpreted as a continuous attempt to avoid despair."[359] **Thus, people are normally driven to pursue security, certitude, and morality in order to overcome the corresponding anxieties of fate and death, emptiness and meaninglessness, and guilt and condemnation.**[360] But these avoidance-strategies only minimize the symptoms while leaving the root problem of existential estrangement from the source of being, of meaning, and of forgiveness unsolved.

Tillich's analysis of the human predicament in *The Courage to Be* implies three crucial human needs: the need for security, for meaning and hope, and for self-acceptance.

> [N]obody can live without hope, even if it were only for the smallest things which give some satisfaction even under the worst of conditions, even in poverty, sickness and social failure. Without hope, the tension of our life toward the future would vanish, and with it, life itself.

> [W]ithout a vestige of self-esteem no one can live, not even he who bases his self-esteem on despairing of himself.[361]

But these needs cannot be fully satisfied apart from participation in the life of what Tillich describes as the New Being.

The human situation is characterized not only by anxieties but also by ambiguities. Tillich distinguishes three basic functions of life: self-integration, the circular movement of life from a center and back to this center; self-creation, the growth function of producing new centers; and self-transcendence, the vertical direction under the principle of sublimity.[362] Because of existential estrangement, these essential functions are countered by the corresponding threats of disintegration, destruction, and profanization. Since "life is neither essential nor existential but ambiguous,"[363] the positive and negative elements are inseparably mixed. Concerning the first of these functions, Tillich notes that "self-centeredness is not selfishness, self-determination is not sinfulness. They are structural descriptions and the condition of both love and hate, condemnation and salvation."[364] Concerning the third, he observes: "The human soul cannot maintain itself without the vertical line, the knowledge of an eternal meaning, however this may be expressed in mythological or theological terms."[365]

Tillich's portrait of the human condition extends to an analysis of the contemporary cultural climate. He criticizes the superficiality of optimistic forms of secularism and the hopelessness of nihilistic forms of secularism.[366] In *The Religious Situation* and *Theology of Culture,* he argues that the three great powers of the industrial society, namely, science, technique, and capitalism, have diminished the transcendent dimension in man's encounter with reality.

> Reality has lost its inner transcendence or, in another metaphor, its transparency for the eternal. The system of finite interrelations which we call the universe has become self-sufficient. It is calculable and manageable and can be improved from the point of view of man's needs and desires. Since the beginning of the 18th century God has been removed from the power field of man's activities. . . . As the universe replaces God, as man in the center of the universe replaces the Christ, so the expectation of peace and justice in history replaces the expectation of the Kingdom of God. . . . Out of this predicament of man in the industrial society the experiences of emptiness and meaninglessness, of dehumanization and estrangement have resulted. Man has ceased to encounter reality as meaningful.[367]

To expose the "structures of evil" that produce social and individual tragedy, Tillich adopted the symbol of the demonic. But Tillich recognized that "the structures of society are creative and destructive at the same time"[368] and advocated the creation of "such a culture and religion as will express the meaningfulness of all reality as a meaningfulness derived from the relation to the ultimate."[369] No secular position, even the ones that are realistic in their understanding of the anxieties and ambiguities of the human situation, is viable without grounding human potential in the ultimate. Instead, Tillich promoted a new realism that would uncover the demonism in the social world and rely upon the transcendent source of meaning and Ground of Being. He called this a "belief-ful realism" to distinguish it from utopian idealism (absolutizing of social programs) and unbelieving realism.[370] He used the word *kairos* to describe the moment of new beginning in which "the eternal breaks into the temporal, and the temporal is prepared to receive it."[371] **In his theology of culture, Tillich struggled for "theonomy," a society characterized by *kairos* in which the ultimate meaning of existence is manifested in its finite structures.** In contrast to "autonomy" (the assertion that man is the source and measure of culture and religion) and "heteronomy" (the assertion that man must be subjected to laws that are alien to his nature), theonomy asserts that the law that is superior to man is also "the innermost law of man himself, rooted in the divine ground which is man's own ground: the law of life transcends man, although it is, at the same time, his own."[372]

Tillich's theology is ontologically centered in that he spoke of the divine as Being itself. All beings are dependent for their origin, meaning, and destiny on the creative Ground of Being.

> Man, together with all things, comes from him who has put all things under man's feet. Man is rooted in the same Ground in which the

universe with all its galaxies is rooted. It is this Ground that gives greatness to everything, however small it may be, to atoms as well as plants and animals; and it is this that makes all things small, however great—the stars as well as man. It gives significance to the apparently insignificant. It gives significance to each individual man, and to mankind as a whole. This answer quiets the anxiety about our small-ness, and it quells the pride of our greatness.[373]

Only the eternal power of Being can provide a basis for meaning and ultimate identity. But what Tillich calls "the Unconditioned" is so transcendent that all reli-gious ideas must be expressed in symbolic terms that point beyond themselves and participate in that to which they point.[374] The phrase *ultimate concern* is Tillich's pri-mary formulation for the conception of God as the Unconditioned.[375] It is through the expression of ultimate concerns that humans have an immediate ontological awareness of the Unconditioned.[376] Tillich contends that "[i]t is the unconditional character of the biblical God that makes the relation to him radically personal. For only that which concerns us in the center of our personal existence concerns us unconditionally."[377]

Tillich wishes to integrate philosophy and theology, and this is particularly evi-dent in his understanding in *Systematic Theology* of the fall as a symbol for the human situation.[378] He is an existentialist to the extent that he asserts that being can only be understood in the light of an analysis of existence, but he parts company with existentialism when he uses his analysis of existence to project a realm of essential being.[379] For Tillich, the fall is the "transition from essence to existence" that is brought about by the human desire to actualize finite freedom.[380] This transi-tion produces a gap between the goodness of essential creation and the nature of actualized creation: "Actualized creation and estranged existence are identical."[381] From this perspective, sin is "universal tragic estrangement, based on freedom and destiny in all human beings. . . . Sin is separation, estrangement from one's essen-tial being."[382] The problem with this analysis is that it tends to merge the doctrines of the creation and the fall to the extent that it equates sin with ontological estrange-ment. Tillich has been criticized for maintaining the pessimistic position that sin is a necessary part of being.[383] Finite human freedom also becomes ambiguous on this account in that it is the *telos* of creation on the one hand, and the inevitable source of human shame on the other.[384]

Tillich often uses the word *estrangement* in place of the more traditional word *sin* because it communicates the idea that humans belong essentially to that from which they are estranged. The state of sin is the state of separation: verti-cally, it is a separation of humanity from the Ground of Being; horizontally, it is a separation of people from themselves and from other people.[385] Because

humans are estranged from God in their personal center, they are bound to sin.[386]

> Sin is our act of turning away from participation in the divine Ground from which we come and to which we go. Sin is the turning towards ourselves, and making ourselves the centre of our world and of ourselves. Sin is the drive in every one, even those who exercise the most self-restraint, to draw as much as possible of the world into oneself.[387]

The inability to overcome the consequences of sin produces despair. "The pain of despair is the agony of being responsible for the loss of the meaning of one's existence and of being unable to recover it. One is shut up in one's self and in the conflict with one's self."[388] In this sense, man is subject to a "bondage of the will" because he cannot heal the disruptions characteristic of estranged existence.

Tillich uses what he calls "the method of correlation" to relate the questions that arise out of the human predicament to God's revelatory answers. He criticizes Barth for denying the human capability of a quest for God and asserts that God's self-manifestation is conditioned by human reception.[389] For Tillich, theology is a dialectic between the existential questions of human finitude and the essential answers of divine revelation. These answers are not derived from but mediated to the human experience of a religious and cultural quest for the recovery of a unity between the finite and the infinite.[390] Humans transcend everything in the historical order and, in spite of their estrangement, belong to an order which is "not transitory, not self-destructive, not tragic, but eternal, holy and blessed."[391] A culture bereft of its religious substance is form without an ultimate source of meaning.[392] **Since people cannot live without meaning and yet rebel against its source, they absolutize relative values by elevating preliminary concerns to the rank of ultimate concern.**[393] But preliminary concerns are finite and should not be maintained as if they were ultimate. Every concern, whether about work, about others, or about pleasure, "tries to become our ultimate concern, our god."[394] Even concern about God can be made a finite concern, "an object among other objects."[395] Human life is characterized by multiple physical, cognitive, aesthetic, social, and political concerns, and each of these can make the false claim of ultimacy in the life of an individual or of a social group.[396]

Needs and wants are illimitable, and when temporal, earthbound concerns take precedence over eternal concerns, people are driven on "from one thing to another and there is no possibility of satisfaction."[397] **Tillich claims that only the fulfillment of the center of one's true being can lead to real satisfaction and joy, but he adds that this fulfillment "does not exclude partial and peripheral fulfillments."**[398] **A mature relatedness in the vertical dimension enhances relatedness in the horizontal dimension.**

There are innumerable concerns in our lives and in human life generally which demand attention, devotion, passion. But they do not demand *infinite* attention, *unconditional* devotion, *ultimate* passion. . . . [Mary] has chosen the right thing, the one thing man needs, the only thing of ultimate concern for every man. . . .

The one thing needed . . . is to be concerned ultimately, unconditionally, infinitely.[399]

This is the fundamental human need, and when this is satisfied, one is no longer overcome by anxiety about the finite concerns of life. The present order must be lived in the light of the coming order.[400]

Since earthly securities are ambiguous, the universal human longing for love and for truth must be directed toward the Ground of unconditioned meaning. In Tillich's terminology, the desire for God as love is *agape,* and the desire for God as truth is *eros.*

Eros drives the soul through all levels of reality to ultimate reality, to truth itself, which is the good itself. . . . *Agape* reaches down to the lowest, forgiving its estrangement and reuniting it with the highest. But *agape* does not contradict the desire for the highest; and a part of this desire is cognitive *eros.*[401]

The ethical passion of biblical religion converges with the ontological passion of philosophy in the God who is the unconditional concern, the "object of surrender, obedience, and assent."[402]

The problem is that the greatest human need, that of relatedness to the Unconditioned, is thwarted by the dilemma of existential estrangement in which no act within the context of this estrangement can overcome it. **Man is utterly unable to break through the bondage of the will to achieve the reunion with God necessary to the fulfillment of his being.[403] The only solution to this problem is divine grace, which occurs in spite of the separation due to sin and results in the reunion of human and divine life.** "Grace is the acceptance of that which is rejected. Grace transforms fate into a meaningful destiny; it changes guilt into confidence and courage."[404] Sin and grace are related, in that grace creates an awareness of sin, while the experience of separation enables one to grasp the meaning of grace. Grace does not destroy human freedom, but in overcoming guilt and estrangement, "it does what freedom under the conditions of existence cannot do."[405]

Grace unites two elements: the overcoming of guilt and the overcoming of estrangement. The first element appears in theology as the "forgiveness of sins," or in more recent terminology, as "accepting acceptance though being unacceptable." The second element appears in theology as "regeneration" or in more recent terminology, as the "entering into the new being" which is above the split between what we are and what we ought to be.[406]

Attempts at self-salvation are futile; participation in the unconditional means living in a "Gestalt of grace."[407] "[W]e ask for a grace as unconditional as the moral imperative and as infinite as our failure to fulfill it."[408] **Affirming the Protestant principle that stresses the infinite distance between God and man, Tillich says that one must actively receive the personal encounter with transcendent reality as a gift.[409] Justification is by grace alone, and grace even creates the faith through which it is received: "we are grasped by grace, and this is only another way of saying that we have faith."[410]**

Faith is "the state of being grasped by an ultimate concern, and God is the name for the content of the concern."[411] The state of faith transcends the drives of the non-rational unconscious as well as the structures of the rational conscious; it is a concern of the whole person, engaging the intellect, emotion, and will.[412] It is in the state of faith that one is able to accept the fact that he is accepted by the power of being-itself.[413] This acceptance, in turn, is the ultimate basis of self-acceptance: **"No one can accept himself who does not feel that he is accepted by the power of acceptance which is greater than he, greater than his friends and counsellors and psychological helpers."[414]**

The "in spite of" character of this acceptance makes it paradoxical, since "it is man in anxiety, guilt, and despair who is the object of God's unconditional acceptance."[415] Since these elements conflict with the affirmation of one's essential nature, the faith to believe that one is accepted requires courage. "The courage to be is the ethical act in which man affirms his own being in spite of those elements of his existence which conflict with his essential self-affirmation."[416] The courage of faith is set in a context of the greatest risk that a person can run:

> For if it proves to be a failure, the meaning of one's life breaks down;
> one surrenders oneself, including truth and justice, to something which
> is not worth it. One has given away one's personal center without hav-
> ing a chance to regain it. . . . This is the risk which is unavoidable if a
> finite being affirms itself. Ultimate concern is ultimate risk and ulti-
> mate courage.[417]

Faith is not characterized by certainty but by hope. Faith is participation in that which is of ultimate concern.[418]

Tillich contrasts the bondage of the old being with participation in the saving power of the New Being in Jesus as the Christ. Christianity announces the presence of a New Reality which overcomes existential estrangement and heals the cleavage between essential and existential being. The term *New Being* points to this restorative principle of the power of being conquering nonbeing, eternity conquering temporality, and grace conquering sin.[419]

> The classical terms for this state are "New Birth," "Regeneration," "being a new creature." Obviously, the characteristics of the New Being are the opposite of those of estrangement, namely, faith instead of unbelief, surrender instead of *hubris,* love instead of concupiscence.[420]

This New Reality beyond the split between essential being and existence is completely manifest in Christ. "What has appeared as our ultimate existential concern has appeared at the same time as the logos of being. This is the fundamental Christian claim and the infinite subject of philosophical theology."[421] The New Being makes its appearance in historical existence in the person of Christ. Tillich's rejection of efforts to reconstruct the historical Jesus out of the New Testament text have led some commentators to interpret him as being willing to accept the possibility that Jesus of Nazareth never lived.[422] But Gilkey argues that this is based on a failure to distinguish the living person *behind* the text from the historian's reconstruction *out of* the text.[423] The former is crucial for Tillich to the validity of the Christian message, while the latter is only of peripheral interest. But Tillich criticizes the tendency to focus attention on the personality of Jesus instead of the New Being that he expresses in his person. "Jesus as the Christ is the bearer of the New Being in the totality of his being, not in any special expressions of it."[424]

All people long for an "unambiguous fulfillment of their essential possibilities," and it is in the self-transcendence of life in the realm of the spirit that this quest is answered.[425] When man is grasped by the unambiguous Spiritual Presence of the New Being, servitude to the ambiguities of life is conquered.

> Unambiguous life can be described as life under the Spiritual Presence, or as life in the Kingdom of God, or as Eternal Life. . . .
>
> The three symbols for unambiguous life mutually include each other, but because of the different symbolic material they use, it is preferable to apply them in different directions of meaning: Spiritual Presence for the conquest of the ambiguities of life under the dimension of the spirit, Kingdom of God for the conquest of the ambiguities of life under the dimension of history, and Eternal Life for the conquest of the ambiguities of life beyond history.[426]

Tillich stresses that there is no human condition that cannot be penetrated by the divine presence. In the reality of the New Being, the anxieties of fate and death, emptiness and meaninglessness, and guilt and condemnation are overcome by participation in divine life, meaning, and grace. It is in the vertical dimension of the New Being that the human needs for security, for meaning and hope, and for self-acceptance find their fulfillment.[427]

This fulfillment takes place in a context of the community of the New Being, and is not given to the separated individual. This community "is primarily a group of people who express a new reality by which they have been grasped."[428] The only way to reach the innermost center of another being is in "a movement that rises first to God and then returns from him to the other self. In this way man's aloneness is not removed, but taken into the community with that in which the centres of all beings rest, and so into community with all of them."[429]

Karl Rahner

Karl Rahner (1904–1984) has been called "the Father of the Catholic Church in the twentieth century" because of the profound influence he exerted on Catholic theology through his teachings and voluminous literary output. The depth and breadth of his theological writings reflect both a commitment to Christian tradition and a concern for relating the implications of this tradition to the issues of contemporary life. Rahner also sought to integrate theology and spirituality, and many of his works combine an evident devotional spirituality with philosophical and theological precision and scholarship.[430]

Rahner's theology is anthropocentrically oriented in his stress on the freedom of human subjectivity and the importance of explicating theological concepts within the framework of contemporary human experience. He begins with the necessary response of affirmation or rejection of the intractable mysteries of divine and human transcendence. The task of theology is to lead people into an awareness of the real nature of human existence and the awesome implications of the freedom to move toward or away from the love of God as the source of personal authenticity.[431]

Rahner speaks of the intellect's pre-apprehension or pre-concept of being (*esse*) as the condition for intuitive human knowing in general. While Aquinas characterized the agent intellect as "the power of forming the first principles of transcendental validity" in the absolute apprehension of being, Rahner argues that this apprehension is not a representation but "an *excessus* beyond the sensibly concretized being to *esse* absolutely."[432] This pre-apprehension of being is the basis for the possibility of the universal concept as well as the objectification of sensory perception, since the capacity for human knowing and the essence of existing objects are both derived from the same ultimate ground of being. "Being itself is the original, *unifying* unity of being and knowing in their *unification* in being-known."[433] The pre-apprehension by which man is a sentient knower is not an a priori knowledge of objects, but the a priori condition of the knowledge of an a posteriori appearance.[434] Thus, "spirit" (*Geist*) is a more original human element than sensible intuition; man is spirit insofar as he is "absolute openness to being in general.

Transcendentality with regard to being in general is the basic constitution of man."[435]

Spirit is the power by which a human reaches beyond the realm of immediate experience and pre-apprehends the metaphysical. Rahner rejects any philosophical position that asserts the existence of innate ideas or immediate intuitions of metaphysical objects and argues that human cognition cannot directly apprehend absolute being. Man cannot know God as an object of reality; the knowledge of God is non-objectively transcendental as the necessary principle by which all human conceptions are made possible.[436] The pre-apprehension of being as the condition for the possibility of objective knowledge implicitly posits the existence of "the thing of which is affirmed absolute 'having being' (that is, of God)" whether this experience of transcendence by the spirit is acknowledged or anonymous.[437] **In his essence, then, man transcends toward God, whose absolute being is the goal of the spirit's desire.**[438] In Rahner's transcendental-existential approach, "anthropocentricity and theocentricity in theology are not contradictories but strictly one and the same thing seen from two different aspects, and each aspect is unintelligible without the other."[439]

The movement toward transcendence is at best an asymptotic approach that is mediated in the mystical experience, not of the subject's own being but of "the infinite horizon of being" in an absolute sense to which the spirit is open.[440] However, man also experiences himself as an inexplicable mystery because "the full depths of being in this self which he experiences exceeds his powers of penetration."[441] **Since he is more than a biological being, man "has needs which are not merely determined by his 'bios'"**[442] **but arise from his essence as a being who has absolute transcendence toward God. Man "does not possess within himself what he essentially needs in order to be himself"**[443] **because he is a mystery whose ultimate reference is to the mystery of God.** His pre-apprehensive receptivity to the self-luminosity of being produces a freedom of spirit which not only surpasses sensibility but also produces a disquieting sense of finiteness and contingency.[444] Human existence is fundamentally ambivalent, suspended as it is between time and eternity and between the world and God. Man is "always exiled in the world and is always already beyond it" because of the appetite of the spirit which strives toward the absolute.[445] **This freedom of spirit creates a freedom of choice by which a person decides what he will finally become. He can suppress the experience of transcendence and devote himself to the affairs and systems of the world. In doing so, he chooses freedom away from the source of freedom and limits the horizon of his openness by refusing the possibility of God's revelatory initiative. Or he can respond in freedom to the deepest movement of his existence and open himself to the transcendent mystery which is the basis of his being.** It is this responsible, free decision that leads one toward the knowledge of God, who can never be known in a neutral fashion. This is a moral and personal knowledge that is founded on the choice to love spirit more than matter. "The concrete knowledge of God is always determined from the start by the way in which man loves and treasures the things presented to him. . . . Thus each man has the God who corresponds to his effort and the manner of that effort."[446] A person deals with himself in freedom and shapes his final state through the unavoidable act of rejecting or accepting the ground of ultimate meaning. God is the source of this freedom, but this freedom becomes truly free only in the choice to grasp the gift of himself in personal love. "He is the freedom of our freedom by the grace of his self-communication, without which our free will could only choose bondage no matter what choice it might make."[447] **The holy mystery called God cannot be manipulated by man and has no need of man, but he is "the One whom we need" whose incomprehensibility is the blessed fulfillment of man.**[448] This choice to move toward or away from God is not conditioned on an awareness of God's historical manifestation in Jesus Christ but is exercised even in the context of one's faithfulness or faithlessness to the dictates of conscience.[449]

It is when one "accepts his own self as it is disclosed and offered to him in the choice of transcendence as interpreted in freedom" before God that he discovers true self-understanding and self-realization because in doing so he has reached beyond himself to the unimaginable God who "stands beyond all multiple world-reality."[450] Man's fulfillment and happiness are found in the acceptance of his own inconceivability in the face of God's inconceivable mystery so that self-transcendence takes place in the power of divine transcendence. Mystery is the definitive factor in human existence; God has created an image of his own infinity deep within human nature, and he calls man away from enslavement to finite things to the fulfillment found only in the abyss of the divine mystery.[451] In the radiant center of human existence, man himself is a mystery which is hidden in the mystery of God.[452] He can only understand himself in the realization of God's self-communication to him, and yet God forever remains incomprehensible, even in the beatific vision.[453] His proper response to this inscrutable mystery is not to understand it (which would be to create an image limited by human rationality), but to accept it and surrender himself to it unconditionally and unreservedly in humility and love. This response of radical commitment requires courage because in this decisive act, one sets out on a "spiritual odyssey upon the sea of God's mystery."[454]

God's mystery is historically mediated in his self-communication of revelation to humanity in Scripture, in the person and work of Christ, and in the community of salvation, the church.[455] But the immediacy of this historically constituted and transcendental knowledge is also "present in the depths of existence in the most ordinary human life."[456] God is not the eternally distant one, but in his revelatory initiative, he acts in grace, calling man to acceptance of his self-communication in Christ.[457] The transcendental experience of "the mystery we call God" offers itself to human freedom through the Spirit of God and through the elevating grace of God, since it is an ultimate goal and an absolute fulfillment of being that is beyond the horizon of human attainment.[458]

> The initial elements of such fulfillment are already present: the experience of infinite longings, of radical optimism, of unquenchable discontent, of the torment of the insufficiency of everything attainable, of the radical protest against death, the experience of being confronted with an absolute love precisely where it is lethally incomprehensible and seems to be silent and aloof, the experience of a radical guilt and of a still abiding hope etc. These elements are in fact tributary to that divine force which impels the created spirit—by grace—to an absolute fulfillment.[459]

This divinising grace of God's absolute self-communication is necessary to the transformation of the human condition because "we need someone who is not as we are, so that we may be redeemed in that which we are."[460]

While Rahner was concerned with theoretical theology, he also sought to demonstrate its relevance to pastoral theology and practical concerns. **On both a theoretical and a practical level, the "universal human need" in Rahner's thought is a relationship with God.**[461] This relationship consists of faith, hope, and love, and each of these is a fundamental human need.

The Need for Faith

Rahner often writes about the contrast between the downward tendency of the human mind toward the finite assertion of earthly life and the elevation of grace that leads toward God as "the goal and end of man's supernatural vocation."[462] The path away from the inwardly spiraling subjectivity that seeks self-mastery and the damnation of only being able to love oneself is a willingness, prompted by grace, to surrender oneself to God in a submission and love borne out of trust, that is, the "exodus of one's own existence out of oneself and toward God—the only route to human happiness."[463] The fullness each person needs is not found in closing in upon oneself but in responding to the summons to come out of oneself and to open one's heart to God, who promises to give himself irrevocably to those who give themselves unconditionally to him. "Fundamentally all sin is only the refusal to entrust oneself to this measurelessness, it is the lesser love which, because it refuses to become greater, is no longer love."[464] To entrust oneself to God is to accept one's creaturely dependence and to break out of the narrowness of human existence by letting go of oneself in the presence of the infinite love which is "utterly beyond our control."[465]

Rahner stresses that this approach to God must be for his own sake, since God cannot be shaped to fit our needs. The "primitive horizontalism" or "anthroegoism" that seeks to reduce God to a mere fulfiller of human needs is "the unique heresy of our time."[466] If belief in God is in any way rationalized by or subordinated to the quest for personal fulfillment, faith is reduced to a self-centered quest that is doomed to failure since "a God who is postulated to exist on the grounds of human needs is and remains in all cases a projection of man himself."[467] It is only when a person renounces self-seeking and loses himself in willing trust and surrender to the mystery of God that he discovers the fulfillment that can never be found as an end in itself but only as a byproduct of the pursuit of God.[468] Faith for Rahner means to include God in one's scheme of things and to depend entirely on God's gracious will; it is "the positive and unconditional acceptance of one's own existence as meaningful and open to a final fulfillment, which we call God."[469] **Faith as the acceptance of the infinite mystery of God and the acceptance of oneself as "the mysterious and gradually revealed gift of the eternal generosity of God" leads to the fundamental fulfillment and consummation of human existence.**[470] In the temporal life-situation, this fulfillment does not preclude conflicts between the "'needs' of society and those of the individual," the tension between happiness and moral duty, or the crosses of pain, illness, and death. Rather, these can be borne in a context of hoping faith.[471]

As the eternal and absolute reality whose personal infinity entered into his world and assumed the finiteness of human existence, Jesus Christ is the focal point of the Christian faith, not just as the bearer of the message but as the content of the message.[472] In Christ the incomprehensible God has given himself to humanity and made it possible for people to be taken into the eternal life of the Trinity; the transcendence of God has been mediated through the finite in the historical manifestation of the God-man who appropriated creaturely multiplicity. This doctrine of God's loving mediation in Jesus of Nazareth is the centrality of the Christian faith. Those who find him also find themselves, since theology and anthropology have met in the loving mediation of the eternal Word of God, Jesus Christ.[473] **In assuming a creaturely status, God has "himself endured our state of need" by taking human fate upon himself and penetrating to the deepest level of man's being.**[474] His redeeming self-surrender has achieved the ultimate possibility of human existence and transformed human despair into acceptance, grace, and hope. It is in Christ alone that God "comes to our help in our state of elemental need" and preserves the dignity of man by bestowing on him an absolute value.[475] As a Catholic, Rahner speaks of his own devotion to the sacred heart of Jesus as the expression of "that reality in which the unnameable mystery which we call God is made present to us as compassionate and self-bestowing proximity."[476] The apostolic witness to the historical manifestation of Jesus affirms that the basis of human existence is God's acceptance of man in love and his provision of truth, life, and eternity to the recipients of grace.[477] Since Christ is the actual absolute and "the decisive existential factor of man's life," the proper human response to him is a loving and unconditional commitment to him in primal trust.[478] By serving him and continuing his life, his followers participate in his destiny.[479]

Rahner relates the need for faith in Christ to the grace and forgiveness of God, who took on human nature and entered into solidarity with man. The human history of rebellion against God, of drawing back from him and refusing to respond to his call, of absolutizing earthly values and minimizing transcendent values, of mistrusting God's direction and focusing confidence in oneself, has led to a condition of guilt, estrangement, and wretchedness that could be redeemed only in the passion and obedient death of the incarnate Word. **The burden of guilt and blame produces a despair and hopelessness that cannot be overcome apart from "the almighty radicalness of divine forgiveness which not only forgives and 'writes off' what 'can no longer be changed' but which can truly redeem the past."**[480] The miracle of God's pardon and acceptance in grace is available through the exercise of one's "fundamental option" of *metanoia* (repentance, or conversion to God through faith and contrition).[481] In Christ the experience of guilt is transformed into the experience of hope in the unmerited work of God that removes this guilt in forgiving grace.[482]

The transcendent mystery of salvation, actualized in the acceptance in freedom of God's self-communication in faith, hope, and love, produces a radical interior change by which a Christian is set free from the bondage of sin, law, and death and brought into the unlimited life of the God of creation and redemption.[483] **Since this salvation comes from God alone and is not subject to the conditions of human control, all "utopian conceptions of salvation-in-this-world are to be rejected as doctrines meriting condemnation."**[484] **Even the act of unconditionally entrusting oneself in freedom to God is a consequence of divine grace.**[485]

As a Jesuit theologian, Rahner accepts the axiom, *"Extra Ecclesiam nulla salus,"* and argues that it is impossible to possess the justifying grace of the Holy Spirit outside the church. The church has been founded by God as the community of the children of God and the continuance of Christ's presence in the world as the socially organized and historically manifest presence of the salvific grace of Christ.[486] Thus, every instance of salvation must in some way be connected with membership in the church; while each individual "works out his own unique, irreplaceable salvation in personal freedom, he always does so by finding his way to the Church."[487] Since the church is "the institutional constitution of the religion of the absolute mediator of salvation," it is the sign of salvation to those who do not belong to it.[488]

In light of this, Rahner warns of a twofold danger to the church:

> There is the possibility of a liberal sell-out of Christianity through a reduction of its vital religious substance to mere secular humanism, for the sake of good relations with the people surrounding such a small Christian community. The opposite danger is the creation of a ghetto of the "holy remnant," those who alone are chosen. That makes it easier to withstand the pressure of secularized society and its atheism, and removes the need to bother about others.[489]

Rahner's answer to the first danger is that Christianity is "the absolute religion, intended for all men," and that no other religion or philosophy has equal validity.[490] His response to the second danger is his teaching on "implicit" or "anonymous" Christianity. There is "a certain stratification" in the reality of the church, consisting of degrees of membership implied by the church's recognition of a *baptismus in voto* (a baptism of desire) which can be explicitly or implicitly willed by those who do not belong to the visible church but who are nevertheless saved by virtue of their moral outlook and intention.[491] This justifying act is understood as the *votum Ecclesiae*, even though the Catholic Church is not its explicit object.[492] Since the grace of God is not confined to the visible church, the statement that there is no salvation outside of the church loses its appearance of arrogance, severity, and exclusivity.[493] God desires the salvation of everyone, and those who look for him "in anonymous hope," whether or not they know the historical name of Christ, find God when they "selflessly follow their conscience" and overcome their selfishness by loving their neighbor.[494] Rahner extends the teaching of Vatican II not only to the practitioners of other religions but even to atheists who live in the grace of justification as "implicit" Christians.[495] Just as one can have orthodoxy without justifying faith in the visible church, so one can be an unorthodox "Christian pagan" who is near to God without realizing it.[496]

The Need for Love

Rahner repeatedly emphasizes the fundamental importance of love of God and neighbor as the all-encompassing act which is central to human living and fulfillment. Interpersonal communication in love with God and others is "the actualization of Christian existence in an absolute sense."[497] **The exercise of love of neighbor, grounded in the love and grace of God, is an act in which a person attains "full creaturely reality" because love of God and love of neighbor constitute an absolute unity.**[498] "Love of neighbor is not only a love that is demanded by the love of God, an achievement flowing from it; it is also in a certain sense its antecedent condition."[499] The mutual conditioning of both expressions of love is such that one without the other is "incomprehensible and unattainable"; there is no love for God that is not already a love for neighbor, and no genuine love for neighbor that is not ultimately an expression of love for God.[500] The two foundational biblical commandments to love God and neighbor require "the demolition of our own selfishness" in that charity does not keep accounts or seek requital.[501] As an unconditional love, its characteristic self-denial breaks a person out of the hell of egotism.[502]

This copenetration of the mysteries of divine and human love and unconditional acceptance is fundamental to the fullness of human living because it actualizes an environment of personal relationships that express the experience of God through grace. It satisfies the human need for genuine community, shared life, and the realization of personhood in interpersonal communication.[503] "If man is a being of interpersonal communication not just on the periphery, but rather if this characteristic co-determines the whole breadth and depth of his existence," then he is intended for community with other persons.[504] Rahner contends that "the human need for institutionalized community extends to religion" and that the church is the visible and historical manifestation of this community of brothers and sisters who are committed to the message of Jesus.[505] Christianity, as an ecclesial religion, provides a sacramental context for the fulfillment of the needs of humans as social beings.[506]

The Need for Hope

Rahner has written extensively on the importance of meaning and hope for authentic human existence. Without these qualities, life becomes "an abyss of absolute emptiness and absurdity" and a "hellish torment" with no foundation for optimism or dignity in the daily round of banalities and hardships.[507] He does not deny the experience of partial purpose and meaning in the goals and experiences of life, but he contends that apart from "a comprehensive actualization of meaning" in God himself, "life ultimately melts away into emptiness, spills into the void. The search and demand for a definitive, all-encompassing meaning is senseless from the start."[508] **A full-orbed meaning and purpose for existence cannot be constructed out of partial meanings but must be found beyond the materials available within the immanent realm.** The Christian finds total meaning outside the boundaries of history by venturing all on a hope that seizes the mystery of God and thereby takes "possession of the mystery of man with absolute optimism."[509] Because of this, Christians are the only people who do not need an "opiate" or analgesic as a façade to conceal an ultimate despair; they have come to understand that essential Christianity is hope, and that their commitment to the promises of God will cause them to "triumph over the risks of human existence with His powerful love."[510]

Christian hope carries its own authentication as an underived mode of knowledge that transcends temporal destiny and embraces an infinite and "absolute future" as one's own.[511] Death is not the final and definitive factor in human existence for those who have accepted in freedom the transcendental hope of resurrection. The absolute future of resurrected existence is nothing less than the living God and a perfect, beatific community with him.[512] Christian hope "demands God himself. Hope will have no gift of God—howsoever wondrous it be, for it will still be finite—through which God announces and represents himself. It must have God himself."[513] The incomprehensible mystery of God is the goal and dynamic of the movement of hope that is founded in the divine promise of unconditional acceptance of the meaning-fulness of the existence of those who accept him in silence and adoration. **The beat-itude of God's impenetrable and unmanipulatable mystery "is bestowed on us only when we affirm and love this holy mystery for its own sake and not ours, when we surrender, and not when we surreptitiously seek to make God a means of our own self-affirmation."[514]**

CHAPTER 2
A CRITIQUE OF THE SIX THEOLOGIANS

Augustine

As one of the most creative theological minds in history, Augustine was the first to develop a fully formed theology that synthesized the classical philosophical heritage with biblical tradition. The combination of original genius, rhetorical skill, personal piety, and philosophical sophistication made him uniquely influential in the history of Western Christianity. His extensive literary corpus provided the formative ideas that guided the Western church and influenced not only medieval theologians like Anselm and Aquinas but also Reformation and more recent theologians such as Luther, Calvin, Pascal, Newman, Niebuhr, Tillich, and Barth. The breadth and wealth of his insights, the skill of his analysis, and the personal dimension of his thought have given him an unparalleled relevance to contemporary concerns, and it is evident from the plethora of recent Augustinian studies that his impact is undiminished.

Augustine was a gifted and skillful synthesizer whose theological models blended Roman, Greek, and biblical influences and made use of highly evocative literary devices to communicate them. He developed a poetic and polyphonic mode of discourse that interspersed prayer, anecdotal and illustrative material, biblical quotations and allusions, narrative passages, conceptual analysis, original expressions, and other rhetorical devices that gave richness and vitality to his words. With few exceptions, however, he was not a systematic thinker. Much of his work is discursive, and though many of his diversions are fascinating, his ideas are sometimes vague and have an aura of ambiguity. **This lack of systematization made it possible for an opponent like Pelagius to quote Augustine against Augustine, but it also meant that Augustine's ideas could exert a great influence upon remarkably disparate theological communities, both Catholic and Reformed (e.g., in their disputes, Erasmus and Luther both appealed to Augustine).** Augustinianism is a comprehensive system of thought that has been derived from the many writings of Augustine, but Augustine was not an Augustinian. He was capable of holding ideas in tension that are usually pulled apart, and because of this, his integration of philosophy, experience, and Scripture, though sometimes forced and fragmented, offered a powerful, suggestive, and fertile source of images and models that evoke truths about the mystery of God. There is a significant interplay in his writings between such diverse elements as faith and reason; personal subjectivity and rational objectivity; and the individual search for God and the corporate expression of the church. These conceptual tensions reflect his incarnational theology of the Word made flesh.

Another reciprocal influence in Augustine's work is his attempted synthesis of both Christian and Neoplatonic elements. This ambitious project involves metaphysical

assumptions that are problematic insofar as they do not properly address the radical difference between the Christian view of God and that of Greek philosophy. While it is true that the supremacy of philosophical thought in Augustine's life was replaced by faith and submission to biblical authority, his writings evince a diluted Neoplatonic metaphysical strain. This is tempered in part by his openness about his own experiences with Manichaeism, Neoplatonism, and Catholicism in the stages of his personal development. Reflection on his spiritual journey became for Augustine a powerful mode of theological inquiry. **The archaeological excavation of his own soul exposed the struggles of his heart as he relentlessly pursued meaning and truth.** Taking this path led him to the realization that his quest would embrace his whole being and not merely his abstract reasoning. By universalizing the dynamics of the human soul in his *Confessions,* he developed a theology of personal engagement in which the quest of the finite seeking the infinite and the flight of the soul to God became paradigmatic of the need for all human activity to be directed toward the possession of the only One who can satisfy the deepest hunger of the heart. With subtlety and artistry, he made it difficult for readers of his passionate process of self-discovery to remain neutral, since they, no less than Augustine, have been created in the image of God and share the same spiritual needs.

Augustine's insistence on the continuity between life and thought, along with his extensive development of the doctrines of original sin, divine sovereignty, and predestination, have led to many psychological appraisals of his life, including charges of morbid introspection and preoccupation with human depravity and powerlessness. These assessments fail to take into account the Augustinian tension between divine sovereignty and human responsibility and between human dignity and human depravity. **In spite of his predestinarianism, Augustine never denied the reality of human freedom and was willing to risk the charges of inconsistency, ambivalence, and ambiguity in his attempt to maintain the balance between prevenient grace and personal responsibility.** In the Augustinian vision, divine grace does not destroy freedom but supports the correct use of freedom.

The twin themes of sin and of grace are central to Augustine's thought, and he develops them with keen insight and balance. He exposes the depth and weight of sin, particularly pride, and this penetrating analysis enables him to see the consequent need for the transforming grace of God. He is pessimistic in his position that no one can ascend to God on the basis of natural ability because of the radical gulf caused by sin, but his optimism is evident in his exposition of the power of divine grace to initiate, motivate, and fulfill the soul's quest for union with God.

To the degree that he adapts a Greek theory of knowledge, Augustine's epistemology is inconsistent with his anthropology, since this approach does not take into account the noetic effects of sin. His epistemology becomes ambiguous when he seeks to amalgamate Greek and biblical approaches to knowledge, but he did maintain a humility concerning the limits of human reason and recognized that the whole person must have faith before he can know or understand. Augustine skillfully extends this insight to the acquisition of moral knowledge in his vision of evil as a turning away from the purposes of God and good as the movement of the will toward the life, light, and love of God. His awareness that people are directed by the objects of their love, and his exposition of the downward love of *cupiditas* in contrast to the upward love of *caritas* are remarkable examples of anthropological discernment. Equally remarkable is his extension of this principle of dominant loves into a brilliant philosophy of history as the dialectic between an earthly and a heavenly city.

His *De Trinitate,* however, may be his greatest achievement because of its extraordinary analysis of the derivative image of God in man as a source of insight that points beyond itself to aspects of the relational dynamics of the Trinity. The rich theological analogies he draws from the nature of human thought, the structure of the mind and of the personality, the experience of self-awareness, and the realm of interpersonal relationships have exerted a substantial and continuing influence in subsequent Christian thought.

Augustine's theological work was shaped by the issues of his time and by his pastoral concern to warn his readers about erroneous teachings and questionable sects. His painful awareness of his own past mistakes enabled him to respond to his opponents with patience and moderation.

Thomas Aquinas

Thomas was an innovator in the sense that he rethought and integrated a wide diversity of influences into a coherent philosophical theology that utilized these sources in new ways. His bold and "modern" adaptation of Aristotelianism led to considerable initial controversy, and his system only gradually won its long-standing and influential place in the church. The resurgence of Thomism in the last century has extended beyond the Roman Catholic Church, and much of this is due to the philosophical work of Jacques Maritain and Etienne Gilson.

Aquinas developed the most comprehensive and unified theology in the history of Christian thought. Like an immense gothic cathedral, his work synthesized and balanced an imposing array of conceptual themes and brought the plethora of the diverging intellectual forces of his day back into a new order that correlated all aspects of reality. Considering that the literary period of his life comprises only twenty years, the scope and vastness of his written output is astonishing. **His work combines what G. K. Chesterton called "organized common sense" with analytical rigor in such a way that his uncanny intuitive ability to distinguish the false from the true was supported by painstaking exposition and argumentation.** In all this Thomas is noteworthy not only for his profundity but also for his practicality and clarity of expression. Although his style is complex and his methods of investigation intensely analytic, his rich and varied writings are clearer than those of most Thomistic commentators. There is a spirit of moderation, graciousness, fairness, and humility about his work, and his intellectual rigor is balanced by a distinct sense of personal spiritual commitment.

The power of the Thomistic synthesis is particularly evident in his *Summa Theologica,* one of the most majestic constructions of the human mind. His superbly articulated synthesis of intuition and logic, faith and reason, unity and diversity, and the biblical and classical is both inductive and deductive, and the broad sweep of its vision encompasses the universal flight from and return to God.

Thomas was, in many ways, an Augustinian, but he sought to amplify and clarify Augustine through insights derived from Aristotle and his Arabic commentators. While embracing, for example, Augustine's understanding of evil as a privation of good and his doctrine of intrinsically efficacious grace, Thomas carefully avoided the Neoplatonic aspects of Augustinianism such as the strong distinction between the soul and the body. On the other hand, though he adapted Aristotelianism in the area of metaphysics, criticisms that Aquinas's philosophy is a baptized version of Aristotle's fail to account for the ways in which he rethought and revised Aristotle. By avoiding the two extremes of complete rejection and uncritical acceptance of Aristotelian philosophy, Thomas was able to develop a theology that built upon Scripture and the traditions of the church but also recognized the importance of observation and investigation of the physical world.

Aquinas is frequently criticized for holding views he never taught, such as a tabla rasa empirical epistemology or the idea that unaided human reason can demonstrate the way to faith. **While he used Aristotelian philosophy as an investigative metaphysical instrument, he was always aware of the limitations of the human intellect and of the need for revelation to raise the mind to the truths of faith. He argued that these truths are not contrary to reason, though they are above reason and thus cannot be attained by it.** By distinguishing more clearly than Augustine between the spheres of philosophy and theology, Thomas was able to inquire into the nature and conditions of existence and to discern the limits of philosophical autonomy. Thus, he could trust the capacity of the human mind within its boundaries while avoiding the mistake of allowing philosophy to corrupt the substance of theology. He accurately understood that faith is not a cognitive achievement but a gift of grace, and that the vocation for which humans were created transcends the powers of human nature.

In focusing his thought on the Being whose essence and existence are one and the same, Thomas developed his profoundly consequential view of analogical predication in religious language. **Although some critics claim that the Thomistic view of analogy leads to equivocation and thus to skepticism, this misses the truth that finite experience cannot be applied to an infinite Being in a univocal way.** Religious language that is similar but not identical is the only way to avoid the extremes of univocal and equivocal predication. By using his method of controlled analogy, Thomas was able to develop a wide and coherent range of theological insights.

Thomas was without peer in reducing the great diversity of philosophical and theological viewpoints of his age into a meaningful and coherent system of thought. But it is precisely this tendency to systematize and coordinate the world of ideas into a self-consistent whole that raises the question of the degree to which the Thomistic view of human happiness is congruent with reality. Only a small percentage of the human race attaches happiness to contemplative activity. Aquinas addresses the mundane needs, goods, and hopes of ordinary people, but treats them almost exclusively as agents that can move a person toward or away from his final end. This can lead to a one-sidedness that underplays the significance and inherent value of primary factors in human motivation.

Aquinas's view that there are many levels of existence conflicts dramatically with the current view among many philosophers that all phenomena can be explained in terms of chemistry and physics. Although Thomas's philosophy was formulated in the medieval era, his work is not a medieval relic. His philosophy stills competes in the world of ideas, and there is in fact a growing number of non-Catholics (e.g., Eric Mascall, Mortimer Adler) who espouse many of his views. His system has been challenged by process theologians like Schubert Ogden and Charles Hartshorne, but modern Thomists have been able to hold their own with critics. Aquinas offered an enduring example of openness to truth regardless of its source, and because of this and the depth of his philosophical investigations, his ideas continue to stimulate thought among a wide range of scholars.

Jonathan Edwards

Edwards was an extraordinarily articulate and skillful thinker whose contributions to philosophical theology and phenomenology of religious experience have justifiably merited the accolade of the greatest religious thinker America has produced. Academic interest in his work has flourished especially since the Second World War, and this is remarkable in view of the widespread deprecation of his work in earlier generations as rigid, misanthropic, and even pathologically obsessed with the wrath of God. More careful scholarship has reappraised this estimate by placing his work in the context of the issues and challenges of eighteenth-century American Christianity, and by uncovering the penetrating and original contributions he made to religious epistemology, metaphysics, moral theory, and psychology. **Although Edwards was misunderstood by his contemporaries and failed in his efforts to defend Puritanism against the encroachments of the liberal theology that would lead to Unitarianism, his carefully articulated vision of reality has an abiding relevance.** His forceful appeal to immediate experience, the profundity of his analysis, and his ability to synthesize logical discourse with affectional fervor make his writings an enduring legacy.

Murray observes that "Edwards divided men in his lifetime and to no less degree he continues to divide his biographers."[1] Some focus on him as a philosopher and apologize for his theological beliefs, which they regard as a bondage to an otherwise great mind. But his philosophical writings were generated by theological controversy, and it would be more accurate to say that his primary concern was clearly religious. His major themes were the consequences of human sin, the person and work of Christ, and the sovereign grace of God. Edwards has been criticized for his views on the nature of virtue, original sin, sovereign election, and his sermonic emphasis on the fear of hell. While he affirmed, in contrast to the Arminians, the doctrine of the perseverance of the saints, the criteria he set forth for recognizing a true Christian were such that few could have any assurance of their salvation. He frequently exhorted his hearers to persevere in their efforts to obtain salvation and to continue in earnestness to the end, in the hope that God may bestow eternal life upon them.[2] The ironic result is that on a practical level there was as much insecurity in Edwards's strong Calvinism as there was in Arminian theology.

Edwards has been criticized for asserting God at the expense of humanity, and there is some truth in the allegation that his preaching and writing evinced a perpendicular piety. In part, however, this was an expression of his conviction that the whole of life and all avenues of intellectual inquiry, including philosophy, the arts, and the sciences, find their integration point in theology. This coherence is rooted in a theological idealism that attributes all things in the universe to the constant volitional activity of God in such a way that the visible universe exists in the divine mind and exhibits this mind and will to created minds. **Strangely enough, Edwards combined this Neoplatonic philosophy with an epistemology that was based upon sensory perception, and this led him to an awareness of the significance of empirical factors in human understanding as well as the limitations of radical empiricism.** Clearly Locke exerted an influence on Edwards's thinking, but the extent of this influence is debatable. Isolated as he was from the intellectual crosscurrents of his time, many of Edwards's ideas were the product of his own direct experience and reflection, and this marked his work with a synthetic and original quality that defies simple classification.

Edwards believed human reason was limited in its ability to comprehend the mind of God and affirmed the necessity of special grace for the attainment of the highest levels of religious and moral truth. While he asserted the deficiencies of reason in view of the deceptiveness of appearances, he nevertheless depended on rational analysis to demonstrate the truth of propositions that were presumably beyond reason's grasp. This inconsistency is mitigated by his admission of temporal paradoxes that point to the need for subordination to the divine perspective conveyed by revelation.

Edwards revitalized and reshaped the ossified Calvinism of his time and infused it with a dynamic of immediacy that apprehended doctrines as living expressions of transforming truth. For him, the awareness of the absolute sovereignty of God was a foundational experience upon which his entire system was based. With great skill he refuted Arminian arguments for the freedom of the will and the ability of human nature to move in the direction of saving faith. He refused to succumb to manipulative revivalist methods because of his predestinarian view of conversion as a miracle of grace. As a proponent of strong determinism, he denied the self-determining power of the will, yet his preaching called people to use their wills to repent of their sins and submit to the claims of Christ. In practice, he treated people as knowing and willing agents, and his sermons utilized language that appealed not only to the mind but also to the emotions and the will.

The caricature of Edwards as a preacher who was preoccupied with the wrath of God and the fires of hell continues to persist, but even his infamous "Sinners in the Hands of an Angry God" sermon counterbalances the motif of wrath with that of the grace of God, who calls people to recognize the precariousness of their condition and receive his mercy. For Edwards, God was not only the source of all rationality but also the unlimited source of loving benevolence. As a theologian of the Great Commandment to love God and others, he taught that a loving encounter with divine truth is the essence of faith. Thus, the central focus of Edwardsean neo-Calvinism turns less on the legal authority and power of God and more on the love and beauty of God. **Since harmony of the soul with God is the ultimate source of human happiness, Edwards perceptively argued that religious experience should be affectational as well as intellectual, and he developed a brilliant phenomenology of spirituality to discern the spirit of truth and the spirit of error.** Unfortunately, there is an ambiguity in his discussions of "experimental religion" that leaves unanswered the relation between the divine and the human and admits that there are no certain signs that religious affections are genuinely of God or counterfeits of Satan. But he sought to integrate the subjective and the objective components of religion by viewing faith as relevant to the whole person in such a way that the rationality of the Word and the subjectivity of the Spirit are brought into harmony. With artistic élan, his exposition of religious experience united mysticism and logic, being and doing, inner life and outward manifestation, faith and practice.

Edwards displayed equal novelty in his integration of moral philosophy with his view of beauty as fundamental to divine being. This aesthetic approach to God as absolute beauty as well as absolute power conceives moral excellence as a spiritual beauty that commends appropriation for its own sake. Edwards's remarkable account of relational dynamism in the being of God is also innovative, as is his creation theology in its quest for a way to place God and the world in a relationship of mutual immanence without compromising divine transcendence.

Søren Kierkegaard

The burden of Kierkegaard's writings is far more relevant and influential in the climate of recent thought than it was during the brief span of his feverish literary career. His work has been a shaping force in current approaches to theology, philosophy, and psychology, but the more pathological and morose aspects of his thought have also been influential among those who developed existential approaches to literature and the arts. **Kierkegaard's thought was intricately bound up with his solitary and tragic life, and his extraordinary stylistic and topical diversity reflects the shadowy reality of doubt, depression, anxiety, fear, despair,**

loneliness, misunderstanding, and rejection through which he passed. His was a tortured and courageous brilliance that defied the cultural and ecclesiastical conventions of his time and offered a new mode of perception and response.

As a polemist, Kierkegaard's rebellion against bourgeois Christianity, Hegelian philosophy, and romantic aestheticism was trenchant and prophetic, but his open attack on the Danish establishment near the end of his life was sometimes strident and frenetic. On the whole, he was not a balanced or systematic thinker, and his work is diffuse and uneven, characterized by passages that are alternatively incisive and turgid. His indirect communication and use of diverse pseudonyms, as well as his literary tricks that obscure the line between the profound and the pretentious, make his work difficult to interpret in places. But since this minimization of consistency and systematic coherence was studied and deliberate, critics who fault him for lacking these qualities actually illustrate Kierkegaardian irony. Kierkegaard predicted that his work would fall into the hands of "the professors," and indeed many attempts by academics to categorize his work have resulted in distorted portrayals. The plethora of conflicting interpretations of his ambiguous, unsystematic, and multilayered writings illustrates the futility of formulating dogmatic resolutions of his views.

Kierkegaard's opposition to rationalistic philosophy took the form of an intense fascination with the paradoxical, and this gives his work an appearance of irrationality. Thus, he is often criticized as merely presenting his position rather than supporting it. But it would be unfair to write him off as an irrationalist or an anti-intellectual. Kierkegaard in fact used cogent arguments to criticize his opponents and support his positions. When he employed paradox, he affirmed the tension it evokes with reason, but his literary strategy does not require that paradox should constitute a formal or logical contradiction. For him the contradiction can be apparent and relative; to embrace its tension is not tantamount to violating the laws of logic. In the same way, Kierkegaard's understanding of subjectivity is not the same as sheer subjectivism; he presented considered arguments for his opposition to philosophical and religious objectivity. Nevertheless, his qualitative dialectic of interiorization underplayed the value of logical connections and resulted in a number of claims that are inconsistent with what he wrote elsewhere, even when his pseudonymous posturing is taken into account. This cavalier approach to inconsistency leads to a lack of logical clarity.

In his attempt to correct the hubris of rationalistic philosophy as well as the compromise and barrenness of institutionalized Christianity, Kierkegaard tended to overstate his case. This is especially evident in his substantial divorce of faith and reason. His distaste for an evidentialist mentality reduced the historicity of Christianity to the bare fact of the incarnation and rebuffed historical investigation as useless and harmful for faith.[3] When faith becomes impervious to rational inquiry, there is no justification for denying any form of epistemic fanaticism. **Kierkegaard's view that faith is inversely proportional to probability and his correlation of passion and uncertainty are unnecessary (people become** passionate about any number of absurd propositions) and foreign to the spirit of New Testament Christianity. The relation between objectivity and subjectivity need not be either/or; it can also be both/and. His division between religious experience and public evidences is unfortunate, since passion and certitude are not antithetical.

On the other hand, Kierkegaard is correct when he contends that human reason must be aware of its own limitations and that when it fails to do so, it succumbs to the arrogance of autonomy. Thus the humility of acknowledging the inadequacy of autonomous reason in the encounter with God is preparatory to the step of faith but does not require the wholesale abandonment of rationality. What must be abandoned is the idolatrous claim that reason can grasp the transcendent object of faith.

Kierkegaard capably illuminated the subjective life of the human spirit with its longings, passions, anxieties, and hopes. He opposed those who minimized the personal and affective dimension of human existence and incisively appealed for a concern with the inward aspects of living rather than a preoccupation with the external. **Even when one acknowledges divine revelation, doctrine must be internalized by the believer so that it leads to personal transformation.** When there is a transition from propositions to implications and from intellectual compliance to passionate concern, doctrine both informs and transforms religious experience.

As a Christian philosopher, Kierkegaard sought to communicate the quest for an eternal *telos* in a context of sin, self-deception, and alienation, and "offered a dialectical mapping of life's terrain as a guide to serious pilgrims" in his phenomenology of the stages on life's way.[4] His three spheres with their internal levels identify the modes of existence in the psychology of the spirit and provide a significant introspective and phenomenological description of the human condition. Kierkegaard's analysis of the struggle to discover freedom and meaning is particularly poignant because it is based on a vision of humanity as finite and temporal with a longing for the infinite and eternal.

The absolute paradox of the intersection of time and eternity in the incarnation is, for Kierkegaard, the central theme of Christianity. Unfortunately, he develops this theme in such a way that he obscures the biblical vision of the grace, mercy, and love of God in the atonement. **His extreme view of transcendence leads to such a metaphysical contrast between God and man that God becomes a featureless absolute. On the other hand, emphasis on the inwardness of subjectivity in his view of humanity leads to an exaggerated individualism that overlooks the communal nature and corporate identity of the church.**

Paul Tillich

Tillich has been ranked by many as the most influential force among North American systematic theologians, and his contribution to twentieth-century theology is comparable to that of Barth, although their approaches are radically different. As a neoliberal who sought to recast the immanental theology of classical Protestant liberalism in a sophisticated system that would speak to contemporary culture, Tillich enjoyed great success. He was an effective apologist who used the thought forms of his time to integrate theology and philosophy in new and penetrating ways that would appeal to modern intelligentsia. Thus he freely borrowed from depth psychology and existentialism in his quest to provide a coherent and practical perspective on the predicament of estrangement and meaning, but he was also aware of the inherent limitations of these approaches in providing answers to the ultimate questions of life. Nevertheless, in his analysis of the human predicament, Tillich sometimes projected the ambiguities of his own inner turmoil onto an outer world that did not feel those ambiguities.

In his work toward a theology of culture, Tillich made a significant contribution to an understanding of how the unconditional finds expression not only in the religious sphere but also in the spheres of philosophy, art, science, psychology, sociology, politics, and the history of ideas. While he analyzed aspects of contemporary culture, he did not develop a systematic theology in this area, and his treatment of the various disciplines lacks methodical rigor and technical precision. Instead, he wrote as a scholarly popularizer whose rhetoric extended beyond his topical analysis. Thus, there is a substantial element of vagueness and obscurantism in his discussions of symbolism and myths, and his attempts to reformulate Christianity in culturally relevant ways often leads to mystification.

Tillich is at his best in his account of the way culture and religion become idolatrous and destructive when the focus of their unconditional loyalty is on finite entities and ideals rather than on the ultimate. **The genius of his message is that all finite concerns must be informed by and become the expression of ultimate concern, and this is the core of his understanding of theonomy.** Tillich wisely discerned that this process entails both subjective and objective components, and he argued that religion must encompass both the concreteness of personal concern and the abstractness of the unconditioned ultimate. He was also willing to embrace other tensions as both/and, such as that between pluralism and commitment, the prophetic (against idolatry of symbols) and the priestly (affirmation of the holiness of symbols), and unlike Barth, theology as both apologetic and kerygmatic.

In his existentialist ontology, Tillich virtually identifies philosophy with ontology and insists upon the inseparability of philosophy and theology. The controversy stimulated by these questionable assumptions is compounded by the eclecticism of his philosophical method. His highly speculative approach conflates the disparate strands of idealism and existentialism, and his use of crucial terms such as *essence* and *nonbeing* is marked by inconsistency and lack of precision.

Tillich's effort to integrate philosophy and theology is also problematic insofar as it makes Christian revelation subservient to a prior ontological analysis in which essence and existence are held in tension. The content of his doctrine of God is derived more from his analysis of being than from revelation. "The shadow of Hegel would fall over Tillich more strongly than the shadow of Christian revelation, or at least the orthodox interpretation of Christian revelation."[5] His method of correlation presupposes an identity between philosophy and theology as correlative aspects of the human quest for being and meaning. When Tillich states that "God answers man's questions, and under the impact of God's answers man asks them," it is not surprising that theological answers and philosophical questions fit together so well in his system, since it is evident that he has shaped the latter by the former. **In some cases, Tillich's philosophical questions have been determined more by this hidden a priori in his system than by a phenomenological analysis of the human/cultural situation. In other cases, his theological answers have been guided more by his philosophical assumptions than by the Christian message.**

Another difficulty stems from the lack of clarity as to the content of the total commitment Tillich calls for; some commentators claim that the object and nature of faith are obscured by his extensive use of symbols and his avoidance of basing assertions about God on scriptural exegesis. Tillich developed a distinctive theory of religious symbolism, but his approach to symbols in terms of "belief-ful realism" eliminates the components of historicity and propositional truth from his revelatory scheme. Christian symbolism becomes an allegory of his ontological/theosophical worldview in such a way that the symbols mediate an immanent power that can be intuited in the depths of life.

The metaphors of God as the Ground or Power of Being are stimulating, but Tillich's equation of God with Being-itself beyond essence and existence is a misguided attempt to reconcile the problem of divine immanence and transcendence. Far from reconciling them, Tillich's approach forces a choice between the absolute Being-itself to which the attribute of existence cannot be applied, and a panentheism in which God is enmeshed in the cosmic process. On a practical level, Tillich appears to lean toward the radical immanentism of the latter. It is not surprising that he minimizes the moral attributes and personality of God.

Because of his view of the estrangement of existence, Tillich equates actualized creation with the fall. This leads to a variety of problems, including that of how essences that do not exist, and do not participate in finitude, can fall. On Tillich's account, existence is not essentially good and is independent of God's creative activity.

Tillich was more faithful to the Christian revelation in his sermons than in his system. His theology failed to account for the biblical picture of Jesus; when he tried "to find new forms in which the Christological substance of the past can be expressed,"[6] the Christological substance was diminished and distorted. The result is a docetic and somewhat gnostic distinction between Jesus and the impersonal Christ as the power of the New Being. Once again, the ontological form of the question predetermined the content of the theological answer. The historical character of the Christian faith is replaced by a philosophical abstraction that capitalizes on the semantic power of Christian symbols while divesting them of their content.

Karl Rahner

Rahner's reputation as the most influential Catholic theologian of the twentieth century is well deserved. His voluminous literary output and the wealth of secondary literature stimulated by his elegant transcendental theology rival that of any contemporary theologian. Influenced by Heidegger and Marechal, Rahner offered a reinterpretation of Aquinas for a secularized age that had lost its sense of the transcendence of God. He developed a creative mediating synthesis that acknowledged the importance of the theological tradition of the church but sought to make it relevant to the exigencies of current thought without acceding to the agenda of secular culture. In avoiding the extremes of traditionalism and modernity, Rahner also resisted the contemporary bias against abstract philosophical theology and used this tool to erect a foundation for an authentic renewal of Catholic theology.

Much of Rahner's work is characterized by a high level of abstraction, a preoccupation with epistemological concerns, and a stylistic density. While these have been sources of criticism, they are not inherent weaknesses in his work but necessary to the rigorous development of his conceptual system. Rahner also made his thought more accessible through interpretive summaries of his views as well as devotionally oriented applications. All his writings are permeated by the unifying theme of the grace or self-communication of God that is mediated through universal human experience. **Rahner skillfully explores the mysterious nature of humanity, arguing that it is unintelligible apart from the transcendent mystery of God.** This mystery is encountered in the ordinary context of historical contingency. His use of the philosophical tool of transcendental reflection demonstrates the human orientation toward the infinite horizon of being and establishes the transcendental conditions for the possibility of human subjectivity and cognition. **On the other hand, critics like George Vass and Hans Urs von Balthasar question Rahner's anthropological approach as predetermining the conditions of supernatural revelation and minimizing the explicitly Christian character of revelatory content.** This is a telling criticism, but it is not fatal to Rahner's method since his transcendental categories are those of grace and divine revelation rather than the Hegelian categories of knowledge and idea. Rahner sought to avoid radical immanentism by arguing that transcendental reflection through human subjectivity does not predetermine the content of the gospel but prepares the way for it.

Rahner has been criticized for his views on anonymous Christianity, particularly insofar as they appear to minimize the need for evangelism. This criticism is mitigated by his response that the proclamation of the gospel is indeed relevant, since it brings anonymous Christians into the depths of their "grace-endowed being by objective reflection and . . . profession of faith which is given a social form in the Church" and leads them toward the fullness of explicit expression of their implicit faith.[7] Therefore the word must be spread not so much to transform people into something which they were not before but to bring them to themselves in the explicit profession of Christian faith.[8] This does not mean that Rahner would declare every person an anonymous Christian, regardless of whether or not he accepts the grace of God; without this acceptance, even in the form of unconditional acceptance of human existence, one remains a real non-Christian, not an anonymous Christian.[9]

Rahner emphasizes the dynamic of open directedness to God in the everyday experiences of life and does not limit the experience of grace to the mediation of specifically mystical moments. **But given the nature of human experience, there is little empirical evidence to support the idea that the ordinary pleasures and limitations of life evoke the kind of transcendental responses his theology predicts.** To some degree there appears to be a conflation of Rahner's own proclivities in his assessment of the movement toward the infinite horizon in the subjectivity of the human spirit.

Another point of vulnerability in Rahner's philosophical theology is his distinction between categorical and transcendental revelation, particularly because this is such a central theme in his system. This relates to the tension between historical immanence and absolute transcendence, and Rahner developed his concept of the supernatural existential to avoid the extremes of extrinsicism (revelation as contradictory to human nature) and intrinsicism (revelation as conditioned by human nature). This concept, however, is peculiar to Rahner and is too ambiguous and elusive to contribute meaningfully to the problem of immanence and transcendence. In innovative ways, he affirmed that God is both immanent and transcendent, but his theory of humanity as the cipher of God has panentheistic overtones insofar as it implies that God's self-expression needs the world and particularly humanity.

CHAPTER 3
A COMPARISON AND CONTRAST OF THE THEOLOGICAL MODELS

A SUMMARY OF THE THEOLOGICAL MODELS OF HUMAN NEEDS

Augustine

Augustinian anthropology is concerned with the image of God in man and the destructive effects of sin that led to the distortion and corruption of this image. Sin always relates to the preference of the created order over the Creator, the pursuit of the mutable and uncertain instead of the immutable and certain, and the quest for the plaudits of men rather than the blessing of God. The original sin of revolting against the source of being and rejection of the divine will by the substitution of one's own has been endlessly repeated in human experience, and the inability not to sin has completely tainted human nature. The consequences of sin are alienation from God, loss of righteousness, and bondage of the will.

Because of this condition of spiritual death, Augustine's assessment of the greatest human need is the grace of God, without which forgiveness and restoration of the divine image would be unattainable. This grace has been manifested in the redemptive work of the incarnate Word, who recreates those who turn to him in faith; this redemption is begun in this world and completed in the resurrected life. It is the grace of God that overcomes the bondage of human will and causes people to turn away from their own futile efforts to the sufficiency that can be found in Christ alone. Divine grace opens the way to the knowledge of the truth about man's real nature and about God as the source and satisfaction of the heart's deepest longing.

In addition to the need for grace, Augustine also writes of the need for the Supreme Good which cannot be found in creation but only in the Creator. One must seek God with the mind and with the heart and desire him above all lesser goods, which can distract and lead one away from the true source of joy and fulfillment. Temporal needs such as health and security are genuine, and their gratification is legitimate so long as one does not get so entangled in the things of the world that they lure one away from the beatitude of the eternal and unchangeable. However, the Supreme Good must not be sought as a means to the soul's felicity but as an end in himself. It is only when God is sought for himself and not for his gifts that the soul also finds the fullness of joy for which it was created. When love of God becomes dominant in one's life and prevails over love of the world, one learns the freedom of obedience to God's will and is gradually conformed to the image and character of Christ. The soul's preoccupation with the love of God for his own sake is the foundation for proper self-love (finding one's blessedness in the Supreme Good) and proper love of others (desiring that they find their joy in God).

Augustine also spoke of the human need for a hope that transcends the promises of earth-bound blessings. Because of the image of God in man, the aspirations of the heart cannot be satisfied by present gratifications, no matter how great, because they are ephemeral and shallow. Only the eternal weight of glory will satisfy the longings of those who realize that they are sojourners on earth and await the city of God. Their hope anticipates by faith that which has not yet been given but which, according to the promises of God, will never pass away when it comes. Any hope that falls short of the vision of God, who is the source of all goodness, is a misplaced hope that will lead not to satisfaction but to sorrow.

Thomas Aquinas

The fallen condition of the human intellect is such that it requires more than natural reason to arrive at the end for which it was created. Aquinas speaks of the human need for divine grace not only in a context of salvation but also for illumination of revelation as well as the faith and determination to pursue God as the true final end of all things. Without God's grace, people will substitute the multiplicity of lesser goods for the unity of the ultimate good and seek felicity in the created order. Grace is also needed for the initiation and perfection of faith, hope, and the love of God. The apprehension of God's essence in the beatific vision as the ultimate good of man will also be made possible by the infusion of the grace of God since this would otherwise be unattainable even in the resurrected body.

With or without the grace of spiritual illumination, God is the anonymous end toward which the will and intellect, as faculties of the rational soul, aspire. The appetite of the will is drawn toward the good as its perfection and ultimate end, while the intellect by its nature tends towards the true. Both faculties are interdependent and find their fulfillment beyond the realm of natural causation in the person of God, the source and essence of goodness and truth. Thomas acknowledges the role of the external goods of the body and the internal goods of the soul in the created order and states that these physical and soulish needs can be placated in such a way that they aid the pursuit of the highest human need of spiritual beatitude. But they can also hinder this pursuit when one becomes too attached to them and seeks them as ends in themselves rather than means by which one is enabled to seek the perfect happiness of knowing God. The multiplicity of finite and imperfect goods can distract the rational creature from its movement toward that alone by which it can be perfected, the infinite good. Those who seek joy and place their hope in temporal and immediate conditions cannot find the happiness they long for because it is realized only in the supernatural apprehension of the glory of God. The final integration point for human beings is not in the immanent order of created things but in the transcendence of the Creator, and Aquinas epitomizes this in the vision of the divine essence.

In addition to the needs for the grace of God and the spiritual beatitude of the vision of God, Aquinas also writes of the need to love God and others, especially in this life. For him, the intellect is higher and nobler than the will, and the happiness of heaven will be more contemplative than affective; human perfection will be found more in the intellectual vision of God than in the love of God. Nevertheless, the two are interrelated and complementary, and since the knowledge of God is analogical and mediate in earthly existence, the love of God prior to the resurrection is more perfect than the knowledge of God since the will can tend directly toward God.

The deepest human needs for the grace, love, and vision of God are all related to the soul's ultimate vocation and perfection in union with God as the Supreme Good.

Jonathan Edwards

For Edwards, the fundamental human need is a restoration of the broken relationship with God, the source of infinite happiness and ultimate blessedness. The fallen condition of the human heart is that of sinfulness and enmity with God, spiritual darkness in the intellect, selfishness in relation to others, and a complete moral inability to satisfy the righteous requirements of a perfect and holy Creator. The defacing of the image of God in man due to the fall has resulted in a nature characterized by depravity and a propensity to evil.

Those who would turn toward God must first acknowledge their unworthiness and sinful condition, and this requires the convicting work of the Holy Spirit. In view of their spiritual and moral guilt, all people are in need of the mercy, grace, and forgiveness that are found in the person and redemptive work of Jesus Christ. The grace of God is sovereign and cannot be elicited by human works or merit; divine grace is prevenient and based solely on the electing purposes of the prescient God. In his sovereignty, God is in debt to no one and would be just to withhold pardon and justification from all men. Solely because of his good pleasure, he elects some to salvation and brings them to the point of faith and regeneration through the power of his Spirit. It is only through the supernatural redemption made available in the atoning death of Christ that the radical transformation from a state of corruption, spiritual death, and condemnation to a position of sanctification, spiritual life, and peace with God is made possible. This sovereign work of God which cannot be determined by the human will does not minimize the reality of the human responsibility to come to the point of repentance and faith in order to enjoy the benefits of forgiveness from the guilt of sin and imputation of the righteousness of Christ.

Edwards also writes of the need to place one's affections and hope in God's promises of a future inheritance for those who are in Christ and not to value the inferior enjoyments of the temporal order above the eternal felicity of heaven. Temporal goods can be possessed and enjoyed without harm insofar as people do not set their hearts on them, but they are utterly inadequate in comparison with the true happiness found in the beauty and love of God. The hope of glory and of unending communion with God should be the wellspring of religious affections.

Søren Kierkegaard

Human anxiety and despair are central Kierkegaardian themes, the former relating to the tension between the temporal and the eternal, and the latter having to do with the consciousness of guilt and sin against God. The existing individual is a composite being, consisting of both psychosomatic and spiritual dimensions, who both exists before God and is absolutely different from God. Sin is related to contentment with the pleasures of the temporal moment and the refusal to aspire toward the higher *telos* of the eternal. Because of the spiritual dimension, temporal pleasures can never satisfy the deep longings of the heart, and this condition leads to a despair that one either hides and internalizes, holds in defiance of the hope of eternity, or grasps as the vehicle that breaks him away from his bondage to the temporal order. The true Christian, as opposed to many who are ensnared in the self-satisfied delusions of Christendom, consciously acknowledges his sinful condition and risks all in a faith that brings him to true selfhood solely through the grace of God. In spite of the destructive effect of sin on the cognitive, affective, and conative faculties, a human still has the freedom of choice to cling in faith or to reject the grace of God.

There is an absolute need not only for the grace of God but also for the person of God, since "man's need for God constitutes his highest perfection." To become conscious of this fundamental need, one must come to the point of recognizing his complete inability to find life or truth through his own resources. Only then can he reach the point of judging the temporal in light of the eternal and attain the single-minded willingness to possess external things with a loose grip in view of their categorical inferiority to the eternal happiness of knowing God. One should not seek God for the happiness he provides, but with the realization that as the highest good, God himself is the reward of those who find him. This single-mindedness of willing one thing above all else is an evidence of divine grace because it is contrary to the finite point of view which is more concerned with a relative rather than an absolute *telos* due to the immanence of the created world.

Similarly, Kierkegaard speaks of the human need for the love of God, which is also the foundation for the satisfaction of the need to love and be loved on the level of human companionship. He adds that it is not selfish to love God because one needs him, since this is the only way in which a person can love God.

In addition to these needs, Kierkegaard discusses at length the need for a faith that is not grounded in objective certainty but in the passion of inwardness. This radical faith takes the risk of appropriating the "absolute paradox" of the incarnation apart from objective certainties or historical proofs. It is the inwardness of faith in the apparent absurdity of the incarnation, atoning death, and resurrection of Jesus Christ as the eternal truth that leads to forgiveness of sins and unlimited hope. This leap of faith is itself a miraculous product of the grace of God.

Paul Tillich

Tillich's analysis of the human condition leads to the three needs of security, meaning and hope, and self-acceptance. The fulfillment of these needs is frustrated by the predicament of existential estrangement from the Ground of Being and the anxieties caused by human finitude. The lack of control over fate and the anticipation of death produce the ontic anxiety of insecurity; the shallowness and emptiness of life that is not centered on ultimate concern produce the spiritual anxiety of meaninglessness and hopelessness; and the ambiguity between good and evil and lack of self-acceptance produce the moral anxiety of guilt and condemnation.

These needs for being, meaning, and forgiveness cannot be satisfied by the pursuit of finite concerns but only through the ultimate concern of relatedness to God as the Unconditioned. The anxieties and ambiguities of the human situation are caused by a separation from one's essential source of being, a transition from essence to existence which Tillich symbolizes as the fall. The sin of estrangement is the state of vertical separation from the Ground of Being and horizontal separation from other people resulting from the universal tendency to turn inward and to center the world in oneself. This sin leads to despair due to the bondage of the will and the complete personal inability to rectify its consequences. Only grace can overcome existential estrangement by creating not only a consciousness of sin and the futility of self-salvation but also the courage to accept oneself by grasping divine acceptance. It is through the courage of faith that one is justified, that is, freed to affirm his own being in spite of the ambiguities of existence.

Grace satisfies the problem of guilt and condemnation, and faith overcomes the dilemma of meaninglessness. People only encounter reality as meaningful when they abandon the effort to center the universe in themselves and ground their potential in the transcendent dimension of eternal meaning. It is radical commitment to the power of Unconditioned Being that opens the way to ultimate meaning and identity and enables people to turn away from finite concerns as the basis of meaning and hope. Nothing less than ultimate, unconditional, and infinite concern can conquer estrangement and bring lasting hope.

The need for security of being is thwarted by the prospect of death but is fulfilled in the saving and restorative power of the New Being, which is manifested in Jesus as the Christ. It is in this New Reality that grace, eternity, and being prevail over sin, temporality, and non-being, and this realization is communal, not individual. The community of the New Being is a manifestation of vertical and horizontal restoration that anticipates the coming order.

Karl Rahner

Rahner's anthropological approach to theology stresses the ambivalence and mystery of human existence in reference to the mystery of God as well as the fundamental need to become open to the transcendent basis of being. One must respond in freedom to the mysterious source of freedom as the ground of ultimate meaning and fulfillment. The alternative to this response is enslavement to the finite order and alienation from the infinite ground of personal authenticity.

In Rahner's thought, a transcendent relationship with "the mystery we call God" is the universal human need, and this relationship consists of the three primary components of faith, love, and hope. The need for faith relates to the turning away from attempts to master one's self and one's environment and a willingness to respond to the love of God in radical trust and commitment. By coming out of themselves and entrusting themselves to the measurelessness of God, people transfer their integration point from finite loves to the limitless love of God and find true dignity, absolute value, and genuine fulfillment. This does not mean that the transcendent God is to be shaped to fit the human receptacle as a cosmic satisfier of human needs, since Rahner emphasizes that God is to be sought for himself and not for his gifts. But when one surrenders in trust and acceptance of his mystery, one discovers that fulfillment is the surplus of this surrender.

The conscious or anonymous focal point of faith is the loving mediation of God in the person and work of Jesus Christ. It is in Christ that the grace and forgiveness of God frees man from his bondage to sin, law, and death and transforms his guilt and despair into acceptance and hope.

The need for love relates to the vertical and horizontal dimensions of love of God and love of neighbor. Rahner sees these as mutually conditioning and copenetrating realities and argues that love, acceptance, and unselfish community with other people is both a reflection and an antecedent of love and communion with God.

The need for hope relates to the actualization of meaning that is necessary for the affirmation of human existence. Authentic hope must transcend the limits of partial and earth-bound meanings and grasp the unlimited scope of the promises of God. The absolute future of beatific community with the mystery of God in unending resurrected existence is the radiance of Christian hope.

DIVERGENCE AND CONVERGENCE IN THE THEOLOGICAL MODELS

The six theologians discussed in chapters 1 and 2 represent a wide range of historical, theological, and philosophical perspectives and differ in a variety of significant ways. Augustine's earlier writings were influenced by Neoplatonic thought, Aquinas sought to synthesize Aristotelian philosophy with Christian theology, Edwards was deeply committed to Calvinistic theology, Kierkegaard's work was shaped by his stance against rationalistic philosophy and institutionalized Christianity, Tillich's existential and cultural theology was a radical departure from traditional theological systems, and Rahner endeavored to relate Catholic theology to contemporary concerns. Their views on the authority and hermeneutics of Scripture range from conservative to liberal, and their positions on the historicity of the person and work of Christ are equally diverse. There is a somewhat greater convergence in their theology of God as immanent and transcendent, but unlike the other five, Tillich's understanding of God as Being-itself is ultimately impersonal. **All of them address the problem of sin and the divine provision of salvation, but they are not all in agreement as to what constitutes sin and salvation as well as the nature of the eternal state.**

In spite of this divergence, there is a remarkable convergence among these theologians in their views of what constitutes the deepest human needs. **All of them arrive, in one way or another, at three needs that are also developed in the New Testament: the need for forgiveness and grace, the need for love and community, and the need for purpose and hope.**

The Need for Forgiveness and Grace

In Augustinian thought, human rebellion against God in pursuing the temporal above the eternal has led to the corruption of the divine image in man and a condition of volitional bondage in which every act is tainted by sin. This corruption and bondage can only be overcome by the grace of God through the redemptive work of Christ. It is through faith in him that forgiveness from the guilt of unrighteousness is found and restoration toward conformity with God is begun. Aquinas concurred with this assessment and added that divine grace is needed not only for salvation but also for illumination of natural and special revelation and the realization that God is the ultimate good toward which the mind and the will must be drawn. Edwards stressed the sinful condition of human nature and the need for forgiveness from the guilt and penalty of sin through the sovereign grace of God in Christ. Even the repentance and faith that lead to justification are gifts of God, for no one, apart from the work of the Holy Spirit, could reach the point of conviction and regeneration.

Kierkegaard also spoke of the problems of guilt and sin before God, but described the human predicament in terms of anxiety and despair, and related these terms to the experience of finitude and inauthenticity. He was especially interested in the inner dynamic of attaining authentic selfhood and fullness of existence through the dialectic of passionate faith in which one ventures everything in believing against the understanding. Tillich's analysis of human anxiety and despair was influenced by Kierkegaard; he developed the problem of existential estrangement and the need to accept God's acceptance in grace. Rahner's understanding of this estrangement shares some elements in common with Tillich but is also informed by a more traditional assessment of the relational separation between man and God caused by sin and guilt and the need of personal forgiveness through repentance and faith in Christ.

The Need for Love and Community

All of the theologians agree that the human heart cannot find its final resting place in the temporal and the finite; only the eternal and infinite can satisfy man's deepest longings. True security and freedom in human existence must be centered on the love and acceptance of God; all lesser loves are unworthy of a person's ultimate concern. The love of God as one's final integration point is also the ground and dynamic of unselfish love on the horizontal level, and it is this love that satisfies the need for genuine *koinonia* and community. The grace of reconciliation with God gives the believer the capacity to love and serve others in a way that manifests divine love.

To some extent, Kierkegaard, Tillich, and Rahner made use of the "correlation method" of theological inquiry in which they saw Christian faith as the answer to the most fundamental questions of life, such as those of security and meaning. Indeed, all of the theologians would agree that without God, human existence is devoid of a true foundation for forgiveness, loving community, and hope. But they also agree that God is not to be sought for his gifts alone, since he is greater than any of his gifts. People need the security of unconditional love and acceptance, and the message of a Creator who knows the thoughts and motives of the human heart and still responds with redemptive grace and absolute forgiveness ultimately and perfectly corresponds to this human need. But this does not mean that unconditional love is in and of itself the supreme good of human existence. The forgiveness, love, and purpose which are offered in the gospel are not ends in themselves but means to the final end of a restored and complete relationship with God, the locus of the heart's deepest longings.

The Need for Purpose and Hope

In their various ways, the six theologians arrive at the human need for a transcendent hope that provides a definitive basis for temporal meaning and purpose. One should regard temporal gratifications and blessings for what they are and view them in the light of the eternal promises of God. Finite concerns can never appease the quest for infinite satisfaction; the soul cannot rest in anything less than the Supreme Good for which it was created. Augustine, Aquinas, and Edwards affirm that the eternal blissfulness of the redeemed community in heaven will center on the glorious vision of God. For Kierkegaard also, the eternal is the highest good, and one must cultivate a single-minded willingness to give up anything on earth in order to gain it; the temporal is only lost temporally, but eternal happiness is gained eternally. Tillich expressed the same thought with the image of commitment to finite and preliminary concerns as opposed to complete devotion to the Unconditioned as the ultimate concern. Any number of personal and social needs and wants can make a false claim of ultimacy, but partial concerns and fulfillments can never provide the transcendent groundwork necessary for eternal meaning. Rahner also wrote of the emptiness and purposelessness of life apart from the actualization of meaning found in laying hold of the mystery of God. The Christian hope of an absolute future of ecstatic communion with the incomprehensible God is the all-encompassing source of temporal and eternal meaning.

Since the need for forgiveness and grace is related to repentance and faith, the theological model of human needs converges in the three theological virtues of faith, love, and hope.

PART 2:
PSYCHOLOGICAL ACCOUNTS
OF HUMAN NEEDS

The eight psychologists selected in this study of psychological accounts of human needs represent two of the three broad theoretical categories developed in Salvatore R. Maddi's comprehensive study, *Personality Theories: A Comparative Analysis.*[1] The conflict model assumes that each person is involved in a continuous opposition between two unchanging forces, and that life is at best a compromise in which these forces are dynamically balanced, and at worst an unsuccessful attempt to deny one of them. The psychosocial version, represented by Freud and Erikson, assumes that one of these forces is inherent in the person and that the other is found in groups or societies.[2] The intrapsychic version, represented by Jung and Rank, theorizes that both opposing forces are inherent within the person.

The fulfillment model assumes that there is only one fundamental force and that it is located within the individual. Ideally, this force manifests itself in greater ways as a person matures. Conflict is not inevitable in this model, and when it occurs, it is a consequence of dysfunctional living. In the actualization version of this model, represented by Maslow and Rogers, the great force is the tendency to express more and more fully the capabilities or potentialities of one's genetic constitution. In the perfection version, represented by Adler and Fromm, the basic force is the tendency to "strive for that which will make life ideal or complete, perhaps even by compensating for functional or genetic weak spots."[3]

Maddi's third broad category is the consistency model in which the emphasis is not on basic forces, but on the attempt to maintain consistency between expectation and feedback from the external world. In the cognitive dissonance version, the crucial elements in the determination of consistency are cognitions such as thoughts, attitudes, and opinions.[4] In the activation version, the consistency or inconsistency relates to the degree of bodily activation or tension that is customary versus that which actually exists.[5] The consistency model is not represented in this thesis, because unlike the conflict and fulfillment theories, it assigns little content to what is inherent in humans, and stresses cognitive or neuro-psychological homeostasis rather than personality attributes.

In addition to the conflict, fulfillment, and consistency models, a fourth "moral model" could be distinguished by considering psychologists concerned with moral development and accountability (e.g., Lawrence Kohlberg, O. H. Mowrer, William Glasser, Karl Menninger). However, their accounts of the core of personality as it relates to human needs are variations on the themes developed in the conflict and fulfillment models. Behavioral psychology (e.g., J. B. Watson, B. F. Skinner) is not discussed because its reduction of human behavior to a scientific technology leaves it little to say about the content of human personality.

In general, this study will focus on what Maddi calls the "core of personality" consisting of those attributes that are common to all people.[6] Core tendencies are the basic motivators of human existence, and core characteristics are the structural entities implied in the core tendencies.[7] By contrast, the "periphery of personality" delineates concrete styles of life that are generally learned rather than inherent and which account for differences among people.[8]

The psychologists who were selected in this study were chosen not only because they exemplify the conflict and fulfillment models of the human personality, but also because of their impact on popular culture as well as their direct and indirect influence on other psychologists and the development of different approaches to psychotherapeutic theory and practice (e.g., ego psychology, object relations theory, and humanistic psychology). As the critiques in chapter 6 will show, it is the author's view that the work of each of these psychologists has strengths and weaknesses, and that there is a wide spectrum in the scientific merit of their work. Nevertheless, all of them have something valuable to contribute to an understanding of the dynamics of behavior. Because of the complexity of the determinants and manifestations of human personality, no single theory is capable of encompassing its rich diversity. Instead, a variety of personality theories has appeared, each theory stressing certain factors and minimizing or ignoring others.

This problem is compounded by the fact that most theoretical assertions are not delineated with enough specificity to support controlled empirical investigation. In addition, the heuristic models used by different therapists lead to different interpretations of the same observations. As well, comparatively little has been done to investigate normal behavioral development; in most cases, the focus of attention has been abnormal behavior, out of which conclusions concerning normal behavior have been extrapolated. Methodological differences also account for the diversity of positions on the genesis, nature, and motivation of psychodynamics, and this is particularly true of the gap between psychologists who see themselves as humanistic and those who do not. As Bugental observed, the former tend to be problem-oriented, while the latter are more technique-oriented.[9] Thus, approaches that are more phenomenological, qualitative, and subjectivist use different criteria for evaluating personality theories and research than those that are more experimental, quantitative, and objectivist. The former develop a more comprehensive conceptualization of personality and psychosocial behavior, while the latter are less vulnerable to vagueness and imprecision.

The cultural background of all the psychologists in this study is a democratic, Judeo-Christian tradition. They have responded in different ways, but their ideas, experiences, and therapeutic work are embedded within this modern Western context.

Because this study will contrast immanent and transcendent approaches to human needs, it will briefly discuss the spiritual and religious position of each of the psychologists as a basis for comparison with the theologians.

CHAPTER 4
THE CONFLICT MODEL OF HUMAN NEEDS

THE PSYCHOSOCIAL VERSION

Sigmund Freud

As the founder of psychoanalysis and the formulator of the first comprehensive theory of personality, Freud has shaped the course of modern thought like few other people. His monumental achievements in developing and applying a systematic method of investigating the human mind led not only to extraordinary insights into the human psyche but also to profound controversy. **Freud recognized that two hypotheses of psychoanalysis, the unconscious nature of most mental processes and the pervasive role of sexual instinctual impulses, were "an insult to the entire world."**[1] His expansion of the concept of sexuality and theory of the development of sexual functioning in early childhood in *Three Essays on the Theory of Sexuality* led to hostile opposition. From Freud's point of view, this resistance to psychoanalysis stemmed more from emotional than intellectual sources.[2]

Freud built and often revised his theories through inductive inferences drawn from decades of psychotherapeutic practice. His principal methods of research were free association, analysis of dreams, individual case studies, and self-analysis. Convinced that there is no clear demarcation between what is psychically normal and abnormal, Freud extended the implications he drew from his study of the disorders of neurotic patients to similar though less pronounced phenomena in the normal life of the mind.[3]

An underlying theme in all of Freud's work is his commitment to a deterministic view of the individual as a complex system that functions on every level in accordance with the laws of nature. He stressed the mutual interplay between psychical phenomena and somatic processes.[4] **The personality is shaped by these processes, especially through the functioning of the primal system of the id. The id is the original personality system from which the ego and the superego are later differentiated.** "It is the dark, inaccessible part of our personality. . . . we call it a chaos, a cauldron full of seething excitations."[5] The id is open to somatic influences and derives its energy from instinctual needs that are psychically expressed in it.[6] Because the id is completely unconscious, it is exempt from the logical laws of thought, its processes are not altered by the passage of time, and it has no knowledge of external reality.[7] **Since the processes of the id strive to gain pleasure and**

reduce unpleasure, the regulatory principle which dominates the id is called the pleasure principle. Increased amounts of energy and excitation are perceived in the id as unpleasure, while pleasure corresponds to decreased excitation.[8] The former is more impelling than the latter,[9] and **the id seeks to reduce tension and return the organism to a condition of relative stability. To accomplish this, it engages in wish-fulfillment by forming an image of an object that will lower the tension caused by an unsatisfied instinctual need. Freud calls this the primary process.**

To meet the demands and threats of the external world, a portion of the id is differentiated into the ego. While the ego borrows its energies from the id, it is unlike the id in that it is aware of external stimuli and capable of directing the activity of the organism to adapt to and modify the outer world.[10] Since "perceptions may be said to have the same significance for the ego as instincts have for the id," the ego functions as the "representative of the external world to the id."[11]

Freud's earlier topographic model of psychic life discriminated between the systems unconscious, preconscious (capable of becoming conscious), and conscious. In that model, the ego coincided with the conscious, though Freud recognized that the greater part of conscious knowledge is often in a state of latency.[12] By the time he wrote *The Ego and the Id* (1923), he replaced the topographic model with a structural model (the id, ego, and superego) and decided that much of the ego is preconscious in the descriptive sense or unconscious in the dynamic sense.[13] The primary process in the id obeys different laws from those of what Freud calls the secondary process in the preconscious ego.[14]

What people show by their behavior to be the purpose and intention of their lives is the striving for happiness.[15]

> Our possibilities of happiness are . . . restricted by our constitution. Unhappiness is much less difficult to experience. . . . An unrestricted satisfaction of every need presents itself as the most enticing method of conducting one's life, but it means putting enjoyment before caution, and soon brings its own punishment. . . . Happiness, in the reduced sense in which we recognize it as possible, is a problem of the economics of the individual's libido.[16]

The strong tendency toward the pleasure principle is opposed by the circumstances of the external world, "so that the final outcome cannot always be in harmony with the tendency towards pleasure."[17] Thus the ego, unlike the id, must find appropriate objects in the external world rather than the mind; it gains control over the demands of the instincts and postpones their satisfaction "to times and circumstances favourable in the external world or by suppressing their excitations entirely."[18] **In this way the ego dethrones the pleasure principle and replaces it with the more modest reality principle.** But this substitution does not eliminate the pleasure principle; instead, it safeguards it by confirming that tension reduction is engineered in realistic ways.[19]

In what Freud terms "the dissection of the psychical personality," an agency of self-observation and conscience splits off from the ego.[20] **This superego represents the values of society particularly as mediated by the parents.** The subsystem of the conscience is associated with attitudes and behavior that have been encouraged and rewarded, while the subsystem of the ego-ideal is associated with attitudes and behavior that have been discouraged and punished. The superego is the heir to the Oedipus complex and is fully developed only after that complex has been surmounted.[21] It "takes over the power, function and even the methods of the parental agency" and can acquire the characteristic of relentless severity.[22] **For Freud, the moral sense of guilt is the expression of tension between the ego and the superego. "From the point of view of instinctual control, of morality, it may be said of the id that it is totally non-moral, of the ego that it strives to be moral, and of the super-ego that it can be super-moral and then become as cruel as only the id can be."**[23] The superego is "always close to the id and can act as its representative vis-à-vis the ego."[24] Because of this, it is more unconscious than the ego.

The three personality systems in Freud's structural model are different processes that normally function in an integrated way. However, **the ego's task in managing and harmonizing the counterclaims of the three divergent forces of the external world, the superego, and the id is a difficult one, and this is why life is not easy.**[25]

All behavior is motivated by the quest for the optimal gratification of instincts within the context of society. Instincts are the "forces which we assume to exist behind the tensions caused by the needs of the id"; while they can never become objects of consciousness, the ideas that represent them can.[26] Human instincts are energized by somatic demands or needs and exert a constant pressure. They are conservative by nature because their aim is to reduce the unpleasure of tension-producing stimulation and to reestablish a state of equilibrium in the organism. The object of an instinct is the thing or condition that is used to satisfy the need and the behavior that takes place to secure it.[27] The instinctual energy is displaceable to any number of objects; "[the object] is what is most variable about an instinct and is not originally connected with it, but becomes assigned to it only in consequence of being peculiarly fitted to make satisfaction possible."[28]

Freud always specified the instinctual content of the id in terms of contrasts. One contrast was between the ego, or self-preservative instincts, and the sexual instincts. The former are related to the preservation of life and the latter are broadly related to the reproduction of the species.[29] Freud gave far more attention to the sexual instincts because they produce greater psychosocial conflict due to their complexity and gradual maturation. The sexual instincts are "numerous, emanate from a great variety of organic sources, act in the first instance independently of one another and only achieve a more or less complete synthesis at a late stage."[30] In Freudian theory, the energy of these instincts (the libido) drives a wide range of psychic phenomena.

Both the self-preservative instincts and the sexual instincts fall within Eros, the basic life instinct.[31] **In his later theory, Freud arrived at a dualism of two fundamental opposing forces: Eros and the destructive or death instinct (Thanatos). While Eros establishes and preserves unities, the death instinct disintegrates connections and destroys things.**[32] Freud did not fully develop his theory of the death instinct and acknowledged the indirect nature of the evidence for it (biological decay, aging, aggressiveness, war).[33] But he maintained that the life and death instincts frequently interact and fuse together in the individual.[34]

Because "psychical acts and structures are invariably overdetermined"[35] (subject to multiple causation), human beings are not completely good or bad; they are "usually 'good' in one relation and 'bad' in another, or 'good' in certain external circumstances and in others decidedly 'bad.'"[36]

> In reality, there is no such thing as "eradicating" evil. Psychological—or, more strictly speaking, psychoanalytic—investigation shows instead that the deepest essence of human nature consists of instinctual impulses which are of an elementary nature, which are similar in all men and which aim at the satisfaction of certain primal needs. These impulses in themselves are neither good nor bad. We classify them and their expressions in that way, according to their relation to the needs and demands of the human community. It must be granted that all the impulses which society condemns as evil—let us take as representative the selfish and the cruel ones—are of this primitive kind.[37]

The outward manifestation of the death instinct is the aggressiveness that is evident in the phenomena of sadism, masochism, and war.[38] To the extent that Eros is brought into play against the destructive instinct through the growth of emotional ties, these phenomena are rendered less pervasive.[39] Nevertheless, Freud denied the existence of any instinct toward perfection in human beings.[40]

The entire personality structure derives its psychic energy from the instincts. As the personality develops, increasing amounts of this energy are drawn from the id to the ego because the secondary process of the ego produces a greater satisfaction of instinctual needs in the context of the external world than does the primary process of the id. Left to itself, the id would invest energy in images or actions (object-choice or object-cathexis) that would not correspond to the circumstances of the outer world. To overcome this deficiency, the reality principle of the secondary process must supercede the pleasure principle of the primary process. This occurs through identification,[41] when the ego draws a correspondence between mental images and physical reality and thereby cathects objects in the external world to satisfy instinctual needs. The earliest and strongest ego cathexes are related to the parents. The ego also employs anticathexes to restrain irrational and antisocial impulses in the id. When anticathexis or repression hinders the cathexis of an object, the psychic energy is displaced to new object-choices. Displacement is a dynamic process that develops the personality and makes civilization possible through sublimation (displacements that are beneficial to cultural development).

The ego is the seat of anxiety because it is threatened by dangers from three directions: "from the external world, from the libido of the id, and from the severity of the super-ego."[42] Reality anxiety corresponds to the first threat, neurotic anxiety to the second, and moral anxiety to the third. As an experience of tension, anxiety leads to a retreat from danger. The danger reaches traumatic proportions when the state of tense excitation cannot be discharged by the efforts of the pleasure principle.[43] Under these conditions of excessive anxiety, **the ego protects itself by means of the defense mechanisms of repression, projection, reaction formation, fixation, and regression.**[44] These defense mechanisms permit the expression in awareness and activity of only those aspects of instinctual demands that are acceptable to society and internalized standards. Repression, the most effective and widely used ego defense, involves the anticathexis of previous object-choices to force them out of consciousness. While a repression "can succeed in inhibiting an instinctual impulse from being turned into a manifestation of affect," the impulse often resurfaces through the process of displacement in the form of substitute cathexes that are disguised in symbolic ways.[45] The instinctual desire looks for substitutes to manifest itself when repressed. "Any fresh advance made by the repressed libido is answered by a fresh sharpening of the prohibition"; but substitutive acts "fall more and more under the sway of the instinct and approach nearer and nearer to the activity which was originally prohibited."[46]

The ultimate course of instinctual dispositions is determined by the experiences of early childhood.[47] The disproportionate attention Freud gives to the first few years of life underscores his view that the personality structure is more or less fixed by the end of the fifth year. The developmental stages of the libido are related to the history of the sexual function. These stages center on the "erotogenic zones" and are diphasic: the pre-genital stages (oral, anal, and phallic) are separated from the genital stage by a period of latency until the time of adolescence.[48] Freud later subdivided these stages and concluded that part of each earlier stage "persists alongside of and behind the later configurations and obtains a permanent representation in the libidinal economy and character of the subject."[49] What Freud called "the early efflorescence of infantile sexual life" is incestuous in nature, and this is particularly evident in the Oedipus complex and castration complex of the phallic stage.[50] Because these wishes are incompatible with reality, they must be overcome in the course of the development of the libido and transformed "from their original auto-erotism through various intermediate phases to object-love in the service of procreation."[51] Similarly, the ego must also undergo a transformation from a narcissistic pleasure-ego into a reality-ego. If the normal development of either the sexual function or of the ego is inhibited, neurotic illness will later ensue.

Psychoneuroses stem from disorders of the ego; when the ego is too weak to cope with the internal and external demands of early childhood, the suppressed sexual instinct is manifested in substitutive phenomena. Neurotics also "prefer psychical to factual reality and react just as seriously to thoughts as normal people do to realities."[52] "Neuroses are extraordinarily rich in content, for they embrace all possible relations between the ego and the object—both those in which the object is retained and others in which it is abandoned or erected inside the ego itself—and also the conflicting relations between the ego and its ego ideal."[53]

Since the crucial factor in the genesis of a neurosis is the relative weakness of the ego,[54] the goal of psychoanalytic treatment is the strengthening of the ego and the enhancement of its organization so that it will draw more psychic energy from the id and become more independent of the superego.[55] In this way, the ego becomes more capable of managing the conflicting forces of the psyche and the external world. Freud's statement, "Where id was, there ego shall be,"[56] refers to the psychoanalytic goal of the progressive conquest of the patient's id by "putting at the disposal of his ego those energies which, owing to repression, are inaccessibly confined in his unconscious, as well as those which his ego is obliged to squander in the fruitless task of maintaining these repressions."[57] Although this goal is often interpreted as bringing unconscious thought into consciousness, in view of the preconscious nature of the ego, it may also be interpreted as the conquest of reality principle functioning over pleasure principle functioning through defenses that decreasingly distort reality.[58] **In psychoanalysis, the therapist forms a pact with the patient's weakened ego against the enemies, "the instinctual demands of the id and the conscientious demands of the super-ego."[59] By avoiding a critical attitude and taking notice of whatever occurs to the patient's mind, the analytic physician engages in a gradual therapeutic process that depends on the development of transference and the overcoming of defensive ego resistances.[60]**

Neuroses not only impair the normal functioning of the individual, but they also frustrate the purposes of civilization.[61] Civilization is based on the replacement of the power of the individual by that of a community; it is achieved through the renunciation of instinctual satisfaction and the transformation of egoistic into social instincts.[62] This occurs through the gradual internalization of external coercion and the consequent strengthening of the superego. Because of this, the price of the advance of civilization is high: "a loss of happiness through the heightening of the sense of guilt."[63] **The extensive sublimation and suppression of instincts demanded by cultural development generates neurotic behavior in those who cannot comply with the demands of civilization.[64] But the abolition of civilization and the consequent state of nature would be far worse;**

"the principal task of civilization, its actual *raison d'être*, is to defend us against nature."[65] Civilization imposes a limit on the manifestations of the destructive and aggressive forces that are present in all human beings.[66] In times of social upheaval these forces become evident: "we are misled into regarding men as 'better' than they actually are. . . . In reality our fellow-citizens have not sunk so low as we feared, because they had never risen so high as we believed."[67]

Another function of civilization is the development of communal systems of thought. **Freud notes the emergence of three great pictures of the universe: animistic (or mythological), religious, and scientific.**[68] In *Totem and Taboo* he attempts to reconstruct the preparation in primitive cultures for the first two of these systems of thought. For him, the totemic institution of exogamy and rules of avoidance for the prevention of incest along with other taboo prohibitions are parallel to the obsessional prohibitions of neurotics.[69] Another analogy with neurotics is the attitude of primitive people toward their rulers that is "derived from a child's infantile attitude to his father."[70] **This infantile model is carried into the development of animism with its humanization of the forces of nature to overcome the sense of helplessness.**[71] **Animism prepared the way for the construction of religion, which Freud regarded as "the universal obsessional neurosis of humanity; like the obsessional neurosis of children, it arose out of the Oedipus complex, out of the relation to the father."**[72] This longing for a father is motivated by the need for protection against the consequences of human weakness.[73]

In Freud's thinking, "the idea of life having a purpose stands and falls with the religious system."[74] **But religious belief is largely based on wish fulfillment and a "delusional remoulding of reality"; religion "imposes equally on everyone its own path to the acquisition of happiness and protection from suffering.** Its technique consists in depressing the value of life and distorting the picture of the real world in a delusional manner—which presupposes an intimidation of the intelligence."[75] **Freud saw no rational evidence for the cosmogony, consoling assurance, and ethical demands of religious teachings.**[76] By contrast, psychoanalysis fits within a scientific and materialistic *Weltanschauung* that is "capable of undreamt-of improvements."[77] Freud's hope was that new discoveries will increase humanity's control over the forces of nature and make easier the satisfaction of human needs in the context of a new social order.[78]

Erik H. Erikson

The widely read books of Erik Erikson (1902–1994) have made him the most popular and influential representative of ego psychology, particularly in his theory of how psychological growth persists throughout the entire course of life. **While his work is largely within a Freudian context, his understanding of eight developmental stages that extend into adulthood is a**

significant point of departure from Freud's view that limits the formative process to the early years of life.

Another important distinction is the psychosocial context of Erikson's perspective on the formation of identity. He criticizes Freud's overemphasis on instinctual energy and neglect of the cultural and historical setting as components in ego synthesis.[79] Psychoanalysis tends to isolate the individual from social factors such as historical era, ethnic group, and economic conditions, and this has led to a false differentiation between the "individual-within-his-family" who projects his infantile family constellation on the "outer world" and the "individual-in-the-mass" who is lost in the aggregate of humanity.[80] Erikson argues that the only adequate way to understand the nature of individual development in a dynamic cultural context is to combine the insights of psychoanalysis with those of the social sciences. Since the individual ego cannot exist apart from the human environment of social organization, it would be as serious a mistake to detach psychoanalytic theory from the social process as it would be to divorce it from the biological process.[81]

Treating the human organism as a homeostasis of three continuous processes, Erikson stresses the importance of recognizing the interaction of the somatic or biological process of systemic organization, the ego process of the coherent organization of experience, and the social process of group organization. These processes correspond to the id, the ego, and the superego, and they "exist by and are relative to each other."[82] Instead of isolating biology, psychology, and the social sciences, clinical training should include insights from all three, since human behavior is codetermined by all of these spheres. Somatic dysfunction, ego anxiety, and the loss of group identity all have a bearing on psychopathology in that each of these can threaten the mutual balance of the whole by asserting autonomy.[83] Individual anxiety not only reflects and produces somatic tension but reflects latent or active social concerns as well. There is a mutual interplay and psychosocial relativity between identity crises experienced in individual life and contemporary historical crises.[84] When this equilibrium is endangered by autonomous strivings in the id, ego, or superego, a condition of psychological dysfunction occurs. Enslavement by the autonomous strivings of the id which produce "excessive demands on ego and society of frustrated organisms, upset in the inner economy of their life cycle,"[85] was the original concern of psychoanalysis. Enslavement by autonomous ego strivings produces "defensive mechanisms which curtail and distort the ego's power of experiencing and planning beyond the limit of what is workable and tolerable in the individual organism and in social organization."[86] The third form of enslavement is by "historical conditions which claim autonomy by precedent and exploit archaic mechanisms within him to deny him health and ego strength."[87] **The problems caused by these imbalances are mollified by what Erikson calls the "mutual complementation" of group identity and ego identity that increases the potential for both ego synthesis and social organization.**[88] **Professional therapy will be of limited value if the culture does not provide the patient with a context for the**

meaningful integration of ego and ethos. Unlike Freud, Erikson does not reduce religion, cultural upheaval, and other mass phenomena to group analogies of individual neuroses, but he does view the history of humanity as a gigantic metabolism of individual life cycles.[89] In his treatment of the psychoanalytic relation of the ego to society, he argues that in addition to individual conflicts, there can be a cultural pathology that inhibits collective identity formation and thereby depletes the "reservoir of collective integrity from which the individual must derive his stature as a social being."[90] This collective integrity is the necessary context in which the individual's sense of being at home in this world can be developed through a coherent assimilation of organic, mental, and social patterns.

Erikson's personality theory stresses the fundamental need for a sense of coherent identity in which the organization of experience in the individual ego produces a self-awareness that has sameness and continuity. This ego identity protects the individual from the danger of the inner and outer discontinuities of the organism and the social milieu and provides a basis for integrating personal endowment and communal meaning.[91] Affection and social rewards reinforce the formation of ego identity, but it can be threatened in times of radical historical change and social upheaval, since somatic tension, social panic, and ego anxiety are interrelated.[92]

Like Freud, Erikson views the ego as an unconscious agency that selects, synthesizes, tests, and integrates perceptions, memories, and actions. While the various selves that make up the composite Self can be made conscious by the "I," the ego can only be known indirectly by its work as an "inner-psychic regulator which organizes experience and guards such organization both against the untimely impact of drives and the undue pressure of an overweening conscience."[93] Thus, the ego screens and balances the extreme impositions of the id and the superego. Erikson distinguishes personal identity and ego identity, the former relating to the perception of spatiotemporal sameness and continuity of existence and the reinforcement of this perception by others. Ego identity, on the other hand, relates to the continuity of the ego's synthesizing methods, that is, the style of one's individuality. Ego identity is enhanced when this style "coincides with the sameness and continuity of one's meaning for significant others in the immediate community."[94] Thus, ego synthesis must be successfully related to group identity; it must coherently organize experience to provide a sense of the reality of the self vis-à-vis social reality.[95] The individual ego is necessarily related to the group ego, which Erikson defines as a "psychosocial 'territory' of trusted mutualities and defined reciprocal negations."[96] An environment of psychosocial equilibrium is the needed context for consistent individual ego development as well as the trans-generational achievement and maintenance of basic values. The mutuality of drives and ego interests accomplished by the joint organization of social processes supports each stage of development within the individual life cycle.

Erikson's theory of personality development appeals to the epigenetic principle which states that there is a ground plan for anything that grows, and that as parts

arise out of this ground plan, each part has "its time of special ascendancy, until all parts have arisen to form a functioning whole."[97] The epigenetic laws of development incorporate a predetermined rate and sequence related to the individual's growing readiness to respond in appropriate ways to social and cultural processes. At each phase of epigenesis, development is codetermined by biological, mental, and social factors, and the ego qualities which emerge enable the individual to "integrate the timetable of the organism with the structure of social institutions."[98] Erikson came to regard the whole life cycle as a unified psychosocial phenomenon with "interliving" life stages that interact with the stages of others. Each stage involves a crisis because of the radical change in perspective that accompanies growing awareness, new forms of vulnerability, and heightened potential. **Erikson's use of the term *crisis* does not refer to impending catastrophe, but to a necessary turning point when development must move in one direction or another, whether in the individual or in the culture at large.**[99]

The process of identity formation in Erikson's stages of human development involves an "evolving configuration" woven out of patterns of characteristic traits that correspond to fixation at each of the eight stages. This configuration of successive ego syntheses and resyntheses integrates "constitutional givens, idiosyncratic libidinal needs, favored capacities, significant identifications, effective defenses, successful sublimations, and consistent roles."[100] The first four phases relate to Freud's psychosexual stages (oral, anal, infantile-genital, latency), but Erikson is less concerned with their biological aspects than with their psychosocial implications. While the final stage in Freudian theory is a genital period that extends from puberty to death, Erikson distinguishes four developmental stages during this period that are virtually unrelated to instinct and libido. **He relates all eight stages to an interpretive scheme that covers expanding needs, a widening radius of significant relations, more highly differentiated capacities, developmental crises, new senses of estrangement along with new dependences and familiarities, new forms of psychosocial strength, and related social institutions that appease the sense of estrangement and guard the strengths originating at each stage.**[101]

Each stage involves a psychosocial crisis which can lead to enhanced or impaired development in the following stages. The first stage is foundational to the rest because the crisis in infancy is that of a basic sense of trust versus a basic sense of mistrust.[102] Each successive stage and crisis is specifically related to an element of social order since the human life cycle and cultural institutions have evolved together.[103] The social sphere corresponding to the first stage is parental care, and the primary institutional safeguard of the sense of trust is organized religion.

In the second stage, experienced in early childhood, the basic task of the ego is the resolution of the crisis of autonomy versus shame and doubt.[104] "The lasting need of the individual to have his will reaffirmed and delineated within an adult order of things which at the same time reaffirms and delineates the will of others has an institutional safeguard in the principle of law and order."[105] In this stage, self-control without loss of self-esteem is the key to "man's basic need for a delineation of his autonomy."[106]

The crisis of the third stage, associated with play age, is the conflict between initiative and guilt.[107] The conscience is established in this stage, and the expanding imagination can lead to guilt feelings that stifle initiative. **The task in this stage is the preparation for a realistic sense of purpose for adult tasks, and this process is assisted in the social order by ideal adult prototypes.**

The fourth stage is the long period of sexual latency in school age during which the development of a sense of industry as opposed to an estranging sense of inferiority due to a lack of recognition of one's efforts is the decisive issue.[108] The capacity for enjoying work is supported by the technological ethos of culture.[109]

The fifth stage, associated with adolescence, must integrate the elements of the previous stages and replace the childhood milieu with that of society.[110] During this time, the ego's task of integration includes "all identifications with the vicissitudes of the libido, with the aptitudes developed out of endowment, and with the opportunities offered in social roles."[111] It is during this crucial stage that the well-known identity crisis occurs with the threat of identity diffusion; a fixation at this stage produces role confusion. The social institution that functions as the guardian of identity is ideology.

Erikson calls the three remaining stages "beyond identity," since they refer to life after adolescence and involve new forms of identity crises from young adulthood to senescence. **The crisis of intimacy versus isolation characterizes young adulthood, the sixth stage.**[112] A growing security in one's forming identity is a necessary prerequisite of true intimacy, which Erikson describes as "a counterpointing as well as a fusing of identities."[113] Fear of losing identity by sharing intimacy can lead to a sense of isolation.

The seventh stage, associated with adulthood, brings the crisis of generativity versus stagnation or self-absorption; the task of the mature person is to develop "a concern for establishing and guiding the next generation."[114] Interpersonal impoverishment occurs when generativity is not achieved.

The final stage relates to senescence; people reach the end of life with a sense of ego integrity only if they have previously attained the qualities of intimacy and generativity.[115] The fruit of the previous seven stages is a meaningful old age characterized by ego integrity, which is the positive alternative to the despair and disgust caused by the lack or loss of accrued ego integration.[116] The social institution corresponding to the eighth stage is philosophy or wisdom.

Erikson develops an epigenetic chart with an eight-by-eight grid to suggest that each of the stages relates to the others either as precursors of the solution of the crisis at each stage or as derivatives of these solutions in the maturing personality.[117] Thus, while the identity crisis relates to adolescence in stage five, identity formation has its precursors in each of the four previous stages and its derivatives in each of the three following stages.[118] On the other hand, "Identity appears as only one concept within a wider conception of the human life cycle which envisages childhood as a gradual unfolding of the personality through phase-specific psychosocial crises."[119]

Erikson acknowledges that his field "deals directly with the immediate needs of men" and that there is "cultural variability as to the inborn and provoked qualities of a need" since humans live more by training and less by instinct.[120] The inner and outer conflicts experienced by the developing personality are necessary for the fulfillment of these needs in the process of attaining psychosocial strength. The requirements of a healthy personality include a growing sense of inner unity, of good judgment (ability to perceive the world and oneself correctly), and of the capacity to do well according to the standards of those who are significant to the individual.[121] These criteria are relative to cognitive and social development in the life cycle, and individual life cycles in turn are related to the generational sequence and to sociocultural structure.[122]

The ground plan of the epigenetic principle as applied to the human life cycle directs the progressive ascendancy of the needed components of personality during the course of the crises of the eight stages in such a way that in the healthy personality, these components merge into a functioning whole. **The eight qualities corresponding to the developmental stages (trust, autonomy, initiative, industry, identity, intimacy, generativity, and integrity) are basic human needs that correspond to an expanding radius of significant relations and social institutions. If any of these needs are frustrated during a psychosocial crisis, fixation can occur at that stage (i.e., the matching dysfunctional qualities of mistrust, shame and doubt, guilt, inferiority, identity diffusion and role confusion, isolation, stagnation and self-absorbtion, despair and disgust), and this will have an effect on the derivatives of that stage.**

In his writings, Erikson particularly emphasizes three of the eight needed components of a growing personality associated with stages one, five, and eight: trust, identity, and integrity. Concerning the first of these needs, a failure to attain basic trust and mutuality will undermine all later development. Erikson proposes that all moral, ideological, and ethical propensities depend on the early experience of trust and mutuality.[123] Through the somatic interchange with the mother, an infant must develop a sense of continuity and sameness that begins to unite the inner and outer worlds. This is a basic wholeness that integrates the inside and the outside with an experience of goodness, and in the developing personality, the communal reinforcement and safeguard of this basic sense of trust is organized religion. Believing as he does that the human life cycle and social institutions have evolved together, **Erikson relates religion to the first-stage conflict of trust versus mistrust that occurs in infancy and shapes all later development in the successive stages. Organized religion socializes and provides a collective reassurance of trust through rituals and "images of primeval superhuman protectors" and "makes comprehensible the vague discomfort of basic mistrust by giving it a metaphysical**

reality in the form of defined Evil."[124] This enhances the feeling of the wholeness of existence and provides a needed sense of goodness that can be trusted.[125] **Erikson disavows the intention of calling religious behavior childish or regressive, but he notes that "large-scale infantilization is not foreign to the practice and the intent of organized religion."**[126] Childhood trust becomes the capacity for faith in the life of the adult, a "vital need" which most commonly finds institutional confirmation in religion.[127]

> What begins as hope in the individual infant is in its mature form faith, a sense of superior certainty not essentially dependent on evidence or reason, except where these forms of self-verification become part of a way of life binding technology, science, and new sources of identity into a coherent world-image. It is obvious that for the longest period of known history religion has monopolized the traditional formulation and the ritual restoration of faith. . . . at the height of its historical function [religion] has played another, corresponding role, namely that of giving concerted expression to adult man's need to provide the young and the weak with a world-image sustaining hope.[128]

Erikson observes that in modern culture, nonreligious ideologies and activities (e.g., social action) are gradually replacing the institutional function of religion as alternative collective provisions for the human need for faith and hope.[129]

The second of the three needs particularly stressed by Erikson is associated with stage five, or adolescence. The formation of a meaningful ego identity, a predominant theme in his writings, is a need that is "reborn with each generation."[130] Erikson approaches the concept of identity from several angles, including individual identity, unconscious striving for a continuity of personal character, ego synthesis, and inner solidarity with a group's ideals and identity.[131] All of these approaches involve both a relationship with oneself ("a persistent sameness within oneself") and a relationship with others ("a persistent sharing of some kind of essential character with others").[132]

The integration that culminates in the formation of a sense of inner identity which should be achieved in adolescence includes but also surpasses the sum of the successive identifications of the earlier childhood years.[133] The experiences of the previous stages culminate in the process of successfully aligning individual drives and endowments with social opportunities, and the sense of ego identity thus attained is a condition of further personal maturation. This process of identity formation, largely unconscious, is located not only in the core of the individual, but also in the core of the communal culture, and thus forms an identity of those two identities.[134] Because of this, the achievement of meaningful inner identity can be threatened by cultural conditions of upheaval and radical social change.

> Industrial revolution, world-wide communication, standardization, centralization, and mechanization threaten the identities which man has inherited from primitive, agrarian, feudal, and patrician cultures. What inner equilibrium these cultures had to offer is now endangered on a gigantic scale.[135]

Social health and cultural stability enhance ego synthesis and provide the necessary provision of balance in which integration of ego stages produces a sense of humanity.[136] Infantile fears and irrational motivation occur when individual identity is threatened due to inadequate association with cultural identity. Psychosocial equilibrium and well-being is necessary to an optimal sense of identity, since personal identity is attained only in the context of a defined group identity.[137] Ideological affirmation is especially important during the process of identity formation in adolescence, and this is normally sought in significant social groups (class, nation, culture). If the environment fails to provide an ideological structure, "the adolescent ego cannot organize experience according to its specific capacities and its expanding involvement."[138]

The task of the ego is to sustain the perception of sameness and continuity in an environment of changing inner and outer conditions so that personal capacities can be integrated with cultural commitments.[139] To maintain this needed sense of totality, the ego develops "modes of synthesis as well as screening methods and mechanisms of defense" by which it restructures experience and action to regain what Erikson calls the synthesis of wholeness whenever it is threatened by the conflicts and uncertainties of life.[140]

Integrity is the third need emphasized by Erikson, and it is associated with stage eight, or senescence. The attainment of identity is not the end of human development; identity continues to adapt to the post-adolescent stages. While psychosocial identity "is necessary as the anchoring of man's transient existence in the here and the now," the individual needs to transcend his identity and move even beyond individuality.[141] **Erikson sees integrity, the acceptance of one's life cycle, as the fruit of the seven previous stages.**[142] **Neurosis is overcome when an individual reaches the point of accepting "the historical necessity which made him what he is" and willingly identifying with his one and only life cycle.**[143] Integrity is characterized by the understanding that an individual life is "the accidental coincidence of but one life cycle with but one segment of history" and the willingness to be responsible in applying the givens of life to the requirements of life.[144] The individual needs to experience fate, with its joys and pains, as something actively cho-

sen in order to attain the ego strength required for a meaningful old age.[145] **The end of the life cycle raises issues of ultimate concerns, but Erikson believes that integrity is replaced by despair and disgust when the individual fails to accept the one and only life cycle as the ultimate of life.**

THE INTRAPSYCHIC VERSION

C. G. Jung

The personality theory developed by Carl Gustav Jung (1875–1961), while initially shaped by Freudian thought, is a distinctive and complex approach that comprehensively draws from a wide range of sources, especially the symbolic content of religions, folklore, and mythology. A strictly systematic approach to Jung's thought is rendered difficult because of conceptual ambiguities, unusual uses of terms, and frequent mystical and religious allusions in his writings. Homans argues that the ideational approach to the work of Jung as an originative psychologist should be counterbalanced by a more contextual approach that considers how personal, social, and religious factors acted as generative forces in the rise of his psychological ideas.[146] **The polarization in the literature on Jung that tends to view him as an "irresponsible deviant from Freud" on the one hand, or an "autonomous thinker who abandoned Freud's dogmatism" on the other, misses the more nuanced interplay between Freud and Jung that influenced the latter's theoretical development.**[147] Jung's break with Freud, stemming in part from Jung's criticism of Freud's pansexual causal reductionism,[148] led to a dramatically different understanding of the psychic process that places more emphasis on spirituality and cultural universals in a contemporary context in which religion has a diminished role in ordering personal and social affairs. Nevertheless, many components of Freudian thought were retained in Jung's portrayal of the tension between the conscious and the unconscious and the tension between the fulfillment of the individual and the demands of conformity to an existing social order.[149]

Jung claims that his concept of the unconscious is exclusively psychological without a philosophical or metaphysical referent.[150] As a product of the evolutionary process, it "shows countless archaic traits," but it is morally and aesthetically neutral and should not be regarded as an enemy to be avoided.[151] **The unconscious can be the source of light as well as darkness; it can be bestial and demonic, but it can also be superhuman and spiritual.**[152] **It is not the unconscious that poses a danger to psychological health, but the repression of its contents due to a one-sided conscious outlook that separates the two realms of the psyche. Jung frequently stresses the need to diminish this dissociation of the personality through a process of assimilating materials that were previously unconscious.**[153] This can be accomplished in part through dream analysis, since Jung regards dreams as sources of information about the inner life that reveal hidden aspects of the personality. They are involuntary psychic processes that provide a true picture of the subjective state in spite of the resistance of the conscious mind in acknowledging it.[154] **In contrast to Freud's view that the primary function of dreams is wish-fulfillment, Jung holds that they are compensatory to the conscious situation in that they articulate material that the mind is not dealing with and thus furnish a symbolic self-portrait of the situation in the unconscious.**

> As a rule, the unconscious content contrasts strikingly with the conscious material, particularly when the conscious attitude tends too exclusively in a direction that would threaten the vital needs of the individual. The more one-sided his conscious attitude is, and the further it deviates from the optimum,

the greater becomes the possibility that vivid dreams with a strongly contrasting but purposive content will appear as an expression of the self-regulation of the psyche.[155]

Jung concluded that the symbols inherent in dreams are also found in mythology, folklore, religion, and art, and his extensive comparative studies in these areas provided him with a broad base of analogies that could be used in understanding the associations of his patients.[156] **He consequently developed the controversial concept that in addition to the personal unconscious, there also exists a collective unconscious which reflects the accumulated culture of humanity, and that far from being a *tabula rasa*, the mind contains specific aptitudes and patterns of apperception that are present at birth.** "Our personal psychology is just a thin skin, a ripple on the ocean of collective psychology."[157]

Unlike the personal unconscious which is derived from the forgotten or repressed materials of personal experience, the contents of the collective unconscious are identical in all people since they are not individually developed but implanted in the psyche through heredity. **Thus, all of mythology is a projection of the collective unconscious. While the conscious mind, or ego, is an "ephemeral phenomenon" of adaptation and orientation of the individual to the environment, a second psychic system, consisting of the personal and collective unconscious, has an indirect but profound effect on consciousness.**[158] Just as the instincts influence human activity apart from rational motivations, so the universal and impersonal forms of the collective unconscious influence imagination, perception, and thinking.[159]

Jung describes the content of the collective unconscious as primordial images or archetypes, which are "dominants that emerge into consciousness as universal ideas."[160] Endless repetition of typical life situations propagated a vast host of predispositions or universal forms without content that cannot become conscious but influence human perception. The archetypes (e.g., the anima, the animus, the shadow, the hero, the mother, the child, God) act like instincts insofar as they modify and affect conscious states, but since their real nature is transcendent, they are very different from the instinctual drives of the organism. Although the instincts (e.g., hunger, sexuality, the drive to activity, and the reflective and creative instincts)[161] and archetypes are polar opposites, they correspond and subsist side by side in such a way that one can be simultaneously driven by instinct and free to be "seized by the spirit."[162] "The archetype as an image of instinct is a spiritual goal toward which the whole nature of man strives" in that the collective unconscious contains the whole corpus of the spiritual evolution of humanity.[163] Since the archetypes mold the personal unconscious, the latter is the only means by which religious experience can be attained.

While Jung argues that the tendency in previous ages was to account for too much in terms of spiritual causation, he decries the modern propensity to overestimate material causation as the only explanation of life.[164] The dimension of spirit[165] must be added to that of instinctual drives and impulses since these alone are not enough to account for the complexity of the human psyche. **Jung criticizes the insufficiency of the causal mechanism of Freudian psychoanalysis and offers in his own analytical psychology an energic account of the dynamics of the psyche. Treating human drives as specific forms of energy, he develops a psychological parallel with the first and second laws of thermodynamics which he calls the principles of equivalence and entropy.**[166] The principle of equivalence relates to the conservation of psychic energy, and states that "for a given quantity of energy expended or consumed in bringing about a certain condition, an equal quantity of the same or another form of energy will appear elsewhere."[167] The principle of entropy states that as tension increases between pairs of opposites, the energy that comes from them also increases. Like the body, the psyche is a self-regulating system that maintains homeostasis; "every process that goes too far immediately and inevitably calls forth a compensatory activity."[168] This compensatory dynamic characterizes the relationship between the conscious and the unconscious, and this opposition provides energy and produces growth. **Thus, conflict is central to Jung's theory, and this conflict is more an intrapsychic rather than a psychosocial conflict.**[169]

In the struggle between the opposites, Jung speaks of progression and regression, and both relate to the human need for adaptation—the former to the conditions of environment and the latter to the conditions of the inner world. **The "vital need" to adapt to the demands of the external world can only be met when one is also adapted to the inner world, that is, by being in harmony with oneself. Conversely, the vital need for this inner harmony can only be met when one is adapted to environmental conditions.**[170] Both of these fundamental needs are associated with the interplay between the conscious and the unconscious. Jung regards the development of consciousness as both a burden and a blessing[171] because it has led to great suffering and tension on the one hand, but it has provided the potential for a more solid foundation of the personality on the other. **Jung is not interested in the one-sided enlargement of the conscious mind with the ego as its center but rather in the pursuit of selfhood. Unlike the ego, the archetype of the self is a new center of the personality, which is midway between the conscious and the unconscious and maintains interaction and communication between these conflicting poles.** Instead of eliminating conflict, Jung calls for the juxtaposition of the conscious and unconscious because increasing tension between the opposites generates a corresponding increase of psychic energy.[172] **It is this dynamic that makes the realization of the whole, or the self, possible, and this realization is what Jung calls the individuation process.**

> Conscious and unconscious do not make a whole when one of them is
> suppressed and injured by the other. If they must contend, let it at least be
> a fair fight with equal rights on both sides. Both are aspects of life.
> Consciousness should defend its reason and protect itself, and the chaotic

life of the unconscious should be given the chance of having its way too—as much of it as we can stand. This means open conflict and open collaboration at once. That, evidently is the way human life should be.[173]

The assimilation of unconscious components enriches the personality and creates a new totality, the self, which comprises far more than a mere ego. The goal of the individuation process is the synthesis of the self, but this does not mean that the ego is to be dissolved in the self; the wholeness of which Jung speaks is the "successful union of ego and self, so that both preserve their intrinsic qualities."[174]

The vital need for engagement in the process of individuation, by which a person balances conflicting polarities and becomes a whole and separate unity instead of a component of collective man,[175] is very real but seldom pursued and is an ideal that is impossible of complete attainment. Psychoanalysis can facilitate the individuation process but is never a cure since the ongoing dynamic of the unconscious prevents any change from being unconditionally valid through the course of life.[176] **Analytical treatment moves through the stages of confession, explanation, and education toward the goal of transformation, but the therapist recognizes that in this process, "the needs and necessities of individuals vary. What sets one free is for another a prison.** There are only individual cases whose needs and demands are totally different."[177] The need for the attainment of selfhood is universal, but the way in which this is best pursued is case specific.

Because individuation requires the confrontation of the conscious with the unconscious, this process of the irrational union of opposites is dependent not on logic but on symbols.[178] Jung referred to this union as the "transcendent function" and often pointed to the mandala as the archetypal image that best symbolizes the wholeness of the self as an attraction of opposites.[179] Because of the assimilation of the archetypes of the collective unconscious in the individuation process, the normal canons of rational discourse are inadequate to account for this interface of immanent and transcendent objects. It can only be expressed in the imagery of symbols and the language of paradox.[180]

Jung regards individual development as the goal of psychotherapy, believing that only in the individual, as the sole and natural carrier of life, can life fulfill its meaning.[181] He is therefore concerned with the danger of individuality being smothered by the collective mind. Because his psychology disdains conformity-inducing forces, many regard it as "an extreme response to the pluralization of modern society."[182] **Jung acknowledges that the dual necessities of nature and culture impinge upon all and that the individual must be related to the community. In this context he uses the archetype of the persona to describe the mask that must be adopted by each person to relate individual consciousness to society and respond to the forces of social convention and mores. The persona is used both to make an impression upon others and to conceal one's true nature, but there is a danger of becoming identified with the persona.[183]** While the persona is necessary to social functioning, it must be secondary to the self. For Jung, social ills like animosity, injustice, and persecution are catalyzed when the persona is dominant because it leads to a lack of self-criticism and the projection of faults onto others.[184] When the self is established as the point of identity between the rational ego and the collective, the rigid persona ceases to dominate, and the individual is no longer determined by the demands of the collective consciousness. The Jungian concept of a self that is not controlled by the power of the social order does not imply that his system rejects social ideals; instead, his psychology claims that cultural advancement occurs when collective beliefs are challenged, and that the individuation process is the key to making this happen.[185]

Jung personally experienced the conflict between the two cultures of religious traditionalism and modern scientific humanism and sought to resolve the tension by synthesizing them in a system that integrates psychological analysis and ancient symbolism.[186] **Disagreement exists among theologians as to whether Jung's system repudiates or is compatible with Christianity, some arguing that it undermines biblical authority,**[187] **and others claiming that it illuminates and enhances the Christian message.**[188] **However, the psychological interpretation of Christianity in works like** *Symbols of Transformation* **and** *Answer to Job* **denounces the scriptural portrait of Yahweh and Christ and rejects** *traditional* **Christianity as inadequate for modern culture.**[189] Nevertheless, Jung's repudiation of traditional Christianity did not prevent him from seeking to assimilate components of it into a new synthesis in which he interpreted Christianity in the light of analytical psychology but concurrently mined it as a source of meaning through its symbolic content. He contended that "the standpoint of the Christian creeds is archaic; they are full of impressive mythological symbolism which, if taken literally, comes into insufferable conflict with knowledge. . . . Is it not time that the Christian mythology, instead of being wiped out, was understood symbolically for once?"[190] When disassociated from authoritarianism and literalism, Christianity provides a meaningful background and context for the individuation process. Thus, Jung rejected religious dogma but maintained an interest in the religious experience in which dogma was rooted and related this experience to the emergence of the archetype of the self as "the god within us."[191]

Insofar as he approached psychology as an empirical science based on the results of comparative research, Jung sought to avoid making metaphysical assertions concerning the existence of any realities toward which the symbols point. Just as the archetype of the hero proves nothing of the actual existence of a hero, so the archetype of God does not affirm the existence or nonexistence of God. The unconscious is "the medium from which the religious experience seems to flow. As to what the further cause of such an experience may be, the answer to this lies beyond the range of human knowledge. Knowledge of God is a transcendental problem."[192] For Jung, archetypes like mana, God, and daimon are synonyms for the unconscious, and the myth of the incarnation speaks of "man's creative confrontation with the opposites and their synthesis in the self, the wholeness of his personality."[193]

On the other hand, Jung wants to avoid the error of psychologism which assumes the nonexistence of God and approaches religious experience through the reductionistic perspective of scientific positivism. Thus, he criticizes the assumption that the idea of God is derived from motives relating to repressed sexuality (Freud) or to the will to power (Adler).[194] He regards the modern tendency to account for everything on physical grounds as an overreaction to the opposite extreme in earlier ages.

> Reason sets the boundaries far too narrowly for us, and would have us accept only the known. . . . We live far beyond the bounds of our consciousness; without our knowledge, the life of the unconscious is also going on within us. The more the critical reason dominates, the more impoverished life becomes; but the more of the unconscious, and the more of myth we are capable of making conscious, the more of life we integrate.[195]

Because religious symbols are derived from the unconscious, they play an important role in Jung's system. These symbols have exerted an enormous and universal influence on humanity because they reflect significant truths about the nature of the psyche.[196] Religions have a positive value in that they enhance people's capacity to respond to numinous symbols in the context of a moral and spiritual tradition. This capacity has diminished in the modern world, resulting in increased disorientation and dehumanization and a sense of isolation in the cosmos.[197]

The diminished power of cultural symbols is due to a combination of the growth of scientific rationalism and the inability of contemporary religion and philosophy to provide people with the "powerful animating ideas" that would give them the security they need in the face of the uncertainties of life.[198] But when the great religions are approached symbolically rather than dogmatically, they become psychotherapeutic systems whose potent images reveal the nature of the soul.[199] They provide insight into the nature of "humanity's black collective shadow" and a more effective way than modern rationalism of dealing with the evil that is lodged in human nature.[200] They also offer a symbolic structure that transcends logic and makes it possible for the consciousness to engage in the irrational union of opposites necessary to the individuation process. Jung uses the God-image, or the union of God and man, as the religious articulation of the wholeness symbolized in the archetype of the self, and the same holds true for the language of individuation.[201]

Ultimately, Jung regards psychoneurosis as "the suffering of a soul which has not discovered its meaning."[202] Although most people do not consciously wrestle with their failure to realize meaning in life, many are experiencing a growing sense of displacement and limitation produced by a culture that is increasingly cut off from symbols of transcendence.[203] Jung's personal concern with the need for meaning was evident throughout his long career, and near the end of his life, he said:

> There is nothing I am quite sure about. I have no definite convictions—not about anything, really. . . . I exist on the foundation of something I do not know. . . . Life is—or has—meaning and meaninglessness. I cherish the anxious hope that meaning will preponderate and win the battle.[204]

According to Jung, Christianity in earlier times provided an escape from the brutality of the ancient world and a structure in which meaning could be found. But the impoverishment caused in recent times by the diminished power of religious symbols has led to a rediscovery of the same spiritual forces in the form of psychological entities, namely, the archetypes of the unconscious.[205] **Since the concepts of the past are no longer adequate, people have turned from religion to psychology to find meaning and direction. But psychology will not effectively assist the needed individuation process unless it recognizes the ongoing importance of numinous symbols which facilitate the synthesis of conscious and unconscious.**

While it is normal in the first half of life to be concerned with biological and social interests, Jung contends that there should be a transition in the second half of life to spiritual concerns in the quest for integration and selfhood.

> **Among all my patients in the second half of life—that is to say, over thirty-five—there has not been one whose problem in the last resort was not that of finding a religious outlook on life. It is safe to say that every one of them fell ill because he had lost that which the living religions of every age have given to their followers, and none of them has been really healed who did not regain his religious outlook. This of course has nothing whatever to do with a particular creed or membership of a church.**[206]

This "unreasoned need" of a spiritual life is met when the archetypes become spiritual guides to the personality as sources of a greater wisdom than that which can be derived from conscious content.[207] The "revelation" thus provided from the inner resources of the psyche offers a transcendent sense of meaning analogous to that offered by the great religions.

Otto Rank

Otto Rank (originally Rosenfeld, 1884–1939) was one of Freud's closest associates from 1906 to 1924. During these years he personally assisted Freud, edited two psychoanalytic journals, and published a number of insightful analyses of myths and legends. His break from Freud's inner circle began with his unexpected publication of *The Trauma of Birth* in December 1923, and his departure from Vienna to Paris in 1926 marked the completion of his break with psychoanalysis.[208] Thus, Rank's writings record the gradual shift in his viewpoints, and this ambiguity, coupled with a writing style that is not always clearly organized, makes his work difficult to synthesize.

The Myth of the Birth of the Hero exemplifies Rank's early psychoanalytical interpretation of mythology in which he explores the analogies in mythical groupings from various cultures and interprets myth as "a dream of the masses of the people."[209] In this book, Rank constructs a standard saga from the hero birth myths and argues that myths are created through "retrograde childhood fantasies" in which the hero symbolically reenacts infantile history.[210] The revolutionary behavior of the hero represents the detachment of the growing individual from parental authority.

In a similar way, Rank's psychoanalytic study of *The Double*, a literary theme which explored the integrity of the self and grew with the development of psychology, traces the folkloric and mythical traditions associated with the cleavage of the ego and the encounter with one's ghostly or real counterpart.[211] According to Rank, the positive evaluation of the double as the soul led to the development of the personality from the self, whereas the negative evaluation of the double as a symbol of death is a symptom of the neurotic exclusion of the idea of death.[212] It is the negative interpretation that dominates literary works on the double, and Rank argues that most of the authors of double stories were pathological personalities. In these stories, the double is antagonistic to its narcissistic prototype who suffers from persecutory delusions. When the hero attempts to destroy his double, it is he who dies instead.[213]

In his Freudian analysis of the various versions of *The Don Juan Legend,* Rank's Oedipal interpretation of Don Juan's seduction of countless women held that these women represent a compensatory substitute for the complete possession of the unattainable mother. Similarly, the men whom he deceives, fights, and finally kills represent the "unconquerable mortal enemy, the father."[214] However, Rank later revised his interpretation of the Don Juan legend when he repudiated psychoanalytic theory and its account of artistic endeavor.[215]

***The Trauma of Birth* is a transitional work in which Rank still attempted to couch his increasingly divergent views within a generally Freudian framework. At this point in his career, Rank was convinced that the birth trauma is the ultimate biological basis of the psychological, and he attempted to replace the theory of multiple stages of fixation with a single locus of fixation, namely, the traumatic incident of parturition.**[216] This is the primal trauma from which all neurotic symptoms emerge since the unconscious is the embryonal state which exists unchanged in the adult ego.[217] All anxieties are partial reflections of the birth anxiety, and the final aim of all pleasures is "the re-establishment of the intrauterine primal pleasure."[218] Since this former source of pleasure is not only unattainable but is associated with the birth trauma itself, it produces a profound psychic ambivalence. The birth anxiety represses the memory of the primal pleasure, while the memory of the previous pleasure experience represses the memory of the painful birth trauma.[219]

***The Trauma of Birth* reduces all neurosis, catatonia, epilepsy, and paranoia to the single primal causality of the repression and return of the birth trauma associated**

with the separation from the mother.[220] In addition, Rank argues that the symbols in dreams and in mythology are related to the same cause. Thus, the myth of the hero relates to prenatal libido (intrauterine primal pleasure) and the creative compensation for the traumata of birth and weaning.[221] Furthermore, during this period, Rank related artistic and other cultural accomplishments as well as philosophy and religion to the trauma of birth. He went so far as to say that "the whole wavering course of history, with its apparently arbitrary and changing phases, [is] subject to the conditions of biological law." History can be understood in terms of "constantly renewed attempts to re-establish by means of the most varied forms of substitutional gratification the lost primal state, and to deny the primal trauma."[222] Essentially all cultural creations, from Plato's philosophy of Eros (yearning for a lost union) to the creation of political systems (paternal domination as a continuance of the primal repression), are related to this primal yearning and primal anxiety.[223] Rank viewed religion as the product of obsessional neurosis and sublimation and understood the idea of a future after death as a projection of life before birth, that is, an everlasting return to the womb.[224]

When he wrote *The Trauma of Birth,* Rank believed he had considerably advanced the understanding of neuroses, but he regarded his theory concerning the centrality of the birth trauma as "a contribution to the Freudian structure of normal psychology, at best as one of its pillars."[225] In his own practice of psychoanalysis, his goal was the "belated accomplishment of the incompleted mastery of the birth trauma."[226] The analytic fixation (transference) related to the mother as the lost primal object, and the reproduction of the birth trauma through the gradual and conscious severance from the analyst as the surrogate, made it possible for the patient to renounce the unattainable mother. The key in the transference process is the use of conscious forces to alter and strengthen the patient's ego relative to the unconscious.[227] In this way, it is possible to free neurotics from excessive domination by the unconscious so that they can live as those who are not neurotic.[228]

The Development of Psycho-Analysis, written during the same period, also emphasized the "detachment of the infantile libido from its fixation on its first objects" through the repetition of the Oedipus relation in the analytic transference.[229] **The ego of the patient must be educated so that it learns that satisfaction of the infantile libido is unattainable. In treatment, the patient's psyche loosens affects from their original objects and displaces them on the analyst who in turn must expose the transference as it progresses so that the patient can eventually be freed from infantile fixation.**[230] Rank believed that this could be best achieved by establishing a definite limit to the length of the treatment so that the resolution of the relationship corresponds to the release of the repressed material. When the patient is freed from repression, anxiety, and guilt feelings, the unwound libido can be put to more normal use.[231] This approach to therapy depends less on the attainment of knowledge than on the acquiring of a deeper conviction based on immediate perception and experience.

With the publication of Volumes II and III of *Technique of Psychoanalysis* (translated into English as *Will Therapy*), Rank's break from the Freudian viewpoint was complete. It was also during this time that he published *Truth and Reality,* the third volume of *Outlines of a Genetic Psychology on the Basis of the Psychoanalysis of the Ego Structure. Will Therapy* and *Truth and Reality* present Rank's post-Freudian understanding of the therapeutic process as well as a psychology and philosophy of human will.[232] In these books, he argues that Freud's therapeutic approach is based upon biological causality and the assumption that the present is determined by the past. This reduces transference to the infantile and interchanges the historically real with the psychologically true.[233] **But there is no therapeutic benefit in seeking to understand the present through the quest for past experiences and events. The content of the past is uncertain because it has been distorted and reinterpreted through reaction patterns. In his new vision of the therapeutic procedure, Rank abandoned historical content and placed the emphasis on present experience rather than recollection of the past through dreams and associations.** The feeling experience in the patient is no longer reduced to a reenactment of the infantile but is seen instead as a means to the growth and development of the personality in the therapeutic context.[234]

By focusing on the present sphere of experience, Rank ceased to view the process of therapy in terms of intellectual training or education; he placed the emphasis on freeing through experience which could in turn lead the patient to insight and self-understanding.[235] He criticized Freudian psychoanalysis as an ideological rather than a dynamic approach because of its principle that knowledge is curative, and that neurosis is cured by making the unconscious conscious. Rank's own "dynamic therapy" explores the present meaning of the analytic situation and comprehends the patient-analyst transference in largely nonsexual terms.[236]

Rank also criticized the Freudian system for its overemphasis of unconscious impulse and minimization of the conscious ego in psychoanalysis.[237] He concluded that the conscious will is the central force in the therapeutic process and that the patient must be regarded as the chief actor. Freudian analysis measures the patient "on a minimum scale" using "primitive fear pictures of the Oedipus and castration complexes together with all related sadistic, cannibalistic and narcissistic tendencies."[238] It is excessively passive in its analytic approach and is bound by the ideological prejudice of the existing order with its social and moral standards. Since it is oriented on the psychology of the "normal" individual, it allows no place for nonneurotic creative expression, and it views the ego in a negative light.[239] Rank believed that by "supporting the individual striving for self-realization" he freed the therapeutic process from the psychoanalytic educational approach that idealizes social conformity.[240] **The human being must be seen not merely as the product of parental and social influences but as a dynamic center of causality who acts and reacts in such a way that he can adapt these forces for his own needs.**

Rank modified and further developed some of the themes in his earlier books like *The Myth of the Birth of the Hero, The Double,* and *The Trauma of Birth,* particularly the theme of primal fears associated with birth and death. **The birth fear is actually a fear of life which Rank associates with the separation and isolation of individual existence. The opposite death fear is the fear of the loss of individuality through union and dependency.** The individual is pulled back and forth by these poles of fear throughout all of life, and this primary ambivalence due to opposing tendencies can never be resolved. Nor, according to Rank, should this tension between individuation and generation be resolved, since it is "the very basis of life."[241] The personality as a whole must be accepted with all of its ambivalence. These and other insights in Rank's thought have influenced Ernest Becker, Arthur Janov (primal therapy), and the clinical theology movement.[242]

Rank arrived at the "neo-Copernican" conclusion that the core component of human personality is the conscious will.[243] "Where Freud speaks statically of id, ego and superego, I speak dynamically of impulse (instinct), emotion and will."[244] For Rank, the will is an autonomous force which organizes and integrates the self in such a way that the personality is not caused by, but acts upon, biological impulses and social drives. Since the individual will has its own dynamic causality, it functions as a "balancing force between impulses and inhibition" and distinguishes the individual from his culture as it creatively shapes human behavior.[245] This account of the will stands in sharp contrast to the psychoanalytic emphasis on past causality rather than present experience as well as psychic determinism due to biological and social forces. **Rank uses the analogy of Newtonian physics versus quantum mechanics to illustrate the difference between Freudian physical determinism and his own understanding of a freedom of the will that transcends lawful causality.**[246] The will differentiates each individual and has a fortuitous and indeterminate quality that cannot be explained by natural or social causes. Psychological approaches that treat the individual as a "statistical average" negate life itself by reducing the personality to an entity that is determined by largely unconscious forces. This denial of personal autonomy justifies neurotic attitudes and allows people to minimize responsibility for the choices they make.[247] By viewing the will as the primary cause of human behavior, Rank elevates the seat of the soul in the modern individual to the conscious level.

Rank contends that Freud and Adler held a negative attitude toward the will by interpreting its exercise in terms of resistance, infantile wish, or masculine protest (Adler's "will to power"). By thus incorporating will into moralistic systems of good and evil, the will came to be regarded as morally guilty and reprehensible. According to Rank, psychology should guard itself against "moralistic values of any kind" and yet it is still under the same bondage to moral principles as religious dogma and philosophic speculation.[248] **The will must not be condemned as evil nor justified as good; the will must simply be affirmed as necessary, especially since any attempts to eliminate it only strengthen its reactions.**[249] The association of will with guilt is reinforced by the dynamics of what Rank calls counterwill. Will first emerges as counterwill against the will of the parents and continues to assert itself against other social forces; this expression of the tendency toward separation and individualization (related to the fear of life) produces guilt because it is in opposition to the equally important tendency toward union and dependency (related to the fear of death). **Rank distinguishes moral guilt, which is generated by violations of social and cultural codes, from ethical guilt, which arises from the unavoidable tension between separation and union. Depending on one's attitude toward this tension, the will can be lost in neurosis, rationalized as compulsive causation, or asserted in creation.**[250] **Rank advocates a mature and creative expression of will which resolves this guilt and reduces the death and life fears.**[251]

There are three personality types which correspond to attempted resolutions of the problem of individuality and unity. The first of these, the neurotic type, leans to the extreme of expressing the tendency toward separation and individualization to the point of excluding the tendency toward union and dependency. Neurotics are fixated on the counterwill, often as a compensatory response to the moral guilt produced by negative responses to will expressions during the developmental years. This leads to a separatistic and hostile attitude toward others and a compulsion to view external reality as a part of their egos.[252] The neurotic strategy fails because it only enhances the sense of guilt and renders one incapable of guilt-reducing surrender and unity.[253] Neurotic types are driven by self-consciousness and discontent with themselves; they are tormented by introspection, turning their will inwardly as counterwill.[254] The increase of self-consciousness in the modern age, coupled with the failure of collective therapies like philosophy and religion to deal effectively with guilt and fear, has led to a significant rise in neuroses.[255]

The average type leans to the opposite extreme of expressing the tendency toward union and dependency to the point of excluding the tendency toward separation and individualization. Unlike neurotics, average types unquestioningly play the roles assigned them by parents and later by society.[256] These people are not bound by the inner torment of guilt because, unlike neurotics, they do not view external conditions as part of themselves. They are motivated more by instinctual satisfaction than by reduction of guilt and fear.[257]

Rank uses the term *artist* to designate the third personality type, because this is the individual who integrates separation and union and minimizes the fears of life and death through creative expression of the will.[258] The artist is the only type who succeeds in the complex task of adaptation; unlike the average type who avoids "the metaphysical problems of human existence" and the neurotic who faces them destructively, the artist faces them constructively by turning the will outside "without wanting to preserve or give out his whole ego undivided in every experience."[259] As the modern equivalent of the hero in literature, the artist "took the traditional folk-tale and lifted it from its superstitious entanglements into a human struggle for self-immortalization through work, that is, self-realization."[260] The artist-hero, through creative expression or exploits, seeks to replace the ego ideal of the masses (e.g., cultural mores) with a new ideal.[261] However, unlike the neurotic, this individualism is only partial because the artist recognizes that constructive expression of personal will cannot be divorced from the collective, that is, from acceptance and authentication by others.[262]

Thus, the neurotic interprets the world according to his "moralistic, guilt ego," while the creative type fashions it according to his "conscious, willing ego."[263] **While the creative person is superior to the neurotic, Rank regards the neurotic as superior to the average person who interprets the world only in a collective sense with no effort toward individuation.** The neurotic "corresponds much more to a miscarried artist (productive person) than to an average man who has not achieved normal development."[264]

There is a bipolarity in every human which creates a tension between man as a biological organism (the natural world) and man as a moral being (the artificial world). One of Rank's therapeutic goals is to liberate the individual from bondage to fatalism as represented by the past, dependency, union, and moral guilt, and to move him toward the self-determination associated with the present, difference, and separation.[265] This translation of compulsion of will into freedom of will occurs when one transcends external influences and actively appropriates reality for individual ends.[266] The birth of individuality is an ongoing process in which the individual is separated from the mass and recapitulates the evolutionary sequence "from blind impulse through conscious will to self conscious knowledge" through a series of births: the child from the mother, the individual from the mass, creative work from the individual, and knowledge from the work.[267] This knowledge relates to the liberation from traditional moral concepts and the formation of one's own ethical ideals. It is the artist type who thus evolves his ego ideal from his creative will affirmation in the face of the paradoxical necessity to live simultaneously in the natural world and the man-made world.[268]

Rank emphasizes the human need to become oneself, to accept one's individual differences, and to have one's individuality accepted by others. The personality must accept itself as an individual, and this justification of one's will is achieved through the love of others. **The "deep rooted need" to be loved and wanted by others harmonizes with the need for self-acceptance.[269] This dynamic of developing and accepting one's individuality instead of altering it is the goal of Rank's "constructive therapy."** The neurotic must stop trying to recreate reality and recreating himself and learn to accept and "make use of the self that has been given to him" with its volitional and emotional autonomy.[270] This requires a positive expression of the will that is not hindered by the guilt feelings associated with counterwill. Rank does not seek to eliminate the fundamental conflict between the universal and the individual, that is, the fear polarity between life and death, because this ambivalence is of therapeutic value.[271] Instead, his therapeutic approach seeks to instill a new attitude toward the self through the experience of present reality, and this is accomplished by freeing the creative self in the end setting of therapy in which the therapist is given up and replaced by the active, constructive utilization of changing reality as an "assistant ego."[272]

The life and death fear polarity relates to another human need, the need for happiness and redemption of guilt. **Rank associates happiness with the pleasurable will affirmation of individualism, but argues that the price of this happiness is the consciousness of ethical guilt. Salvation or redemption, on the other hand, relates to the diminishing of this guilt consciousness through the abrogation of individualism and will affirmation in the quest for "likeness, unity, oneness with the all."**[273] The gradual development of individual consciousness in the human race and the corresponding loss of unity with nature and the unconscious led to the association of creative will affirmation with sin, guilt, and rebellion against God. In Rank's interpretation of religious myths, the creative will is personified in God; those who exercise it become guilty of arrogating divine prerogatives for themselves. Heroic myths, on the other hand, seek to justify this creative will expression by glorifying its deeds. Both extremes illustrate the unavoidable human tension between the poles of nothingness and godlikeness, between causal compulsion and godlike freedom, nature and spirit, force and will.[274] The concept of ethical guilt associated with awareness of the "divine power of creation" as one's own power of will causes the individual to try to deny his will in order to justify it, and this is the purpose of the "universal redemption therapies" of religion and philosophy.[275] The average type accepts these universal attempts at guilt justification, but the neurotic rejects these norms as well as his own. The creative type accepts his individual will but cannot eliminate the inner conflict and guilt which this affirmation produces. His quest for happiness is frustrated by his need for guilt redemption, and if his individuation reaches the point where he can no longer find redemption in universal ideologies, only death will release him from self-conscious guilt.[276]

Thus, there is a human need for belief in a worldview with its outer and inner illusions with which one can build a sense of control and security.[277] **The different levels of illusion (e.g., art, religion, philosophy, science, sport, play, and love) lift man "out of himself" and enable him to accept the appearance of reality as truth.**[278] Truth for Rank is an intellectual representation of the will and has little to do with reality; it is what an individual believes or affirms. Doubt represents the conscious counterwill since it is what one denies or rejects.[279] The milieu of civilized man "is no longer the natural reality, the opposing force of an external world, but an artistic reality, created by himself which we, in its outer as in its inner aspects, designate as civilization."[280] **These rational and artificial structures are an essential part of human existence, but the irrational forces of the natural world must be accepted as equally vital, since one's destiny is simultaneously determined by both principles.**[281] **The need to balance one extreme with its**

counterpart in a both-and rather than either-or understanding is a theme that appears in most of Rank's work.

Rank also discusses the human need for belief in immortality in the face of the reality of death. Each individual has a fundamental need to expand "beyond the realm of his self, his environment, indeed, early life itself."[282] This can be satisfied in creative or in destructive ways on the level of human relationships, cultural ideologies, or religious ideologies, but "[t]he ego needs the Thou in order to become a Self."[283] For Rank, the idea of God as the ultimate Thou evolved from totemistic systems in which the individual soul was united with the collective soul.[284] **A supernatural worldview was necessary to provide symbolic support to the need for assurance of eternal survival since "[m]an, no matter under how primitive conditions, never did live on a purely biological, that is, on a simple natural basis."[285] Spiritual belief has been used for millennia to conquer death, the greatest obstacle encountered by freedom of will.** The idea of the soul was brought into being by the denial of death and the "universal need for immortalization" and permanency.[286] However, the new god of truth in the modern era has raised doubt regarding the existence of the soul; psychological ideology has been supplanting religious and moral idealogy through progressive self-consciousness.

> Psychology is the soul's worst enemy, because in creating its own consolation for death it becomes compelled by the self-knowledge it creates to prove that the soul does not exist. Thus it becomes both a scientific "psychology without a soul" and a kind of overburdening of the inner spiritual self which, with no support from an inherent belief in immortality, goes to pieces in a way the neuroses show so well.[287]

Scientific psychology denies the soul and offers "substitute objects not only for man's lost belief in the soul but for man who lost that belief."[288] But a soulless psychology cannot replace what it seeks to destroy without destroying itself.[289]

> We are born in pain, we die in pain and we should accept life-pain as unavoidable, indeed a necessary part of earthly existence, not merely the price we have to pay for pleasure. . . . Man is born beyond psychology and he dies beyond it but he can *live* beyond it only through vital experience of his own—in religious terms, through revelation, conversation, or re-birth.[290]

CHAPTER 5
THE FULFILLMENT MODEL OF HUMAN NEEDS

THE ACTUALIZATION VERSION

Abraham H. Maslow

Abraham Maslow (1908–1970) is recognized by many as the most influential contributor to the development of what he has called humanistic, third-force psychology. **At the outset of his career, there were only two major forces in psychology: the experimental approach of behavioristic psychology and the clinical, psychoanalytic approach. Through his study of human nature, Maslow grew increasingly dissatisfied with these approaches and sought to replace them with a more holistic-dynamic account of human beings that stresses an innate tendency to move toward higher levels of growth and fulfillment.**

Maslow was influenced by the organismic theory of Kurt Goldstein and Andras Angyal and by the thinking of Gordon Allport and Carl Rogers, but he was clearly one of the predominant architects of the rapidly growing humanistic movement in modern psychology. Maddi considers Maslow's position a variant on the fulfillment model because in it fulfillment is the most important but not the only directionality in the person.[1] In addition to the maturation tendency toward actualization of inherent potentialities, Maslow also recognizes in the core of personality a survival tendency to satisfy physical and psychological needs. He employs Goldstein's term *self-actualization* to describe the fulfillment tendency and maintains that this tendency builds upon rather than conflicts with the survival tendency.

Maslow insists that psychologists have focused too much of their attention on human weakness and pathology and have largely overlooked the stronger and healthier side of human nature. Because clinical studies primarily deal with people who, for various reasons, are mentally and emotionally impaired, they result in a jaundiced view of humanity that neglects virtues like creativity, love, well-being, egotranscendence, courage, and warmth. According to Maslow, what is called "normal" in psychology is really a psychopathology of the average.[2] **By concentrating his research on psychologically healthy and creative people, he sought to develop the other half of the picture and to provide a psychological foundation for humanistic values.**

Maslow's approach is holistic in that it views the individual as an integrated, organized whole.[3] Because of this, he is critical of a mechanistic scientific psychology like behaviorism because of its tendency to fragment and compartmentalize the person. Though he does not propose to eliminate mechanomorphic science, he argues that nothing short of a humanistic science will do justice to the study of the whole person. This personal science must integrate issues like consciousness, purpose, identity, and values.[4] Agreeing with Bronowski,[5] Maslow states that science is based on human values and is itself a value system; there are no disinterested observations.[6] Further, the long-held dichotomy between the cognitive and the conative, the rational and irrational, the objective and the subjective, is overplayed. These need not be at odds with each other but can be cooperative and synergic.[7]

Along these lines, Maslow makes a number of assumptions regarding inner human nature, including the following: it is biologically based and largely unchangeable; it is in part unique to the individual and in part species-wide; it is scientifically discoverable; it is essentially good or at least neutral; it should therefore be encouraged and actualized; it is weak and subtle and can be easily overcome by habit, cultural pressure, and wrong attitudes; but it rarely disappears.[8] **Since many theorists assumed that human instincts must be controlled because they are bad or antisocial, Maslow's assumption that the tendencies of the inner nature are basically good was a relatively novel conception.**[9] On this account, neurotic and socially pathological behavior is ultimately attributable to external environmental conditions that lead to ignorance, wrong attitudes, and habits that block the actualization of the essential nature. **Maslow rejects the usual approach that derogates desire and need and criticizes traditional instinct theory, arguing that destructiveness and aggression are not primitive impulses or human instincts.** Instead, the basic human needs are instinctlike and ethically positive or at least neutral.[10] This is true of the two core tendencies of personality, namely, survival and actualization.

Maslow appeals to anthropological evidence to support his assertion that the fundamental or ultimate desires of human beings are manifested in different ways but appear to be universal rather than culturally determined. Basic needs are more common among humanity than are superficial desires or behaviors.[11] **Maslow draws a distinction between basic needs and "metaneeds," the former being deficits in the organism which must be filled up if one is to function in a healthy way.**[12] Unsatisfied deficit needs breed illness, and thwarting or threatening them produces psychopathological results. This is not the case with everyday conscious desires which are merely symptoms or surface indicators of the more basic needs.[13] When ordinary desires or neurotic needs are frustrated, it makes little difference for ultimate health, but the gratification of basic needs like safety or love is necessary for health.[14] The beneficial phenomena that are largely determined by the gratification of basic needs are numerous.[15]

It is useless, according to Maslow, to draw up an atomistic list of human drives or needs. Depending on the specificity of analysis, such a list could contain anywhere from one to a million needs and would give the mistaken impression that they are mutually exclusive.[16] **The only sound basis for classifying of motivational life is a hierarchical arrangement of constant fundamental needs. At the bottom of this hierarchy are the physiological needs that relate to the homeostasis of the organism. The second level consists of the safety needs, including security, stability, protection, freedom from fear and anxiety, structure, order, law, and so on. At the third level are the belongingness and love needs. These relate to the longing for acceptance, relationships, roots, and intimacy. Fourth are the esteem** needs, which are classified into two subsidiary sets. **The first set includes the desire for strength, achievement, adequacy, mastery and competence, and the second set includes the desire for reputation, prestige, status, and importance.**[17] The hierarchical arrangement of these needs is based on the principle of relative prepotency so that the needs on one level must be satisfied before those on the next level can motivationally dominate the organism. Because of these dynamics, people rarely reach a state of complete satisfaction; as soon as one need is satisfied, it is replaced by another.[18]

Maslow acknowledges that depending upon the individual, there can be exceptions to his hierarchical arrangement. For instance, there are people for whom self-esteem is a more powerful motivator than love. One cause of reversal of the hierarchy is that when a need has been satisfied for a long time, it may be underevaluated.[19]

In addition to this flexibility, it is also unnecessary for a need to be completely satisfied before the next need emerges. Maslow observes that most people are partially satisfied and partially unsatisfied in all their basic needs at the same time and adds that "a more realistic description of the hierarchy would be in terms of decreasing percentages of satisfaction as we go up the hierarchy of prepotency."[20]

Just as the lower levels of basic needs are prepotent over the higher, so the basic needs as a whole are prepotent over the metaneeds. That is, the deficiency needs must be satisfied to a large extent before the growth needs can dominate the person. Maslow's general rubric for the metaneeds or growth needs is the self-actualization tendency. He defines this as "ongoing actualization of potentials, capacities and talents, as fulfillment of mission (or call, fate, destiny, or vocation), as a fuller knowledge of, and acceptance of, the person's own intrinsic nature, as an unceasing trend toward unity, integration or synergy within the person."[21] Although this tendency is more subtle than the survival tendency, it is more important since it relates to the enhancement of life and not merely to the maintenance of life. **Because the relative satisfaction of the deficiency needs is the necessary prerequisite to the process of self-actualization, the two core tendencies are not in conflict.** But Maslow lists sixteen qualitative differences between them:

1. The higher need is a later phyletic or evolutionary development.
2. Higher needs are later ontogenetic developments.
3. The higher the need the less imperative it is for sheer survival, the longer gratification can be postponed, and the easier it is for the need to disappear permanently.
4. Living at the higher need level means greater biological efficiency, greater longevity, less disease, better sleep, appetite, and so on.
5. Higher needs are less urgent subjectively.
6. Higher need gratifications produce more desirable subjective results, that is, more profound happiness, serenity, and richness of the inner life.
7. Pursuit and gratification of higher needs represent a general healthward trend, a trend away from psychopathology.

8. The higher need has more preconditions.
9. Higher needs require better outside conditions to make them possible.
10. A greater value is usually placed upon the higher need than upon the lower by those who have been gratified in both.
11. The higher the need level, the wider is the circle of love identification: the greater is the number of people love-identified with, and the greater is the average degree of love identification.
12. The pursuit and the gratification of the higher needs have desirable civic and social consequences.
13. Satisfaction of higher needs is closer to self-actualization than is lower-need satisfaction.
14. The pursuit and gratification of the higher needs leads to greater, stronger, and truer individualism.
15. The higher the need level the easier and more effective psychotherapy can be: at the lowest need levels it is of hardly any avail.
16. The lower needs are far more localized, more tangible, and more limited than are the higher needs.[22]

In addition to his hierarchy of deficiency and growth needs, Maslow also discusses what he calls basic cognitive needs by which he means the desire to know and to understand, and the need for an aesthetic dimension. This has been misconstrued as an affirmation of a higher need than self-actualization,[23] but it is really an attempt to distinguish cognitive and conative needs while at the same time affirming their interrelation.[24]

Unlike the basic needs, the metaneeds have no hierarchy since they are all equally potent and can be mutually substituted. These metaneeds are: truth, goodness, beauty, wholeness, dichotomy-transcendence, aliveness, uniqueness, perfection, necessity, completion, justice, order, simplicity, richness, effortlessness, playfulness, and self-sufficiency.[25]

Maslow's concept of self-actualization is closely related to what he calls a currently active future because it includes the concepts of potentiality and hoping and of wishing and imagining. The future exists now in the person in the form of ideals, hopes, duties, goals, unrealized potentials, destiny, and so forth.[26] The self-actualized person is characterized by qualities like superior perception of reality, increased acceptance of self and others, spontaneity, autonomy, fresh appreciation, human kinship, ethics, humor, creativity, resistance to enculturation, and resolution of dichotomies.[27] **Maslow seeks to correct the impression that "self-actualization" implies selfishness rather than altruism or that it neglects the ties to other people and society. The dichotomy between individualism and altruism is resolved in self-actualizing people, in that they are "simultaneously the most individualistic and the most altruistic and social and loving of all human beings."[28]**

Maslow stresses the differences between being bent on deficiency need gratification and being growth dominated or "metamotivated." The deficiency or coming-to-rest conception of motivation does not adequately account for those people who are predominantly growth-motivated. While deficit-needs are shared by all humans, self-actualization is idiosyncratic, since every person is different.[29] **The self-actualizer approaches relationships and perceives reality in ways that transcend those who are motivated by deficiency needs. This is especially true in the case of the "peak experiences" that are associated with self-actualized individuals. These moments of highest happiness and fulfillment produce a form of cognition (Cognition of Being, or B-cognition) that is distinct from ordinary cognition (Cognition of Deficiency, or D-cognition).**[30] B-cognition is more holistic, intense, absorbing, rich, ego-transcending, self-validating, desirable, receptive, awe-inspiring, and integrative than D-cognition, and the person in the peak experiences is more in touch with the actualizing metamotivations.[31] As Clippinger observes, peak experiences are similar to those found in religion and mysticism.[32] They cannot be forgotten or summoned at will, and they temporarily merge what ought to be into what is. **But B-cognition carries its own dangers, such as its incompatibility with action and responsibility. Because of this, Maslow maintains that not only B-cognition but also D-cognition is necessary to the concept of self-actualization.**[33]

Self-actualization as an expression of full humanness is biologically based. Thus, it is "(empirically) normative for the whole species rather than for particular times and places, i.e., it is less culturally relative. It conforms to biological destiny, rather than to historically-arbitrary, culturally-local value-models as the terms 'health' and 'illness' often do."[34] Built into the inner nature is a biological pressure toward fuller and fuller being. This directional tendency, Scroggs and Douglas note, is "reminiscent of the Aristotelian enteleché—a built-in purpose or direction that the organism pursues and that will unfold invariably, unless something blocks or thwarts it."[35]

Maslow's stress on the physiological source of the actualizing tendency is consistent with Goldstein's organismic theory, but he also adds the psychological concomitant of the tendency of the person to make choices that satisfy basic needs and metaneeds.[36] But these choices are not made out of a self-conscious sense of one's destiny. Rather, there is an unconscious dimension to motivation, and this is particularly true of behavior related to growth and self-actualization.[37] While most behavior is overdetermined or multimotivated,[38] there are forms of behavior that are unmotivated. Coping behaviors (striving, doing, achieving, trying, purposiveness) are related to the deficiency needs and are motivated.[39] Expressive behaviors (being-becoming, existing, growing) are related to the metaneeds and are not consciously motivated.

Because of this, the metaneeds are more subtle and equivocal than the deficiency needs, and there are many factors that can inhibit self-actualization. Maslow views human needs as fragmented remnants rather than the whole instincts found in lower animals. They are instinctlike capacities and potentialities that leave room for doubt, uncertainty, and conflict.[40] **It is a difficult psychological achievement even to be aware of our true needs. And the higher the need, the weaker and more easily suppressed it is by learned cultural and environmental** forces.[41] There is little hope of self-actualization in the absence of adequate physiological provision, safety and security, love and acceptance, and competence and respect. **Ungratified deficiency needs have a regressive power, and even when these needs are sufficiently gratified, this is no guarantee that self-actualization will occur. Growth requires courage in the face of threat and risk, and the pull toward safety and self-protection against pain, fear of the unknown, and loss is inimical to the dynamics of growth.**

Safety needs are prepotent over growth needs, but unbridled gratification of these needs can be as regressive and psychopathological as inadequate gratification. Thus, the forces of growth and regression are in dialectic tension.[42] On this account, it is not surprising that Maslow could find few people who met his criteria for self-actualization. He estimated that perhaps only one in one hundred or two hundred reach this goal.[43]

The dividing line between the inspirational and the scientific is not always clear in Maslow's writings. He regarded the Third Psychology as "one facet of a general *Weltanschauung,* a new philosophy of life, a new conception of man."[44] **In effect, he sought to clothe a metaphysical framework with the garments of a presumably scientific psychology. This becomes especially evident in the following statement about humanistic psychology: it is "transitional, a preparation for a still 'higher' Fourth Psychology, transpersonal, transhuman, centered in the cosmos rather than in human needs and interest, going beyond humanness, identity, self-actualization, and the like."[45] Maslow in fact regarded his third-force psychology as a secular surrogate for religion:**

> The human being needs a framework of values, a philosophy of life, a religion or religion-surrogate to live by and understand by, in about the same sense that he needs sunlight, calcium or love.
>
> Without the transcendent and the transpersonal, we get sick, violent, and nihilistic, or else hopeless and apathetic. We need something "bigger than we are" to be awed by and to commit ourselves to in a new, naturalistic, empirical, nonchurchly sense.[46]

The peak experiences are the sacraments of this new religion, because they are "life-validating, i.e., they make life worth while. These are certainly an important part of the answer to the question, 'Why don't we all commit suicide?'"[47] Another aspect of Maslow's psychological worldview is his attempt to construct a humanistic value system that has no reference

to a transcendent source. The ultimate value in his "descriptive, naturalistic science of human values" is self-actualization, the "far goal toward which all men strive."[48] The good is anything that moves one in the direction of the actualization of the inner nature.

Carl R. Rogers

During the course of his lengthy career, Carl Rogers exerted an ever-broadening influence on the development and popularization of humanistic psychology. According to his own account, the enormous popular response to his work is largely because he expressed an idea whose time had come. This central idea in his writings is

> the gradually formed and tested hypothesis that the individual has within himself vast resources for self-understanding, for altering his self-concept, his attitudes, and his self-directed behavior—and that these resources can be tapped if only a definable climate of facilitative psychological attitudes can be provided.[49]

The essence of Rogers's therapeutic approach is the creation of a set of conditions that will enable a person to utilize and express the inward, growth-directed tendency that is fundamental to the human organism.

Unlike psychoanalysis, Rogerian therapy did not develop within a medical context; it is comparatively easy to learn and requires fewer sessions to be of benefit to the client. For these reasons, it has been widely used by clinical psychologists and counselors. However, Rogers recognizes that his approach does not fit traditional psychological theory and consequently has had less impact within the academic community. His theory of therapy and of personality is far removed from the mechanistic view of behaviorism and the pessimistic view of psychoanalysis. It shares more in common with the existential and humanistic psychologists who stress the phenomena of becoming and growth. He found the Freudian view unconvincing and was influenced instead by theorists like Kurt Goldstein, Harry Stack Sullivan, Andras Angyal, Abraham Maslow, Gordon Allport, and Rollo May, who related behavior to one's self-view.[50]

Rogers has produced the most rigorously developed and comprehensive account of humanistic psychology. At first, however, he resisted theoretical formulation in favor of a phenomenological method that emphasized personal experience, perception, and feelings. His major concern in the first years of his clinical relationships was the development of methods and skills that produced effective results.[51] Following his conviction that "theory, to be profitable, must follow experience, not precede it,"[52] Rogers waited until he and his colleagues had amassed extensive clinical experience before beginning to crystallize a distinctive theoretical perspective. Two other reasons for his initial reticence in this area are his concern that theory, once constructed, often becomes dogma, and his strong emphasis on human freedom.

Rogers believes in what he calls "the fundamental predominance of the subjective" and argues that while there is no such thing as objective truth, the machinery of science is the best way to avoid self-deception.[53] He views scientific research as the disciplined effort to discover order in the phenomena of subjective experience through systematic theoretical thinking. More than anyone else, Rogers has conducted and stimulated research on the nature of the self and the process of change and has grown increasingly confident that almost any aspect of psychotherapy can be scientifically

investigated. Even though psychotherapy is "a deeply subjective existential experience in both client and therapist, full of complex subtleties, and involving many nuances of personal interaction,"[54] the changes that occur in therapy are amenable to research investigation. He and his associates have utilized a number of methods to integrate subjective experience and objective research, and these include content analysis of recorded and transcribed therapy interviews, measurement of operationally defined variables, the use of William Stephenson's "Q-technique" of statistically sorting statements about a person's self-image, standardized tests of clients in therapy, and rating scales designed to measure attitudes of the therapist and changes in the client.[55]

Rogers first developed a theory of therapy, and this became the basis for his subsequent theories of personality, of the fully functioning person, and of interpersonal relationships. His most systematic exposition of his theoretical framework appeared in 1959,[56] and since that time, the bulk of his effort has been directed to applying this approach to other human activities. He has expressed the hope that the evidence of future research will eventually replace the various "schools" of psychotherapy with a more holistic approach that incorporates whatever is factually verified.[57] He believes that in the long run, the humanistic view will take precedence over the behavioristic view.[58]

Rogers used the term *client-centered therapy* to distinguish his approach from other therapeutic methods. For him, a "client" is one who voluntarily seeks help for a problem without relinquishing responsibility for the situation.[59] The term *nondirective* is also used to describe his method of counseling, but Rogers later came to prefer the label *person-centered approach* as he extended its application to people in all contexts.[60]

In his theory of therapy, Rogers arrived at three basic conditions that must be fulfilled by the therapist in order to facilitate a process of change in the client. First, the therapist must be genuine and transparent with the client, open to the feelings and attitudes that occur within, and able to communicate them when appropriate.[61] Rogers uses the term *congruent* to describe this acceptance of one's feelings and lack of façade. Counseling effectiveness diminishes when the therapist defensively behaves in a way that is incongruent with his or her inner feelings. This attitude of self-acceptance and openness requires ongoing personal growth on the part of the therapist.[62]

The second condition for the therapist is what Rogers calls "unconditional positive regard" for the client. This involves a warm, acceptant, and positive attitude toward the client that does not fluctuate with the client's behavior. The therapist "prizes" and cares for the client but does so in a nonpossessive way that permits the client to be separate.[63] In this way, the feelings and needs of the client are respected, and the therapeutic relationship gives him the freedom to be what he is. The second condition depends on the first, because "a person can implement his respect for others only so far as that respect is an integral part of his personality make-up."[64] The therapist must accept himself before he can accept others. This atmosphere of acceptance and respect without evaluation allows the client to experience a feeling of safety, knowing that she will be accepted by the therapist regardless of the attitudes she expresses.

The third condition is empathic understanding, that is, the ability and willingness of the therapist to sense the moment-to-moment feelings and personal meanings of the client from the latter's internal frame of reference. This requires a sensitive and nondirective reflection of the client's attitudes that frees him from the threat of external evaluation and recognizes him as a person who is in process of becoming.[65] In this way, the therapist manifests a belief in the worth and significance of the client and becomes an alter ego of the client's attitudes and feelings. Acceptance and understanding are emotional phenomena, not intellectual ones. To permit oneself to understand another person in this way is rare and risky because it can lead to change.[66] **Rogers stresses that the attitudes and feelings of the therapist are more important to the therapeutic process than his theoretical orientation and techniques.**

These three conditions are skills that require effort to cultivate, but they do not involve diagnosis of the client's condition. Psychological diagnosis is notably absent in the Rogerian approach. Rogers objects that it is not only unnecessary but in some ways even detrimental, in that it increases dependent tendencies in the client and makes the effectiveness of therapy rest on the professional expertise of the therapist.[67] **Rogers also wishes to minimize the amount of transference that takes place between the client and therapist because, contra Freud, he holds that transference and projection are not necessary to the therapeutic process but in fact hinder the growth of the client.**[68] Unconditional positive regard provides security in the relationship but not dependence. While positive and negative transference attitudes are unavoidable, these do not typically develop into transference relationships in client-centered therapy.

When the client experiences a supportive relationship with the therapist that is characterized by congruence, unconditional positive regard, and empathic understanding, she gradually becomes able to listen to herself and accept her feelings and attitudes. Paradoxically, the prerequisite to change is that she first learns to accept herself as she is. Rogers notes that "to the degree that each one of us is willing to be himself, then he finds not only himself changing; but he finds that other people to whom he relates are also changing."[69] **When the therapeutic conditions are met, the client is increasingly free to express and explore her feelings. This leads to the discovery of internal conflicts brought about by incongruity between some of her experiences and her concept of self. For the first time, she is able to experience consciously the feelings which were previously distorted in or denied to awareness because of the continued unconditional positive regard of the therapist.**[70] **Slowly, her concept of self is reorganized and becomes increasingly congruent with her experience.** Since fewer experiences can be threatening to her concept of self, there are fewer perceptual distortions and denials, and consequently, decreased anxiety and defensiveness.[71]

Rogers has developed a continuum of seven stages of process in psychotherapy to illustrate and quantify this gradual shift from incongruence to congruence in the client.[72] **On one end of the continuum, the client has a static and rigid self-structure and is unwilling to communicate self; on the other end, the client's self-structure is flexible and adapts to experience.** He moves from stasis to process and from remoteness to enhanced relationships as he becomes increasingly aware of his internal experiencing.

Among the outcomes of the therapeutic process in which the client experiences himself as being fully received throughout, Rogers includes the following: openness to experience; perceptions that are more realistic and differentiated; movement away from façades, from meeting external expectations, and from pleasing others; experiencing of the potential self (the client discovers that he can *be* his experience); the full experiencing of an affectional relationship; the liking of one's self; movement toward self-direction and self-trust; and movement toward being in process.[73]

Based on his clinical experience, Rogers came to the conclusion that the core of personality is not negative but positive. Though Rogers was raised in a conservative Protestant home and later spent two years at Union Theological Seminary, he abandoned his earlier religious orientation and especially any concept of the sinfulness of man. He also rejected the Freudian position that human instincts, if permitted expression, would lead to destructive and antisocial behavior.[74] Man is not "a beast who must be controlled but an organism able to achieve, through the remarkable integrative capacity of its central nervous system, a balanced, realistic, self-enhancing, other-enhancing behavior."[75] He argues that his positive view of human nature has an empirical rather than a philosophical foundation, and in spite of the fact that the main source of incompatible evidence comes from the clinical experience of the Freudian group, it has been his experience that "persons have a basically positive direction."[76]

According to Rogers, the problem of destructive and antisocial behavior stems from the defensiveness and aggressiveness associated with inadequate self-concepts. When people begin to accept themselves, they can also appreciate and accept others, and this leads to enhanced communication and cooperation. People who are in touch with their feelings and accept them with their complexity find that these feelings mingle and harmonize in a balanced way. A person who is free to express his natural potentialities will act in a rational, constructive, and social way.[77]

Thus, the real issue at the bottom of each person's problems is how to get in touch with the real self. Since the core of personality is positive, an individual is most fulfilled when she can fully express what she actually is.[78] The whole person-centered approach rests on a basic trust in human beings and in human experience. Rogers claims that "when an activity *feels* as though it is valuable or worth doing, it *is* worth doing. Put another way, I have learned that my total organismic sensing of a situation is more trustworthy than my intellect."[79]

Rogers always has placed a strong stress on freedom of thought in his own life and practice. For him, experience is the highest authority, not the evaluations or dictates of

others. He minimized the role of external judgments and authorities and encouraged people to follow their internal locus of evaluation.[80] Thus, one of the indices of growth in a client is that "the individual moves away from a state where his thinking, feeling, and behavior are governed by the judgments and expectations of others, and toward a state in which he relies upon his own experience for his values and standards."[81]

The process of change in the person-centered approach is based on what Rogers calls "the forward-moving forces of life itself." His whole psychotherapeutic system centers on an inherent tendency in the organism toward maintenance and enhancement that provides the motivation for development and growth.[82] Thus, the therapeutic process is "the achievement by the individual, in a favorable psychological climate, of further steps in a direction which has already been set by his growth and maturational development from the time of conception onward."[83] Therapy simply releases and facilitates an already existing but blocked tendency of the organism toward psychological development. Rogers summarizes the essence of his approach in these words:

> [W]hen we provide a psychological climate that permits persons to *be*— whether they are clients, students, workers, or persons in a group—we are not involved in a chance event. We are tapping into a tendency which permeates all of organic life—a tendency to become all the complexity of which the organism is capable.[84]

Rogers has called this the "actualizing tendency" and claims that it is present not only in human beings but in all living organisms. Goldstein, Angyal, and Maslow held similar views about the actualizing tendency and influenced Rogers's thinking in this key area.[85]

While this organismic pressure or forward-moving tendency is always present, it is an inherent potentiality that is not intuitively evident to people from their own experience. The growth tendency "may become deeply buried under layer after layer of encrusted psychological defenses; it may be hidden behind elaborate façades which deny its existence; but it is my belief that it exists in every individual, and awaits only the proper conditions to be released and expressed."[86] In a suitable psychological climate, this tendency is released and becomes actual rather than potential.

Rogers has developed an extensive set of constructs for use in his theories of therapy and personality, and two of the most important are the organism and the self.[87] **For Goldstein, the self is virtually the same as the organism, but Rogers clearly distinguishes the two.**

Each individual is an organism who exists as the center of a changing world of experience. The organism reacts to this perceptual or phenomenal field in accordance with a single basic tendency to actualize, maintain, and enhance the experiencing organism. Behavior is "the goal-directed attempt of the organism to satisfy the experienced needs for actualization in the reality as perceived."[88] These needs are both physiological and psychological, and all behavior is directed to meet present needs.[89] **Thus, behavior is best understood from the internal frame of reference of the individual.**

Part of the actualizing tendency is the movement toward differentiation in which a portion of the total perceptual field becomes differentiated and symbolized in an awareness of being and functioning that Rogers calls the self, concept of self, or self-structure. **The self is a fluid and changing gestalt which is available to awareness though not necessarily in awareness.**[90] **While the inherent potentialities of the organism are genetically determined, the self-concept is socially determined.**

Rogers eventually drew a distinction between the actualizing tendency of the organism and the self-actualizing tendency, the latter being a psychological manifestation of the genetically determined organismic tendency. Thus, there is only one underlying forward-moving tendency in the organism, but it is blocked when a person inadequately perceives and symbolizes (represents in awareness) his feelings and experiences. The greater one's self-awareness, the more he is able to make conscious choices that are consistent with the subconscious organismic choices that are guided by the evolutionary flow.[91]

Although the organism is ultimately guided by a single motive, it has a number of needs that are subservient to the actualization tendency.

> [T]o me, it is meaningful to say that the substratum of all motivation is the organismic tendency toward fulfillment. This tendency may express itself in the widest range of behaviors and in response to a wide variety of needs. To be sure, certain basic wants must be at least partially met before other needs become urgent.[92]

In his theories of therapy and personality, Rogers focuses his attention on two critical needs: the need for positive regard and the need for self-regard.[93] **The first could be inherent or learned, but the second "develops as a learned need developing out of the association of self-experiences with the satisfaction or frustration of the need for positive regard."**[94] These needs are particularly relevant to the client-centered approach to therapy which depends on the provision of unconditional positive regard and an atmosphere of security, acceptance, respect, and empathic understanding. All individuals have basically the same needs, but these needs are often not permitted conscious symbolization.[95] However, they prompt behavior even when they are not consciously experienced.[96]

The needs for positive regard and self-regard are frustrated when conditions of worth are imposed on a person by significant others. The individual organizes these conditions into her concept of self and so develops incongruence between self and experience. Experiences that are contrary to conditions of worth are incorrectly perceived or denied to awareness so that they are not organized into the self-structure. Because the organism is able to subceive (experience without conscious awareness) experiences that are inconsistent with the distorted self-structure, this incongruence produces psychological maladjustment, threat, and defensive behavior (distortion and/or denial of experience that threatens the self). Under certain circumstances (e.g., an experience that suddenly exposes one's incongruence), the defensive process cannot prevent the experience from being accurately symbolized in awareness. When this occurs, the organism's self-structure becomes disorganized, producing varying degrees of anxiety. Reintegration, the reversal of this process, takes place in the therapeutic context of unconditional positive regard and empathic understanding.[97]

In his theory of the fully functioning person, Rogers "pictures the end-point of personality development as being a basic congruence between the phenomenal field of experience and the conceptual structure of the self . . ."[98] **The fully functioning person is one who perceives and symbolizes all experiences accurately in awareness, so that the self-concept is congruent with experience. The self and personality emerge from experience rather than experience being distorted to fit a preconceived self-structure.**[99] This person's need for positive regard and positive self-regard are met through the experience of unconditional positive regard and empathic understanding in relationships with significant others.

Under these conditions, the fully functioning person will have these characteristics: an increasing openness to experience without defensiveness; the experience of himself as the locus of evaluation rather than his introjections from others; no conditions of worth and hence the experience of unconditional self-regard; increasing trust in his organism; growing congruence between the self and the ideal self (the self-concept which the individual would most like to possess); increasingly existential living, that is, willingness to be a process rather than a product or a static entity; ability to creatively adapt to each situation; ability to accept and live with others in the maximum possible harmony because of the rewarding character of reciprocal positive regard.[100] Thus, Rogers's view of the good life is not a fixed state of virtue, contentment, happiness; nor is it a state of drive-reduction, or tension-reduction, or homeostasis. Rather, it is a fluid process, a direction, "a continually changing constellation of potentialities."[101] For Rogers, "life, at its best, is a flowing, changing process in which nothing is fixed."[102] The fully functioning person has the freedom to adapt to his environment to provide the maximum satisfaction of his deepest needs; such a person, for Rogers, is a "fit vanguard of human evolution."[103]

During the course of his career, Rogers extended the principles of the therapeutic relationship to all human relationships. "No longer am I primarily interested in individual therapeutic learning, but in broader and broader social implications."[104] In his theory of interpersonal relationships, he outlined the conditions, process, and outcome of a deteriorating relationship and of an improving relationship, and all of these correspond to his theory of therapy.[105] **The three conditions of genuineness, acceptance, and empathy are relevant to any situation in which the development of the person is a goal.**[106] Rogers and his associates have applied the person-centered model to group therapy, family life, play therapy, education and learning (e.g., student-centered teaching), group-centered leadership and administration, group tension and conflict, interpersonal and intergroup communication, creativity, and encounter groups.[107]

Beyond this, Rogers's approach has increasingly become a philosophy of life and not merely a psychological model. This is especially evident in his book, *A Way of Being,* where he writes, "I am no longer talking simply about psychotherapy, but about a point of view, a philosophy, an approach to life, a way of being, which fits any situation in which *growth*— of a person, a group, or a community—is part of the goal."[108] He recognizes that "the basic difference between a behavioristic and a humanistic approach to human beings is a *philosophical* choice."[109] **According to the Rogerian perspective, there is no evil, no genuine guilt, and no valid external judgments. Each person is her own authority for truth and values, and human nature can be trusted.** In fact, humans are wiser than their intellects: "our organisms as a whole have a wisdom and purposiveness which goes well beyond our conscious thought."[110] In the broadest context, the actualization tendency in each organism is actually part of a greater formative tendency at work in the universe.[111]

Rogers also exhibited a growing spiritual interest, and he came to see his thinking as a bridge between Eastern (especially Taoism) and Western thought.[112] He embraced the idea of multiple realities, that is, millions of separate, individual perceptions of reality.[113] Like those in the transpersonal psychology movement, he grew interested in paranormal phenomena, meditation and altered states of consciousness, ESP, biofeedback, telepathy, precognition, clairvoyance, holistic health, and experience of union with the universal.[114] These vast resources of "nonconscious intelligence" are part of human potential. The emerging "person of tomorrow" will be characterized, among other things, by a yearning for the spiritual.[115]

THE PERFECTION VERSION

Alfred Adler

Although originally associated with Freud, Adler moved away from the instinctivism of psychoanalysis and pioneered in the formulation of social psychology. He emphasized social relations rather than biological determinants in the development of the personality. **The primary source of human motivation is derived from social factors rather than inborn instincts. Thus, Adlerian theory would more accurately be called a context psychology than a depth psychology.**

In his earliest writings, Adler accepted Freudian drive psychology with its focus on objective external determinants of the unconscious, but he gradually revised his position into a more subjectively oriented approach to the personality. While he acknowledged many of Freud's observations, he interpreted them less literally, especially in the area of sexuality. His replacement of the sex drive with a more psychological and internally caused striving called the "masculine protest" led to his break with Freud in 1911 and the formation of his own group, which came to be known as Individual Psychology.

Adlerian theory stresses the conscious dimension of the personality and is holistic, subjectifying, and organismic in its conception. By contrast, Freudian theory minimizes the conscious dimension and is more atomistic, objectifying, and mechanistic in its conception.[116]

Adler's ideas clearly influenced a number of other theorists like Erich Fromm, Karen Horney, and Harry Stack Sullivan, whose conclusions share more in common with his own than with those of Freud.[117] There are also a number of parallels between Adler's theory and the field theory of Kurt Lewin, particularly in Adler's stress on dynamic relational forces.[118]

One important theme in Individual Psychology concerns the nature of formative influences in childhood. The family atmosphere during the early years of life has a significant bearing on whether an individual will develop a constructive or destructive approach to relationships throughout the rest of her life. A crucial role of the mother is in the provision of the earliest and greatest experience of love and fellowship that the child can have.[119] Her skill or lack of skill exerts a profound influence on all the child's potentialities. Another formative influence is the family constellation, which largely involves the child's birth-order position. Adler's clinical experience led him to the conclusion that children of the same family are not formed in the same environment because they are treated in different ways depending on their order of birth and sibling relationships. Adler was a clinician, not an experimentalist, but his birth order theory has stimulated research that has been partly corroborative.[120]

When environmental or hereditary factors make it difficult for a person to adapt, feelings of inferiority arise. At first, Adler wrote about organ inferiority and the attempt to overcompensate for biologically caused weaknesses. He then expanded his notion of inferiority to include psychological feelings of inferiority that arise from social disabilities associated with what was regarded as the feminine role. He spoke of the masculine protest as a method of overcompensation for the inferiority feeling that takes the form of a striving on the part of both men and women for the qualities of strength, competence, and achievement that are attributed in our culture to masculinity.[121] **Adler later generalized his concept of inferiority to include any feeling of inadequacy in any area of life. Since humans are pushed by the need to overcome their inferiority, these feelings can often be a constructive force in living because they motivate the individual to strive for higher levels of functioning.**[122]

Adler mentions a number of human needs, including the need for security. "By security we do not consider only security from danger; we refer to that further coefficient of safety which guarantees the continued existence of the human organism under optimum circumstances, in very much the same way that we speak of the 'coefficient of safety' in the operation of a well-planned machine."[123] Another human need is that of significance. "Every human being strives for significance; but people always make mistakes if they do not see that their whole significance must consist in their contribution to the lives of others."[124] Security and significance are clearly related to the social and communal life, and a meaningful existence can only be maintained by the favorable conditions offered by the social life. "The communal need regulates all relationships between men."[125] The human need for love and affection is also related to the social life and finds its original expression in the desire of children to be fondled, loved, and praised. The affectional tendency is "the psychological apparatus which the child can bring into play to achieve satisfaction, and the way in which he bears lack of satisfaction represent [*sic*] an essential part of the child's character."[126]

Since the feeling of inferiority frustrates the fulfillment of these needs, Adler came to propose that the striving for superiority or perfection is the fundamental tendency of the human personality. However, his ideas were considerably modified in the course of his writings. He originally concluded that the aggression drive was more important than the sexual drive but then abandoned drive psychology and replaced the aggressive drive with what he called the will to power. He observed that the intensive striving for power is generated in family education that spurs on the ambition of the child and awakens ideas of grandeur in his mind.[127] For example, children quickly become experienced in finding out the means by which they can best succeed in occupying attention.[128] The will to power is later expressed in the masculine protest.

In the next stage in his thinking, Adler replaced the will to power with the striving for superiority. At this point, he maintained that the feeling of inferiority causes a striving for recognition and superiority. "It is the feeling of inferiority, inadequacy, insecurity, which determines the goal of an individual's existence."[129] The striving for superiority is a prepotent dynamic principle which underlies every human action and contribution to culture. The struggle to reach an advantageous position is "the key to the whole personality."[130] The basic force behind all human activity is the striving from a felt minus situation "below" to a felt plus situation "above."

In the final stage of Adler's thinking, he modified the concept of superiority to include expressions that are less self-interested and more consistent with social interest. In this sense, the goal of striving for superiority is really the pursuit of completion or perfection and has been compared to Goldstein's and Maslow's principle of self-actualization.

The philosophy of Hans Vaihinger influenced Adler's theory of personality. Vaihinger presented a form of idealism called fictionalism that regarded ideational constructs, or fictions, as having inherent value for human life, even though they are only more or less consistent with reality. From this, Adler derived his concept of fictional finalism, meaning that the basic human tendency is movement in the direction of a future goal, namely, the ideal of perfection or completion.[131] **For Adler, people are motivated more by their expectations of the future than by their past experiences.**[132] "Individual Psychology insists absolutely on the indispensability of finalism for the understanding of all psychological phenomena. **Causes, powers, instincts, impulses, and the like cannot serve as explanatory principles. The final goal alone can.**"[133]

The striving for perfection is not the realization of an inherent organismic potentiality; instead, it is a fictional goal of mitigating feelings of inferiority and enhancing the self-esteem of the individual.[134] The fictional goal of superiority or perfection is the subjective cause of psychological events and is manifested in innumerable ways depending on the characteristics of the person. For Adler, the final fictional goal is the perfection of mankind, the creation of an ideal community.[135]

This goal-directed, teleological character of psychic movements is ultimately the creation of the individual. "This teleology is self-imposed. It arises in the psychological organ and must be understood as a device and as the individual's own construction."[136] Adler contends that a person's fictional goal is formed within the first few months or years of life, and he notes that this can give the false impression that character and personality are hereditary.[137] It is influenced by hereditary and environmental factors, particularly social influences, but it is not fully determined by them. "It is neither heredity nor environment which determines [the individual's] relationship to the outside. Heredity only endows him with certain abilities. Environment only gives him certain impressions."[138]

Thus, Adler denies "the causal significance of situation, milieu, or experiences of the child," and proposes an antimechanistic view of the personality.[139] Although he did not use the term, his principle of internal, subjective causation was a version of "soft" determinism. **The "creative self" makes its own self-ideal and personality; the child creatively utilizes her objective situation to form a subjective opinion of the world and herself.**[140] **"Meanings are not determined by situations, but we determine ourselves by the meanings we give to situations."**[141] **Hence, childhood experiences are not as important as the manner in which the child judges and assimilates them.**

Because of his emphasis on the creativity of the self, Adler's formulations were more idiographic than nomothetic. With few underlying explanatory constructs, his is more of a field theory than a class theory. Each personality is unique in construction and expression, and every case must be approached with this in mind. Adler stressed not only the uniqueness but also the unity of the organism in his theory of personality. "What is missing from psychoanalysis is the very first requisite for a science of psychology—a recognition of the coherence of the personality and of the unity of the individual in all his expressions."[142] Adler found this coherence in what he called the "law of movement" that depicts the goal-directed behavior of the individual. The unitary self strives for a personally determined goal and is expressed in a pattern of characteristics shaped by the need to move from a felt position of inferiority to one of superiority or perfection. This pattern is what Adler termed the "style of life." All of a person's experiences "must fit into his style of life, into the mosaic of his life's pattern."[143] This "life curve" or "spiritual curve" provides a unified picture of the entire movement of an individual, since all of his habits and symptoms are consistent with the fictional goal of superiority that is expressed in his unique style of life.

While this life goal is commonly shared, there are millions of variations in individual styles of life, or ways of striving for this goal.[144] **Each person organizes herself according to her subjective view of life that has been formed by the creative self, but some styles of life are more sound and consistent with reality than others.** "In the end we shall not be able to find a single human expression which is not filled with the purposiveness of the mind."[145] The underlying purpose behind all behavior is the achievement of security, satisfaction, and completeness.[146] Even behavior that appears to be inconsistent with this purpose (e.g., laziness), can be shown upon further analysis to be part of the individual's strategy for superiority.[147] If this behavior is ineffective, it is because it reflects an inappropriate style of life.

Adler notes that the style of life, the individual's "unified and crystallized pattern of behavior," is reached by the end of the fifth year of life.[148] Because of the stability of this scheme of apperception that consistently interprets experiences, it is difficult to correct mistakes in the meaning given to life. These mistakes are made because the meaning is formed in the child's mind by groping and guesswork. "The child is caught in the trap of his perspectives and repeats unceasingly his original mental mechanisms and the resulting actions."[149] Thus, an individual can deviate from his life pattern of behavior only with great difficulty. It is hard for human beings to know themselves and to change their styles of life. Habits and attitudes are symptomatic of underlying life goals; they change when the goal changes.[150] Only rarely will a person be forced by the consequences of his mistakes to make such a revision on his own.[151]

An additional complication is that a person's fictional goal is often unconscious in nature; people generally veil their real goals from themselves. "Nobody knows his own goal of superiority so that he can describe it in full."[152] Unlike Freud, Adler stressed the centrality of consciousness in the personality, but he recognized the reality of the unconscious. The goal of superiority or perfection is not unconscious because of repression, but because something has not been understood or has been withheld from the understanding.[153] As long as it is not understood, it is unassailable to the criticism of experience. A person may not understand her guiding self-ideal or style of life, but she pursues it and remains bound to it; it is evident in all her "postures, attitudes, movements, expressions, mannerisms, ambitions, habits and character traits."[154] Every action, every dream, is in some way a strategy for fulfilling one's goal.[155]

Human beings live in the realm of meanings and experience their circumstances in ways that are consistent with the significance they attach to them.[156] The goal of the individual has a profound effect on his perception, memory, imagination, fantasy, and dreams; all of these are goal-directed by the striving for security, significance, and superiority.[157] There are, for example, no "chance memories," since individuals unconsciously choose to remember only those events that are consistent with their styles of life.[158]

Next to the striving for superiority and perfection, the concept of social interest or social feeling is the most important factor in Adler's Individual Psychology.

> These two tendencies, the social feeling, and the individual striving for power and domination, influence every human activity and color the attitude of every individual in his striving for security, in his fulfillment of the three great challenges of life: love, work, and society.[159]

The social feeling "which binds man to man" is a universal human phenomenon; every person is socially embedded. The individual striving for superiority is always in the context of the rule of communal life.

In his earlier thinking, Adler's "will to power" was a driving force that was in conflict with social interest. He later concluded that the individual striving for superiority and perfection is socially neutral and can be pursued within the context of social interest.

> In the realm of individual living, man will strive for the perfection of
> himself, and in the realm of group living, he will strive for the perfection
> of society. The individualistic and social expressions are simply different facets
> of the same tendency to strive for superiority.[160]

Because of this, the individual striving for superiority need not be selfish interest pursued at the cost of social interest. People's significance must consist in their contribution to the lives of others; this is the only heritage that endures.[161] "The only salvation from the continuously driving inferiority feeling is the knowledge and the feeling of being valuable which originate from the contribution to the common welfare."[162] Thus, for Adler, a genius is a person of supreme usefulness to society and the most cooperative of human beings.[163]

The inborn ability to cooperate must be trained and exercised. Since the mother is the child's first bridge to social life, her function is to develop this potentiality and to spread the social interest to wider circles.[164] **When the social feeling is insufficiently developed in a child, it is extremely difficult for her to cultivate community consciousness as an adult. Without this spirit of cooperation, she will have problems in one or more of the three basic ties of every human being: occupational, social, and sexual.**[165]

The child has only a brief time in which to develop her psychic habits, and immature techniques of adjustment can lead to mistaken responses to her environment. **The three greatest childhood sources of mistaken meanings are organic infirmities, pampering, and neglect.**[166] These conditions can overburden the child and produce a neurotic disposition. Under normal circumstances, feelings of inferiority actually stimulate healthy striving and development. But in these situations, inferiority feelings can reach a pathological level because the child is overwhelmed by a sense of inadequacy. The resulting inferiority complex or compensatory superiority complex expresses a private frame of reference that is not congruent with reality.[167] The neurotic individual is more concerned about self-esteem and his personal quest for superiority than the normal individual who has a more developed social interest and relates his pursuit of satisfaction to the welfare of the community.

The pathological fear in the neurotic of the loss of self-esteem leads to a striving for self-enhancement that draws from rather than contributes to the group in which he lives. In this case, his goal of personal superiority is only a semblance of the more commonly acceptable individual goal of perfection.[168] Unlike the healthy person, the neurotic believes in his fiction and does not use it to attain a goal in reality.

Since the root cause of neurotic behavior is undeveloped social interest, people who approach the problems of occupation, friendship, and sex without the confidence that they can be solved by cooperation are failures in society.[169] To protect their self-esteem and hidden goal of personal superiority, neurotics engage in safeguarding behavior. This is especially characterized by the aggressive character traits of vanity, ambition, depreciation, accusation, jealousy, envy, avarice, and hate.[170] "All character traits reveal the degree of social interest."[171]

The Adlerian method of treating the neurotic patient begins with understanding the patient's style of life. The therapist accomplishes this through a series of diagnostic approaches plus the use of empathy, intuition, guessing, and verification.[172] She must look below the surface and discover the mistake made in the whole lifestyle rather than treat symptoms or specific expressions.

Using the patient's fictional goal as the key to understanding, the therapist must communicate this understanding to the patient. "The physician must grasp the special structure and development of that individual life with such accuracy, and express it with such lucidity, that the patient knows he is plainly understood and recognizes his own mistake."[173] **Finally, the therapist must help the patient revise his view of the meaning of life (his guiding fiction) to better satisfy reality and create a behavior pattern more appropriate to the fulfillment of the patient's needs.**[174] This involves awakening the patient's social interest by winning his good will through a relationship of cooperation, encouragement, and an unconditional expression of social interest.[175] In this way, the therapist belatedly assumes the maternal function.

Adler was concerned with finding ways of preventing maladjustment in adults by correcting mistaken styles of life formed by children under family upbringing. He believed that the best way to accomplish this was not through parents but through teachers trained to create an

atmosphere in the schools that would encourage the development of social interest and reshape mistaken outlooks. He was also interested in other aspects of social psychology, including crime and related disorders, social hostility, and war.[176]

Erich Fromm

Because of the clarity and scope of his writings, Erich Fromm's numerous books have been widely read. He adapted Freudian insights from the observation of individuals and applied them to the psychological understanding of groups.[177] **Fromm's concern with the interaction of psychological, economic, and ideological factors in the social process was heavily influenced by the social theory of Marx.**

Fromm focused on the existential dilemma that arises from the uniqueness of human existence and the inherent contradiction between the coexistence of animal and human

natures. The nature or essence of humanity is "not a specific substance like good or evil, but a contradiction which is rooted in the very conditions of human existence."[178] Since the instinctual equipment of humans is incomplete, survival depends on the development of speech and tools. At the same time, the human being is characterized by self-awareness, awareness of others as others, awareness of the past, and of death in the future. "Man transcends all other life because he is, for the first time, life aware of itself."[179] Thus, humanity is both in and out of nature, "partly divine, partly animal; partly infinite, partly finite."[180] **This biological and psychological dichotomy between missing instincts and self-awareness generates an existential conflict that requires a solution that can be either regressive or progressive.** One can attempt to transcend separateness and achieve unity by returning to nature, to animal life, or to one's ancestors. The alternative to this archaic solution is the progressive task of developing the full humanity within oneself.[181] **The deepest human tendency is the movement away from animal limitations toward the fulfillment of human possibilities.** "The necessity to find ever-new solutions for the contradictions in his existence, to find ever-higher forms of unity with nature, his fellowmen and himself, is the source of all psychic forces which motivate man, of all his passions, affects and anxieties."[182]

The animal aspect of humans is characterized by physiological needs (e.g., hunger, thirst, and sexual needs) that must be satisfied. But the satisfaction of these instinctual needs is insufficient for happiness or even sanity, since human beings are uniquely bound up with psychic needs that also must be satisfied.[183] These needs transcend those of animal origin and require a new harmony to replace the lost harmony with nature.[184] Thus, while humans are shaped by the economic and social structure of society, this adaptability is limited by the nature of their psychological needs.[185] **Fromm distinguishes between purely subjectively felt needs, some of which are harmful to human growth, and objectively valid needs that are consistent with the requirements of human nature.**[186]

The physiologically conditioned needs are essentially aspects of an underlying need for self-preservation. Since this need must be satisfied under all circumstances, it forms the primary motive of human behavior.[187] The psychological needs, on the other hand, are not rooted in bodily processes, but "in the very essence of the human mode and practice of life."[188] Fromm lists a number of these psychological needs, including the needs for relatedness or unity, for rootedness, for transcendence, for identity, for a frame of orientation and devotion, for effectiveness, for excitation and stimulation, and for the development of a character structure.

The need for *relatedness* is the necessity to unite and be related to other human beings. "This need is behind all phenomena which constitute the whole gamut of intimate human relations, of all passions which are called love in the broadest sense of the word."[189] The only approach to unity that can be successful without having a crippling effect is the kind of love that provides a union with another person while retaining a personal sense of separateness and integrity.[190] The failure of any kind of relatedness is narcissism, which is "the essence of all severe psychic pathology."[191]

The need for *rootedness* is cognate to the need for relatedness but more specifically associated with biological ties. This need for the security of natural roots can be satisfied regressively in a pathological attachment and fixation to the mother, or it can be satisfied progressively in the experience of the brotherhood of man.[192]

The need for *transcendence* relates to the phenomenon of self-awareness; it is the need to transcend the state of the passive creature. The regressive answer to the need for transcendence is to destroy life and thus to transcend it, but the progressive solution is creative activity. "The satisfaction of the need to create leads to happiness; destructiveness to suffering, most of all, for the destroyer himself."[193]

The need for a sense of *identity* is satisfied when humans sense themselves as the subject of their actions. People identify with nation, religion, class, and occupation, but these lead merely to herd conformity and are substitutes for a truly individual sense of identity. As with the other needs, this need for identity is so imperative that people could not remain sane if they did not find some way of satisfying it.[194]

Since Fromm defines *religion* as "any group-shared system of thought and action that offers the individual a frame of orientation and an object of devotion," the need for a *frame of orientation and devotion* is, for him, a religious need.[195] Humans need to construct comprehensive and cohesive mental pictures of the world that serve as frames of reference from which they can discern where they stand and what they ought to do.[196] Without such cognitive maps, people would be unable to organize the impressions that impinge upon them; "even if a man's frame of orientation is utterly illusory, it satisfies his need for some picture which is meaningful to him."[197] **Humans not only need maps but also goals as guides for action. Hence the need for an object of total devotion, which serves as "a focal point for all our strivings and the basis for all our effective—not only our proclaimed—values."[198]** This object of devotion, whether irrational and idolatrous, or rational, motivates conduct and gives meaning to life. It provides a sense of equilibrium and harmony in the world.

The need for *effectiveness* is the basic motivation to be competent in the world, to produce genuine effects and accomplishments. When this need is frustrated, one feels a sense of powerlessness and inadequacy. In interpersonal relations, this existential need can be regressively manifested in effecting fear and suffering or progressively manifested in effecting love.[199]

In his discussion of the need for *excitation and stimulation,* Fromm distinguishes between a "simple" stimulus that is rooted in one's neurophysiological organization and produces a drive, and an "active" stimulus of a psychological nature that results in a striving for a goal.[200] While the former leads to immediate and passive response, the latter produces an active and mutual relationship between the stimulus and the responder. **The need for excitation and stimulation can generate destructiveness and cruelty, or it can be expressed in love and productive interest.**

The need for the development of a *character structure* arose as a substitute for the loss of instinctive adaptation in humans. **"Character is the specific structure in which human energy is organized in the pursuit of man's goals; it motivates behavior according to its dominant goals: a person acts 'instinctively,' we say, in accordance with his character."**[201] Character-conditioned drives and strivings are so strong that they appear to a person as natural reactions. According to Fromm, social character is formed by cultural means and mediates the process of transforming general psychic energy into specific psychosocial energy.[202]

While people are motivated to satisfy each of these existential human needs, their attempts to do so can lead them in positive or negative directions. With the severance of the primary bonds which provided a sense of security, people experience themselves as separate entities from the world. **They can attempt to overcome the consequent state of aloneness by progressing to the "positive freedom" of relating to the world by spontaneous expressions of love and work, or they can regress, as most people do, by shrinking from their freedom in an attempt to eliminate the alienating gap between themselves and the world.**[203] The feeling of individual isolation and powerlessness in modern society is too frightening for the average person. Since people cannot go on bearing the burden of "freedom from," they must try to escape from freedom altogether unless they can progress from negative to positive freedom.[204]

The two primary mechanisms of escape from freedom are submission to a leader and compulsive conformity to a group.[205] Fromm offers a historical analysis of social developments to illustrate these mechanisms and the dialectic character of freedom. Structuralized societies like the medieval social system give people security instead of isolation, but at the cost of freedom. The demise of this system and the development of new economic forces in Renaissance culture led to greater freedom but also increased isolation, anxiety, and opportunities for tyranny.[206] The economic development of capitalism produced a spirit of restlessness, doubt, and insecurity; at the same time the doctrines of Lutheranism and Calvinism offered solutions that enabled people to cope with this increasing insecurity.[207] According to Fromm, the theology of the Reformation "expressed the feeling of freedom but also of insignificance and powerlessness of the individual"—the cost of religious certainty was self-humiliation and complete submission to an overwhelming power.[208]

The continued development of capitalistic society led to an increase in the ambiguous freedom that brought with it not only greater independence and self-reliance but also a growing sense of isolation and anxiety. Fromm uses the psychology of Nazism to illustrate authoritarianism as a mechanism of escape from freedom and also discusses the phenomenon of automaton conformity in modern society as an alternative mechanism of escape.[209] While traditional freedom must be preserved and increased, "we have to gain a new kind of freedom, one which enables us to realize our own individual self, to have faith in this self and in life."[210] The spontaneous activity of positive freedom is the only way to overcome the problem of isolation without sacrificing the integrity of the person.

In order to adjust to the requirements of society, people find different ways of adapting their inner needs to external demands. Fromm characterizes the resulting social orientations as productive or nonproductive and describes five social character types. He originally designated four of these orientations (receptive, exploitative, hoarding, and marketing) as nonproductive but later placed them on a continuum ranging between productiveness and nonproductiveness.[211] In addition, the various orientations blend, since no person exclusively manifests a single orientation.[212]

The productive character is life affirming; it is the aim of human development. "Productiveness is man's ability to use his powers and to realize the potentialities inherent in him."[213] Apart from those who are mentally and emotionally crippled, every human being is capable of a productive attitude and relatedness. **Thus for Fromm, curing in psychoanalysis means removing the obstacles which prevent people from being effective and productive.**[214]

Fromm extensively discusses the emotional and cognitive dimensions of productive love and thinking. The person who loves productively is concerned more with increasing his or her capacity to love than with being loved by others.[215] This is not easy to do since productive love is an art that requires mastery of both theory and practice. The qualities of discipline, concentration, patience, and supreme concern that are necessary to the practice of an art are rare in our culture.[216] Productive love is an active giving of oneself and is characterized by the qualities of care, responsibility, respect, and knowledge.[217] In contrast to symbiotic union, mature love is union under the condition of preserving one's integrity and individuality. Since productive love requires the affirmation of one's own life, self-love is actually the opposite of selfishness.[218] "Love is possible only if two persons communicate with each other from the centre of their existence, hence if each one of them experiences himself from the centre of his existence."[219]

Productive thinking is characterized not only by involvement and responsiveness of the thinker toward an object but also by the ability to see and respect the object in a realistic and comprehensive way.[220] **A productive thinker is more concerned with being than with having.** Having and being are two fundamental modes of experience, and both are potentialities of human nature. While the biological urge for survival tends to further the having mode, "selfishness and laziness are not the only propensities inherent in human beings." There is also "an inherent and deeply rooted desire to be: to express our faculties, to be active, to be related to others, to escape the prison cell of selfishness."[221] Because this desire is repressed in many societies, abandoning the false security of the having mode to find one's true identity in the being mode is risky and heroic.[222]

"All passions and strivings of man are attempts to find an answer to his existence or, as we may also say, they are an attempt to avoid insanity."[223] Fromm argues that the satisfaction of the pleasure drive and the pursuit of individual egoism are unsatisfactory attempts to answer the problem of human existence. This problem is aggravated by the human awareness of mortality and the fact that the brevity of life does not permit the full realization of human potentialities. **"It is part of the tragedy of the human situation that the development of the self is never completed; even under the best conditions only part of man's potentialities is realized. Man always dies before he is fully born."**[224] For Fromm, the only way to overcome the fear of dying is by not hanging on to life or experiencing life as a possession. **The fear of death and craving for immortality can only be conquered by a radical shift from the having mode to the being mode.**[225] **The deepest human need is to overcome the anxieties of separateness and helplessness before the forces of nature and society. Productive loving and thinking are the answer to this underlying problem of human existence.**

> There is only one solution to his problem: to face the truth, to acknowledge his fundamental aloneness and solitude in a universe indifferent to his fate, to recognize that there is no power transcending him which can solve his problem for him. Man must accept the responsibility for himself and the fact that only by using his own powers can he give meaning to his life. . . . There is no meaning to life except the meaning man gives his life by the unfolding of his powers, by living productively.[226]

Since all organisms have an inherent tendency to actualize their potentialities, the goal of life is the realization of these powers. People are not passive pawns of circumstance; within limits, they can choose to influence and control their conditions. "Man's main task in life is to give birth to himself, to become what he potentially is."[227]

Contending as he does that "psychology can not be divorced from philosophy and ethics nor from sociology and economics,"[228] Fromm relates his psychological system to the problem of ethics. **He criticizes Freud for taking a relativistic position with regard to values and affirms that humans cannot live without values and norms.**[229] Fromm draws a distinction between authoritarian ethics and humanistic ethics. According to him, the former is based on irrational authority, while the latter is based on rational authority. The source of irrational authority is power over people, but the source of rational authority is competence. In contrast to authoritarian ethics, the sole criterion of ethical value in humanistic ethics is human welfare.[230] Thus, the source of norms for ethical conduct must be derived from the inherent qualities of humanity; humanistic ethics must be based on "the science of man." **Although there is a lengthy tradition of humanistic ethics (e.g., Aristotle, Spinoza, Dewey), it was Freud who laid the foundations for a modern science of character with his discovery of a method by which he could study the total personality.**[231] **Based on post-Freudian psychology, a system of objectively valid norms can be developed. "Humanistic ethics is the applied science of the 'art of living' based upon the theoretical 'science of man.'"**[232] The good in this approach to ethics is the affirmation of life and the use of one's powers; that is, the productive character is the ideal of humanistic ethics.[233]

Fromm also contrasts authoritarian and humanistic conscience. Authoritarian conscience, like its counterpart in ethics, is based on irrational authority. The guilt feelings induced by rebellion against the authority's rule are used by the authority to increase dependency. The equation of sin with disobedience is part of the authoritarian structure and, according to Fromm, leads to a vicious and dehumanizing circle of disobedience, repentance, punishment, and renewed submission.[234] "The scars left from the child's defeat in the fight against irrational authority are to be found at the bottom of every neurosis."[235] **Humanistic conscience, on the other hand, is "the expression of man's self-interest and integrity."**[236] Its goal is the enhancement of productiveness, and increased productiveness in turn strengthens conscience.[237]

Fromm defines *religion* as "any system of thought and action shared by a group which gives the individual a frame of orientation and an object of devotion."[238] **Religion is an attempt to answer the problem of human existence, and it can be based on either rational or irrational faith.** According to Fromm, rational faith is a firm conviction based on productive intellectual and emotional activity that is founded on the potentialities of people.[239] Irrational faith, on the other hand, is "the belief in a person, idea, or symbol which does not result from one's own experience of thought or feeling, but which is based on one's emotional submission to irrational authority."[240] **As with ethics and conscience, so also with religion: the primary contrast is between authoritarian and humanistic expressions. Authoritarian religion is based on the transfer to God of the infantile attitude of the child toward his father.**[241] Submission to a controlling power offers the masses a measure of satisfaction and security.[242] It also provides a sense of hope, and Fromm illustrates this in his exposition of the dynamics of the early Christian community. "The first Christians were a brotherhood of socially and economically oppressed enthusiasts held together by hope and hatred."[243]

Fromm rejects authoritarian religion and promotes the secular faith of humanistic religion:

> [I]t is not true that we have to give up the concern for the soul if we do not accept the tenets of religion. The psychoanalyst is in a position to study the human reality behind religion as well as behind non-religious symbol systems. He finds that the question is not whether man returns to religion and believes in God but whether he lives love and thinks truth. If he does so the symbol systems he uses are of secondary importance. If he does not they are of no importance.[244]

Humanistic religion is "centred around man and his strength"; in this context, religious experience is "based on one's relatedness to the world as it is grasped with thought and with love."[245]

> Man's aim in humanistic religion is to achieve the greatest strength, not the greatest powerlessness; virtue is self-realization, not obedience. Faith is certainty of conviction based on one's experience of thought and feeling, not assent to propositions on credit of the proposer. The prevailing mood is that of joy, while the prevailing mood in authoritarian religion is that of sorrow and of guilt.

Inasmuch as humanistic religions are theistic, God is a symbol of man's own powers which he tries to realize in his life, and is not a symbol of force and domination, having power over man.[246]

To illustrate humanistic religions, Fromm cites early Buddhism, Taoism, the teachings of Isaiah, Jesus, Socrates, Spinoza, certain trends in the Jewish and Christian religions (particularly mysticism), and the religion of Reason of the French Revolution. Thus, humanistic religion can be theistic or nontheistic, and both authoritarian and humanistic expressions can be found within the same religion.[247] **Fromm prefers the nontheistic version and contends that the true goal of psychoanalysis is consistent with the best expression of religion, namely, to help the patient in the discovery of truth and the development of his or her capacity for love.**[248] **For him, the most rational faith is faith in oneself; only then can one have faith in others and in humanity as a whole.**[249]

Fromm's faith in humanity is based on his position that destructiveness is only a secondary potentiality in mankind, and that the primary potentiality is positive. **People only become evil if the proper conditions for their growth and development are lacking; the degree of destructiveness is proportionate to the degree to which the unfolding of a person's capacities is blocked.**[250] Thus, Fromm holds a "rational faith in man's capacity to extricate himself from what seems the fatal web of circumstances that he has created."[251] But for this to take place, there must be a realization of this primary potentiality that Fromm calls "a radical change of the human heart."[252] The physical survival of the human race depends on this change, but this is possible "only to the extent that drastic economic and social changes occur that give the human heart the chance for change and the courage and the vision to achieve it."[253] Fromm outlines the conditions for human change and the character structure of the "new Man" that must emerge.[254]

Fromm does not define psychological health and productiveness in terms of adjustment to society since "there is a discrepancy between the aims of the smooth functioning of society and of the full development of the individual."[255] While society frustrates the proper development of humans by making demands that are contrary to their needs, it is nevertheless possible to create a society that supports the fulfillment of these needs.

If the economic and political spheres of society are to be subordinated to human development, the model of the new society must be determined by the requirements of the unalienated, being-orientated individual. . . . Basic research on the nature of needs that has hardly been touched will have to be done by the new science of Man.[256]

Fromm sets an agenda of radical changes in the social structure that are necessary to the emergence of the new society of genuine humanistic socialism. This will require a conversion to a noninstitutionalized, nontheistic, humanistic "religiosity" without religion that enhances being and productiveness.[257]

CHAPTER 6
A CRITIQUE OF THE EIGHT PSYCHOLOGISTS

Sigmund Freud

While Freudian theory is vulnerable to criticisms of being unscientific and too reductionistic (though behaviorists criticize it for not being reductionistic enough), classic psychoanalysis does offer a comprehensive system of personality, pathology, and therapy that has made a lasting contribution to an understanding of human behavior, especially in such areas as defense mechanisms, the reality of unconscious mental dynamics, and the psychodynamics of dreams. Freud's work was characterized by originality, boldness, and power of communication. In his theory of neurosis, he captured the tragic dimension of human existence, particularly in the self-destructive antithesis of instinctual conflict. The locus of these destructive impulses is internalized in the individual and not merely derivative from civilization. In this respect, Freud's portrayal of the human condition has more depth than romantic humanism and yields significant points of correlation with the Christian understanding of sin, guilt, and the need for redemption.

Regarding Freud's theory of personality, there appears to be no unified structure or functional unity between the id, the ego, and the superego, and these personality components are described in intuitive and literary terms that elude scientific analysis. Instead, they are often personified as homunculi that operate in monochromatic ways, yielding a theory that does not adequately account for the richness, complexity, and diversity of human personality.

In spite of his commitment to a scientific worldview, Freud's ideas were less objective and scientific than he liked to think. His theory was based more on clinical impressions than on controlled empirical methods. The accumulation of data and presentation of conclusions is unsystematic, the terms and concepts are often vague and difficult to test and measure, and thus the scientific status of psychoanalysis is questionable at several points. This is true of the death instinct which critics regard to have been prompted more by personal considerations and a desire for theoretical consistency than by empirical evidence. It is also true of Freud's speculative account of the libidinal development of women that largely ignored sociocultural factors. His constructs are stimulating but not concrete or explicit enough to be formulated into operational definitions or subjected to rigorous experimental testing. In addition, the bulk of his theory is derived from observations of neurotic people, and this limits the validity of his conclusions concerning human behavior.

In spite of its unverified assumptions, however, Freud's theory has stimulated further systematic research on the nature of personality, and ego-analytic psychologists as well as object-relations theorists owe much to his work. This leads to an ambivalence: while much of Freudian psychoanalysis defies rigorous testing, it does appear that Freud developed a number of valid hunches. Unfortunately, his system resists falsification because it has internalized ready answers to criticisms, describing such disagreements as resistance and quickly dismissing alternative approaches to interpreting behavior. It is a system that explains too much too readily, and it is built on a doubtful model that relates psychodynamics to instinctual aggressive and sexual drives in a context of tension-reduction rather than stimulation.

While Freud recognized the need to avoid "the Scylla of underestimating the importance of the repressed unconscious, and the Charybdis of judging the normal entirely by the standards of the pathological,"[1] classic psychoanalysis tends to be a one-sided perspective that generalizes from data relevant only to neurotic states of mind. In addition to this overemphasis on psychopathology, Freudian theory is weakened by its pansexualism, in spite of Freud's protests to the contrary.[2] Part of the difficulty here has been the broad and somewhat ambiguous way in which Freud spoke of sexuality. In any case, his assumptions about sexuality as the primary motivator of human behavior, his virtual exclusion of the role of the mother, and his tacit reinforcement of a patriarchal mentality are problematic.

In a number of ways, Freud's work reflects the rationalistic materialism of the late nineteenth century with its deterministic outlook. Trapped in the inexorable cycle of biological and sociological events, the individual must continually resort to defensive behavior to manage ongoing conflicts and the anxieties that stem from them. Because the individual is not consciously aware of the defensive processes that underlie his or her behavior, the Freudian account makes it difficult to escape a profoundly pessimistic conclusion about the validity of human rationality and actions. This is aggravated by Freud's conflation of evolutionary teleology and psychological intentionality regarding primal instincts.

The extended duration of therapy in analytic treatment can enhance rather than mitigate narcissism, particularly since Freud's psychology of the unconscious minimizes the volition associated with conscious responsibility. Freud's hopes for the future related to the protection of the autonomy of the individual from unconscious threats, but his excessive expectations led to unrealistic utopian scenarios and a disillusionment consistent with his pessimistic and in some ways misanthropic view of humanity with its "naive self-love." This pessimism is reflected in his conviction that tension and lack of harmonious reconciliation will always characterize human goals.

Freud's attempt to develop a psychogenesis of religion as a projection of human relationships and fears will be discussed in chapter 8.

Erik H. Erikson

Erikson built creatively upon the Freudian foundation, and with his emphasis on the nature and development of the ego as well as the individual's relationships with others, he made a significant and lasting contribution to the school of ego psychology. His explication of the development of personality throughout the stages of the life span and his discussions of the strivings of the ego for competence and adaptation to the social milieu are insightful and often original. This is particularly true of his writings on the identity crisis, the life cycle, and the sociocultural dynamics that contribute to neurosis. Books like *Toys and Reasons* and *Gandhi's Truth*[3] illustrate his innovative ability to apply the principles of neo-Freudian analysis to topics as diverse as symbolic conflict resolution in the play of children on the one hand and psychosocial biography on the other. Erikson had a remarkable breadth of knowledge and a talent for integrating psychoanalytic thought with contemporary sociological and anthropological theory. **However, his compelling literary style, while slanted toward the popular and anecdotal, often suffers from an unsystematic presentation as well as insufficient discrimination in the use of materials.**

Without abandoning his allegiance to Freud, Erikson diverged from Freudian theory as he progressively deemphasized the role of instincts in favor of the contribution of parents and society to the development of personal identity. In this process of reacting against Freudian pessimism concerning human nature, Erikson's pendulum swung too far in the opposite direction. **In his quest for a new emphasis on health as opposed to the psychopathology of neurosis, he embraced a belief in progress, of ego strength, and of other-centered functioning that is sometimes naive in its minimization of skepticism.** It does not follow, for example, that people should uncritically pursue integration with social groups or develop increasingly inclusive identities. His genial faith in humanity and in the epigenetic progress toward wisdom in the life cycle indicates a profound degree of selectivity in his appeal to the history of human development, socialization, ideas, and values. **His faith in the positive and hopeful components of human nature is in some measure a needed corrective to Freud but in other ways limits the incisiveness of his critique of human selfishness and destructiveness.**

Erikson's most lasting contribution to ego psychology is his detailed account of the psychosexual stages of life that offers a substantial amplification of Freud's phases and transcends them by extending the analysis of ego development beyond adolescence to the striving for competence and adaptability in adulthood. His analysis provides more objective criteria for the assessment of psychic maturation as well as a fruitful scheme for further research and empirical testing of developmental hypotheses. On the other hand, his psychosocial model reflects contemporary American culture, and this may limit its applicability to other contexts.

By relating behavior to relational and cultural factors, Erikson has overcome the instinctual bias of Freudian theory, but his interpretive scheme tends to underplay biological, chemical, and genetic components of mental illness. His understanding of identity formation as an outcome of intrapsychic and communal responses focuses on the concept of self-sameness and continuity, but his account of "ego-identity" remains elusive, impressionistic, and ambiguous.

Erikson's theorizing, like that of the other psychologists in this study, often extends beyond the territory of psychology to that of ethics and metaphysics without acknowledging the epistemological shift this represents. In moving from the sphere of scientific inquiry to that of philosophic inquiry, he tacitly gives the impression that the latter is grounded in the former. Facing a culture that is losing a common ideology that undergirds human aspirations and the quest for meaning, his work on the relationship between ego and moral development implicitly appeals to values that are ultimately grounded in a religious understanding of human dignity and worth. His more cosmic affirmations allow room for the transcendent dimension, but in practice tend to reduce theology to ideology and religion to the mutuality of trust.

Another philosophical component of Erikson's thinking is his combination of an Aristotelian essentialism with an evolutionary adaptive scheme in his epigenetic ground plan of differential ascendancy in the components of ego maturation. In his response to the demands of the sociocultural environment, the individual's adaptive ability is limited by predetermined potentials that are manifested in a developmental sequence. Erikson's attempt to synthesize an evolutionary adaptive scheme with preexisting potentials is not rigorous or systematic and offers no account of the incipience of new epigenetic potentials.

C. G. Jung

As an original, creative, and prolific thinker, Jung was ahead of his time, and it has taken decades for his theories to become a significant source of influence on North American culture. At the time of his death in 1961, Jung's ideas were beginning to extend beyond a small circle of followers to a wider audience, and in recent years this process has taken on great momentum. Jung's impact on modern thought extends beyond his field, since his discoveries and theories relate to all aspects of human life and seek to relate psychology to a sympathetic approach to myth and spirituality that integrates Eastern and Western concepts.

Jung was a compelling and charismatic person, a tenacious explorer of unknown territory, and a brilliant expositor of the diverse materials he attempted to synthesize. His fertile intellect and facile grasp of different disciplines led to a variety of contributions to the study of personality, including the concept of the "complex," the use of word association tests, an archetypical approach to dream material, and the study of the entire life span with an emphasis on the problems associated with the second half of life. His dynamic theory of psychological types with its typology of introversion and extroversion and identification of the patterns of sensing, feeling, thinking, and intuitive is a significant contribution to personality theory that has been supported by research evidence related to the Myers-Briggs Type Indicator.

Jung's diversity and eclecticism is both a strength and a weakness. In a time of increasing specialization, Jung's approach offers a depth and wealth of insights from disciplines as disparate as philosophy, art, literature, music, anthropology, medicine, and

comparative religions in an attempt to synthesize rather than atomize these diverse materials. However, his preoccupation with the movement toward wholeness and individuation and his fascination with mandalas, eastern mysticism, alchemy, and occultism led to the development of a speculative, complex, and esoteric psychological theory with unavoidably metaphysical overtones. **The core concepts of Jungian theory are difficult to define and empirically evaluate.** These constructs are not developed rigorously enough to yield specific hypotheses that can be tested against objective criteria. This is particularly true of Jung's concept of the collective unconscious which continues to be speculative, particularly since the appearance of similar symbols in diverse cultures does not demonstrate ancestral etiology.

These problems are amplified by the fact that **Jung invested Freudian psychoanalytic terms with different meanings and became increasingly vague and imprecise in the conceptual structure of his later work.** He did not attempt to harmonize his earlier and later ideas, and there are problems with ambiguities and inconsistencies in his expositions (e.g., the interface between psyche and spirit).

Jung's grandiloquent explanatory system essentially overlooks the biological and sociocultural components in the causation and reinforcement of psychopathology. These somatic and social variables have a greater impact on human behavior and psychopathology than Jungian theory acknowledges. Clinical psychologists today are more inclined to recognize that behavioral problems are multiply determined.

On the other hand, Jung sought to confront the questions of meaning and purpose, and addressed the predicament of senselessness and aimlessness that often surfaces in the second half of life. He was incisive in his observation that the care of souls has been overlooked in an increasingly secularized age that has little room for the universal questions in its epistemic structure. He correctly noted that the problems of isolation and despair become accentuated in a culture that has largely abandoned the ideological coherence provided by shared religious convictions. **Unlike most personality theorists, Jung explicitly recognized the importance of spiritual concerns, but his attempt to resurrect spiritual symbolism that is devoid of creedal content led him to an amalgam of psychology and spirituality that approximates a rival religion that replaces dogma with the contents of the unconscious.** His radical reinterpretation of religious symbols as archetypal symbols of transformation and individuation that direct the energy of the psyche toward the goal of wholeness and selfhood is intentionally devoid of an objective basis grounded in transcendent reality. Instead, the archetype of the God-image as a symbol of totality becomes experientially indistinguishable from the archetype of the self. This leads to a wholesale abandonment of external authority and personal accountability as well as a profound distrust of rationality in the quest for self-actualization. **Yet Jung advocated an uncritical and implicit trust of the unconscious as a reliable guide to growth in wholeness and meaning. This profound faith in the unconscious as the deepest source of wisdom is rooted in a romanticized apprehension of archaic archetypal materials.**

Jung's openness to the realm of the ineffable and the numinous has made him an increasingly popular figure in religious circles, but his excessive emphasis on the mystical journey within can lead to a form of gnosticism that centers on the subjective and intuitive and trivializes the objective and historical components of reality. **The Jungian quest for selfhood can also lead to an exaggerated individualism and a minimization of interpersonal relations. Jung's followers claim that self-realization automatically enhances relations with others, but there is no assurance that concentration on the individual psyche promotes social concern.**

Jung's focus on the nonrational unconscious in the pursuit of meaning led him to an understanding of morality as nonobjective and numinous. With such a nonnormative stance, **Jung was ambivalent toward evil and attempted to understand it in terms of the archetype of the shadow. This approach fails to confront the power of personal and structural evil and reduces it to a "shadow side" that should be acknowledged and accepted in the quest for psychic wholeness. Taking his cue from the East, Jung came to see evil as a part of the good and added Satan into the Godhead by altering the Trinity into a mandala or quaternity and making this quaternity a symbol of the self.** This speculative revisionism is characteristic of Jung's freehanded reinterpretation of religious symbols and myths to suit his psychologized vision of reality. By naively reinterpreting historical realities as projections of psychological needs, Jung overreacted to the modern materialistic and rationalistic view of the universe. **He spurned the idea of God as an objective transcendent reality and turned instead to primal symbols stripped of their transcendent referents.** This psychologized spirituality reduces the search for meaning to an inner journey, and it is not surprising that his thought appeals to those of a more mystical or religious bent rather than those who are concerned with propositional logic. **Although Jung claimed that he was not making metaphysical statements, his psychologized interpretation of reality is essentially metaphysical, and certainly more compatible with pantheism or monism than with theism.** But because his writings are ambiguous, difficult, and unsystematic, Jungian jargon continues to proliferate in Christian as well as New Age circles.

Otto Rank

In recent years, there has been a revival of interest in Rank's work and a growing acknowledgement by psychologists of the indirect influence and farsightedness of his ideas. His contributions until recently were largely ignored or forgotten because of anti-Rank stigma in the Freudian establishment, the relative brevity of his life, and the density of his literary output. Rank's writings are hampered by their stylistic vagueness and by their ill-defined and enigmatic use of terms such as *will, artistic,* and *creative.* **But his reputation has been gathering momentum as more theorists recognize that Rank's once-radical views actually anticipated many aspects of mainstream psychodynamic theory.** Rank was ahead of his time, and several aspects of his conceptual legacy, particularly his understanding of the tension between life and death, speak with particular relevance to the present. His innovative ideas offer a rich source of heuristic material for clarification of psychological theory and for research investigation, and this has been underscored by the fact that several aspects of his psychology have been unwittingly rediscovered by later theorists and therapists. **Ernest Becker has been an influential force in the renewed appreciation of Rankian theory, and the presence of Rank's theoretical insights in the work of psychologists like Fromm, Maslow, and Rogers is now being recognized.**

One of Rank's lasting contributions to psychological theory is his recognition of the importance of the preoedipal mother-child relationship in the development of the personality. **His association of neurosis with the ambivalence of desiring to return to prenatal existence and fearing the repetition of the trauma of separation, as well as his view of analysis as probing the existential memory of this preverbal state, have become seminal ideas that have been further explored in recent object relations theory. However, he overstated his case in *The Trauma of Birth* when he elevated the trauma of parturition into a universal psychosocial explanation.**

Another significant Rankian contribution is his emphasis on volition as the organizing force that creatively expresses individual personality in a way that transcends genetic or instinctual determination. Rank perceptively argues that human relationships become meaningful only in a matrix of mutual deliberateness and conscious choice. His understanding of the will as a transformational agent of creative self-determination that is also dynamically interrelated to the sociocultural milieu and the somatic substratum was a significant precursor to later ego psychology. Rank's will therapy focuses on the strengthening of the personality and the manifestation of creative and responsible behavior that is based not only on given but also self-chosen factors. **However, his tripartite scheme of neurotic, average, and artistic types is too rigid and forced.**

Rank correctly discerned that psychology defies explication solely in terms of the natural sciences since humans live in ways that express the social forces of civilization and thus transcend biological explanation. Psychology must move beyond a mechanistic or biological frame of reference and incorporate subjective and creative factors including volition, ethics, religion, art, and other cultural phenomena. **Rank persuasively argues that modern psychologists who deny the existence of the soul cannot avoid substitute soulish objects and manifestations, and that even self-styled "scientifically objective" psychologies incorporate tacit moral systems.**

Rank's psychological approach is culturally oriented and seeks to integrate and appreciate human values. **His high level of cultural awareness and extraordinary ability to analyze myths and legends enabled him to use literature as a vehicle for examining the varieties of human experience.** He understood that the humanities offer a way of access into human consciousness that can be more direct than the way of scientific investigation and that the tendency toward specialization among psychologists limits their access to this fruitful source of insights that can supplement and enrich psychodynamic theory.

Rank is particularly helpful in his insights concerning awareness of death and the quest for meaning as the consequences of awareness of life. He saw that the reality of death is in fact a test of the meaning and significance of life and related the development of symbolic structures that provide a sense of solace and affirmation to the pursuit of immortality. This will to live, as opposed to the Freudian Thanatos instinct, animates a universal urge to survive biologically, culturally, or spiritually.

Rank's innovative approach to the therapeutic relationship stresses the present process of responsible choice in creating one's own personality as opposed to deterministic past causality. By focusing on dynamic relationship and experiencing of the present more than ideological interpretation and knowledge of the past, he envisioned therapy as a mutual relationship in which creative solutions to the patient's problems are sought in a context of creative affirmation and positive choice. **Because of this personal component of subjective and objective responses between analyst and patient, Rank came to see the therapeutic process as more of an art than a science.** This method of therapy transcends the analytical approach of undoing infantile repressions and offers greater potential for change because of its relational setting and insistence on conscious volition.

On the other hand, Rank tended to overreact to the mechanism and determinism of Freudian theory by swinging to the opposite end of the theoretical spectrum. After his departure from Freud, he failed to acknowledge the debts he owed to his former mentor and proceeded to become increasingly antipsychoanalytic. **He undervalued the role of the unconscious as well as genetic factors in personality development, and this hampered the explanatory value of his theoretical system.** Nor did he acknowledge the contradiction between his earlier and later ideas or give an account of his transition to a voluntaristic and humanistic perspective. **He so devalued his past association with Freud that he arrived, in his final period, at an anti-intellectual approach to psychology. He came to deprecate self-knowledge and argued in** *Beyond Psychology* **that humans live in irrational ways and that attempts to understand human behavior are futile.**

Abraham H. Maslow

Maslow made as significant a contribution as any psychologist or social scientist to the affirmation of the generally neglected potentialities of human beings. As a consequence, his books have been influential not only in the psychological arena but also among professionals in management, marketing, counseling, and education. He formulated a number of fruitful concepts and terms (e.g., need hierarchy, metaneeds, peak experiences, synergy, deficiency and being motivation, self-actualization), and some of these have flowed into popular discourse.

Maslow's work was more a corrective than it was a refutation of psychoanalytic theory and therapy; he sought to address the healthy side of personality that was neglected by the Freudian emphasis on the neurotic side. He is to be commended for attempting to steer a course between orthodox psychoanalysis and behavioristic psychology, but **his position is vulnerable to criticism in several areas, particularly because his theorizing and speculations often went far beyond the available empirical data. One problem concerns the structure of his need hierarchy.** Although he acknowledges that order reversals occur, **the structure appears to be too rigid to take the rich diversity of human personality and behavior into account. In addition, his definition of psychological health does not fundamentally represent the psychology of women.** It is also questionable whether his hierarchy of needs adequately represents the essential human needs, particularly because his brief account of the basic cognitive needs is not sufficiently integrated in the rest of his theory, thus leaving the stress on the conative at the expense of the cognitive. The emphasis of the existential psychologists like Victor Frankl and Rollo May on the quest for meaning and the inner fear of nonbeing is largely overlooked in his work.

Another difficulty is the questionable basis for his assumptions regarding the inner nature. **In his attempt to correct the negative perspective on human nature that resulted from psychoanalysis and the preoccupation with psychopathology, he appears to have swung the pendulum to the opposite extreme by focusing his attention on the healthiest examples he could find and drawing most of his conclusions from them,** as if such a sample would provide a suitable population for making generalizations about the motivational potential of humanity. **He assumes without empirical warrant that the inner nature is good or neutral, and that this nature should therefore be brought out and encouraged rather than suppressed.** His formulation of growth-through-delight rests, as he admits, on "the faith that if free choice is *really* free and if the chooser is not too sick or frightened to choose, he will choose wisely, in a healthy and growthward direction, more often than not."[4] This sanguine faith-posture does not fully address the issue of evil and the dark side of humanity. **Maslow conceded that he was unable to explain how human cruelty fit into his system, and near the end of his life, he expressed his hope to arrive at an understanding of this psychological puzzle.**[5] In effect, Maslow became less a psychologist and more a humanistic philosopher who theorized about human nature and morality and whose hope was in the evolution and manifestation of human potential. He freely speculated about ultimate values and the need for a new system of thought that would function as a kind of religion centered on the uniting of humanity.

Maslow's contention that the actualization tendency is a growth motivation is questionable. While deprivation motivation relates to the repairing of deficits and the reduction of organismic tension, growth motivation deals with enrichment and realization of capabilities or ideals. Maddi argues that growth motivation as an idea is logically inconsistent, because a motive involves a goal state and therefore implies deprivation unless the goal has been achieved.[6] Setting aside the question of the logical validity of this argument, Maslow escapes it when he speaks of the unmotivated nature of expressive behaviors like growth and actualization. The problem is that he is not always consistent and clear in his terminology, for example, when he speaks of metaneeds and metamotivation. This gives an impression of a quasimotivational quality in the growth needs that is not consistent with his discussion of the nature of expressive behavior. If the actualization tendency is in fact unmotivated, his suggested eight ways to self-actualize make little sense.[7]

There is also the problem of Maslow's criteria for whom he considers to be self-actualized. He did not take the basic precaution of having a control group when he investigated his self-actualized subjects. He runs a circular course when he selects these people on the basis of his own criteria and then uses them to provide empirical evidence for his claims about the nature of the self-actualized individual. Nor does he consider the antecedent conditions that produce peak experiences.

While Maslow does not state that a given need must be completely satisfied before the next need in the hierarchy can become dominant, his theory does indicate that the basic needs must be gratified to a reasonable extent as a precondition for actualization. **However, there are many counterexamples of people who have achieved significant levels of creativity in spite of minimal fulfillment of one or more of their basic needs. This remains a problem for this theory even if it is claimed that these people would have reached even greater heights if their deficit needs had been adequately fulfilled.**

Carl R. Rogers

Rogers's profound influence in the field of counseling and psychotherapy was due not only to his skills in writing, speaking, and management of encounter groups but also to the many innovations he introduced to the therapeutic arena. His nondirective approach, his emphasis on listening and empathic understanding, and his view of people seeking help as clients rather than patients challenged the prevailing approach to psychotherapy and enhanced the relational component of therapy. By emphasizing the active and responsible participation of the client, Rogers created a climate in which the client is accorded dignity and equality with the therapist. **Person-centered therapy is commendable insofar as it views people as purposeful, holistic beings who become more fully functional in response to the therapeutic triad of empathy, congruence, and unconditional positive regard.** Its emphasis on living in the existential present, openness to experience, and commitment to the process of growth are also positive and health-oriented virtues.

Person-centered therapy is quintessentially humanistic not only in practice but also in philosophy; it is an all-embracing approach to life that transcends the boundaries of psychology and makes sweeping judgments against virtually all forms of external authority and conventional religion. Its emphasis on intuition, feeling, and permissiveness, and its disenchantment with parental and cultural values in the quest for actualization, propagates an anarchistic and individualistic form of humanism.

The Rogerian model of therapy and personality is built upon a naive type of phenomenology that accepts self-reports on face value.[8] Because of the problems of

defensive and deceptive behavior, such reports of inner experiencing are often distorted and unreliable. For the most part, Rogers overlooked the significant role played by unconscious processes in affecting human behavior and self-image. This uncritical acceptance of self-reports calls into question the validity of some of the research conclusions reached by Rogers and his followers. Another factor that has influenced these conclusions is the degree to which the very process and reflective techniques of client-centered therapy has shaped the data.

Rogers eventually departed from his early emphasis on scientific method and research design, and few significant research advances have been achieved by the Rogerian group since the definitive presentation of his theory in 1959. Since that time, Rogers spent more time as a popularizer and less time as a researcher. Hans Strupp notes that Rogers and associates moved away from a scientific foundation in the direction of a growing irrationalism.[9] But the aura of authority derived from the scientific status of psychology remained even while Rogers made bolder applications of his model in the realms of philosophy and religion.

Another problem concerns the circularity of proposing that inherent potentialities determine behavior while at the same time advocating the use of observed behavior as the measuring operation which reveals the inherent potentialities.

> With such an approach, you as a theorist can never be shown to be wrong, and because it is logically impossible to show you are wrong, it can never be determined that you are right either. Acceptance of such a circular position can only occur on the basis of faith, or intuition. It is necessary to be able to say what a person's inherent potentialities are by some logical or empirical means that are independent of the behavior to be explained by these potentialities.[10]

Indeed, Rogers fails to describe the nature of the organism and the organismic potentialities that are to be actualized. Because of this, his concept of the actualizing tendency is very general and slippery. The genetic determinants of action which are central to his theory are unspecified.

The whole Rogerian system climaxes in the fully functioning person, but when he describes the person who emerges from the therapeutic process (e.g., openness to experience, an internal locus of evaluation), he denies the normative nature of these characteristics and refuses to call them goals.[11] **In this respect, his emphasis on human freedom and avoidance of any form of external evaluation introduces a self-defeating element in the purpose of the therapeutic process.** He may not call these characteristics of the emerging person "goals," but he uses them as the criteria for therapeutic success. External norms, values, and standards may be minimized in theory, but they are necessary in practice.

Rogers's crucial assumption of natural balancing forces within each person that act to make self-interest coincide with the interests of others is questionable and empirically unsupported. He takes for granted that the pursuit of the fulfillment of personal needs, providing that the individuals concerned are "fully functioning," will not lead to a collision of needs. **The spirit of individualism and self-indulgence in the Rogerian approach is so pervasive that process takes precedence over committed and permanent relationships.** The predominant guide in this process is not rationality but feeling and intuition. This reflects a naive view of human nature that erroneously contends that there is only one drive for human personality and that this actualization drive always operates in good and positive ways. Thus, all conflict, dysfunctionality, and pathological behavior are attributed to external forces and trivialized into a loss of contact with the organismic valuing process. **This faith in the personal capacity to direct one's own life leads to an inadequate analysis of the depths of human estrangement and suffering.**

Rogerian theory promotes an inflated view of the self as the center of ontology, epistemology, and ethics. Truth is determined by the inner subjectivity of the individual, and the highest moral imperative in this system is personal wholeness. Rogers consistently deprecates sources of authority outside of the self, and yet his account of the nature of the self is slippery and amorphous. He champions freedom of choice and responsiveness to the totality of experiencing, but his system reduces these experiences of freedom to the instinctually driven and deterministic organismic valuing process. At the core level, the so-called self-actualization process is driven by biologically rooted instincts.

Alfred Adler

As an early reaction against Freudian instinctivism that sought to build upon and move beyond Freud's observations, Adler's work is of crucial importance to personality theory. His thinking has influenced a number of other theorists in the areas of social psychology, field theory, Gestalt psychology, family therapy, and rational-emotive therapy, but much of this influence is indirect, and it is difficult to determine the degree to which the numerous affinities of Adler's ideas with those of current ego psychology can be attributed to the impact of Adler himself. Nevertheless, Adler's system is more popular now in the United States and Europe than it has been since its inception.

Adler's concepts of the creative self and social interest, as well as his stress on the conscious mind, provided a needed corrective to psychoanalytic theory. He departed from the analytical and atomistic approach of Freudian personality theory and developed a more holistic account of individuals that ties in broader social, cultural, and economic factors and incorporates people's projected life plans. In doing so, he arrived at a better balance of individuals and the relational contexts in which they are rooted and find their meaning. **By moving from an abnormal to a general psychology, Adler sought to restore the sense of humanitarianism, dignity, creativity, and awareness that had been threatened by the psychoanalytic perspective of human nature.**

Adler anticipated and in some cases laid the groundwork for the arrival of important trends in psychotherapy. These include the problems of gender identity in society, the mechanism of overcompensation, the influence of birth order and the family constellation as determinants of personality, the role of the individual's inner image in defective functioning, the nature of psychological tasks that must be fulfilled in life, the psychology of the pampered child, and the importance of aggression in human behavior. **His books, however, are poorly organized; they are inconsistent and uneven, lacking a comprehensive plan of presentation, and written in a rambling and somewhat pedantic style. The case histories tend to be repetitious and one-sided, and the informality and simplicity of his analysis leaves Adler open to the criticism of superficiality and theoretical meagerness.** The intuitive and common-sense nature of Adlerian psychology is especially evident in its humanitarian focus on social interest, but the logic of this expression of psychic energy as an extrapolation from his earlier theories of power and perfection is vague. **The simple formulas associated with correcting the problem of emotional isolation and undersocialization as the primary index of psychopathology can lead to a shallow analysis of the human condition.**

In his attempt to restore dignity to the personality, Adler made man the center of reality and overreacted to Freud in his emphasis on social and environmental factors and minimization of biological and unconscious factors in character formation. **His postulation of a dialectic union of egoism and altruism and his assumption that a proper development of social feeling is a matter of education evinces a certain naiveté concerning human nature and fails to take into account the complexities of intrapsychic phenomena and motivation.** Leaning toward an idealistic view of humanity, Adler assumes that virtually all maladjusted behavior stems from inadequate development of the inborn tendency toward social interest. Since this deficiency is brought about by environmental factors associated with the child's upbringing, responsibility for inappropriate behavior is always projected outside of the individual. This creates the problem of a lack of accountability and rests on the assumption that internal change is externally induced.

Adlerian psychology views the individual's striving for superiority as the key to the style of life and the pattern of behavior that one adopts. **While feelings of inferiority and striving for superiority are components of behavior, they do not account for the rich complexity of the human personality.** In Adler's system, compensation for the real or imaginary sense of inferiority becomes a Procrustean bed in which the bulk of behavioral phenomena are fitted. Compensatory strivings surely account for some behavioral traits, but there are many aspects of symptomatology and psychodynamics that are rooted in other causes.

Individual Psychology's holistic theory of personality improved upon Freud insofar as it incorporated purposive ambitions and meaning structures. **Adler's system offers a balance between the extremes of hard determinism and libertarianism, but the apparent teleology of future goals is mitigated by his view that outcomes are often different from conscious aspirations.** But Adler could not resist the temptation to extrapolate his fictional finalism on the individual level to a communal goal of perfection as a transcending evolutionary impetus in the historical sphere. **Thus, his position on the psychology of religion is that God is simply "a concretization of the idea of perfection, greatness,** and superiority," and that "God, as man's goal, is the harmonic complementation for the groping and erring movements on the path of life."[12] His claim is that Individual Psychology arrives at the same conclusion as the great religions concerning the need to increase social interest but does so in a scientific way and proposes a scientific technique.[13] This is a reductionistic position that assumes that scientific knowledge has supremacy over other forms of knowledge. **Indeed, Adler's own work was not strictly scientific but was based on clinical observation and intuition rather than scientific experimentation. He offered little empirical evidence for his theories, relying instead on broad extrapolations from frequently repeated case examples.**

Erich Fromm

As one of the most popular and influential psychoanalysts in America, Fromm applied the breadth of his interests and variety of his literary output to an analysis of the problems of contemporary life. His personality theory, like Erikson's and Adler's, is socially oriented, and it is also enriched by his knowledge of cultural anthropology and his use of historical analysis as a psychological tool. His sociobiological synthesis is the product of his bold attempt to overcome the demarcation between psychology and anthropology. **Fromm's conclusion that relatedness is the key problem of psychology and that human behavior is a learned response to social conditions enabled him to transcend the instinctual boundaries of the Freudian system.** Not only did he minimize the biological determinants of human behavior and the role of instincts, but he also effectively challenged the orthodox model of psychosexual development along an ontogenetic sequence. **But Fromm carried his reaction against Freudian excesses so far that in his minimization of the part that unconscious motivation plays in human behavior, he lost some of the valuable insights gained through the psychoanalytic theory of the unconscious.** Nevertheless, his indebtedness to Freud is evident in all of his writings, including those penned after he broke away from his original Freudian outlook.

Fromm's cultural observations are insightful but limited insofar as they are confined to a single cultural heritage and do not account for the origins of personality types within a culture. His psychological analysis of history is creative and ingenious but overblown, and it suffers from a lack of correspondence with historical data, particularly in the motif of freedom and escape. His political philosophy is shaped by Marxist ideology and underestimates the role of noneconomic causal forces in shaping modern culture. **Fromm is also vulnerable to the criticism of building his theoretical system more on moralism and philosophy than on empirical techniques and scientific data.** His supporters reply by appealing to his sociopsychological study on *Social Character in a Mexican Village,* but much of his theory remains speculative. **On the other hand, Fromm was correct in his dispute with excessively positivistic approaches to psychology, sociology, and anthropology, and his attempt to synthesize interdisciplinary insights to provide a frame**

of reference that cannot be derived from any single discipline is commendable. Thus, he was willing to move beyond the idea of objective knowledge to an affirmation of universal moral guidelines in which scientific insights can be contextualized.

Fromm rejected Freud's death instinct and argued that aggression and destructiveness are not inherent parts of human nature but are only manifested when basic needs are frustrated. **While his description of the authoritarian personality has become a fruitful contribution to personality theory, his position that pathological societies are responsible for distorted expressions of human nature rests on an excessively optimistic conception of the person.** He does not adequately account for how otherwise rational and self-conscious people consistently create social conditions that are irrational and destructive. **In addition, the reforms he proposes for the achievement of a sane society are politically and economically unrealistic and utopian.** His sanguine view of human nature appears to be derived more from his philosophical and political commitments than from psychological research. Nevertheless, Fromm was aware of the tragic side of human existence; in spite of his view that people are primarily good, he held that this goodness is not actualized apart from conditions that are not manifested in the prevailing context of social injustice, physical privation, and emotional insecurity.

Although opposed to external authoritarian ideologies and structures, Fromm embraced the idea of objective ethical norms. He cogently argued that people become victimized by internal and external forces when civilization abandons faith in guiding moral principles. But he failed to provide an adequate account of the origin and locus of these ethical standards; his autonomous humanism speaks with the voice of moral authority but is grounded only in relative and immanent categories. **Fromm's own hostility to all forms of authoritarianism as destructive of freedom is based in part on his misunderstanding of Protestant theology and the Reformed view of the sovereignty of God.** He erroneously assumes that this implies the degradation and relative worthlessness of man in the face of an arbitrary and oppressive omnipotence and concludes that it is masochistic to submit to such a sadistic being. He then assumes a causal connection between this account of Protestantism and the development of capitalism and modern totalitarianism such as Nazism. Such sweeping claims and tendentious arguments are characteristic of Fromm's psychoanalytical purview of history and cultural development. His hostility to traditional expressions of religion, particularly Christianity, is a theme that often appears in his books, but this does not mean that he is opposed to religion per se. Instead, Fromm advocates a nontheistic and humanistic religion that is essentially a mystical atheism. By combining rational insight with mysticism, his self-psychology retains a tenuous and revisionistic connection with his Tanakh and Talmudic roots. In this way, Fromm affirms his presupposition of the autonomy of man over against the ultimacy of God and elevates it to the status of a religious surrogate.

CHAPTER 7
A COMPARISON AND CONTRAST OF THE PSYCHOLOGICAL MODELS

A SUMMARY OF THE PSYCHOLOGICAL MODELS OF HUMAN NEEDS

Sigmund Freud

Freud's largely deterministic approach to personality theory was shaped by a perspective of rationalistic materialism which viewed the individual as a complex system of energies and forces that reflect somatic and social influences. In his structural model of psychic life, it is the task of the ego to mediate between the incessant counterdemands of the id and the superego. The primal personality system of the id is driven by the constant pressure of somatic demands or needs that are instinctually energized. The internal dynamic of libidinal energy profoundly influences psychic phenomena in a variety of ways, particularly through the primary process of the pleasure principle, which seeks to reduce tensions induced by unmet instinctual needs. The superego represents an entirely different set of forces that are generated by social and cultural values and primarily internalized in the psyche through parental influence. The conscience and ego-ideal associated with the superego are the sources of a moral sense of guilt which can impinge upon the ego with an unyielding severity.

In addition to the forces of the id and the superego, the ego must cope with the realities of the external world and modify the primary process of the pleasure principle with the secondary process of the reality principle, which seeks optimal gratification of the instinctual needs within the context of realistic social constraints. The counterclaims of the divergent forces of the id, the superego, and the external world produce neurotic, moral, and reality anxieties that the ego seeks to manage through defense mechanisms. The less these defense mechanisms distort reality, the more effectively the reality principle functions as a modifier of the pleasure principle. Eros, the basic life instinct, relates to the quest for the satisfaction of somatic needs, the reduction of anxiety, and the striving for happiness within the context of human society. This requires the normal growth of the sexual function and the development of the ego from a narcissistic to a reality-oriented system. At the same time, this adaptation to the realities of a communal context necessitates an exchange of diminished happiness for the security of civilization, including the heightening of the sense of guilt and acquiescence to communal ideologies. Those who cannot successfully comply with these social constraints due to disorders of the ego exhibit neurotic behavior that can only be corrected through therapeutic enhancement of the ego's strength and organization.

In addition to the life instinct of Eros, Freud theorized an opposing instinct of destruction and death, called Thanatos, which is manifested in aggressive and warlike behavior as well as the penchant to return to the inanimate state. For him, the principal purpose of civilization is to restrain these primal and aggressive forces, but the cost of civilization is the reduction of instinctual satisfaction on the individual level and the communal illusions, guilt inducement, and repression caused by animism and religion that have characterized human history until the advent of modern science. While religion offers the idea of purpose in life, it is based upon illusion and reality distortion. Science offers a better foundation for modern civilization, and Freud believed that psychoanalysis fits within the scientific worldview.

Erik H. Erikson

Erikson's psychosocial approach to personality theory stresses the codetermination of human development and behavior by somatic, mental, and social processes, which correspond to the id, the ego, and the superego. Because of this, it is necessary to consolidate insights from biology, psychology, and the social sciences to understand human behavior, since organic disorder, ego anxiety, and lack of group identity can contribute to psychopathology. Ego synthesis and social organization are complementary; on the one hand, a sense of coherent identity is attained in a context of collective integrity. On the other hand, the social milieu reflects individual development, since the human life cycle and social institutions have evolved together. Successful growth through the eight developmental stages in the life cycle requires psychosocial equilibrium at each phase so that the ego is able to integrate the organism with the social ethos. The eight stages and their associated crises of ego synthesis and resynthesis relate to an expanding radius of needs, capacities, relations, and social institutions. While Erikson associates the eight qualities of trust, autonomy, initiative, industry, identity, intimacy, generativity, and integrity with the developmental stages in human personality, he particularly stresses the three needs of trust, identity, and integrity that correspond with the first, fifth, and eighth stages.

The need for trust and mutuality is foundational to all later moral, ethical, and ideological development; childhood trust engenders the capacity for mature faith. The sense of goodness that can be trusted, as well as the experience of hope and faith, is generally reinforced through the social institution of religion, although there are other collective reinforcements of trust, faith, and hope.

The need for meaningful ego identity is a dominant theme in Erikson's work, particularly as it relates to ego synthesis through ideological affirmation in a context of group identity. This synthesis sustains the sense of sameness and continuity within a changing environment and protects the individual from many of the dangers of internal and external disruption. Ego identity organizes experience and sustains a sense of the self in relation to social reality.

The need for integrity relates to the acceptance of the validity and ultimacy of one's life cycle along with the responsibility this entails. An ego integration that transcends individual identity provides the strength and wisdom needed for a meaningful old age.

C. G. Jung

In Jung's account of the tension between the unconscious and the conscious, the psyche draws energy from this tension and engages in compensatory activity when the conscious attitude becomes too one-sided in its repression of the unconscious dynamic. As the primal psychic system, the unconscious contains materials that are prerequisite to psychological health but that the conscious mind would assess as both primitive and spiritual, demonic and divine. Because of the processes of evolution and cultural adaptation, Jung theorized the existence of a collective as well as a personal unconscious in each individual that influences perception, imagination, and cognition. The universal images or archetypes of the collective unconscious shape the personal unconscious and, together with the instincts, drive the psyche.

The ego, or personal consciousness, developed in response to environmental conditions and the human need for adaptation to the demands of the external world. Jung also wrote of the need for inner harmony or adaptation to the inner world through the homeostasis of the conscious and the unconscious. These fundamental needs for inner and outer adaptation are mutually dependent and relate in turn to the need for selfhood or individuation by which a person maintains a creative tension and communication between the opposite poles of the personality. The self is synthesized when conscious and unconscious processes are assimilated in a new totality, but this individuation process is an ideal that can never be fully attained.

In addition to the conscious-unconscious tension, Jung also addressed the tension between individual fulfillment and the necessity of some measure of conformity to social and cultural reality. While one must adopt a persona in order to relate to social conventions, he warned against the danger of becoming more identified with the persona than with the self. It is only as an individual that one can find meaning in life, since subservience to collective consciousness leads to dissociation from the unconscious and absorption into the mass mind.

The individuation process requires the use of symbols as the vehicle by which the irrational union of the opposite poles of consciousness and unconsciousness can be achieved. Since archetypal images are transcendent, Jung called this the transcendent function and viewed the wholeness of the self as a union of immanent and transcendent objects. In his analytical psychology, he attempted to synthesize components of modern psychology and ancient religious imagery by symbolically reinterpreting Christian and other religious traditions, eliminating the dogma but maintaining the archetypal materials that were derived from the collective unconscious. These numinous symbols of transcendence, when divested of the trappings of religious traditionalism, facilitate the individuation synthesis of conscious and unconscious and provide a spiritual basis for meaning in life.

Otto Rank

As Rank departed from his originally Freudian perspective, he replaced his earlier view of birth as the primal trauma from which neuroses emerge by an emphasis on the centrality of conscious will in his theory of personality. In doing so, he moved from an ideological and past-oriented therapeutic approach to an experiential, present-oriented understanding of the transference process between patient and analyst. Having rejected the Freudian emphasis on unconscious impulses, Rank came to regard the conscious will as the autonomous force by which the personality acts upon somatic impulses and social inhibitions. It is this dynamic causality of the will that enables the individual to be liberated from the bondage of parental and social conformity and to adapt biological and social forces in the quest for self-realization. As the primary locus of human behavior, the will transcends deterministic causality.

Rank discussed the opposite fears of life and death in terms of a continuous tension between separation, isolation, and individuation on the one hand and union, dependency, and generation on the other. The will can mediate between these two poles, but it can never eliminate the inner ambiguity; nor should it, since this tension between the individual and the relational is the basis of life. The neurotic type seeks to resolve the tension by expressing the tendency toward separation and excluding the tendency toward union, while the average type does the opposite. It is only the artistic type who maintains the tension and adapts to the demands of life through creative expression of conscious will. The artist-hero moves toward self-determination by replacing mass ideals with individual ideals without abandoning the need for authentication and acceptance by others. This creative will affirmation leads to the birth of individuality and separation from the mass while still negotiating the requirements of the cultural milieu. The human need to accept one's individuality is counterbalanced by the human need to be loved and accepted by others.

Rank also writes of the counterbalancing human needs of happiness and redemption of guilt. Since he relates "ethical guilt" to the tension between union and separation, any increase in happiness caused by growth in individualism is offset by a greater consciousness of ethical guilt. But the price of redemption is reduction in happiness through the renunciation of individualism and absorption in a universal ideology. The "universal redemption therapies" of religion and philosophy have, until recent years, satisfied the need for believing in a truth system or worldview that provides a sense of security and a ground for believing in immortality in spite of the reality of death. This need has been threatened by the gradual replacement of earlier ideologies with a soulless psychological ideology.

Abraham H. Maslow

Maslow's humanistic and holistic approach to personality theory recognizes the two core tendencies of survival and actualization. The survival tendency of personality is related to basic or "deficit" needs that are constant and fundamental and must be adequately gratified for healthy functioning of the organism. Psychopathological symptoms appear when these deficit needs are unsatisfied. Maslow arranges basic needs hierarchically with physiological needs at the bottom, safety needs (e.g., security, stability, structure) on the second level, belongingness and love needs (e.g., acceptance, relationships, roots, intimacy) on the third level, and esteem needs on the fourth level. There are two sets of esteem needs: the first set includes the desire for strength, achievement, adequacy, and competence, and the second set includes the desire for prestige, status, and recognition. This need hierarchy is based on the principle of relative prepotency which states that lower-level needs must be satisfied before higher-level needs become motivationally dominant. Maslow acknowledges that there are individual exceptions to this arrangement and that later needs emerge before earlier needs are fully gratified. In fact, he associates higher levels of need with lower levels of satisfaction.

The second core tendency of personality is actualization, and Maslow relates growth needs or "metaneeds" to this disposition toward personal fulfillment. The self-actualization tendency toward life enhancement builds upon the survival tendency toward life maintenance, but it is more subtle. The growth needs (truth, goodness, beauty, wholeness, dichotomy-transcendence, aliveness, uniqueness, perfection, necessity, completion, justice, order, simplicity, richness, effortlessness, playfulness, and self-sufficiency) presuppose the relative satisfaction of the basic needs and are not hierarchically arranged. The Being-cognition associated with those who are growth dominated is on a higher and more fulfilling level than Deficiency-cognition, but both forms of cognition are necessary to self-actualization. There is a dialectic tension between the forces of growth and regression, and few people meet Maslow's criteria for actualization and B-cognition.

Carl R. Rogers

Rogers's "person-centered approach" emphasizes an inherent forward-moving or actualization tendency in the human organism toward becoming and growth in which behavior is directed to meet physiological and psychological needs. The actualizing tendency of the organism is genetically determined, but the actualizing tendency of the self is socially determined and can therefore be blocked through inaccurate symbolization of experience. While the core of the personality is positive, the experiences of guilt, defensiveness, and aggressiveness are caused by inadequate self-concepts. It is therefore essential for one to get in touch with the real self in order to become a fully functioning person who accepts oneself and is thereby able to accept and cooperate with others. This need for positive self-regard is conditioned upon the equally fundamental need for unconditional positive regard by significant others.

In his client-centered therapy, Rogers concluded that three conditions must be met by the therapist to facilitate positive change in the client: congruency (genuineness and openness) with one's feelings, an unconditionally accepting attitude toward the client, and empathic, nondirective, and nonjudgmental understanding of the client's attitudes. Rogers later applied these therapeutic criteria to all personal relationships and concluded that healthy psychological functioning is threatened by anything other than unconditional ascriptions of worth and by external judgmental standards and authorities. Each person should develop values and standards more through personal experience than through the judgments and expectations of others. But this needed positive self-regard and acceptance are facilitated in a context in which one experiences unconditional positive regard and empathic understanding from other people.

When these needs for self-acceptance and acceptance by others are met, this engenders a congruence between experiential phenomena and conceptualization of the self. The growth-directed self-actualization tendency is then freed to move a person toward a fully functioning state characterized by harmonious relationships with others, existential or process living, and ongoing creative and even spiritual development.

Alfred Adler

The Individual Psychology of Adler is a holistic and social psychology that focuses on the social factors that influence the development of the personality in the early years of life and traces the behavioral implications of these factors in later years. The formative experiences of maternal love and the birth-order position in the family constellation can lead to feelings of inferiority that can threaten the fulfillment of basic psychological needs such as security, love and affection, and significance. But feelings of inferiority and inadequacy can be constructive insofar as they motivate individuals to compensate by striving for higher functional levels. In view of the human need to overcome inferiority, Adler theorized that the central tendency in the personality is the striving for superiority or perfection. This is expressed in the will to power which Adler associated with the "masculine protest." The quest for recognition and superiority is a goal-driven dynamic which underlies all human behavior. Adler later came to regard this core tendency as a striving for completion or perfection that is not inimical to social interest.

This teleological behavior is motivated by a "fictional finalism" of goals which the individual constructs early in life to reduce inferiority feelings and enhance self-esteem and completion. The goal-directed movement in each individual's behavior is the source of coherence in the personality and is expressed in a unique pattern or style of life. Individuals who adopt inappropriate life patterns are unable to adapt successfully to social interest because their unconscious fictional goals are incongruent with reality. The neurotic's guiding fiction must be revised to create a behavior pattern that is consistent not only with the need to overcome inferiority and to strive for self-enhancement but also with the requirements of cooperation with social interest, particularly in the three basic areas of occupation, friendship, and sexuality. Adler's discussion of the human needs for security and significance are directly related to the social and communal life since significance and meaning in life consist in an individual's contribution to the lives of others.

Erich Fromm

The deepest human need, according to Fromm, is to overcome the existential conflict that arises from the duality of animal and human natures in each person. This dilemma produces the anxieties of separateness and helplessness before the forces of nature and relates to the tendency to transcend the animal aspect by fulfilling human possibilities. While physiological or instinctual needs like hunger, thirst, and sexuality must be satisfied, humans also have a set of psychological needs that are aspects of the overriding motivational need of preservation and development of the self.

All of the psychological or existential needs are motivators of human behavior, and each of them can be pursued in a progressive or a regressive manner. The need for relatedness is the personal necessity to experience love and unity with other human beings. Its progressive expression is a union that retains a sense of separateness, and its regressive expression is narcissism. The need for rootedness pertains to the security of biological ties; it is satisfied progressively in the experience of the brotherhood of man and regressively in pathological fixation to the mother. The need for transcendence, or self-awareness, can be pursued progressively in creative activity or regressively in the destruction of life. The need for identity is met when people sense themselves as the subject of their actions, but it can be regressively satisfied in herd conformity. The need for a frame of orientation and devotion refers to the necessity of cognitive maps, personal goals, and objects of total devotion that give direction and meaning to life. This need is met regressively in irrational objects of devotion and progressively in rational objects. The needs for effectiveness, for excitation and stimulation, and for a character structure also have destructive and productive manifestations.

Fromm writes of the productive character who affirms life through love and work and who strives to realize his inherent potentialities even though the development of the self is never completed. Productive love affirms one's own life while giving oneself to another, and productive thinking emphasizes a desire to be and not merely to have. It is only in productive loving and thinking that humans can accept personal responsibility for themselves and find meaning in the actualization of their potential. To this end, they should develop a humanistic rather than an authoritarian reference point for authority, ethics, and conscience, and place their faith in themselves and in humanity as a whole for the realization of their primary potentiality and the development of a new society of being-oriented individuals.

DIVERGENCE AND CONVERGENCE IN THE PSYCHOLOGICAL MODELS

Although Freud had his antecedents in the exploration of the unconscious and the development of psychiatry,[1] his influence on subsequent psychological theory and practice is unparalleled. **In varying degrees, Freud left his mark on each of the other psychologists discussed in chapters 4 and 5, in spite of the fact that most of them repudiated significant aspects of his work.** Those who were originally a part of Freud's inner circle (Adler, Jung, and Rank) criticized Freud's thinking and methods on a number of levels. **Jung's appraisal includes the following:** Freud's psychology is an expression of his own psychic constitution; his pansexualism is a causal reductionism that relegates virtually all human behavior, including culture, to sexual instincts and repression; his exclusive emphasis on inexorable biological drives and forces allows no room for the transcendent dimension and prevents him from understanding religious experience; his teaching is one-sided in that it generalizes from neurotic states of mind; his excessively cognitive methods extinguish the mystery of the individual self and leave modern man bereft of authentic consolation; and he never assesses his materialistic premises or assumptions.[2] **Freud, for his part, criticized Jung for being excessively irrational, inconsistent, and optimistic, and Adler for being too systematic and for neglecting the unconscious by viewing everything from the perspective of the ego.[3] Jung and Rank criticized Adler on the same grounds, and Rank was in essential agreement with Freud's appraisal of Jung.[4]** Rank argued that the therapeutic process must be raised from the sphere of intellectual training to that of experience, and that "[i]t is neither the infantile (Freud), nor the guiding purpose (Adler), nor the unconscious made conscious (Jung) that counts, but the therapeutic experience itself."[5]

To some extent, modern psychoanalysis has mollified the problem of growing divergence among theorists by incorporating the insights of Adler and Rank with those of Freud in a less atomistic and more existential context that simultaneously includes the cognitive, emotional, and conative dimensions of therapy.[6] Nevertheless, this does not eliminate the deep-rooted philosophical, theoretical, and methodological differences among these psychologists. **One area of divergence is the extent to which the unconscious is recognized as a motivating force in human behavior.** Fromm, for example, criticized Adler for his inability to see beyond the rational and teleological components of behavior and for his failure to descend from surface motivators to "the abyss of irrational impulses" as Freud had done.[7] Rank, on the other hand, took exception to Freud's minimization of the conscious ego and his excessive stress on the unconscious impulse in psychoanalysis.[8]

Another area of divergence is whether tension increase in the personality is desirable or undesirable. Freud viewed increased amounts of energy and excitation as unpleasurable to the id, which seeks to reduce tension-producing stimulation and bring the organism to a condition of homeostasis.[9] Jung also regarded the psyche as a self-regulating system that attempts to maintain a state of equilibrium, but he believed that the entropic dynamic of compensatory activity between the conscious and the unconscious is a source of energy and growth. For him, increasing tension between these opposites enables the realization of the self and makes the individuation process possible.[10] Rank considered the unavoidable bipolar tension between separation/individuation/freedom/will and union/generation/compulsion/force as the basis of life.[11] Rogers held that psychological health is not a matter of tension-reducing equilibrium but a process of increasing potentiality.[12]

The eight psychologists also diverge on the question of their assessment of human nature. In general, the conflict theoreticians are more negative in their appraisal of the inherent nature of man than the fulfillment psychologists. Freud was especially mistrustful of people, and Jung tended to agree with his evaluation of man's shadow side while still recognizing the profound complexity and double-sided nature of the psyche.[13] Maslow and Rogers, on the other hand, believed that this perspective is jaundiced due to a psychopathology of subjects who are mentally and emotionally dysfunctional.[14] They argued that human nature is essentially positive and tends toward the wholeness of self-actualization and fullness of being that realizes virtues such as love, creativity, courage, and well-being. In their thinking, pathological behavior is attributable to harmful environmental conditions; human nature itself can be trusted.[15] Fromm took a mediating position in his claim that the essence of humanity is neither good nor evil but a dichotomous tension between animal and human natures.[16]

Despite these and other significant areas of divergence (e.g., the question of the individual in relation to the social process), **it is possible to discover a degree of convergence on the issue of human needs by observing that each of the psychologists had something to say about four basic areas of needs: survival needs, identity needs, relational needs, and ideological needs.**

Survival Needs

Freud identified survival needs as somatic or instinctual needs which exert a constant pressure and seek to maintain a state of equilibrium in the organism. The self-preservative instincts and sexual instincts fall within the basic life instinct of Eros. Erikson also acknowledged libidinal needs as part of the biological process of systemic organization that corresponds to the id, and he stressed the reciprocal influence of somatic, mental, and social factors in the development of the personality. Jung spoke of instinctual drives and impulses such as hunger, sexuality, and activity as well as reflective and creative instincts, but argued that material causation must not be overestimated; instinctual drives must be supplemented by a transcendent dimension to account for the intricacy of the human psyche. Rank reacted against the biological causality of Freud's therapeutic approach. While he recognized the role of instinctual and biological needs, he argued against any psychic determinism due to these forces. Maslow discussed a survival tendency to satisfy physical and psychological needs that exists at the core of personality. He theorized that inner human nature is biologically grounded and that human instincts are at least ethically neutral. His first two levels of basic needs, the physiological and safety needs, are necessary for survival. Rogers emphasized an inner, growth-directed actualizing tendency that moves the organism toward the satisfaction of both physiological and psychological needs. Adler's reaction against Freud led him away from the biological factors of instinctivism to social factors as the primary determinants of human behavior. He did, however, speak of organ inferiority as well as the need for security that promotes the continued existence of the human organism. Fromm related physiologically conditioned needs such as hunger, thirst, and sexual needs to the animal aspect of human nature. But he contended that survival needs extend beyond the physical, since the satisfaction of psychic needs as well as instinctual needs is necessary for human happiness and sanity.

Identity Needs

In Freud's thought, identity relates to the object-cathexes of the ego with appropriate circumstances in the outer world; the ego must replace the pleasure principle with the reality principle in order to harmonize the conflicting forces of the id, the world, and the superego. As the organization of the ego is strengthened through defenses that decreasingly distort reality, it becomes more independent of the superego and draws more energy from the id. Erikson's personality theory emphasizes the need for a sense of coherent ego identity that protects the individual from organic and social discontinuity. He relates ego identity to group identity, since the style of one's individuality must organize experience in a psychosocial manner. In Jung's thought the need for adaptation to the inner world and the outer world through harmony with oneself and with environmental conditions is met in the individuation process, which requires a reciprocity between the conscious and the unconscious. For Jung the self is the true center of the personality and is midway between these opposing forces. The individuation process does not eliminate the ego but unites it to the self. Rank regarded the conscious will as the dynamic personal locus of causality which is capable of organizing and integrating the self in such a way that it can creatively act upon biological instincts and social forces. The process of becoming an individual occurs as one engages the conscious will to differentiate the self from the collective without losing authentication from others. In Maslow's hierarchy of needs, the fourth level or esteem needs, as well as the metaneeds that are associated with self-actualization, all relate to identity. Actualization of human potential in the direction of fuller being leads to increased integration in the personality and to acceptance of one's intrinsic nature. The identification need for positive self-regard in Rogers's personality theory is met when one's concept of self becomes increasingly consistent with the phenomenal field of experience and less dependent on the value judgments and expectations of others. A fully functioning person has a self-concept that is congruent with experience. Adler's Individual Psychology emphasizes the conscious forces in the personality and deals with the problem of identity in terms of the striving for recognition and superiority in order to overcome feelings of inadequacy. Fromm describes the need to overcome the anxieties caused by helplessness before natural forces and separateness from society. Humans need to transcend the state of passivity and achieve a sense of identity and self-awareness as the subject of their actions. Authentic identity is not attained by herd conformity but by productive loving and thinking.

Relational Needs

Freud recognized the necessity of diminishing personal happiness and instinctual satisfaction on the individual level in favor of social instincts in order to sustain a level of civilization that defends humanity against the destructive and aggressive forces that would otherwise become rampant. This requires the transformation of the ego from a narcissistic pleasure orientation into a reality-ego that is consistent with the requirements of a social context. Erikson's psychosocial approach to personality theory stresses the reciprocal relationship between group identity and ego identity in which somatic drives and ego interests are integrated with social processes throughout the developmental life cycle. The early experience of basic trust and mutuality is essential to all subsequent development. Jung acknowledged the necessity of the individual to be related to the communal and cultural context. Individual consciousness is conjoined with social forces by means of the persona, but Jung warned against an overidentification with the persona and the consequent absorption of individuality into the collective mind. Rank's bipolar tension between the fear of life with its separation of individual existence and the fear of death with the loss of individuality in union and dependency is an unresolvable ambivalence. Creative expression of conscious will cannot be isolated from the collective, since there is a need for affirmation and authentication. It is through the love of others that acceptance of the self with its individual differences becomes possible. In Maslow's hierarchical scheme of basic needs, relational needs correspond to the third level, namely, the belongingness and love needs of intimacy, acceptance, and rootedness. The growth needs that correspond to the self-actualization tendency also include relational components, and Maslow argues that self-actualized people are not narcissistic but altruistic. Rogers's person-centered approach stresses the need for unconditional positive regard by others as the foundation for self-acceptance. He extended the three therapeutic conditions of genuineness, acceptance, and empathy to all situations of personal development. Adler related the needs for security and significance to favorable conditions in the social and communal life. Since every individual is socially embedded, meaningful existence cannot be attained without satisfaction of the communal need for love and affection. Fromm's list of existential human needs includes the needs for relatedness and rootedness. Productive loving requires an active giving of oneself to others while simultaneously preserving one's integrity and individuality.

Ideological Needs

According to Freud, civilization has produced three communal systems of thought that portray the universe in animistic, religious, and scientific terms. The mythology of animism led to the development of religion, which provides a sense of protection and an ideological basis for purpose in life. Since religious belief is based on illusion and wish fulfillment, the new social order must be founded on the ideology of a scientific worldview. Erikson regarded organized religion as the collective safeguard and ideological support of the need for basic wholeness and trust. Childhood trust provides the basis for the adult's vital need of faith, which also relates to the need for integrity and wisdom in accepting the ultimacy of one's life cycle. Jung believed that when religions are approached symbolically and not dogmatically, they are of great value in providing a sense of meaning in life. Their numinous symbolic content provides a context for the individuation process because religious symbols are archetypes of the collective unconscious. Rank affirmed the human need for belief in worldviews that create a sense of control and security. Systems of imaginative projection such as art, religion, and philosophy enable individuals to embrace the appearance of reality as truth. Rank also emphasized the need for a belief in immortality that transcends the reality of death. He argued that cultural and religious ideologies that sustain the idea of the soul are being eroded by a soulless psychology. Maslow spoke of the basic cognitive need to know and understand and to have a philosophy of life, a religion, or a surrogate for religion that provides a framework of values and a sense of the transpersonal and transcendent. Rogers stressed freedom of thought and discouraged reliance on external judgments and authorities in favor of personal experience and intuition. Nevertheless, he acknowledged the necessity of a philosophy of life and came to see his own psychological system as a worldview that synthesizes Eastern and Western perceptions of reality. Adler's concept of fictional finalism emphasizes the teleological nature of personality that is motivated by future goals. Every style of life expresses purposive behavior, and ideological goals profoundly shape perception and imagination. Fromm discussed the ideological need for a frame of orientation and devotion. A cognitive map is required to organize impressions into a frame of reference, and an object of total devotion is needed as a goal and focal point for action. Faith can be rational or irrational, but it is essential to finding an answer to the problem of human existence.

PART 3:
THE THEOLOGICAL AND
PSYCHOLOGICAL ACCOUNTS

CHAPTER 8
A COMPARISON AND CONTRAST OF THE THEOLOGICAL MODELS AND THE PSYCHOLOGICAL MODELS

This concluding chapter will begin with **a convergence and divergence study of the theological and psychological models of human needs.** In addition, it will consider **the metaphysical and moral assumptions held by the psychologists, psychological accounts of theism and theological accounts of nontheism, the role of human needs in the justification of religious belief,** the problem of self-interest and self-love, and the differences between immanent and transcendent solutions to human needs.

A STUDY OF THE CONVERGENCE AND DIVERGENCE OF THE THEOLOGICAL AND PSYCHOLOGICAL MODELS

In a comparative study like this, it is important to avoid reading psychology into theology and theology into psychology. As the next section will discuss, **the psychological models are based upon metaphysical and moral assumptions, even though many psychologists are reticent to acknowledge the philosophical rather than scientific status of such assumptions. These presuppositions are often radically different from those held by most theologians, resulting in disparate meanings behind identical terms.** Some psychotherapeutically oriented theologians, however, have succumbed to the temptation to assume ideological congruence based on surface similarities and to draw theological conclusions from current psychological theorizing.[1] These caveats notwithstanding, there are legitimate parallels between the theological and psychological models of human needs. In part, this is to be expected; since both approaches are considering the same subject, overlap in their anthropological inferences is inevitable. In addition, Western civilization and perceptions have been profoundly shaped by Christian thought, and all of the psychologists in this study, including those with a Jewish background, have been influenced by the symbols and institutions of Christendom.

Theological approaches to psychology range along a continuum from one extreme of uncritical acceptance to the opposite extreme of wholesale rejection. Some conservative theologians believe that all psychological theorizing is suspect because of the metaphysical and epistemological foundations upon which it is based, whereas more liberal theologians tend to welcome psychological insights on the nature and needs of man. **In their attitudes to psychology, Rahner leaned toward the side of distrust and Tillich toward the side of affirmation, but neither went to the respective extremes. As Ernest Becker sought to show, there is a definite relationship between psychiatric and religious perspectives on**

reality, and this is well illustrated in the work of Kierkegaard, whose analysis of the human condition was post-Freudian, even though he wrote in the 1840s.[2] The real contribution of psychology to modern culture is its penetration into the archaeology of "the basic psychobiological infrastructure behind our subjectivity."[3] **Applied correctly, the psychological dimension enriches rather than diminishes theological insights concerning human nature, just as theological awareness deepens psychological acuity; processes in the natural order and God's action in the world should be viewed as both/and rather than either/or.** Modern psychology has illuminated the fundamental psychological tendencies and needs that people bring to their experience, and this has provided a vocabulary and comprehension that some theologians have used in an attempt to integrate the theological doctrines of creation and anthropology with psychological insights. It has been observed, for example, that the human functions of cognition, affect, and conation correspond to creed, cultus, and code, and relate to Tillich's three existential anxieties (meaninglessness, death, and behavior/guilt).[4] Tillich believed that Jung's distinction between the fixed archetypal potentialities and the variable symbols in which the potentialities present themselves offered a solution to the problem of continuity and change in religious symbols.[5] Erikson's psychology of identity has been related to Rahner's theology of anonymous faith.[6] Others have drawn parallels between psychological growth models and personal religious development—Erikson's psychosocial stages model and Maslow's needs hierarchy have been compared with Loevinger's model of ego development, the developmental stages outlined by Kohlberg, and Fowler's structural developmental model of faith.[7] There is some value in this approach, but without a cautious recognition of its assumptions and limitations, it is easily overstated.

The conflict model of personality, with its tensions between the conscious and the unconscious, childhood and selfhood, and self and society, may be a more appropriate model of the personality before conversion than the fulfillment model. Theological anthropology generally associates the fallen state with spiritual, personal, and social alienation; on this account, the conflict is intrapsychic *and* psychosocial, and it is "theopsychic" as well. By the grace of God, the core of personality can be changed, and thus the fulfillment model may be a more apt description of the personality after conversion.[8]

In this study, **the theological models of human needs acknowledge the nature of physical needs and converge in the three essential need areas of forgiveness and grace, love and community, and purpose and hope. The psychological models converge in the four basic need areas of survival needs, identity needs, relational needs, and ideological needs. Despite the differences in presuppositions, vocabulary, and proposed solutions to the satisfaction of these needs, there is a correspondence between the theological models and the psychological models.**

Both theologians and psychologists recognize survival needs. Since these needs are physiologically based, they must be gratified to a minimal extent if the organism is to endure. There is a difference of opinion as to the content of these survival needs, in that some theorists like

Fromm believe that they extend beyond the level of organic or physical needs to psychic needs such as security (Adler) and safety (Maslow).

The need for forgiveness and grace in the theological models corresponds to the identity needs in the psychological models. From a theological perspective the human condition is characterized by alienation, estrangement, volitional bondage, and personal guilt caused by the pursuit of finite and temporal concerns above the ultimate and eternal concern of communion with the infinite Creator. The way of forgiveness and restoration of the divine image was initiated by God's grace in the redemptive work of Christ and must be appropriated in the personal response of repentance and faith. Those who respond in this way to the grace of God become a part of the new creation with a new identity and destiny as members of God's family. They are no longer defined by the temporal and immanent order but by the eternal and transcendent, and this new identity as people who have been forgiven and enjoy peace with God is the source of substantial healing of relationships with others.

The psychological models also confront the experience of guilt and estrangement in light of the quest for identity, but they define these words in different ways than the theological models and propose alternative methods of overcoming the problem of alienation. As discussed earlier, some psychologists view identity in terms of individuation, while others see identity in terms of self-actualization. **The conflict model approaches identity as the product of psychosocial or intrapsychic adaptation, while the fulfillment model stresses the actualization of human potential through the acceptance of one's intrinsic nature. But both psychological models see guilt as a product of cognitive dysfunction or tension with social mores.**

The need for love and community in the theological models corresponds to the relational needs in the psychological models. The theological models approach this need on the vertical as well as the horizontal dimensions, the former providing the foundation for the latter. The unconditional love and acceptance of God in Christ is the foundation of the security, freedom, and significance of those who respond to him in faith, and this relationship should be tangibly expressed in fellowship and community with others that is characterized by mutual love, acceptance, and servanthood.

In the psychological models, both conflict and fulfillment theorists acknowledge relational needs in view of the reality of a social and cultural context in which each individual must cope. In general, the conflict theorists stress the process of becoming a fully functioning individual within the given contingencies of social embeddedness, while the fulfillment theorists emphasize the centrality of love, affection, empathy, and uncritical acceptance, arguing that basic needs can only be satisfied interpersonally.[9]

The need for purpose and hope in the theological models corresponds to the ideological needs in the psychological models. Temporal existence is enriched and enlarged by the hope of unending life in the presence of God and in continual fellowship with the community of the redeemed. Resurrected life is the answer to the apparent meaninglessness caused by death, and finite concerns take on a new perspective when one embraces the promise of an eternal destiny in communion with the Supreme Good for which the soul was created and without which it can never find true satisfaction or rest.

The psychological models relate ideological needs to the pursuit of meaning and purpose in life. They generally agree that people need a philosophy or a religious ideology that will provide them with a sense of faith, purpose, and hope in spite of the fact that such religious or cultural beliefs are essentially irrational and illusory. Most of the psychologists observe that more scientific and secular ideologies are replacing the function served by the great religions since the latter are losing their hold on contemporary culture. Rank and Jung were less optimistic than the others about the potential of the new soul-denying cognitive systems to provide an adequate foundation for meaning and purpose in view of the certainty of finitude and death.[10]

Thus, there is a general correspondence between the need areas recognized by the theological models and those recognized by the psychological models. **But there are significant areas of divergence between the theologians and psychologists, including their views of human nature, guilt, morality, the meaning and purpose of life, and human destiny.** The theologians stress that humans are more than biological or psychological beings and that they cannot be reduced to products of genetics, environment, and historical/social conditions. There is also a transcendent and spiritual dimension to human nature which is systematically overlooked or rationalized by immanentist modes of explanation. Some psychologists like Frankl acknowledge that in view of the fear of nonbeing, "spiritual aspirations . . . should be taken at face value and should not be tranquilized or analyzed away,"[11] but most regard these aspirations as illusory. **While the theologians would acknowledge that human existence is shaped by genetic, physiological, social, and behavioral factors, they would add spiritual factors to the list and argue that humans cannot be accounted for in terms of isolated elements but must be seen from a whole-person perspective.** Psychologists have a tendency to so emphasize present reality that they minimize the quest for an ultimate meaning in view of the finality of death; theologians are more subject to the opposite tendency of so focusing on the final end of man that they underplay present reality.[12]

In general, the theologians in this study approach human nature from a radically different standpoint than that of the psychologists; many of the latter, particularly the humanistic psychologists, assume an inherent goodness in man and blame undesirable behavior on environmental and social conditions or on a failure to actualize one's inner potentialities. Most psychoanalysts deny the theological account of the human condition in their approach to estrangement, anxiety, and guilt as illnesses that can be cured rather than objective states of alienation, and their denial of the actual existence of personal and moral guilt.

Tillich engaged in extensive dialogue with therapists like Erikson, Rogers, Fromm, Hobart Mowrer, and Rollo May, and believed that the movements of existentialism and depth psychology are of great value for theology because of their revelation of hidden

levels of reality in human existence. **But he was critical of psychology on a number of points and maintained that psychoanalysis may be able to cure people of special difficulties, but it cannot cure them of guilt, emptiness, meaninglessness, or the terror of life and death.**[13] It is religion, not psychology, that must show a final way to those who must decide about the meaning and aim of their existence.[14] Tillich also criticized Freud's pain-pleasure principle and doctrine of libido as an inadequate reinterpretation of the theological account of concupiscence.[15] The Freudian exposition of human creatureliness combines genuine insight on man's existential predicament with a fallacious theory of his essential nature.[16] Tillich also took issue with existential psychology for attempting to reduce the essence of humans to their existence and questioned the predominantly individualistic perspectives of the personality theorists.

Rahner argued that while psychology offers many insights on what it is to be human, it cannot define the human person; the mystery of what it is to be a person cannot be reduced to refined psychological concepts.[17] **Rahner criticized psychological attempts to explain away guilt, affirming that while psychoanalysis can cure a measure of sickness and suffering, it is only through God that people can be delivered from guilt. People cannot liberate themselves by means of their own resources; if guilt is removed, it must be because of divine forgiveness.**[18]

Although modern psychology has made a significant contribution to a deeper understanding of human drives, cognition, emotion, behavior, and willing, theologians like Augustine, Aquinas, Edwards, and Kierkegaard understood many of these implications and, like Tillich and Rahner, would have recognized areas of convergence and divergence between psychological and theological anthropology.

METAPHYSICAL AND MORAL ASSUMPTIONS IN THE PSYCHOLOGICAL MODELS

Psychologists generally claim that their systems are scientific because they are derived from empirical data, whereas theologians begin with a commitment to a religious philosophy of life. **But as Browning, Vitz, and others have observed, psychologists frequently shift categories from the scientific to the philosophical and the normative in their use of metaphors of ultimacy and theories of moral obligation.**[19] By blurring the conceptual boundaries between science and broader worldview considerations, psychologists are often unaware of their own metaphysical and moral presuppositions as they invoke the authority of science to authenticate their opinions.

The work of each of the psychologists in this study was shaped by metaphysical and moral assumptions. Freud developed a mechanistic and naturalistic model of instinctual tension-reduction that drew upon images from electronics, hydraulics, and organic evolution.[20] While Ricoeur argued that Freud held an intersubjective as well as a mechanistic model of the mind, the former consistently drifted toward the latter.[21] **Freud's life and death instincts were metaphors of ultimacy that served as a metaphysical substitute for a religious cosmology and reflected his rationalistic materialism.**[22] His view of moral obligation was an ethical egoism of civilized detachment.[23]

Erikson asserted that he left metapsychological questions to experts in these areas,[24] **but his own discussions on religion and ethics refute this claim.** In his own commitment to a humanist worldview, he believed that human potentialities are clouded by the archaic fears associated with religious dogma and traditions.[25] **Erikson thought that such "systems of superstition and exploitation" caused people to look for ultimate concerns in the transcendent when they would be better served by a perspective that looks for such concerns in the sphere of the immanent and immediate.**[26] Erikson was committed to a generative ethics that related mental health to the capacity to care for succeeding generations. He believed that his ethic of mutuality was based on a more universal standard of perfection and would "mediate more realistically between man's inner and outer worlds than did the compromises resulting from the reign of moral absolutes."[27] Thus, he sought to replace past systems of absolutist ethics with an ethical relativism based on world maintenance through the generational sequence.

Jung's writings are dotted with religious and ethical judgments, but he was more conscious than most psychologists of the metaphysical and moral metaphors and assumptions that necessarily undergird psychological theorizing. In his quest to capture the power of spiritual symbols and make them available to psychological analysis, he rejected traditional Christianity but attempted to reinterpret religious symbols in a nonauthoritarian way for use in the individuation process. **Although he sought to avoid metaphysical assertions, his psychological model incorporated metaphors of ultimacy that relate to the ontological dualism of good and evil, the self as the god within man, and the meaning of life.**[28] He also espoused a theory of obligation that could be called a nonhedonistic ethical egoism: "the actualization of one's unique archetypal ground plan and its epigenetic timetable."[29] But this self-realization of archetypal potentialities is inconsistent with his view of the duality of good and evil in human beings, and Jung does not specify the means by which the individuation process of the self could be coordinated with the archetypal needs of others.

Humanistic psychologists like Maslow and Rogers held a far less complicated view of the process of personal growth than did Jung or Rank. Instead of the conflicts of polar ambivalence, they adopted the metaphor of ultimate harmony of potentialities in a single actualizing force. In their eudaemonistic ethical egoism, fulfillment is gained when people are true to their own deepest selves, and individual fulfillment is, in turn, complementary to the self-actualization of others. The organismic self-actualization tendency becomes a moral imperative in this psychological model because it replaces external systems of moral judgment, especially those making absolutist claims, with the inner actualizing tendency as the most reliable guide to decision making and the enhancement of life.[30]

As their careers progressed, Maslow and Rogers came to regard their psychological models as part of a larger philosophy of life which became increasingly monistic in character.[31] Fromm's secular faith of humanistic religion was also nontheistic and vigorously opposed to traditional, institutionalized religion, but his was more of a secular/scientific humanism than a cosmic humanism. Fromm also developed a very definite agenda for the transformation of society into a humanistic socialism through a humanitarian rather than authoritarian ethical system that is based upon a "science" of human welfare.[32]

The psychologists' views of human nature range from the pessimism of Freud to the ambivalence of Jung and Rank to the guarded optimism of Erikson, Adler, and Fromm to the unbounded optimism of Maslow and Rogers. Each of the psychologists claims that his work is founded on empirical observation and scientific research, yet it is evident that their conclusions are profoundly influenced by philosophical and ethical considerations that are not scientifically supportable. It is self-deceptive, even for a scientist, to believe that one is epistemologically, metaphysically, or morally neutral; as Storr noted, "It is impossible to make observations of any kind without an assumed framework."[33] **Like other disciplines, psychology is fraught with presuppositions, and to assume a posture of scientific objectivity that ignores these presuppositions is to invite obfuscation, misconception, and delusion.**

The psychologies in this study have become secular alternatives to the Judeo-Christian worldview and often serve as religious surrogates for the psychotherapists who embrace them as well as their patients.[34] They are marked by a consummate refusal to consider the option that religious claims could have any real, objective truth. It is not surprising, then, that most psychology texts virtually ignore the philosophical, moral, and religious implications of personality theory.[35] Maddi's comprehensive graduate text on personality theory completely omits reference to religious motivation in his discussion of both the core and the periphery of personality. Even when psychologists (whether atheists or believers) study religious conversion, they generally ignore the possibility that God may have had anything to do with the process.[36] In part, this assumption stems from a methodological approach that assumes that a "scientific" method is the only valid avenue of psychological inquiry. But this is to don epistemological blinders that overlook other forms of knowledge such as philosophical, historical, moral, personal, and religious knowledge, each having its own contributions, limitations, and appropriate means of investigation.[37] This inevitably leads to a vicious circle between method and metaphysics.

The very nature of psychological interpretation is such that it "cannot penetrate to the absolutely final or first reality."[38] When psychology transcends its limitations and assumes the shape of a worldview with its own metaphysical and moral stance, it unavoidably formulates its own orienting mythology.[39] Under the cover of ordinary knowledge, it challenges theology by discussing matters of ultimate concern, but framing them within the mystique of "an eschatology of immanence in which the insides of nature will erupt into a new being."[40]

Building on the assumption that God is in eclipse in modern culture, the new psychological belief system replaced the absolute mystery of the transcendent with the relative mystery of the immanent.[41]

PSYCHOLOGICAL ACCOUNTS OF THEISM AND THEOLOGICAL ACCOUNTS OF NONTHEISM

The metaphysical presuppositions held by the psychologists in this study are particularly evident in their accounts of religious behavior and experience. **Freud's assessment of religion in** *Totem and Taboo* **and** *The Future of an Illusion,* **summarized in chapter 3, exerted a profound influence on subsequent psychoanalytic theory.** In Freud's thought, religion serves the important functions of maintaining a sense of control over the forces of nature by personifying those forces and justifying the cost of civilization's diminishment of instinctual gratification by sanctioning social institutions and offering the promise of future compensation. It also provides a cosmic father figure, created in the image of man, that can reduce anxiety and satisfy basic human needs such as provision and security.[42] **Religion creates a sense of purpose in life, but it is an illusion based on human wish fulfillment that keeps people in a socially infantile state.** It is a collective neurosis that once served an important purpose but must now be superseded in the modern era by a more reasonable foundation for civilization. **Freud did not reject religion because it fulfills psychological needs but because of his belief that it has no rational foundation.** Many of his followers, however, went beyond him in denying religious truth claims because of their assessment of these claims as the product of the unconscious wishes of those who hold them.[43]

Erikson viewed organized religion as a social institution that offers a collective reassurance to those whose anxieties accrue from their infantile past. This institution relates to the need for trust and a sense of goodness that develops in its more mature form into a faith in a coherent world image. Religion "has shrewdly played into man's most child-like needs, not only by offering eternal guarantees for an omniscient power's benevolence (if properly appeased) but also by magic words and significant gestures, soothing sounds and soporific smells—an infant's world."[44] Like Freud, Erikson divorced religion from evidence and reason.

Jung held a more positive attitude toward religion than Freud or Erikson and believed that spiritual concerns are necessary to the quest for selfhood. The numinous symbols of religion facilitate the synthesis of conscious and unconscious in the individuation process because of their archetypal significance. However, in his psychological reinterpretation of religion, Jung repudiated the institutions and doctrines of traditional Christianity, arguing that Christian mythology should be interpreted symbolically. Since archetypes like God are derived from the collective unconscious and reflect the spiritual evolution of humanity, it is through them that spiritual experience is gained. Jung's view that the archetypes are synonyms for the unconscious did not cause him to assume the nonexistence of God, but he believed that the existence of an objective reality behind religious experience is beyond the boundaries of human discernment.

In Rank's account of religion, God evolved as the personification of the creative will, and spiritual belief in the soul gradually developed as part of a mythology that assures collective or individual survival and permanence through the denial of death. The need for immortality in view of the finality of death reached its fullest expression in Christianity, which replaced both biological and social fatherhood by spiritual fatherhood and gave the ancient Oriental mother-cult a new meaning, leading to a "timeless and stateless spiritual philosophy of two ever-opposed principles."[45]

Maslow and Rogers were interested in substituting a secular and immanentistic philosophy of life for traditional religion, believing that external judgment and authority should be replaced by trust in the actualization tendency. In their vision of a secular religion, the realization of human potential is part of a greater transpersonal formative tendency at work in the universe.

Adler viewed the idea of God as a culturally evolved expression of the concept of perfection and superiority, a corporate fiction that provides a goal of harmonious social interest. Like Freud, he believed that the modern world requires a more scientifically enlightened substitute for religion. Fromm saw the need for a frame of orientation and devotion as a religious issue and believed that it could be satisfied by either a rational or an irrational faith. He criticized traditional religious expressions as irrational and authoritarian in contrast to the rational and humanistic religion of secular faith in human strength. **Fromm associated authoritarian religion, particularly Protestantism, with herd conformity, humiliating submission, infantile attitudes, and feelings of insignificance and guilt.**[46]

In general, then, the psychological accounts of religious belief, particularly Christian theism, include the following: religion evolved as a human response to the fear of nature and death, personifies these forces in an attempt to control and placate them, involves infantile wish projection, offers relief from guilt and anxiety, provides a sense of purpose and hope of immortality, and creates a communal ideology that sanctions social institutions. This explanation has much in common with functionalist accounts of religion (such as that of Emile Durkheim) that religion developed in response to the need for social stability and legitimizes corporate structures through a common mythology.[47] The functionalist analysis acknowledges the sociological function that religion serves and is more positive than psychological accounts that reduce religion to an oppressive atavism from primitive tribalism.

The ascendancy of psychology was proportionate to the sociocultural decline of religious ideology. The meaning vacuum left by the secularization of modern culture had to be filled by a religious surrogate, and psychology has often attempted to fill this gap.[48] Theologians have responded to this challenge on a number of levels, including that of turning the tables by arguing that if there is a psychology of theism, there is also a psychology of nontheism.

When the questions of the existence of God and the ontological status of religious claims are reduced to an issue of practical meaningfulness in the lives of adherents, theologians and philosophers of religion respond that subjective meaning cannot decide the question of objective reality. **Some psychologists are guilty of committing the genetic fallacy when they assert that their accounts of religious origins are tantamount to a refutation of religious beliefs. These beliefs satisfy deep psychological needs, but this proves nothing about the validity or falsehood of their truth claims, nor does it affirm that they are ultimately based on these needs.** And even if any of the psychological accounts fully explained the origin of religion, it would be a daunting task to establish that it in fact originated in this way, since this is a matter of history rather than philosophy or psychology. **The real issue is not why people fear the contingencies of their existence but why there are beings in a contingent universe who are concerned with problems of contingency.**[49] Historical religions confront the problem of how to bear the end of life, and Becker (who sought to integrate insights from Freud and Kierkegaard) argues that if they lose their grip on people's lives, people still need what classical religions have provided, namely, a lived creative illusion that does not lie about the genuine experience of guilt and the existential terror of life and death.[50]

While the correlation method in theology sees Christianity as the answer to the questions surfaced in the deepest moments in human experience, theologians argue that the God of Christian theism is not merely a job description, shaped to solve and placate the problems of human existence. They contend that God is not an anthropomorphic projection; humanity is defined by the God of creation and revelation, not the other way around, and he must be sought for himself, not for his gifts. Prayer is not a matter of autosuggestion, and "the word 'father' is not the projection into the infinite of childish, subjective concepts which aim at a prerational domination of his existence, but is authorised by a God who, working in everything, liberated his creatures to his own freedom and love."[51] Rahner claims that Christians are the only people who do not need to reach for an opiate or an analgesic because they can be "willing to drink the chalice of the death of this existence with Jesus Christ" since they understand that in Christ this earthly existence passes through death into life.[52]

The reductionism of psychological and sociological interpretations of religious belief is a sword that can cut both ways; just as theism may satisfy deeply felt longings, so atheism may appeal to the human quest for autonomy, the illusion of control, and the fear of moral accountability before a personal Creator. Theologians have observed that the infinite-personal God of Judeo-Christian theism is not the comforting and reassuring kind of being that people would want to invent. Personal encounter with the omnipresent, omniscient, omnipotent, holy, and awesome *mysterium tremendum* can be an overpowering and profoundly traumatic ordeal of disintegration and nakedness as the experiences of Job, Habakkuk, Isaiah, Daniel, Paul, and others testify.[53] Exposure to and by the numinous gaze of God is an unsettling encounter that can lead to repentance, but the threat of God's moral excellence and sovereignty also produces the response of rebellion. Edwards's assessment of the human condition is that "men naturally are God's enemies."[54] This is consistent with the account of human rebellion in Romans 1 that could be described in psychological terms as the *trauma* of divine holiness ("For the wrath of God is revealed from heaven against all ungodliness and wickedness of men"), the response of *repression* ("who by their wickedness suppress the truth. For what can be known about God is plain to them, because God has shown it to them"), and the *substitution* of religious surrogates that reshape and distort the threat of God with images that are more palatable to human wishes.[55]

Thus, both predispositional and presuppositional issues are involved in religious and secular belief systems, and the question of the rationality of religious versus secular belief cannot be settled by psychodynamic considerations.[56] If the psychologists' position that religious belief is based solely on need fulfillment is true, this would indeed pose a serious challenge to the plausibility of theological truth claims. But the fiat dismissal by psychologists of the rationality of religious belief is based on the unfounded assumption that there is no weight to the evidential and rational arguments that have been refined for centuries by theologians, apologists, and philosophers of religion. It is true that some theologians (e.g., Kierkegaard and Barth) have taken a more fideistic approach to theism than others, but this does not diminish the abundance of rational evidence that has been offered in defense of the Christian worldview.

THE ROLE OF HUMAN NEEDS IN THE JUSTIFICATION OF RELIGIOUS BELIEF

As the perception that religion has become rationally and culturally deficient grows in the modern era, it becomes increasingly difficult for people to commit themselves to an ideology based upon the transcendent and invisible. Christian apologetics address this popular conception, and an effort of unprecedented proportion and sophistication has been underway in recent years by apologists and philosophers of religion to challenge this perception and to demonstrate the superior credibility, coherence, and comprehensiveness of the theistic worldview in the pluralistic marketplace of competing explanatory constructs.[57] In the past several decades, Christian apologists have developed a variety of evidential, rational, presuppositional, and subjective arguments in defense of the faith, and there has been a growth in combinationalist apologetics that synthesize many lines of argument. The phenomenological argument for the justification of religious belief from the nature of human needs may not be convincing on its own, but it can supplement a combinationalist apologetic. While it is beyond the scope of this section to develop this argument, a cursory sketch of some of its prominent features will be made.

Psychological Factors in Belief Acquisition and Validation

1. An excessive disjunction between rational inquiry and personal faith overlooks the fact that the mind/heart distinction is slippery. The dichotomy between an algorithm and an irrational leap falsely assumes that cognition and affection are entirely separate domains of mental life, when in reality, every emotional state has a component of knowledge and every cognitive state has a component of feeling.[58] This cognitive-affective fusion means that cumulative reasoning is person-relative; there is a personal participation of the knower in all acts of understanding.[59] To build up the case for any proposition, informal evidences must be trusted, since "the rationality of holding a belief is not entirely a matter of its epistemic justification."[60] Classical evidentialism neglects the critical role that personal values and psychological factors play in belief acquisition. But personal knowledge does not rule out rational inquiry; a comprehensive approach to knowing integrates rather than dichotomizes personal experience and rational reflection.[61] Different modes of validation such as reason, personal experience, and practicality can be mutually supportive in a whole-person approach that includes the analytic and the intuitive modes and allows for tacit as well as explicit knowing.[62]

2. Faith is a universal experience that involves the risk of commitment beyond knowledge. All people, including the atheist and the scientist, are committed to some kind of worldview (whether articulated or not) in a way that is incommensurate with rational proof. But the component of faith need not eliminate a quest for rationality, since both can be present. Faith and rationality can be viewed as a dialectical process in which faith seeks understanding and leads to it, while understanding generates faith and deepens it.[63] **Pojman notes that from a biblical perspective, "there is just enough evidence for a person passionately concerned but not enough to produce a comfortable proof."**[64] Religious belief requires decisive rather than interim assent because it involves not merely belief about, but belief in; the object of the former is a proposition, but the object of the latter is a person.[65] There is a qualitative difference in believing a person that includes deeper levels of trust and hope. In the absence of apodictic certainty, mature faith is forged in a context of doubt, particularly since religious belief entails the commitment to temporal risk for eternal gain.[66]

3. Religious belief and behavior are motivationally overdetermined in that multiple factors, including human needs, are involved in the processes of conversion and growth in faith. Psychological categories and interpretations cannot account for the complexion of subjective experience involved in religious belief and practice.[67] The huge constellation of diverse psychological, social, and cultural factors that influence religious belief renders each case unique and unpredictable. These factors include: socio-economic status; personal values; temperament and personality mode; mental capacity; response to cultural influences; socially shared set of meanings; levels of conflict; suggestibility; religious background; level of cognitive dissonance; cultural belief system; extent of self-esteem; sense of security; psychological adjustment; strategies of accommodation; exposure to manipulation, exploitation, and coercion; psychogenic interests; attitude toward authority; and unsatisfied survival, identity, relational, and ideological needs.[68] In view of this, group comparisons and correlational statistics should be supplemented by N=1 (single case) methodology.[69] While functionalist reasons (e.g., personality integration, guilt, and fear reduction) may be involved in religious belief, they do not wholly account for it.

4. The whole complex of people's belief structure strongly influences the way in which they devise and weigh theories; their analysis of arguments for or against religious belief is affected by the subjective commitments they bring with them.[70] The extremes of nonperspectivism (evaluation of evidence is uninfluenced by one's conceptual framework) and hard perspectivism (reason can only have intramural significance, since different fiduciary frameworks make interchange between worldviews impossible) can be avoided by the more realistic course of soft perspectivism that recognizes the role of conceptual frameworks in evidential evaluation but still allows communication between frameworks because of shared rules of inference, basic beliefs, and sympathetic imagination.[71] Thus, **one's evaluation of the rational merit of theistic arguments depends on one's personal experiences and cognitive framework; the teleological argument may be persuasive to person A, mildly compelling to person B, and unconvincing to person C.**[72] **Each person has a distinctive noetic structure that involves complex valuational attachments to beliefs depending upon depth of ingress or centrality in the personality. The greater the ingress of belief, the more difficult it is to dislodge it.**

5. There is a reciprocal relationship between belief and behavior, attitude and action, thought and experience. The simultaneous dynamics of living necessitate a circularity that has no beginning. Thus, faith is both a source of action and a consequence of action; acts of obedience and worship influence belief, and belief properly leads to behavioral response. **Kierkegaard's radical volitionalism stresses active risking in hope more than knowledge and creedal affirmation; for him, objectivity without subjective response is an enemy of Christian faith.** Most philosophers of religion affirm that religious beliefs are more than propositions, since they involve how people think and how they live. The biblical mutuality of faith and works stresses that faith is not merely a matter of mental assent or rational reflection but a way of life. Christian faith is relational in that it involves trust and commitment to a personal being.

The Relevance of Human Needs to the Rationality of Religious Belief

1. While theistic apologetics is usually concerned with objective and rational evidence, arguments for religious belief can also be based on the affective dimension of human existence, including aspirations for more than this world can offer, and the quest for meaning and purpose. The argument from human needs offers subjective evidence that functions as an important component in a cumulative case for religious belief built on human experience.[73] Other strands of subjective evidence that can be woven together into a strong cumulative and multidimensional argument include the experience of conflict between good and evil in human nature, mystical experiences of a numinous nature, experiences of spiritual immanence, correlations between mental health and adjustment to spiritual reality, and the facts of psychical research.[74]

2. *The argument from human needs is not postulating the existence of God on the grounds of human needs since this would reduce God to an anthropomorphic projection.* As Rahner observed:

> that approach in which we invoke the idea that we cannot manage either at the individual or the social level without the idea of God has to be viewed with the utmost caution and critical realism. . . . When theism is invoked as a postulate for shaping the world in a way that makes the course of human life in it reasonably humane and tolerable, it almost inevitably arouses the suspicion in the mind of modern man of being a fictitious ideology. It is quite useful, but for that very reason incurs the suspicion of being a mere fiction. The question of whether we believe in God certainly has some importance too for human living in its fully concrete reality. But if we attempt to persuade either ourselves or another to believe in God precisely *in order that* these very real advantages ensuing from belief in God may be gained, then in the majority of cases today the psychological mechanism which we seek to set in motion in this way will fail to function in view of the fact that the world as we experience it is so terrible.[75]

Instead, the argument states that the satisfaction of human needs in the lives of those whose trust and hope are in God constitutes legitimate subjective evidence that reinforces the religious commitment they already have. **It is not that God exists as a cosmic satisfier of human needs but that human needs are part of God's created order and by their nature can only be fully met when humans are rightly related to their Creator.**

3. *If it is claimed that the satisfaction of human needs offers evidential justification for religious beliefs, it is necessary to examine religious experience to discern the extent to which needs are satisfied in the lives of believers relative to unbelievers.* Along these lines, it is relevant to note that most of the psychologists in this study acknowledge the role and importance of some form of religious belief or at least a secular surrogate for religious belief. **At the same time, it is also necessary to give an account of counter instances in which religious belief, far from satisfying psychological needs, actually appears to stifle and narrow the personality.** There are many religious believers whose lives appear to be joyless and legalistic and whose personalities are characterized by a hard carapace of defensive strategies. Since the inception of Christianity, believers have been aware of the problems of hypocrisy, legalism, and dead orthodoxy, but they maintain that these distortions do not diminish the fact that, on the whole, religious belief makes a significant difference in the need areas of faith, hope, and love.

4. Theism offers a better solution to the basic identity needs, relational needs, and ideological needs of humans than secular and religious alternatives. It provides an ultimate and personal foundation for identity and morality as well as a cure to the problem of personal guilt through divine forgiveness. It answers the relational need for love and community through restoration of man's broken relationship with God, which in turn makes the *agape* of God available for the restoration of relationships and community with others. And it meets the ideological need by opening "a horizon of expectation" to those who have staked their final purpose and hope on the character and promises of God.[76] In contrast, secular alternatives like scientism and humanism offer only finite meanings and temporal purposes; man is reduced to a sociobiological vehicle programmed to preserve its selfish genes; the universe becomes a closed system in an irrational and impersonal universe that will ultimately undergo entropic dissolution; values are at best subjective and relative; humanity is subject to the idolatry of chance that allows no room for the transcendent; and the vision for the future wavers between the extreme of presumption in an illusory hope of the self-mastery of the human race in a secular eschatology of progress through linear time and the opposite extreme of despair (e.g., the hopelessness of existentialism).[77] **Religious alternatives to theism in which ultimate reality is personal but not infinite (e.g., polytheism, Mahayana Buddhism) or infinite but not personal (e.g., monism, Theravada Buddhism, the New Age Movement) are also unable to fully satisfy human needs. Beyond survival needs, human needs in the final analysis are relational (identity needs and ideological needs cannot be satisfied in a relational vacuum).[78] And the only sure foundation for unlimited meaning and security of hope in a contingent universe is an absolute, infinite, and sovereign being.** Theism, with its belief in a God who is both personal and infinite, can best meet human needs because it corresponds to the deepest human aspirations of unending existence in a creative personal context.

5. The argument from desire or "Sehnsucht" mentioned in C. S. Lewis and developed by Peter Kreeft is also relevant to the issue of human needs since it relates to the lack of perfect contentment in this life and the longing for a joy that transcends any earthbound experience or comprehension.[79] As Kreeft outlines the argument,

> The major premise of the argument is that every natural or innate desire in us bespeaks a corresponding real object that can satisfy the desire.
>
> The minor premise is that there exists in us a desire which nothing in time, nothing on earth, no creature, can satisfy.
>
> The conclusion is that there exists something outside of time, earth, and creatures which *can* satisfy this desire.[80]

The defense of this argument is beyond the compass of this study, but the concept is reminiscent of the Augustinian "vision of human life as a quest for infinite satisfaction, fueled by a torrent of desire that cannot rest in anything less"[81] as well as Tillich's apologetic strategy of exposing existential questions to which Christianity provides an answer.

THE PROBLEM OF SELF-INTEREST AND SELF-LOVE

An extended discussion of human needs raises the problem of self-interest and self-love; is it wrongfully self-centered to be concerned with the satisfaction of one's psychological needs? The answers to this question range along a continuum from the pole of absolute detachment from the interests of self in complete ascetic abandon, to the opposite pole of egocentricity and idolatry of the self. The former has an anticreation orientation along the lines of Manichaean dualism, while the latter is a case of autonomous self-worship. Both theologians and Christian psychologists have criticized humanistic psychology for moving toward the second extreme. They charge that psychologists have placed such an emphasis on becoming an independent, self-actualizing individual that they have lost sight of what it means to be a person in relation. Adler's Individual Psychology, Jung's individuation process, Rank's creative individual, and Fromm's man for himself find their epitome in the Maslow/Rogers vision of self-esteem and actualization of human potential.[82] Since the self with its unlimited potential is virtually a god, the sacrament in Rogers's secular invitation to be born again is self-actualization, and the purpose of life is one's own personal development.[83] It is not surprising, then, that humanistic psychologists regard the Christian practice of self-denial and sacrificial service as obstacles rather than agents of personal growth. On their account, fulfillment is attained through the realization of wants and is blocked by conformity and obedience to the will of another (whether God or man). Thus, Fromm criticizes what he takes to be the Protestant view that self-love is synonymous with selfishness, claiming that they are in fact opposites, since those who do not love themselves cannot love others.[84] **Maslow, Rogers, and Fromm dispute any bifurcation between individualism and altruism because they believe that "self-actualizing people are simultaneously the most individualistic and the most altruistic and social and loving of all human beings."**[85]

One of the fundamental differences between the psychologists and the theologians in this study is that the latter believe that human love at its best and most profound must be a reflection of divine love; the natural loves of affection, friendship, and *eros* are incomplete and inadequate unless they are empowered by the divine love of *agape*.[86] While *agape* involves self-sacrifice for the good of others, it need not eliminate personal benefit or fulfillment, because it is expressed through the mutuality of natural human loves in such a way that the outcome is both divine and human.[87]

One's concept and evaluation of self-love depends on one's view of human nature. Those who hold a negative view (Freud) will see self-love in narcissistic terms; those with an ambivalent view (Jung and Rank) see it in ambiguous terms; those with a positive view (Erikson, Adler, and Fromm) see it as beneficial; and those with a completely optimistic view (Maslow and Rogers) see it in terms of actualization and altruism. While the psychologists in this study deny an absolute foundation for objective truth and morality, the theologians see both the dignity and depravity of humanity since they relate man to God as the ultimate ground of the true, the beautiful, and the good. **As Pascal observed, the grandeur of man is in his creation in the image of God, but the degradation of man is in his moral and spiritual rebellion against his Creator; thus, there is no place for despair or room for pride for those who repent of their sin and receive God's grace in forgiveness.** When founded on the love of God, loving oneself as a creature is appropriate, but self-love is misappropriated when it is elevated above the love and claims of God, for then it idolatrously usurps divine authority.

    The theologians agree that God must be loved for himself and not for his benefits, but they also affirm that when the Supreme Good is loved above all other goods, one is delivered from the devouring egoism which distorts self-love without losing the desire for joy. Only when this desire is subordinated to the desire for God does it find its own fulfillment as well.[88] "The human being attains his or her fulfillment in one single, total act of his or her existence: in the love of God for his own sake. But this fulfillment is, precisely, only reached when not it but God is sought."[89] Thus, **Bernard of Clairvaux distinguished four degrees of love: man loves himself for his own sake, loves God for man's own blessing, loves God for God's own sake, and loves himself for God's sake.**[90] It is in this way that one finds life by losing it for Christ's sake.[91] **In the New Testament, self-denial is not an end in itself but the means of weaning the human heart from the pursuit of lesser goods to the Supreme Good for which it was created.**[92] **But it requires a miracle of grace for one to surrender selflessly to God in faith, hope, and love.**[93]

    Western Christianity since Augustine has been criticized by some observers as being excessively concerned with individual issues such as the introspective conscience and how God works redemption on the personal rather than corporate level.[94] Yet the biblical picture is not distorted by concern on the personal level, but when the personal is separated from the communal in such a way that people are seen as autonomous centers of knowing and judging rather than persons whose humanity is manifested in relatedness and mutual dependence on others.[95] It is through bonds of commitment to others that people become fully human, and the true source of unconditional commitment in self-giving love is not the organismic self-actualization tendency, but the unconditional love, acceptance, and forgiveness of God.[96] **When people love God completely (above all other loves, and for himself, not for his gifts), they become capable of loving themselves correctly (seeing themselves as God sees them—forgiven, beloved of God, children of light) and loving others compassionately (with selfless *caritas*). The more clearly they discover that their needs for identity, love, and hope are met in Christ, the freer they are to love and serve others unconditionally.**[97] They are no longer bound to manipulate relationships in the quest for need fulfillment since it is their Creator and Redeemer who satisfies their needs for security and significance.[98]

IMMANENT VERSUS TRANSCENDENT SOLUTIONS TO HUMAN NEEDS

One's view of needs, particularly the solution to how they can best be fulfilled, depends on one's view of reality, that is, the nature and destiny of human beings and the universe in which they live. As discussed earlier in this chapter, worldviews are unavoidable, and each person, whether a scientist, a psychologist, or a theologian, must account for the universality of moral and mystical experience in terms of the metaphysical and axiological presuppositions he brings to the evidence. The atheist claims that moral and religious experience should be seen as being "taken out of oneself" rather than originating from beyond oneself, while the theist holds that this experience points to God's action in the world.[99] The former may think he is applying Occam's razor to the phenomenological evidence, while the latter would criticize this approach as reductionistic. When scientific naturalism eliminated teleology as a heuristic construct, methodological reductionism spread to other disciplines such as ethics, philosophy, theology, and psychology.[100] Psychologists who disavow the spiritual realm must eliminate the spiritual or frame it in terms of the psychological, and this reductionistic method assumes *ab initio* that reports of the existence of a dimension beyond the space-time continuum must be spurious or misguided. This results in a conceptual flatness, as Browning observes in his comparison of the basic metaphors of the Christian faith with the metaphors of ultimacy of the modern psychologies. In contrast with the richness and multi-dimensionality of the former, "[t]he deep metaphors of the modern psychologies—life or death, harmony, natural selection, etc.—tend to be singular and one dimensional."[101] When psychology eliminates the transcendent, "the soul's center of gravity may be transferred from the center—from the point of personal responsibility in the presence of the Unconditioned—to the impersonal, unconscious, purely natural sphere."[102]

It is helpful to recognize multiple levels of description when seeking to account for human behavior, just as a poem can be viewed on many levels such as markings of ink on paper, alphabetical letters, words, grammar and syntax, or an aesthetic creation.[103] Each of these levels yields truth about the poem, but none of them are exhaustive of the whole. Thus, religious conversion can be interpreted in terms of sociocultural influences, but this level of description does not exclude higher or lower levels. Clearly, there is an asymmetry about these levels of description, since the more comprehensive levels can account for the lower, but the lower levels cannot account for the higher without distorting or debunking them. **Another way of viewing this is to think of reality as "comprised of simultaneously interpenetrating dimensions arranged according to a hierarchy of richness and comprehensiveness" so that the spiritual realm is "*contiguous* with the rest of experience without its being reducible to it."[104]**

Post-Enlightenment society has been increasingly characterized by the cultural phenomena of secularization, privatization, and pluralization.[105] In the modern pluralistic context of competing ideologies, three major worldviews have become prominent: scientific (secular) humanism, cosmic humanism (monism/pantheism), and theism. When theism is abandoned, as it was by each of the psychologists in this study, the dominant remaining options are scientific humanism (Freud, Adler, Rank, Erikson) and cosmic humanism (Jung, Maslow, Rogers, and Fromm moved in this direction). The conflict theorists tended toward the scientific version of humanism while the fulfillment theorists tended toward the cosmic version.

The rapid territorial expansion of scientific humanism in cultural ideology was aided by the claim that modern science "destroyed the old public, objective and cosmological kind of religion" so that religious beliefs and values no longer fit with a scientifically coherent picture of the world.[106] From the point of view of the modern scientific consciousness, Judeo-Christianity seems preposterous, and the idea of the supernatural should be jettisoned; there is "no room in the Cosmos for an absolutely transcending objective mind and an absolutely transcending God."[107] **This epistemologically reductionistic attitude that science is the only trustworthy form of knowledge has created its own mythology and value system in which the evolution and continuance of the human species has become a substitute for personal immortality.** But the materialistic worldview of scientism, despite its evolutionary and technical optimism, diminishes the cosmos to the impersonal plus time and chance and offers no solutions to the human predicament and its existential estrangement.[108] In view of the need for a unifying philosophy of life and the "unsuppressible and unquenchable thirst for religious myth and moral order," humans cannot live consistently with the logical implications of scientistic presuppositions, since they offer no realizable metaphysic of personal hope.[109] It is therefore no wonder that the scientifically oriented psychologists project these meanings into their work. Nor is it any surprise that several of the psychologists moved through a transition from scientific toward cosmic humanism during the course of their careers, since this offers the attractive ideology of being part of a cosmic evolutionary process and the semantic mysticism of transcendence without any personal responsibility or accountability.

While most philosophers criticize the naturalistic fallacy of generating ethical values from science by deducing what ought to be from what is, this has not deterred a host of scientists and psychologists from developing elaborate value systems, often "open-ended," from an immanentistic rather than Archimedian vantage point.[110] Some of these values are smuggled in from the residue of convictions derived from Christianity that have shaped Western civilization,[111] but others are diametrically opposed to a theistic value system. For example, in theism, personal identity is eternal and derived from the divine; one's relationship with God defines self-worth. But in the clinical-humanistic approach, identity is ephemeral and mortal; relationships with self and others define self-worth. In the former, love, affection, and self-transcendence are primary, and service and self-sacrifice are central to personal growth. In the latter, personal needs and self-actualization are primary, and self-satisfaction is central to personal growth.[112] **Theonomous and autonomous accounts of personal fulfillment are radically different, not only in their solutions to human**

needs but also in cognate areas like the human condition, the purpose of life, and meaning in view of death.

There are different ways of reacting to the problem of human finitude: one can hide from limitation and death, deny it, or accept it in meaning or despair.[113] Becker observes that the widespread problem of neurosis in modern life relates to "the failure of all traditional immortality ideologies to absorb and quicken man's hunger for self-perpetuation and heroism."[114] With the "disappearance of convincing dramas of heroic apotheosis," modern man "became psychological because he became isolated from protective collective ideologies."[115] Few people can find contentment with a conscious awareness of ultimate irrationality and meaninglessness as Sartre, Gide, Beckett, Camus, Ionesco, Kafka, and other creators of literature of the absurd would attest. Mascall argued that "if you try to find the ultimate meaning of the world simply within it you will fail, and then, if you refuse to look for it anywhere else, you will say that the world does not make sense. If you develop a neurosis as a result, this will be the effect of your conclusion rather than its cause."[116] The futility of Sisyphus resonates with the human condition of longing for one's life to have made a cosmic difference in a universe that is utterly indifferent. People cannot live without some kind of hope that there is abiding value in their lives or that it will turn out well in the end; but when everything is reduced to the sphere of immanence, to matter in interaction in a mechanistic and self-contained system of cause and effect, there is no ultimate and abiding ground of hope that corresponds to this human aspiration.[117] This is why terms like "peak experiences," "being cognition," "self-actualized individuals," "fully functioning person," "person of tomorrow," "rational faith," and "productive love and thinking" have a dishonest ring to them; they do not authentically deal with the universal fear of nonbeing or the painful question of meaning that plagues those who have not opted for the hedonism of escapism.[118] To avoid the Scylla of despair and hopelessness, psychologists often fall into the Charybdis of personal or futuristic presumption. But in the absence of the absolute Mystery that humans need:

> All the analysis in the world doesn't allow the person to find out *who he is* and why he is here on earth, why he has to die, and how he can make his life a triumph. It is when psychology pretends to do this, when it offers itself as a full explanation of human unhappiness, that it becomes a fraud that makes the situation of modern man an impasse from which he cannot escape. . . . Modern man needs a "thou" to whom to turn for spiritual and moral dependence, and as God was in eclipse, the therapist has had to replace Him—just as the lover and the parents did.[119]

This psychological dishonesty is not limited to concerns of meaning and mortality but extends to a rationalization and shallow reinterpretation of the profound and ubiquitous experience of guilt. **The problem of guilt cannot be reduced to neurotic infantile fantasy, to the fear of life, or to violation of arbitrary social conventions. Psychotherapy can indeed address the problem of neurotic guilt, but it cannot eliminate the residue of existential guilt** manifested in the symptoms of alienation and relational estrangement.[120] **This alienation is rooted in freedom, not determinism, and it cannot be cured without personal acknowledgement of responsibility and the forgiveness of others.** Humans are powerless to overcome the gap between what they are and what they would be, but this impotence does not eliminate the problem of personal culpability.

In the absence of a transcendent metaphysic, psychologists are left with immanentistic solutions in their attempt to respond to the tragic vision of Freud. But their solutions are hardly different from the usual bromides about the self-mastery of the human race: we must take charge of our own fate, rise above ourselves, and rule our environment and our destiny. Freud hoped that scientific discoveries would lead to a greater mastery of nature and an improved social context. In the interim it is the task of psychoanalysis to cure neurotic misery so that people need only experience the common misery of reality. The best one can do is to work and to love. Erikson stressed the importance of attaining trust and identity as well as integrity, that is, the willingness to accept the ultimacy of one's only life cycle. People should experience the joys and sorrows of fate as something they have actively chosen and accept the responsibilities of nurturing the next generation. Jung believed that humans must attain selfhood through the individuation process of uniting the opposite forces of the conscious and the unconscious. Through the symbolic structure of the great mythologies and religions, the archetypes can guide the personality in the quest for the integration of the self. Rank supported the individual striving for self-realization through the exercise of conscious will and acceptance of the ambivalence in the personality between individuation and generation. He advocated a creative will expression that diminishes the life-and-death fears through the integration of union and separation. Individuals should accept the pain of life as unavoidable and try to overcome it through animating personal experience. Maslow believed in the essential goodness of human nature and encouraged its expression and actualization. People's basic or deficiency needs must be satisfied so that they can be dominated by growth need or metaneed motivation. This self-actualization tendency can lead to peak experiences and a new form of cognition. Rogers held that the core of personality is positive and that when people experience unconditional positive regard, they learn to listen to themselves and to accept their attitudes and feelings as they are. People become fully functioning self-actualizers when they experience self-regard and enhanced cooperation with others. According to Adler, humans need security as well as a sense of significance through their social contribution to the lives of others. Since everyone strives for superiority and perfection, they need fictional goals that will enable them to overcome inferiority and attain a sense of social worth. Fromm asserted that the problem of finitude and mortality can be overcome through productive loving and thinking (shifting to a being mode from a having mode). When people acknowledge the reality of their aloneness in the universe, they can find meaning in their lives by accepting responsibility for themselves, believing in themselves, and giving birth to the potential that is within them.

These solutions essentially distill down to the following advice: we should accept life with all its hardships, ambiguities, and joys; we should accept ourselves as we are and others as they are; at the same time, we should try to become whole, integrated, creative, and productive people; and we should accept the fact of our mortality and make the most out of life. **These simplistic solutions to the complexities and depths of the human condition are reminiscent of Aldous Huxley's admission near the end of his life: "It is a bit embarrassing to have been concerned with the human problem all one's life and find at the end that one has no more to offer by way of advice than 'Try to be a little kinder.'"**[121] With the crumbling of communal ideologies of heroism, dignity, vision, and hope, these psychologists have sought to validate the self through their own creative illusions and *causa-sui* projects in an attempt to overcome the threats and vulnerabilities of reality.[122] But illusions that have no metaphysical grounding are only therapeutic through a course of self-deception; those who become aware of what they are find them unsatisfying, since people cannot consciously live and die for what they know to be a hoax.

This is not to deny the important and sometimes acute perceptions these personality theorists had concerning human traits and behavior. The problem is that when these true insights are embedded in a reductionistic worldview, the solutions the psychologists offer become superficial. Emancipation from belief in the transcendent does not bring happiness; it brings either despair or denial of creatureliness. Without God, people are limited to finite meanings and substitute ends in a milieu of resignation, escapism, or futile attempts to create absolutes within a bounded condition. But the ineradicable longing for mystery, majesty, dignity, hope, and transcendent power cannot be found in the identities, relationships, and secular ideologies of the world. The yearning for ecstasy and awe remain and can only be satisfied in an unbounded personal context of faith, hope, and love. **In the Christian vision, death is not extinction, but the birth canal into a larger world in which the whole person—body, soul, and spirit—will be transformed and completed in an unlimited future of unending felicity.** Because of the image of God, humans manifest a transcendence within immanence which no earthbound source of identity, purpose, or hope can fully satisfy. As some of the psychologists observed, being is indeed more fundamental than doing; but one's sense of being, identity, and personhood must be defined by God and not the world. **Human destiny is bound up in God, or as Dante expressed it in the conclusion of *The Divine Comedy*, "the love that moves the sun and the other stars."** Those whose faith and hope are in God understand that their "life cycle" does not end with death, and that this temporal existence is the sojourn of a pilgrim who awaits the inexhaustible satisfaction of the vision of the infinite-personal source of all that is true, beautiful, and good.[123] It will not be "the self-actualized individual" or "the man for himself" who beholds the divine vision, but it will be persons in community with God and with one another who share the corporate joy of heaven.[124]

Rank understood, as did Kierkegaard before him, that humans are religious and not merely biological beings, and that psychology must give way to theology.[125] No one can simultaneously embrace a reductionistic and a theistic worldview; a choice must be made, since there is no neutral ground between autonomy and theonomy. God uses the pulley of unfulfilled longing to draw people away from idolatrous attachment to the created order to the beatific vision that will satisfy every human need.

The Pulley

When God at first made man,
Having a glass of blessings standing by,
"Let us" (said he) "pour on him all we can;
Let the world's riches, which dispersèd lie,
Contract into a span."

So strength first made a way;
Then beauty flow'd, then wisdom, honour, pleasure.
When almost all was out, God made a stay,
Perceiving that alone of all his treasure
Rest in the bottom lay.

"For if I should" (said he)
"Bestow this jewel also on my creature,
He would adore my gifts instead of me,
And rest in Nature, not the God of Nature:
So both should losers be.

"Yet let him keep the rest,
But keep them with repining restlessness;
Let him be rich and weary, that at least,
If goodness lead him not, yet weariness
May toss him to my breast."

—George Herbert (1593–1633)

APPENDIX

A SUMMARY OF HUMAN NEEDS IN THE NEW TESTAMENT

The New Testament teaches that God is the source of all biological and spiritual life, and that humans, as God's offspring, must ultimately look to him for the satisfaction of their physical and spiritual needs. While physical needs like food, drink, clothing, and shelter are matters of genuine concern and are not to be minimized, the Gospels and Epistles stress that the deepest human needs are not material but spiritual; the claims of the kingdom of God must take precedence over all other claims. Those who enjoy the benefits of a salvific relationship with God should pursue him above all other concerns, knowing that during the time they are pilgrims and sojourners on the earth, they can look to him for the provision of their temporal needs. Those who are in Christ have nothing and yet possess all things; they recognize their stewardship, not ownership, of the time, abilities, and material goods with which they have been entrusted, and trust in God rather than their own abilities or resources to meet their needs on all levels.

Of the three fundamental spiritual or relational needs that emerged from the study of human needs in the New Testament (discussed in chapter 1), **the first is the need for forgiveness and grace.** In his preaching on the kingdom of God, Jesus addressed the need for repentance and salvation to individuals and to the nation of Israel as a whole. Religious externalism led to the false belief that ritual observance creates a condition of righteousness before God, but Jesus went deeper than outward action and applied the Torah to the thoughts and motives of the human heart. Arguing that the source of defilement is not external but internal, he spoke of the need of forgiveness from the guilt of sin and the creation of a new heart through the blood of the new covenant which he offered in his sacrificial death for the sin of the world. It is only through the grace and forgiveness of God that a person can be delivered from the bondage of sin, slavery, and death and transferred into the kingdom of light. There is no middle ground between sin and righteousness, slavery and freedom, death and life; apart from the grace of God, people are in a condition of spiritual death in which they are "children of wrath" who are alienated from God because of their transgression of his ordinances and enslavement to the power of sin. The universality of sin leads to a condition of condemnation of both Jews and Gentiles before a God of holiness. The solution to this human plight is the forgiveness and restoration available in Christ, but this necessitates an acknowledgement that the quality of life acceptable to God cannot be attained through human merit or good works but only through divine grace. Christ's offer of newness of life and freedom from the dominion of sin requires the response of repentance; people must acknowledge their need to be forgiven and act on Jesus' words by receiving his gift of eternal life. This spiritual healing is available to those who admit that they are sinners and are in need of the mercy and grace that is available through the redemptive work of the Son of God. This appropriation of Jesus' person and work cleanses believers from the defilement of sin and brings them into the family of God as sharers of his life.

The second human need in the New Testament is the need for love and community. Those who accept the apostolic testimony concerning Jesus Christ and enter by faith into the benefits of the new covenant discover the satisfaction of restored *shalom* with God. By putting him above the quest for temporal gain and recognition, they find their lives by losing them for God's sake. On the other hand, those who pursue self-satisfaction become entangled in the manifold concerns of temporal affairs and fail to understand that love, joy, and peace are the overflow of the pursuit of God and cannot be fully attained as ends in themselves.

As bearers of God's image, people are relational beings who need not only a restored relationship with their Creator but also a restored relationship with one another. Those who are recipients of the mercy and grace of God in Christ enjoy his unconditional love and acceptance, and this is the basis on which they are called to love others even as they have been loved by their Lord. The clearest expression of their love for God is the love they manifest toward one another, and in this way, sacrificial love and compassion become the central element of Christian living. Because they have been forgiven, they are commanded to forgive those who have sinned against them and to seek the forgiveness of those against whom they have sinned. Their new identity in Christ is the foundation for a loving and holy communal life expressed in the metaphors of a family and a body. This community of Christ's followers is exhorted to pursue a unity of mutual love, service, encouragement, kindness, forgiveness, giving, and compassion. Where there is unity of fellowship in a covenant community of believers, there are a joy and love that demonstrate the mercy and grace of God and transcend socioeconomic barriers because of the equality each member has in Christ.

The third human need in the New Testament is the need for purpose and hope. The Gospels and Epistles consistently emphasize that the things which are unseen are more fundamental than those which are visible, since the former are temporal while the latter are eternal. The afflictions and adversities of this world cannot be compared with the glory that is to be revealed because the inheritance of those who are in Christ is imperishable and incorruptible. As members of God's household, they have embraced a transcendent source of identity and security that assures them that their lives have purpose and significance. They are ambassadors of the new creation in Christ, and they anticipate their resurrection at his advent and unending life in his presence. Their hope is not founded on the vacillating and uncertain circumstances of earthly existence, but on the unchanging character and promises of God. The hope of those who have been reconciled to God reaches beyond the boundaries of this world to everlasting life.

HUMAN NEEDS IN THE NEW TESTAMENT

This appendix is a study in biblical anthropology that particularly focuses on the New Testament accounts of what human beings need in order to be whole and fully functioning persons.

Before proceeding, six points are necessary to delineate the boundaries of this survey of human needs in the New Testament:

1. This study will not deal with the problem of ascription regarding the authorship of the Gospels and Epistles. "The Pauline corpus," for example, will include all the Epistles traditionally ascribed to Paul.

2. A survey of human needs in the Old Testament is beyond the scope of this study.

3. An attempt will be made to avoid the kind of psychological exegesis that inserts modern categories related to individual and group psychology into the New Testament text.[1]

4. Recognizing that post-Augustinian and post-Lutheran psychological analyses of needs may be anachronistic with regard to the first-century concerns that underlie the writing of the New Testament, a brief description of the primary historical issues that form the background to the Gospels and Epistles will be included.

5. The scope of this appendix requires it to be hermeneutically and theologically oriented. While it is not primary exegesis, an effort has been made to make it compatible with the historical context while concurrently considering what the text renders possible to someone for whom the history of the church has happened.

6. This study does not seek to read an atomistic list of human needs from the text of the New Testament but rather to discern overlapping areas of emphasis that are relevant to human maturity and fulfillment.

THE GOSPELS AND ACTS

Preliminary Concerns

The last decade has seen the rapid development of what has been called the "third quest" for the historical Jesus of first-century Palestine.[2] Working as historians with the growing knowledge of second-temple Judaism, scholars like Meyer, Sanders, Theissen, Borg, and Wright have gained new insights into the religious, social, and political implications of the life and teaching of Jesus.[3] In this way, the actions and teachings of Jesus have been increasingly related to the Jewish social and political concerns of his time, and not limited, as they have traditionally been, solely to moral and spiritual issues.[4]

Although there are areas of disagreement among the historians of the third quest, the growing consensus is that Jesus sought to renew Israel and that his message was addressed to Jewish and Palestinian society.[5] Jesus "regarded his own teaching, not just as religion for the individual or for a church within the nation, but as a national way of life which the nation could disregard only at its mortal peril."[6] The predominant Jewish expectation of his time was nationalistic and temple centered; the hope was that God would enable Israel to defeat the Romans so that righteous Israel would be vindicated before the pagan nations. The Old Testament imagery that God would rule the world through Israel (e.g., Zech. 14; Isa. 11:60–62) had become distorted into a rationale for a narrow nationalism and a religious exclusivism. It was because of this that Jesus warned his contemporaries of the divine judgment that would come upon them if they continued on their nation-centered path. Paradoxically, Israel's quest for political deliverance through a separatist understanding of holiness was leading directly to their demise at the hands of Rome as God's instrument of judgment. **Jesus offered to fulfill the Jewish hope, but he radically redefined the content of that hope. In place of the exclusivistic "holiness code" which stressed separation and preservation of revelation, Jesus sought to explode the boundaries of Israel's self-centered understanding with an inclusive "mercy code" that related true holiness to the paradigm of divine mercy and compassion (e.g., Luke 6:27–36; Matt. 5:38–48).**[7]

Because of this redefinition, Jesus was perceived as a threat to the established order (cf. Luke 4:16–30); he was not meeting the needs the Jews wanted their Messiah to meet. In spite of this rejection and his warnings of judgment upon the nation, Jesus identified himself with Israel, including her outcasts with whom he had table-fellowship. In his crucifixion he took the judgment he had pronounced against Israel upon himself "so that, in his vindication, Israel may find herself brought through the judgment and into the true Kingdom, may see at last the way to life and follow it while there is yet time."[8] In this way he inaugurated the kingdom of God that was promised in the prophecies of the Old Testament even though he was rejected by the nation to whom the promises were made.[9] The people who responded to Jesus and his message had become the nucleus of the Israel of the new age,[10] and as foreseen by Isaiah and Zechariah (e.g., Isa. 2:2–3; Zech. 8:23) and fulfilled in Acts (1:8; 10:1–11:18), this kingdom would soon expand to include the Gentiles. This new order would coexist with the old until the consummation, and it would consist of people whose restoration to a normal relationship to God is reflected in individual transformation and collective embodiment of the mercy they have received. This community is the heir of Israel, having grown out of that people and having responded to their call.[11]

On this account of the message of Jesus, it is clear that his teaching went beyond individual morality and piety, and extended to the corporate problems and needs of Israel. As Yoder observes, "The personhood which he proclaims as a healing, forgiving call to all is integrated into the social novelty of the healing community."[12] This has often been overlooked because of the "tendency to reinterpret the national in terms of the individual" as the church moved away from its original Palestinian setting.[13] But there is a danger of overreacting to the excessive individualism that has characterized some Protestant interpreters and moving to the opposite extreme of denying that Jesus addressed individual as well as corporate needs. The preaching of Jesus concerning the kingdom of God addressed human needs at all levels, and in different contexts, Jesus applied the need for repentance and salvation to individuals (John 3:3–21; 5:24) and to the nation (Matt. 4:17; 11:20–24). **Jesus was concerned with both the transformation of the heart and the transformation of Israel. His teaching about purity of heart had definite social and political implications, and his summons to the people of God to manifest mercy as a historical community required the response of the individuals within that community.[14] This interweaving of individual and corporate needs is the perspective taken in the survey that follows.**

The Synoptic Gospels

Physical needs

The writers of the Synoptic Gospels recognized both physical and spiritual needs. In the Synoptic accounts of the Sermon on the Mount, Jesus assured the multitude that God is the sovereign sustainer of his creation and knows that his earthly children need food, clothing, and shelter.[15] He is able to provide for their physical needs, and even more than an earthly father, he is willing to give what is good to those who ask him.[16] Thus, people need not be anxious about these physical needs when they depend upon God as their sustainer who knows what they need before he is asked.[17] The Lord's prayer appropriately includes petitions for both physical and spiritual needs, since God is the source of all physical and spiritual life.[18]

The miraculous signs recorded in the Synoptic Gospels authenticated the preaching of Jesus and demonstrated the breadth of his authority and his ability to satisfy every human need. These powers were signs of the new age and evidences that the kingdom of God had come among those who beheld them.[19] They were acts of restoration that portrayed the healing of the whole person in the kingdom of God.[20]

Jesus manifested his ability to provide for the physical needs of his followers in the feedings of the five thousand and the four thousand with baskets of broken pieces left over after the crowds had been satisfied.[21] He can therefore provide for those who look to him to meet these needs, and this is illustrated in his commendation of the attitude of the poor widow who contributed everything she had to the temple treasury and thus had to look to God to meet her physical needs.[22]

Beyond the basic physical needs for food, shelter, and clothing, Jesus particularly focused on the need for physical healing. He declared in his Nazareth manifesto that he came to provide release from physical and spiritual bondage.[23] When the imprisoned John the Baptist sent disciples to ask Jesus if he was the Messiah whose coming he had announced, Jesus responded by pointing to the diseases he cured, including leprosy and paralysis, and to his restoration of hearing to the deaf and sight to the blind.[24] The breadth of Jesus' healing ministry is illustrated in the Synoptic accounts of his curing a diversity of afflictions ranging from pains, fever, hemorrhages, and epilepsy, to the restoration of those who were dumb, lame, and maimed, as well as liberation from physical and mental illnesses ascribed to demonic bondage.[25] Even the physical resurrection from the dead is adumbrated in the narratives of Jesus' resuscitation of individuals who had died.[26]

Spiritual needs

While Jesus ministered in these ways to the physical needs of those who came to him, his compassion and pity were even more deeply moved by the spiritual ignorance and destitution of the multitudes who were "harassed and helpless, like sheep without a shepherd."[27] Physical concerns were important in his ministry, but spiritual needs were more fundamental. **He made this clear in the way he used the physical healing of the paralytic as a means of demonstrating his more significant spiritual authority to forgive sins.**[28] The same principle is evident in Jesus' call to Peter and Andrew to leave their fishing nets and become fishers of men and also in the temptation narratives in which Jesus overcame the seduction to place the appetite for food, power, and wealth above the desire to do the will of his Father.[29]

Jesus frequently exhorted his hearers to place a higher priority on their spiritual well-being than on their material prosperity. Declaring that a person's life does not consist in the abundance of his possessions, he used the parable of the rich fool to illustrate the futility of the one "who lays up treasure for himself, and is not rich toward God."[30] The parable of the rich man and Lazarus and the Synoptic accounts of the rich young ruler develop the same theme.[31] One cannot simultaneously serve God and earthly wealth.[32]

The spiritual needs for forgiveness and a right relationship with God and others were focal points in the teaching and ministry of Jesus.

Forgiveness

Unlike other renewal movements that intensified the Torah in the direction of a separatist understanding of holiness, Jesus characteristically applied the Torah to the thoughts and intentions of the human heart.[33] He argued that a person is not defiled by external things but that the source of sin and defilement is internal. Corrupt thoughts and practices such as envy, slander, pride, murder, adultery, coveting, and deceit do not arise from foods and practices that are ritually unclean, but from within the human heart.[34] This perception of the human condition is consistent with Jesus' emphasis on the need for repentance and forgiveness. The creation of a new heart, the basic theme of the Jeremiah 31:31–34 promise of a new covenant (cf. Ps. 51:10), is necessary because of the problem of inner defilement.

In view of this, people must acknowledge their need to be forgiven. Forgiveness is spiritual healing, but "those who are well have no need of a physician."[35] Those who regard themselves as righteous, like the Pharisees Jesus accused of placing religious observance above the practice of mercy, will not discern their need for forgiveness. Only those who admit that they are sinners will seek spiritual healing. This is the point of Jesus' parable about the tax collector who, in contrast to the self-righteous Pharisee, said, "God, be merciful to me a sinner!" and found the divine forgiveness he sought.[36] A similar contrast is found in the Lukan account of the woman whom Jesus forgave in the Pharisee's house.[37]

Jesus' mission is encapsulated in Matthew's birth narrative with the words, "he will save his people from their sins."[38] Luke's basic concern is also with "the salvation established by the work of Jesus as an experience available to man."[39] Jesus told his disciples that the purpose for which he came to earth was to seek and to save the lost and to give his life as a ransom for the forgiveness of sins.[40] His offer of spiritual healing was based on the sacrifice he anticipated with increasing frequency as the time drew near. Unlike those Pharisees whom he accused of imposing heavy burdens upon others, particularly in their tendency to place ritual integrity above humanity, Jesus offered the light yoke of forgiveness and mercy to those who would come to him.[41] But his offer required a response; those who came to him had to recognize their need to be forgiven and turn to God in repentance. Both John the Baptist and Jesus spoke of the imminence of the kingdom of heaven and warned their listeners to repent of their sins, since repentance and forgiveness are necessary for deliverance from the bondage of sin and entrance into the kingdom of God.[42] This response of repentance was required on both an individual and a corporate level.[43]

Jesus repeatedly stressed the need to respond to his invitation, particularly in view of the mounting opposition to his message by the religious and political leaders of the nation during the course of his ministry. The builders were rejecting the chief cornerstone and were seeking to enter the kingdom by the wide way that leads to destruction.[44] The parables of the marriage feast and the banquet made clear that an invitation is not enough; a person must act on Jesus' words.[45] In the imagery of the parable of the sower, Jesus sowed the seed of the word, but the result depends upon the conditions and receptivity of the soil.[46] Consistent with his use of parables, Jesus affirmed that spiritual truth must be revealed; it is hidden from those who would reject it but revealed to those who would respond in faith.[47] One must receive the kingdom of God like a child or not enter it at all.[48]

A right relationship with God

In addition to the need for forgiveness, the Synoptic Gospels also communicate the need for an obedient and loving relationship with God. There are a number of facets to this relationship, including responsiveness to the spiritual direction and nourishment that is provided by the continuing presence of the shepherd.[49] This requires obedience to the demands of discipleship, particularly in following Jesus above all else.[50] He called his followers to a purity of heart that is centered on God rather than the multiplicity of finite concerns. He exhorted them to lose their lives for his sake in order to find them,[51] to be more concerned with their relation to God than with human appearances and approval,[52] to love him more than any earthly relationships,[53] to pursue him before anything else,[54] and to hunger and thirst for righteousness rather than worldly gain.[55] As in the parables of the hidden treasure and the pearl of great value,[56] the one who is pure in heart chooses one thing and treasures it above all other goods. "[O]ne thing is needful. Mary has chosen the good portion, which shall not be taken away from her."[57] **The one thing needful is to put the claims of the kingdom above all other claims. One must "seek first his kingdom and his righteousness"; those who pursue the spiritual above the material do not have to be anxious about physical needs like food, drink, clothing, and shelter, because "all these things shall be yours as well."**[58]

Jesus used the metaphor of stewardship to depict people's true relationship to earthly goods. A steward does not own but manages the property of another and is therefore accountable to the owner. He is responsible to be faithful in his use of the time, talent, and treasure that have been entrusted to him.[59] Maintaining this perspective of God's ownership of all things and looking to him rather than the world as the source of security requires a radical trust in God and a cessation of striving.[60] Jesus recognized the natural human tendency to be more concerned with pleasing men than with pleasing God.[61] This problem is only overcome when a person lets go of finite centers and turns to God as the supreme object of faith and hope.[62] The true reward for the follower of Jesus is not on earth but in heaven, and it is there that treasures should be laid up.[63]

A right relationship with others

People need not only a restored relationship to God but also a restored relationship to one another, and Jesus taught that the former provides the basis for the latter. In his summary of the law and the prophets, he said that one should love God completely and others compassionately.[64] He told his followers to "[l]ove your enemies, do good to those who hate you, bless those who curse you, pray for those who abuse you. . . . And as you wish that men would do to you, do so to them."[65] Because they have been forgiven their sins against God, they in turn should forgive those who have sinned against them and seek the forgiveness of those against whom they have sinned.[66] Jesus viewed service to the needs of others as service to God and encouraged an attitude of humility rather than arrogance, selfish ambition, or competition.[67]

The physical and spiritual needs listed above are interrelated in the Synoptic Gospels since the claims of Jesus have a bearing on every human need.[68] Jesus' ministry of physical provision and healing is directly associated with his offer of spiritual healing, that is, forgiveness of sins.[69] Forgiveness, in turn, provides the basis for entering into a right relationship with God, and a loving and obedient relationship with God is the foundation of a loving relationship with others.

The Gospel of John

Physical needs

While the physical needs for material sustenance and physical healing appear in John's Gospel, they are given less emphasis here than in the Synoptics. The series of typical stories in John 1–12 generally stress spiritual over physical concerns, particularly the need for a response of belief in Jesus' testimony concerning himself as the means of regeneration into newness of life. Although the sign narratives in these chapters relate to material provision (changing the water to wine in chapter 2 and feeding the multitude in chapter 6), physical healing (the nobleman's son in chapter 4, the paralytic in chapter 5, and the man born blind in chapter 9), and overcoming death (the raising of Lazarus in chapter 11), these physical events are used in this Gospel to authenticate the preaching and teaching of Jesus and to elicit the response of faith in his person and work. For example, after he fed the multitude, Jesus exhorted the people who followed him to the other side of the sea to be more concerned about spiritual than physical nourishment.[70] He presented himself as the bread of life that came down from heaven to provide eternal life for those who partake of him.[71] Similarly, he offered living water from the well of salvation to the Samaritan woman and to the crowds at the feast of Tabernacles and told his disciples that his food is to do his Father's will.[72] After claiming to be the light of the world, he healed the man who was blind from birth and offered him the greater light of believing in him.[73] The healings of the nobleman's son and the paralytic are also associated with exhortations to believe, Jesus' works bearing witness that the Father had sent him.[74] The accounts of the raising of Lazarus and the resurrection of Jesus are used to substantiate Jesus' claim to provide both biological and spiritual life to those who believe in him.[75]

Thus, the Fourth Gospel acknowledges human needs on the physical level but uses them to point to the dominical offer to satisfy spiritual needs.

Spiritual needs

Like the Synoptics, John's Gospel underscores the need for a right relationship with God, but it puts this on a more global level, stating that in order to enter into such a relationship, one must become a new person. This theme is most clearly developed in the dialogue between Jesus and Nicodemus in chapter 3 in which Jesus argued that without the new birth of the Spirit, one cannot enter the kingdom of God.[76] People stand condemned because of their sin, and in this state they will face the judgment of God and perish.[77] As the Son of God and the Lamb of God who takes away the sin of the world, Jesus came to provide salvation from this peril and the way of entrance into a living relationship with God in which one enters into the Father's family as a spiritual child.[78]

The Synoptic Gospels speak of the need for forgiveness, but John is more inclined to use the positive and negative imagery of sharing the life of Jesus and his Father and deliverance from the bondage of sin. This bondage is described in terms of slavery, darkness, and death.[79] There is thus no greater need than to gain freedom from this condition of spiritual judgment and death and to enter into eternal life.[80]

The seven "I am" statements in this Gospel not only emphasize the divine nature of Jesus and the need to respond to him but also portray the meaning of being born anew. As the bread of life, Jesus provides physical and spiritual nourishment.[81] As the light of the world, he offers enlightenment to those who are in darkness and calls people to respond to the light of his words by following him.[82] As the door and as the good shepherd who lays down his life for the sheep, he is the means of entry as well as the provider of the identity, security, and sustenance needed by his flock.[83] As "the resurrection and the life" and "the way, and the truth, and the life," Jesus guides his people out of falsehood into the truth and is the source of life who offers to overcome both spiritual death and (in the resurrection) physical death.[84] And as the true vine, he provides rootedness, vitality, and spiritual fruit to those who abide in him and become conduits of his life in the same way that a branch draws its life from the vine.[85]

John's Gospel is permeated with the opposing motifs of light and darkness, love and hate, life and death, truth and lies, righteousness and sin, freedom and slavery, and belief and disbelief. These stark contrasts between the forces of good and evil stress the lack of middle ground and are consistent with the Gospel's stated purpose of bringing the reader to the point of acceptance of the apostolic testimony concerning the person and work of Jesus ("these are written that you may believe that Jesus is the Christ, the Son of God, and that believing you may have life in his name").[86] The new birth takes place when a person responds to Jesus by believing that he is the Christ. This concept of belief or appropriation of Jesus' person and message runs throughout John's Gospel. As in the eucharistic discourse in chapter 6, one must either accept or reject Jesus' offer to find life by partaking of his body and blood.[87] This is done by receiving him, an act which John equates with believing in his name.[88] The importance of recognizing that Jesus is the Christ and responding in faith is communicated through the series of signs and responses to the signs (acceptance and rejection) in John 2–12 and in Jesus' recorded interactions with people and groups (e.g., the woman at the well and the Samaritans).[89] The Fourth Gospel repeatedly stresses that belief in Jesus as the Christ leads to eternal life and failure to receive his sayings leads to spiritual death.[90]

In his meditation on being in him, Jesus told his disciples to look to him as the source of comfort, provision, peace, friendship, truth, joy, love, life, and protection.[91] In this way, by becoming a new person in Christ, one discovers that the need for a right relationship with God is satisfied. The fulfillment of this need, in turn, provides the basis for the fulfillment of the need for restored relationships with others. Those who find identity, purpose, and hope in Christ are secure enough to serve and love others. Jesus' new commandment to his followers to love one another as he loved them makes self-sacrificing love and compassion the essence of the Christian life.[92] When this kind of love is manifested, it produces a unity in the community of believers that bears witness to the world.[93]

The destiny of human beings is to be where Jesus is—in the bosom of the Father. Jesus' high priestly prayer in John 17 expressed his desire that those who believe in him may be in the Father just as Jesus is in the Father and that the unity this relationship produces would so display the Father's life that it would have a missionary dimension to a watching world.

The Book of Acts

As a continuation of the narrative of the Gospel of Luke, Acts provides an account of the transitional period during which the gospel spread from Jerusalem to a substantial portion of the Roman Empire. Like the Gospels, Acts relates the salvific work of Jesus to both physical and spiritual needs.

Physical needs

In his sermon in the Areopagus, Paul argued that the Creator of the world has no needs since he is the source of all life. Since all humans are his offspring, they must look to him for biological and spiritual life.[94]

The apostolic preaching of the gospel of Christ in Acts was often accompanied by signs and wonders, including physical healings of the sick, the lame, and the paralyzed, and liberation from demonic bondage.[95] In the early Christian church, physical needs for nourishment and shelter were being cared for by the community of believers, at first by selling possessions and goods and distribution of the proceeds by the leadership to those who had need, and later by organized collections for the poor and needy.[96]

Spiritual needs

As in the Gospels, the spiritual need for a right relationship with God is given greater significance in Acts than physical concerns, although the latter are not minimized. Thus, the apostles manifested a willingness to suffer physical punishment and death if necessary in order to continue teaching and preaching Jesus as the Christ.[97] The theme of salvation through the person and work of the crucified and resurrected Jesus is the predominant theme in the apostolic kerygma in Acts.[98] Associated with this theme is the need for a response of recognition of Jesus as the Christ and repentance for the forgiveness of sins.[99]

THE PAULINE CORPUS

Preliminary Concerns

Just as there has been a growing awareness in recent years of the relationship between Jesus' preaching concerning the kingdom of God and Jewish literature and sociopolitical concerns, a similar development has taken place with regard to the influence of Jewish thought-forms on the Pauline corpus. The majority view had long been that Paul was opposed to Jewish ideas and influences because of the "legalism" with which they were associated. This view began to be challenged when an increasing understanding of first-century Rabbinic Judaism began to be applied to Pauline studies.[100] Some scholars have swung to the opposite extreme by claiming that Paul had virtually no negative critique of Judaism,[101] but almost all are agreed that the Pauline corpus has been influenced by Palestinian Judaism to a greater extent than had previously been thought. In light of this, it is important to avoid the kind of hermeneutical anachronisms that occur when the original meaning of the text in its first-century context is overlooked. While the epistles have implications that reach far beyond their original settings, the initial occasions and meanings must be taken into account to avoid the problem of reading twentieth-century views into first-century material.[102]

The increased recognition in current scholarship of the ideological impact of the Old Testament and Jewish apocalyptic materials upon Pauline theology does not mean that the latter can be comprehensively reduced to the former. In his Christology, soteriology, and eschatology, Paul frequently alludes to the traditional imagery and concepts of Jewish theology, but these are adapted to serve and illuminate the redemptive work of God in Christ.[103] Paul's encounter with the risen and exalted Jesus on the road to Damascus[104] profoundly shaped his gospel of reconciliation. Kim argues that this revelatory experience, combined with Jewish theology and the Christian kerygma, provided the basic content of Pauline theology.

> [T]he revelation of the crucified Jesus of Nazareth as enthroned at God's right hand proved to Paul that through the cross he has superseded the Torah as the medium of the divine revelation and salvation and therefore that he is the one who had formerly been described as Wisdom. So, the Son of God who was revealed to Paul on the Damascus road is the content of his gospel. . . .[105]

Associated with this revelatory encounter was the commission to carry the name of Jesus "before the Gentiles and kings and the sons of Israel."[106] The message that Jesus is the Christ has significant implications for the relationship between Jewish and Gentile believers that are developed in a number of the Pauline Epistles. Paul sought to expose the error of those Jewish believers in Jesus who failed to see that the new covenant inaugurated since the coming of the Messiah included not only Jews but also Gentiles in a single new community.[107]

There has been a growing recognition among New Testament scholars that this issue is the real context out of which the doctrine of justification by faith emerged in the Epistles of Paul. Since both Jews and Gentiles are justified by the same faith in Christ, the Gentiles are full heirs to God's promises to Israel; in the kingdom of God, the place of Gentile believers is just as secure as that of Jewish believers. This is an important corrective to the centuries-old approach to Pauline interpretation that limits the discussion to how individuals are to be saved and ignores the first-century issues and questions. However, in view of the richness of the thematic development of salvation and the cognate concepts of redemption, propitiation, justification, reconciliation, and sanctification in the New Testament epistles, it would be just as erroneous to attempt to reduce all this material to the single dimension of the Jewish-Gentile relationship in the body of Christ.[108]

The Pauline corpus is the primary source material for gaining an understanding of the nature and constituency of the earliest church.[109] Meeks, Theissen, and Malherbe agree that the congregations to which Paul addressed his epistles "generally reflected a fair cross-section of urban society."[110] The social structure of Hellenistic primitive Christianity encompassed an unusual diversity of strata, interests, and customs. Those who embraced the apostolic kerygma experienced profound social change as they found a new source of identity and a new basis for cohesiveness and fellowship in the Christian community.[111] **The early church was a corporate movement that often transcended socio-economic barriers by according equal membership to Jews and Gentiles, slaves and freemen, males and females.[112] The basis for this equality is their common participation in the body of Christ into which they have all been incorporated by divine grace through faith in Christ and in which they share the same hope.[113]** In spite of this, there has been a tendency, particularly among Protestant biblical interpreters, to minimize this corporate dimension when the discussion turns to the issue of righteousness. The assumption that justification, the establishment of a right relationship between God and men, has its primary referent on the individual level, has been challenged in recent years by scholars who wish to relate righteousness to the larger social and cosmic dimensions.[114] Blame for the excessive emphasis on individualism with respect to salvation has centered on Augustine and Luther because of their application of the Pauline doctrine of justification to the problem of the introspective and penitential conscience.[115] By contrast, Ridderbos relates the transition from the "old" to the "new man" to the history of the redeemed community; "it is a matter here not of a change that comes about in the way of faith and conversion in the life of the individual Christian, but of that which once took place in Christ and in which his people had part in him in the corporate sense. . . ."[116]

While Christian truth is arguably a corporate expression that is distorted when limited to a purely individualistic setting,[117] it would be just as erroneous to restrict the Pauline doctrine of justification to the corporate context. As Yoder acknowledges:

> We are objecting to a particular polemical application of the traditional doctrine, which used it to *exclude* the ethical and social dimensions. By echoing scholars who have rediscovered the missing dimensions we are not denying the personal. We are denying that it can most adequately be spoken about in abstraction from the rest, as certain recent Western traditions have assumed.[118]

The doctrines of justification and sanctification in the epistles were relevant in their initial context both to the needs of individual believers and to the needs of the church as a corporate historical community. Provided that their first-century meanings are not overlooked, they also have a relevance to the varying concerns of later cultural contexts such as the longing for incorruption in the ancient world, the quest for forgiveness and freedom in the Middle Ages, and the search for meaning and purpose in life in the contemporary context.[119]

Physical needs

The Pauline Epistles, unlike the Gospels and Acts, do not record incidents of physical healing, although reference is made in 1 Corinthians to the spiritual gift of healing in the body of Christ.[120] **In the realm of physical concerns, the Epistles emphasize the active role of the community of faith in providing for those who are in need.** This includes the practice of service and hospitality, regular provision for widows, financial support of those who preach and teach, and collections for "the needs of the saints."[121] Citing the example of the churches of Macedonia, Paul encouraged sacrificial giving in the churches for those who needed relief and assured his readers that in doing so they could confidently look to God to provide for their needs.[122] When the Philippian church sent a gift to him when he was in prison, he thanked them for their sacrifice and told them that "God will supply every need of yours according to his riches in glory in Christ Jesus."[123] Paul commended the practice of contentment and thanksgiving to his readers in the wavering circumstances of abundance and abasement.[124]

Spiritual needs

Paul frequently stressed that spiritual concerns, and particularly the progress of the gospel, were of far greater significance to him than physical concerns. He expressed his willingness to suffer hunger and thirst, inadequate clothing and shelter, physical danger and persecution, and social slander and disrepute for the sake of the advancement of the gospel of Christ.[125] The suffering and deprivation he and his colaborers endured did not lead them to despair because they regarded them as a vehicle by which the grace of God would be extended to the lives of others.[126] He perceived the afflictions endured by those who sought to propagate the gospel as momentary and slight in comparison with the "eternal weight of glory beyond all comparison."[127] **In spite of the sensory evidence of the physical world, the unseen spiritual reality anticipated by those whose hope embraces the promise of a new mode of existence in the presence of God is more substantial because it is eternal not transient.** While acknowledging the needs associated with bodily existence, the apostle places a greater stress on the immortality and quality of life that will characterize those who are "at home with the Lord."[128] Paul's assurance of the transformation from humility to glory in the resurrection of the body was a motivating force in his thinking and behavior and caused him to regard temporal attainments as inconsequential in comparison with the possibility of enduring rewards at the judgment seat of Christ.[129] Those who enjoy the "in Christ" relationship have nothing and yet possess everything; they are stewards, not owners of the world's goods, but possess "every spiritual blessing in the heavenly places" and look to God for the provision of their temporal needs.[130] Rather than comparing themselves with others, they are called to contentment even during times when they have nothing more than food and clothing.[131] The desire for material prosperity is inconsistent with the Pauline understanding of the believer's earthly purpose, particularly because no physical possessions can be brought into the next world. Those who are rich in good deeds are the only ones who are laying a good foundation for the future.[132]

The Pauline corpus frequently underscores the problem of the universality of human sin and the consequent condemnation of both Jews and Gentiles before a perfect and holy God. This is the theme of Romans 1:18–3:20 in which moral and religious Jews are depicted as being in the same bondage to sin as Gentiles who do not have the law. The law brings the knowledge of sin but does not enable one to overcome it and actually underscores the futility of human works in the achievement of a state of righteousness before God.[133] Apart from the grace of God, people are spiritually dead through the trespasses and sins in which they walk, and are by nature children of wrath.[134] In their natural state, they are not only helpless to do that which is pleasing to God but manifest an estrangement and hostility of mind and are at enmity with God; in consequence, they are separated from Christ, "having no hope and without God in the world."[135] **Hence, the greatest human need from a Pauline perspective is to overcome this state of alienation and spiritual death or separation from God. But his epistles stress that this need cannot be met through human efforts, even if one is religious and zealous to accomplish good works. The dilemma is that people fall short of the character of God in thought, word, and deed and are thus incapable of putting themselves back into a right relationship with God. At the same time, God cannot accept that which is contrary to his character, and this raises the problem of how a righteous God can accept sinners. Paul's answer is the doctrine of justification by faith, and it is most explicitly developed in Romans 3:21–5:21.** God manifested his righteousness apart from the law in the person and work of Jesus Christ and offers the righteousness of Christ to all who receive this gift of grace.[136] It is through divine rather than human initiative that the means of reconciliation, propitiation, and redemption has been provided.[137] Those who have been reconciled to God in Christ are part of the new creation and fellow heirs with Christ in anticipation of the time when the whole creation will be "set free from its bondage to decay and obtain the glorious liberty of the children of God."[138]

In his book *Paul and Palestinian Judaism,* Sanders takes issue with Bultmann, Conzelmann, and Bornkamm by arguing that Paul's thought in passages like Romans 7 and Philippians 3 "did not run from plight to solution, but rather from solution to plight."[139] The conclusion that Jews and Gentiles are all in need of a Savior is not derived from a prior awareness of this need but from the conviction that such a Savior had actually been sent by God. Having embraced this conviction, Paul then deduced the inadequacy of all other approaches to salvation. According to Sanders, then, Paul's anthropology is the byproduct of his Christology and soteriology and not the other way around. The Pauline message is not descriptive of man but prescriptive in that it is intended to elicit the response of faith among those to whom Christ is preached.[140]

Sanders is correct in saying that in Pauline thought, theology is more determinative of the fullness of human need than anthropology, but it would be going too far to contend that apart from a conviction concerning the divine solution, there could be no awareness of the human plight. In Romans 1:18–23, Paul argues that because of external revelation in nature and internal revelation in the human heart, the world is not characterized by ignorance of the true God, but rather by suppression of this truth in unrighteousness. Nor, according to Romans 2:12–16, are people ignorant of the problem of sin because their God-given conscience bears witness to their inability to live in conformity with their own standards, let alone God's.[141] The problem, however, is the human tendency to disavow or suppress this knowledge and the consequent delusion that one can attain a quality of life that is acceptable before God solely through human merit. Paul repeatedly repudiates this perception in his epistles and stresses the universal need for the grace of God and the futility apart from this grace of overcoming the state of spiritual alienation caused by rebellion against the divine will. Justification before God cannot be achieved by performance or effort but through faith in Jesus Christ, and Paul's gospel calls all people—Jews and Gentiles—to transfer their hope and trust from their own works to the work of Christ.[142] It is in this way that one enters into the benefits of the new covenant inaugurated by Christ and participates in the life of the Spirit with the people of God.[143]

The Epistles of Paul employ both juridical and participatory statements to develop the theme of righteousness by faith. The human condition without Christ is described in terms of trangression of the ordinances of God and enslavement to the power of sin. Those who are in the flesh cannot please God since they are under sin and condemned by the law of God.[144] Hence there is the need for a transfer from one lordship to another: from transgression to expiation, and from dominion to freedom.[145] Those who have been reconciled to God in Christ have entered into a new relationship characterized by peace rather than emnity with God and enjoy the benefits of a new position of holiness and blamelessness by virtue of the life of

Christ within them.[146] Their calling is now to manifest in their practice the new identity they have found in Christ, and this is the ongoing process of sanctification, or growth in the Spirit.[147] All who have participated in the benefits of Christ's death and resurrection have been delivered from the old aeon and have become ambassadors of the age to come whose mandate is to extend the invisible geography of the new creation.[148] Thus, for Paul, justification from the penalty of sin and deliverance from the power of sin are eschatological realities that presently manifest the powers of the age to come.[149]

In Pauline thought, the gospel fulfills not only the need for reconciliation but also the need for a hope that transcends the finite boundaries of this world. The believer's hope is fixed on an "eternal weight of glory" that is not worthy of comparison with the "slight momentary affliction" endured in the temporal state.[150] God has given "eternal comfort and good hope through grace" to those who have put their faith in "Christ Jesus our hope."[151] As they anticipate the second advent, their hope is in the character of God and the realization of his promises.[152] Their identity and hope in Christ satisfy the need for security that cannot be met in earthbound circumstances and relationships. This is the theme of Romans 8:19–39; the intercessory work of the Spirit and the Son assures believers that nothing in heaven or earth will be able to separate them from the love of God. This hope and security extend to the redemption of the whole person: body, soul, and spirit.[153] Paul's expectation of the resurrection from the dead was an essential motivator that governed his life and ministry. The resurrection of Christ is the foundation for his hope in the resurrection of the dead and of the faithful who are alive at the *parousia,* and he uses this anticipation of triumph over mortality as a source of assurance and comfort to the Corinthians and Thessalonians.[154]

The Pauline corpus consistently encourages the cultivation of an eternal rather than a temporal perspective as well as an awareness of human accountability before God. Since there is "no condemnation for those who are in Christ Jesus,"[155] this is not prompted by a fear of punishment but by the desire for rewards. For Paul, this desire is a legitimate component of the believer's motivational structure.[156]

One of the most prominent themes in the Epistles of Paul is the need for spiritual growth and nurture. "For this is the will of God, your sanctification."[157] He frequently exhorts his readers to pursue those things that will lead to their sanctification, including setting their minds on the Spirit and on the things above, walking and living by the Spirit, being transformed by renewing their minds, clothing themselves with Christ, growing into maturity, cleansing themselves from defilement, acting in accordance with the new nature, putting on the whole armor of God, increasing in love, living by faith in Christ, putting to death the lusts of the old nature, and living in a way that is pleasing to God.[158] **"The way to maturity for the people of God does not lie in their becoming Jews but rather in their drawing out and applying to personal and communal life the meaning of the death and resurrection of Jesus Christ."[159] The process of growth in spiritual maturity is the path to the restoration of the image of the Creator. This restoration is made possible not by human**

attainment but through the adequacy that comes from God.[160] The people of God have been given every resource necessary for their growth into conformity with the character of Christ through the expression of their new identity in him in their attitudes, actions, and relationships.[161] This extends to a willingness to minister to the needs of others in the spiritual community. Paul uses the metaphors of a family and a body to communicate the dynamic of interdependence and mutual edification in the development of mature communities as well as mature individuals. He exhorts those who are in Christ to live in unity and to love one another, forgive one another, encourage one another, be kind to one another, do good to one another, build up one another, serve one another, look to the interests of one another, bear the burdens of one another, pray for one another, and live in peace with one another.[162]

THE GENERAL EPISTLES, HEBREWS, AND REVELATION

Like the Pauline corpus, the General Epistles are far more concerned with spiritual rather than with physical needs. James, for instance, stresses the importance of viewing human existence from an eternal rather than a temporal perspective. "Let the lowly brother boast in his exaltation, and the rich in his humiliation, because like the flower of the grass he will pass away."[163] The quotation from Isaiah 40:6–9 in 1 Peter 1:24–25 illustrates the same perspective: "All flesh is like grass and all its glory like the flower of grass. The grass withers, and the flower falls, but the word of the Lord abides for ever." The Epistle to the Hebrews likewise reminds the readers of their willingness to endure abuse, affliction, and the plundering of their property because they knew they "had a better possession and an abiding one."[164] Thus, those who suffer for the name of Christ can rejoice not only insofar as they share his sufferings but also because they can anticipate the glory that is to be revealed.[165] Peter instructs his readers to cast their worldly anxieties on God because he will care for their needs and exalt his people at the proper time.[166] The deepest needs are spiritual, not material, because they pertain to that which will endure.

Each person will give an account to God who is ready to judge the living and the dead, and in view of this judgment, there is a universal need for cleansing from the defilement of sin that renders all guilty before God.[167] The General Epistles affirm that this is the purpose for which Christ came.[168] Hebrews teaches that Christ, whose once-for-all sacrifice provided the redemption that could not be obtained through the sacrificial system of the Mosaic covenant, is the mediator of a new and better covenant. Since his is an enduring priesthood, he continually delivers and intercedes for those who draw near to God through him.[169] Through his perfect sacrifice for the sins of his people, he became the source of salvation to all who obey him and purifies their conscience from dead works so that they can die to sin and live to righteousness.[170] **Those who have become children of God through faith in Christ have a new source of identity in the one who partook of their nature, bore their sorrows, and understands their weaknesses and temptations.**[171] **Such a high priest and mediator is fully** capable of providing the mercy and grace to satisfy every human need. He has called his people out of darkness into light, made them a chosen race and a royal people, loved them unconditionally as his children, made them overcomers of the world, and given them assurance of new and unending life in Christ.[172]

This new identity in Christ provides a source of security and significance that transcends earthly felicity; God "is able to keep you from falling and to present you without blemish before the presence of his glory with rejoicing."[173] These epistles teach that a relationship with Christ satisfies the human need for purpose and hope, because the Christian's inheritance in him will endure forever.[174] When this hope is fixed on the character and promises of God, it provides a source of stability, refuge, and encouragement during times of adversity and uncertainty. It is a "sure and steadfast anchor of the soul" and a source of assurance that believers will inherit the divine promises.[175] Those who have seized this living hope are purified by it and motivated to pursue lives of holiness and godliness as they wait for the promises to be fulfilled at the *parousia*.[176] These promises are associated with the imagery of rewards for those who seek God, and those who are motivated to pursue the promises and rewards of God are willing to take the risks of faith and undergo temporal loss for eternal gain.[177] In the beatific vision, there will no longer be hunger, thirst, pain, or death, for "God will wipe away every tear from their eyes."[178]

This transcendent hope is used by the writers of the General Epistles to stimulate a willingness among the readers to pursue lives that are expressive of spiritual maturity and Christlike character.[179] These epistles frequently stress holiness of conduct and growth in the truth,[180] and this is the foundation upon which ministering to the needs of others is based. Faith in Christ is best expressed in acts of love, service, encouragement, sacrificial giving, and hospitality to others.[181]

CONCLUSIONS

The Need for Forgiveness and Grace

The New Testament portrait of human nature recognizes and incorporates the twin pulls of the material and the transcendent. **On the one hand, people are compared to "a mist that appears for a little time and then vanishes."[182] In this respect, they resemble the lower animals and share the same physical needs. On the other hand, humans are reflexive moral agents and spiritual beings who have been made in the likeness of God.[183] Thus, they are both continuous and discontinuous with the rest of creation, and there is an ongoing tension between these two states.[184]** The New Testament repudiates the opposite extremes of self-degradation and arrogance.[185] The former is inconsistent with its teaching that men and women have been called into a covenant relationship with God and have true dignity and purpose because of the image of Christ after which they are recreated and the destiny offered them. The latter overlooks their creaturely finitude and the tragedy of the moral distortion engendered by rebellion against the divine will. The peaceful ordering of the original creation has been broken, and the greatest human need is the restoration of this *shalom* with the Creator. But peace with God cannot be attained by human initiative; it can only be accomplished through the forgiveness and grace offered in the redemptive work of Christ. "Therefore, since we are justified by faith, we have peace with God through our Lord Jesus Christ. Through him we have obtained access to this grace in which we stand, and we rejoice in our hope of sharing the glory of God."[186] In their fallenness, humans are bent away from their Creator, and this spiritual alienation is manifested in intrapersonal and interpersonal alienation as well as estrangement from the natural order. These consequences could only be reversed by the grace and healing that proceeds from God. "In this is love, not that we loved God but that he loved us and sent his Son to be the expiation for our sins. Beloved, if God so loved us, we also ought to love one another."[187] **Apart from divine grace, the resources of human nature would be incapable of overcoming the infinite abyss separating people from the attainment of beatitude in possessing God as the object of perfect happiness.[188] In breaking the spell of the fall, Jesus opened the way to a restored relationship with God, whereby people are no longer slaves to the dehumanization of sin but children of God and fellow heirs with Christ.**

The Need for Love and Community

Ephesians 2:12 describes the plight of those who are without Christ in terms of relational alienation; they are "strangers to the covenants of promise, having no hope and without God in the world." The New Testament solution to the human dilemma is not a quest for self-fulfillment, since this would in fact exacerbate the problem by encouraging the individual to disregard others or manipulate them by using them as a means to their end of attaining self-fulfillment. **Instead, the writers of the New Testament stress the need for the realization of the love and community that reflects the divine attribute of a harmonious unity whose inmost being is the activity of loving relationships.[189] Since God is a relational being, the restoration of his image in fallen humanity through the redemptive work of Christ is manifested not only in the healing of the vertical relationship between God and sinners, but also in the dynamic of loving and being loved in the horizontal relationships of people in communion.[190]** Thus, the encounter with Christ is not a matter of ego-enhancement, but of deriving a new basis for identity that gives one such a foundation for security, purpose, and hope that one is enabled to love and serve others unconditionally.[191] The enjoyment of a loving relationship with God produces right relationships with others, since human love at its best and most profound is a reflection of divine love. "It is by becoming a person, one who can respond to God and to his fellow men, that we rediscover our unity within the human race."[192] The New Testament doctrine of the Trinity provides the foundation for personhood in created beings, and this personhood is expressed in relationships.[193] Macmurray observes that "[i]t is only in relation to others that we exist as persons; we are invested with significance by others who have need of us; and borrow our reality from those who care for us. We live and move and have our being not in ourselves but in one another. . . ."[194] In the Gospels and Epistles, wholeness is portrayed in terms of the restoration of relationships with God and others that liberates the person from individualism and egocentricity. The new identity in Christ is expressed within a context of community and fellowship united by a common source of life, a common purpose, and a common hope.[195] The realization of the self is not found as an end in itself, but as the byproduct of the pursuit of a right relationship with God and others. "For whoever would save his life will lose it, and whoever loses his life for my sake will find it."[196] Life is found not in ego-enhancement, but in receiving Christ's life and expressing it in concern for the needs of others.[197]

The Need for Purpose and Hope

Paul argues in 1 Corinthians 15 that the resurrection of Jesus Christ is the foundation for the Christian hope of redemption and resurrection. If the dead are not raised, earthly existence would have no ultimate meaning; "If in this life we who are in Christ have only hope, we are of all men most to be pitied. . . . Let us eat and drink, for tomorrow we die."[198] It is because of their identification with Christ in his death and resurrection that believers participate in a transcendent hope and are already a part of the new order of creation.[199] Their life is "hid with Christ in God," and this life is Christ himself.[200] This is what Paul calls "the riches of the glory of this mystery, which is Christ in you, the hope of glory."[201] The New Testament portrays Christ not only as the foundation but also as the actual fulfillment of the Christian's hope. Even now the believer rejoices in hope of sharing his glory while anticipating all that will be associated with his second advent. This "now" but "not yet" of hoping in that which is not seen is "entirely superior to and distinct from the failing strength of man's natural hope."[202] It eclipses the travail, disappointments, and uncertainties of earthly existence and overcomes the futility, injustice, and despair of life rooted only in the soil of the temporal. As Kemp observes:

> Man's need and hope is for a living sense of partnership with the Eternal, that the Eternal should wear a human face and admit man into his friendship here and now; and that from this partnership man should derive a positive value which crowds out the futility felt by him in his isolation, replacing it with deep and abiding satisfaction.[203]

The essence of beatitude in the New Testament is the possession of the vision of God in an enduring relationship with the Creator and Redeemer.[204]

SELECTED BIBLIOGRAPHY

Adams, James Luther. *Paul Tillich's Philosophy of Culture, Science, and Religion.* New York: Harper & Row, 1965.

Adams, James Luther, Wilhelm Pauck, and Roger Lincoln Shinn, eds. *The Thought of Paul Tillich.* San Francisco: Harper & Row, 1985.

Adler, Alfred. *The Individual Psychology of Alfred Adler.* Edited by Heinz L. Ansbacher and Rowena R. Ansbacher. New York: Basic Books, 1956; Harper Torchbooks, 1964.

_____. *Understanding Human Nature.* Translated by W. Béran Wolfe. Greenwich, Conn.: Fawcett Publications, 1927, 1954.

_____. *What Life Should Mean to You.* Translated by Alan Porter. New York: Perigree Books, 1958.

Aldridge, Alfred Owen. *Jonathan Edwards.* New York: Washington Square Press, 1964.

Allen, Diogenes. "Motives, Rationales, and Religious Beliefs." *American Philosophical Quarterly* 3 (1966).

_____. *The Reasonableness of Faith.* Washington: Corpus Books, 1968.

Allport, Gordon W. *The Individual and His Religion.* New York: Macmillan Company, 1950.

_____. *The Person in Psychology.* Boston: Beacon Press, 1968.

Angyal, Andras. *Foundations for a Science of Personality.* New York: Commonwealth Fund, 1941.

_____. *Neurosis and Treatment.* New York: John Wiley & Sons, 1965.

Aquinas, Thomas. *Summa Contra Gentiles.* Translated by Vernon J. Bourke. Notre Dame, Ind.: University of Notre Dame Press, 1975.

_____. *Summa Theologica.* Translated by Fathers of the English Dominican Province. London: Burns & Oates, 1947–48.

Arbaugh, George E., and George B. Arbaugh. *Kierkegaard's Authorship.* London: George Allen & Unwin Ltd., 1968.

Argyle, Michael, and Benjamin Beit-Hallahmi. *The Social Psychology of Religion.* London: Routledge & Kegan Paul, 1975.

Audi, Robert, and William J. Wainwright, eds. *Rationality, Religious Belief, and Moral Commitment.* Ithaca, N.Y.: Cornell University Press, 1986.

Augustine. *Confessions.* Translated by R. S. Pine-Coffin. Harmondsworth, Middlesex: Penguin Books, 1961.

_____. *The City of God.* Edited by Vernon J. Bourke. Translated by Gerald G. Walsh, Demetrius B. Zema, Grace Monahan, and Daniel J. Honan. Garden City, New York: Image Books, 1958.

Banks, Robert. *Paul's Idea of Community.* Grand Rapids: William B. Eerdmans Publishing Company, 1980.

Barbour, Ian. *Myths, Models and Paradigms.* London: SCM Press, 1974.

Battenhouse, Roy W., ed. *A Companion to the Study of St. Augustine.* New York: Oxford University Press, 1955.

Becker, Ernest. *Escape from Evil.* New York: Free Press, 1975.

_____. *The Birth and Death of Meaning.* London: Collier Macmillan Publishers, 1971.

_____. *The Denial of Death.* New York: The Free Press, 1973.

Berger, Peter L. *A Rumor of Angels.* Garden City, N.Y.: Doubleday & Company, 1969.

_____. *The Sacred Canopy.* Garden City, N.Y.: Anchor Books, 1967.

Bergin, Allen E. "Psychotherapy and Religious Values." *Journal of Consulting and Clinical Psychology* 48 (1980).

Bernard of Clairvaux. *The Love of God.* Edited by James M. Houston. Portland, Ore.: Multnomah Press, 1983.

Bobgan, Martin, and Deidre Bobgan. *The Psychological Way/The Spiritual Way.* Minneapolis: Bethany Fellowship, 1979.

Bonner, Gerald. *God's Decree and Man's Destiny.* London: Variorum Reprints, 1987.

Borg, Marcus J. *Conflict, Holiness and Politics in the Teachings of Jesus.* New York: Edwin Mellen Press, 1984.

Brome, Vincent. *Jung.* New York: Atheneum, 1978.

Bronowski, Jacob. *Science and Human Values.* New York: Harper & Row, 1956.

Brown, David. *The Divine Trinity.* London: Duckworth, 1985.

Brown, Hanbury. *The Wisdom of Science.* Cambridge: Cambridge University Press, 1986.

Brown, Norman O. *Life Against Death: The Psychoanalytical Meaning of History.* New York: Viking Books, 1959.

Browning, Don S. *Religious Thought and the Modern Psychologies.* Philadelphia: Fortress Press, 1987.

Budd, Susan. *Sociologists and Religion.* London: Collier Macmillan Publishers, 1973.

Bugental, James F. T. *Challenges of Humanistic Psychology.* New York: McGraw-Hill Book Company, 1967.

Burke, Thomas J., ed. *Man and Mind: A Christian Theory of Personality.* Hillsdale, Mich.: Hillsdale College Press, 1987.

Burleigh, John H. S. *Augustine: Earlier Writings.* Philadelphia: Westminster Press, 1953.

Burnaby, John. *Amor Dei.* London: Hodder & Stoughton, 1938.

Burrell, David B. *Aquinas: God and Action.* Notre Dame, Ind.: University of Notre Dame Press, 1979.

Burston, Daniel. *The Legacy of Erich Fromm.* Cambridge, Mass.: Harvard University Press, 1991.

Carnell, Edward John. *The Burden of Søren Kierkegaard.* Exeter, Devon: Paternoster Press, 1965.

Capps, Donald, and James E. Dittes, eds. *The Hunger of the Heart: Reflections on the "Confessions" of Augustine.* West Lafayette, Ind.: Society for the Scientific Study of Religion, 1990.

Chenu, M.-D. *Nature, Man, and Society in the Twelfth Century.* Translated by Jerome Taylor and Lester K. Little. Chicago: University of Chicago Press, 1968.

Cherry, Conrad. *The Theology of Jonathan Edwards: A Reappraisal.* Garden City, N.Y.: Anchor Books, 1966.

Clark, Ralph W. "The Evidential Value of Religious Experiences." *International Journal for Philosophy of Religion* 16 (1984).

Clark, Walter Houston. *The Psychology of Religion.* New York: Macmillan Company, 1958.

Clayton, John Powell. *The Concept of Correlation: Paul Tillich and the Possibility of a Mediating Theology.* Berlin: Walter de Gruyter, 1980.

Coan, Richard W. *Hero, Artist, Sage, or Saint?* New York: Columbia University Press, 1977.

Cole, John. "Holy Trinity a Light amidst Darkness." *The Times,* 5 May 1988.

Collins, James. *The Mind of Kierkegaard.* Princeton, New Jersey: Princeton University Press, 1983.

Cooper, John C. "The Basic Philosophical and Theological Notions of St. Augustine." *Augustinian Studies* 15 (1984).

Copleston, Frederick. *A History of Philosophy.* 6 vols. Westminster, Md.: Newman Press, 1960.

Cosgrove, Mark P. *Psychology Gone Awry.* Leicester: Inter-Varsity Press, 1979.

Cox, David. *Jung and Saint Paul.* New York: Association Press, 1959.

Crabb, Lawrence J., Jr. *Basic Principles of Biblical Counseling.* Grand Rapids: Zondervan Publishing House, 1975.

_____. *Effective Biblical Counseling.* Grand Rapids: Zondervan Publishing House, 1977.

Cupitt, Don. *The Worlds of Science and Religion.* London: Sheldon Press, 1976.

D'Arcy, M. C. *The Mind and Heart of Love.* New York: Henry Holt and Company, 1947.

_____. *Thomas Aquinas.* London: Ernest Benn Limited, 1930.

Dawkins, Richard. *The Blind Watchmaker.* Harlow, Essex: Longman Scientific & Technical, 1986.

_____. *The Selfish Gene.* Oxford: Oxford University Press, 1976.

Delattre, Roland André. *Beauty and Sensibility in the Thought of Jonathan Edwards.* New Haven, Connecticut: Yale University Press, 1968.

De Prospo, R. C. *Theism in the Discourse of Jonathan Edwards.* Cranbury, N.J.: Associated University Presses, Inc., 1985.

De Wulf, Maurice. *The System of Thomas Aquinas.* New York: Dover Publications, Inc., 1959.

Deane, Herbert A. *The Political and Social Ideas of St. Augustine.* New York: Columbia University Press, 1963.

Dodds, Michael J. *The Unchanging God of Love.* Fribourg, Switzerland: Éditions Universitaires, 1986.

Edwards, David L. *A Reason to Hope.* London: Collins, 1978.

Edwards, Jonathan. *A Treatise on Religious Affections.* Grand Rapids: Baker Book House, 1982.

_____. *Freedom of the Will.* Edited by Paul Ramsey. New Haven, Conn.: Yale University Press, 1957.

_____. *The Works of Jonathan Edwards.* 2 vols. Edinburgh: Banner of Truth Trust, 1974.

Eliade, Mircea. *Myths, Dreams, and Mysteries.* Translated by Philip Mairet. New York: Harper & Row, 1960.

_____, ed. *The Encyclopedia of Religion.* 16 vols. New York: Macmillan Publishing Company, 1987.

Ellenberger, Henri F. *The Discovery of the Unconscious.* New York: Basic Books, Inc., 1970.

Elwood, Douglas J. *The Philosophical Theology of Jonathan Edwards.* New York: Columbia University Press, 1960.

Emmanuel, Steven M. "Kierkegaard on Doctrine: A Post-Modern Interpretation." *Religious Studies* 25.

Erikson, Erik H. *Childhood and Society.* 2nd ed. New York: W. W. Norton & Company, 1963.

_____. *Gandhi's Truth: On the Origins of Militant Non-violence.* New York: W. W. Norton & Company, 1969.

_____. *Identity and the Life Cycle.* New York: W. W. Norton & Company, 1959.

_____. *Identity: Youth and Crisis.* New York: W. W. Norton & Company, 1968.

_____. *Insight and Responsibility.* New York: W. W. Norton & Company, 1964.

_____. *Toys and Reasons.* New York: W. W. Norton & Company, 1977.

Evans, C. Stephen. "Is Kierkegaard an Irrationalist? Reason, Paradox, and Faith." *Religious Studies* 25.

_____. *Philosophy of Religion: Thinking about Faith.* Downers Grove, Ill.: InterVarsity Press, 1985.

_____. *Preserving the Person.* Downers Grove, Ill.: InterVarsity Press, 1977.

_____. *Subjectivity and Religious Belief.* Washington: University Press of America, 1982.

Ferenczi, S., and Otto Rank. *The Development of Psycho-Analysis.* Translated by Caroline Newton. Madison, Connecticut: International Universities Press, 1986.

Fiering, Norman. *Jonathan Edwards's Moral Thought and Its British Context.* Chapel Hill, N.C.: University of North Carolina Press, 1981.

Figgis, John Neville. *The Political Aspects of S. Augustine's "City of God."* London: Longmans, Green, and Company, 1921.

Forsyth, James. *Freud, Jung, and Christianity.* Ottawa: University of Ottawa Press, 1989.

Fowler, James W. *Stages of Faith and Religious Development: Implications for Church, Education, and Society.* New York: Crossroad, 1991.

_____. *Stages of Faith: The Psychology of Human Development and the Quest for Meaning.* New York: Harper & Row, 1981.

Frankl, Viktor E. "Address before the Third Annual Meeting of the Academy of Religion and Mental Health, 1962." In *Discovering Man in Psychology: A Humanistic Approach.* Edited by Frank T. Severin. New York: McGraw-Hill Book Company, 1973.

Freud, Sigmund. *Psychoanalysis and Faith: Dialogues with the Reverend Oskar Pfister.* New York: Basic Books, 1963.

_____. *The Essentials of Psycho-Analysis.* Edited by Anna Freud. Translated by James Strachey. Harmondsworth, Middlesex: Penguin Books, 1986.

_____. *The Pelican Freud Library.* 15 vols. Angela Richards and Albert Dickson, gen. eds. Translated and edited by James Strachey. Harmondsworth, Middlesex: Penguin Books, 1973–86.

Fromm, Erich. *Man for Himself.* London: Ark Paperbacks, 1986.

_____. *Psychoanalysis and Religion.* London: Victor Gollancz, 1951.

_____. *The Anatomy of Human Destructiveness.* New York: Holt, Rinehart and Winston, 1973.

_____. *The Art of Loving.* London: Unwin Books, 1962.

_____. *The Crisis of Psychoanalysis.* New York: Holt, Rinehart and Winston, 1970.

_____. *The Dogma of Christ.* London: Routledge & Kegan Paul, 1963.

_____. *The Fear of Freedom.* London: Ark Paperbacks, 1984.

_____. *The Heart of Man.* London: Routledge & Kegan Paul, 1964.

_____. *The Sane Society.* London: Routledge & Kegan Paul, 1956.

_____. *To Have or to Be?* London: Abacus Classic Library, 1979.

Funk, Rainer. *Erich Fromm: The Courage to Be Human.* New York: Continuum Publishing Company, 1982.

Geisler, Norman. *Christian Apologetics.* Grand Rapids: Baker Book House, 1976.

Gill, Jerry H. *Faith in Dialogue.* Waco, Tex.: Jarrell (Word Books), 1985.

Gilson, Etienne. *The Christian Philosophy of St. Thomas Aquinas.* Translated by L. K. Shook. London: Victor Gollancz Ltd., 1957.

Glen, J. Stanley. *Erich Fromm: A Protestant Critique.* Philadelphia: Westminster Press, 1966.

Glover, Jonathan. *What Sort of People Should There Be?* Oxford: Oxford University Press, 1984.

Goldstein, Kurt. *Human Nature in the Light of Psychopathology.* Cambridge, Mass.: Harvard University Press, 1947.

González, Justo L. *A History of Christian Thought.* rev. ed. Nashville: Abingdon Press, 1971.

Grabmann, Martin. *Thomas Aquinas.* Translated by Virgil Michel. New York: Longmans, Green and Co., 1928.

Grant, W. Harold, Magdala Thompson, and Thomas E. Clarke. *From Image to Likeness.* New York: Paulist Press, 1983.

Greenberg, Jay R., and Stephen A. Mitchell. *Object Relations in Psychoanalytic Theory.* Cambridge, Mass.: Harvard University Press, 1983.

Grenz, Stanley J., and Roger E. Olson. *20th Century Theology.* Downers Grove, Ill.: InterVarsity Press, 1992.

Gross, Martin L. *The Psychological Society.* New York: Random House, 1978.

Guiness, Os. *The Gravedigger File.* Downers Grove, Ill.: InterVarsity Press, 1983.

Gutting, Gary. *Religious Belief and Religious Skepticism.* Notre Dame, Ind.: University of Notre Dame Press, 1982.

Hägglund, Bengt. *History of Theology.* Translated by Gene J. Lund. St. Louis: Concordia Publishing House, 1968.

Hall, Calvin S., and Gardner Lindzey. *Introduction to Theories of Personality.* New York: John Wiley & Sons, 1985.

_____. *Theories of Personality.* 3rd ed. New York: John Wiley & Sons, 1978.

Hall, M. H. "A Conversation with Abraham H. Maslow." *Psychology Today,* July 1968.

Hankey, W. J. *God in Himself: Aquinas' Doctrine of God as Expounded in the "Summa Theologiae."* Oxford: Oxford University Press, 1987.

Hannay, Alastair. *Kierkegaard.* London: Routledge & Kegan Paul, 1982.

Hauerwas, Stanley. *A Community of Character: Toward a Constructive Christian Social Ethic.* Notre Dame, Ind.: University of Notre Dame Press, 1981.

Hausdorff, Don. *Erich Fromm.* New York: Twayne Publishers, 1972.

Helm, Paul. *The Varieties of Belief.* London: George Allen and Unwin, 1973.

Heron, Alasdair I. C. *A Century of Protestant Theology.* Philadelphia: Westminster Press, 1980.

Hick, John, ed. *The Existence of God.* New York: Macmillan Company, 1964.

Hoitenga, Dewey J., Jr. *Faith and Reason from Plato to Plantinga.* New York: State University of New York Press, 1991.

Holmes, Arthur F. *Contours of a World View.* Grand Rapids: William B. Eerdmans Publishing Company, 1983.

_____. *Faith Seeks Understanding.* Grand Rapids: William B. Eerdmans Publishing Company, 1971.

Holyer, Robert. "Human Needs and the Justification of Religious Belief." *International Journal for Philosophy of Religion* 17 (1985).

Homans, Peter, ed. *Childhood and Selfhood.* Cranbury, N.J.: Associated University Presses, Inc., 1978.

_____, ed. *The Dialogue between Psychology and Theology.* Chicago: University of Chicago Press, 1968.

_____. *Jung in Context.* Chicago: University of Chicago Press, 1979.

_____. *Theology after Freud.* Indianapolis: Bobbs-Merrill Company, Inc., 1970.

Hopper, Jeffery. *Understanding Modern Theology.* Philadelphia: Fortress Press, 1987.

Horton, Michael Scott, ed. *Power Religion.* Chicago: Moody Press, 1992.

Hostie, Raymond. *Religion and the Psychology of C. G. Jung.* New York: Sheed and Ward, 1957.

Hudson, W. D., ed. *The Is-Ought Question.* London: Macmillan, 1969.

Hughes, Phillip Edgcumbe, ed. *Creative Minds in Contemporary Theology.* Grand Rapids: William B. Eerdmans Publishing Company, 1966.

Hughes, Sister Eileen Dolores. "The Christian Perspective on Individuation: Psychological and Spiritual Helps for the Journey to Wholeness." *The Journal of Pastoral Counseling* 22 (1987).

Imhof, Paul, and Hubert Biallowons, eds. *Karl Rahner in Dialogue.* Translated by Harvey D. Egan. New York: Crossroad Publishing Company, 1986.

Jeeves, Malcolm A., ed. *Behavioural Sciences: A Christian Perspetive.* Leicester: Inter-Varsity Press, 1984.

_____. *Psychology and Christianity.* Downers Grove, Ill.: InterVarsity Press, 1976.

Jenson, Robert W. *America's Theologian.* New York: Oxford University Press, 1988.

Johnson, Howard, and Niels Thulstrup, eds. *A Kierkegaard Critique.* New York: Harper & Brothers, 1962.

Johnson, Maxwell E. "The Place of Sacraments in the Theology of Paul Tillich." *Worship* 63 (1989).

Johnson, William. *The Search for Transcendence.* New York: Harper & Row, 1974.

Jolivet, Regis. *Introduction to Kierkegaard.* Translated by W. H. Barber. London: Frederick Muller Ltd., 1950.

Jones, Stanton L., and Richard E. Butman. *Modern Psychotherapies.* Downers Grove, Ill.: InterVarsity Press, 1991.

Jung, C. G. *Answer to Job.* Translated by R. F. C. Hull. London: Ark Paperbacks, 1954, 1984.

_____. *Memories, Dreams, Reflections.* Edited by Aniela Jaffé. Translated by Richard and Clara Winston. rev. ed. New York: Vintage Books, 1963.

_____. *Modern Man in Search of a Soul.* London: Routledge & Kegan Paul, 1933; Ark Paperbacks, 1984.

_____. *Psychological Reflections: An Anthology of His Writings 1905–1961.* Edited by Jolande Jacobi. London: Routledge & Kegan Paul, 1971; Ark Paperbacks, 1986.

_____. *The Collected Works of C. G. Jung.* 20 vols. William McGuire, ed. London: Routledge & Kegan Paul, 1969.

_____. *The Undiscovered Self.* Translated by R. F. C. Hull. New York: Mentor Books, 1958.

_____, et. al. *Man and His Symbols.* Garden City, New York: Doubleday & Company, 1964.

Kegley, Charles W. *The Theology of Paul Tillich.* New York: Pilgrim Press, 1982.

Kellenberger, J. "Three Models of Faith." *International Journal for Philosophy of Religion* 12 (1981).

Kelsey, Morton T. *Christo-Psychology.* London: Darton, Longman & Todd, 1982.

Kemp, E. W., ed. *Man: Fallen and Free.* Hodder & Stoughton, 1969.

Kendler, Howard H. *Historical Foundations of Modern Psychology.* Philadelphia: Temple University Press, 1987.

Kierkegaard, Søren. *Attack upon "Christendom."* Translated by Walter Lowrie. Princeton, N.J.: Princeton University Press, 1944, 1968.

_____. *Christian Discourses.* Translated by Walter Lowrie. Princeton, N.J.: Princeton University Press, 1940.

_____. *Concluding Unscientific Postscript.* Translated by David F. Swenson and Walter Lowrie. Princeton, N.J.: Princeton University Press, 1941.

_____. *Crisis in the Life of an Actress.* Translated by Stephen Crites. London: Collins, 1967.

_____. *Edifying Discourses.* Edited by Paul L. Holmer. Translated by David F. and Lillian Marvin Swenson. N.Y.: Harper Torchbooks, 1958.

_____. *Either/Or.* 2 vols. Translated by David F. Swenson, Lillian Marvin Swenson, and Walter Lowrie. Princeton, N.J.: Princeton University Press, 1944, 1959.

_____. *Fear and Trembling.* Translated by Howard V. Hong and Edna H. Hong. Princeton, N.J.: Princeton University Press, 1983.

_____. *For Self-Examination.* Translated by Walter Lowrie. London: Oxford University Press, 1941.

_____. *Johannes Climacus or De omnibus dubitandum est.* Translated by T. H. Croxall. London: Adam & Charles Black, 1958.

_____. *Judge for Yourselves!* Translated by Walter Lowrie. London: Oxford University Press, 1941.

_____. *Philosophical Fragments.* Translated by David F. Swenson and Howard V. Hong. Princeton, N.J.: Princeton University Press, 1936, 1962.

_____. *Purity of Heart Is to Will One Thing.* Translated by Douglas V. Steere. New York: Harper Torchbooks, 1958.

_____. *Repetition.* Translated by Howard V. Hong and Edna H. Hong. Princeton, New Jersey: Princeton University Press, 1983.

_____. *Søren Kierkegaard's Journals and Papers.* 7 vols. Edited and translated by Howard V. Hong and Edna H. Hong. Bloomington, Ind.: Indiana University Press, 1978.

_____. *Stages on Life's Way.* Translated by Walter Lowrie. Princeton, N.J.: Princeton University Press, 1940.

_____. *The Concept of Anxiety.* Edited and translated by Reidar Thomte and Albert B. Anderson. Princeton, N.J.: Princeton University Press, 1980.

_____. *The Concept of Irony.* Translated by Lee M. Capel. London: Collins, 1966.

_____. *The Point of View for My Work as an Author.* Translated by Walter Lowrie. N.Y.: Harper & Row, 1962.

_____. *The Sickness unto Death.* Edited and translated by Howard V. Hong and Edna H. Hong. Princeton, N.J.: Princeton University Press, 1980.

_____. *Training in Christianity.* Translated by Walter Lowrie. Princeton, N.J.: Princeton University Press, 1941.

_____. *Works of Love.* Translated by David F. Swenson and Lillian Marvin Swenson. London: Geoffrey Cumberlege, Oxford University Press, 1946.

Kilpatrick, William Kirk. *Psychological Seduction.* Nashville: Thomas Nelson Publishers, 1983.

_____. *The Emperor's New Clothes.* Westchester, Ill.: Crossway Books, 1985.

Kimble, Gregory, Michael Wertheimer, and Charlotte White, eds. *Portraits of Pioneers in Psychology.* Washington: American Psychological Association, 1991.

Kirk, Kenneth E. *The Vision of God.* 2nd ed. London: Longmans, Green and Co., 1932.

Klein, Dennis B. *Jewish Origins of the Psychoanalytic Movement.* New York: Praeger Publishers, 1981.

Klotsche, E. H. *The History of Christian Doctrine.* rev. ed. Grand Rapids: Baker Book House, 1979.

Koch, Sigmund, ed. *Psychology: A Study of a Science.* 3 vols. New York: McGraw-Hill Book Company, 1959.

Kohlberg, Lawrence. "Implications of Moral Stages for Adult Education." *Religious Education* 72 (1977).

_____. "Moral Stages and Moralization: The Cognitive-Developmental Approach." In *Moral Development and Behavior.* Edited by Thomas Lickona. New York: Holt, Rinehart and Winston, 1976.

Kotenskey, Ronald L. *Psychology from a Christian Perspective.* Nashville: Abingdon, 1980.

Kreeft, Peter. *Fundamentals of the Faith.* San Francisco: Ignatius Press, 1988.

_____. *Heaven: The Heart's Deepest Longing.* San Francisco: Ignatius Press, 1989.

Kress, Robert. *A Rahner Handbook.* Atlanta: John Knox Press, 1982.

Küng, Hans. *Freud and the Problem of God.* Translated by Edward Quinn. New Haven, Conn.: Yale University Press, 1979.

Langer, Jonas. *Theories of Development.* New York: Holt, Rinehart and Winston, Inc., 1969.

Lasch, Christopher. *The Culture of Narcissism.* New York: W. W. Norton & Company, 1979.

Lee, Sang Hyun. *The Philosophical Theology of Jonathan Edwards.* Princeton, N.J.: Princeton University Press, 1988.

Levine, Charles, Lisa Jakubowski, and James Côté. "Linking Ego and Moral Development: The Value Consistency Thesis." *Human Development* 35 (1992).

Lewis, C. S. *Mere Christianity.* New York: Macmillan Publishing Co., 1943, 1945, 1952.

_____. *The Pilgrim's Regress.* Grand Rapids: William B. Eerdmans Publishing Company, 1933, 1958.

_____. *The Weight of Glory and Other Addresses.* Grand Rapids: William B. Eerdmans Publishing Company, 1949.

Lieberman, E. James. *Acts of Will: The Life and Work of Otto Rank.* New York: Free Press, 1985.

Lindzey, G., C. S. Hall, and M. Manosevitz, eds. *Theories of Personality: Primary Sources and Research.* 2nd ed. New York: John Wiley & Sons, 1973.

Loevinger, Jane. *Ego Development.* San Francisco: Jossey-Bass, 1976.

MacKay, Donald M. *Brains, Machines and Persons.* Grand Rapids: William B. Eerdmans Publishing Company, 1980.

_____. *Human Science and Human Dignity.* Downers Grove, Ill.: InterVarsity Press, 1979.

Macmurray, John. *Persons in Relation.* London: Faber and Faber Limited, 1961.

Maddi, Salvatore R. *Personality Theories: A Comparative Analysis.* 4th ed. Homewood, Ill.: Dorsey Press, 1980.

Malherbe, Abraham J. *Social Aspects of Early Christianity.* 2nd ed. Philadelphia: Fortress Press, 1983.

Malony, H. Newton, ed. *Current Perspectives in the Psychology of Religion.* Grand Rapids: William B. Eerdmans Publishing Company, 1977.

Maritain, Jacques. *Moral Philosophy.* London: Geoffrey Bles, 1964.

_____. *The Person and the Common Good.* Notre Dame, Ind.: Notre Dame Press, 1966.

Marty, Martin E. *The Modern Schism.* London: SCM Press, 1969.

Mascall, E. L. *The Christian Universe.* New York: Morehouse-Barlow Co., 1966.

Maslow, Abraham H. *Eupsychian Management.* Homewood, Ill.: Richard D. Irwin, Inc. and The Dorsey Press, 1965.

_____. *Motivation and Personality.* 3rd ed. New York: Harper & Row, 1987.

_____. *The Farther Reaches of Human Nature.* New York: Viking Press, 1971.

_____. *Toward a Psychology of Being.* 2nd ed. New York: Van Nostrand Reinhold Company, 1968.

McFadyen, Alistair I. *The Call to Personhood.* Cambridge: Cambridge University Press, 1990.

McKelway, Alexander J. *The Systematic Theology of Paul Tillich.* London: Lutterworth Press, 1964.

Meadow, Mary Jo, and Richard D. Kahoe. *Psychology of Religion.* New York: Harper & Row, 1984.

Mehl, Peter J. "Despair's Demand: An Appraisal of Kierkegaard's Argument for God." *Philosophy of Religion* 32 (1992).

Meyer, Hans. *The Philosophy of St. Thomas Aquinas.* Translated by Frederic Eckhoff. London: B. Herder Book Co., 1946.

Miles, Margaret Ruth. *Augustine on the Body.* Missoula, Mont.: Scholars Press, 1979.

Miller, Perry. *Jonathan Edwards.* Westport, Conn.: Greenwood Press, 1949.

Mohler, James A. *Late Have I Loved You: An Interpretation of Saint Augustine on Human and Divine Relationships.* N.Y.: New City Press, 1991.

Moltmann, Jürgen. *Theology of Hope.* London: SCM Press, Ltd, 1967.

Monahan, William B. *The Psychology of St. Thomas Aquinas.* London: Ebenezer Baylis & Son Ltd., n.d.

Moreland, J. P. *Christianity and the Nature of Science.* Grand Rapids: Baker Book House, 1989.

_____. *Scaling the Secular City.* Grand Rapids: Baker Book House, 1987.

Morris, Lynne, ed. *The Christian Vision: Man in Society.* Hillsdale, Mich.: Hillsdale College Press, 1984.

Murray, Iain H. *Jonathan Edwards: A New Biography.* Edinburgh: Banner of Truth Trust, 1987.

Myers, David. *The Human Puzzle.* San Francisco: Harper & Row, 1978.

_____, and Malcolm A. Jeeves. *Psychology through the Eyes of Faith.* San Francisco: Harper & Row, 1987.

Neel, Ann. *Theories of Psychology: A Handbook.* Cambridge, Mass.: Schenkman Publishing Company, Inc., 1977.

Newbigin, Lesslie. *Foolishness to the Greeks.* London: SPCK, 1986.

Newport, John P. *Paul Tillich.* Waco, Texas: Word, Incorporated, 1984.

_____. *The Other Side of 1984.* Geneva: World Council of Churches, 1983.

Niebuhr, Reinhold. *The Nature and Destiny of Man.* 2 vols. New York: Charles Scribner's Sons, 1941.

Notterman, Joseph M. *Behavior: A Systematic Approach.* New York: Random House, 1970.

Nye, Robert D. *Three Views of Man: Perspectives from Sigmund Freud, B. F. Skinner, and Carl Rogers.* Monterey, Calif.: Brooks/Cole Publishing Company, 1975.

Nygren, Anders. *Agape and Eros.* Philadelphia: Westminster Press, 1953.

O'Connell, Robert J. *St. Augustine's Early Theory of Man.* Cambridge, Mass.: Belknap Press, 1968.

O'Connor, D. J. *Aquinas and Natural Law.* London: Macmillan & Co., 1967.

Oden, Thomas C. *Kerygma and Counseling.* San Francisco: Harper & Row, 1978.

O'Donnell, James Joseph. *Augustine.* Boston: Twayne Publishers, 1985.

O'Donovan, Oliver. *The Problem of Self-Love in St. Augustine.* New Haven, Conn.: Yale University Press, 1980.

O'Mahony, James E. *The Desire of God.* London: Longmans, Green and Co., 1929.

Otto, Rudolf. *The Idea of the Holy.* Translated by John W. Harvey. 2nd ed. Oxford: Oxford University Press, 1950.

Peacocke, A. R. *Creation and the World of Science.* Oxford: Clarendon Press, 1979.

Peerman, Dean G., and Martin E. Marty, eds. *A Handbook of Christian Theologians.* Nashville: Abingdon Press, 1965.

Pegis, Anton C. *At the Origins of the Thomistic Notion of Man.* New York: Macmillan Company, 1963.

Pelikan, Jaroslav. *The Melody of Theology: A Philosophical Dictionary.* Cambridge, Mass.: Harvard University Press, 1988.

Pembroke, Neil. "God in the Life-Cycle: An Integration of Karl Rahner's Theology of Anonymous Faith and Erik Erikson's Psychology of Identity." *Journal of Psychology and Christianity* 9:1 (Spring 1990).

Percy, Walker. *Lost in the Cosmos.* New York: Washington Square Press, 1983.

Petitot, L. H. *The Life and Spirit of Thomas Aquinas.* Chicago: Priory Press, 1966.

Philp, H. L. *Jung and the Problem of Evil.* London: Rockliff, 1958.

Pieper, Josef. *On Hope.* San Francisco: Ignatius Press, 1986.

Pittenger, Norman. *Saint Thomas Aquinas: The Angelic Doctor.* New York: Farnklin Watts, Inc., 1969.

Plantinga, Alvin. *God and Other Minds.* Ithaca, N.Y.: Cornell University Press, 1967.

_____. *God, Freedom, and Evil.* Grand Rapids: William B. Eerdmans Publishing Company, 1974.

_____. *The Nature of Necessity.* Oxford: Clarendon Press, 1974.

_____, and Nicholas Wolterstorff, eds. *Faith and Rationality: Reason and Belief in God.* Notre Dame, Ind.: University of Notre Dame Press, 1983.

Pojman, Louis P. *Kierkegaard as Philosopher.* Swindon, Wiltshire: Waterleaf Press, 1978.

_____. *Religious Belief and the Will.* London: Routledge & Kegan Paul, 1986.

_____. *The Logic of Subjectivity.* University, Ala.: University of Alabama Press, 1984.

Polanyi, Michael. *Personal Knowledge.* Chicago: University of Chicago Press, 1962.

_____. *The Tacit Dimension.* Garden City, N.Y.: Anchor Books, 1966.

Progoff, Ira. *The Death and Rebirth of Psychology.* New York: McGraw-Hill Book Company, 1956, 1969.

Rahner, Karl. *Belief Today.* Translated by M. H. Heela, Ray and Rosaleen Okendon, and William Whitman. New York: Sheed and Ward, 1965, 1967.

_____. *Christian at the Crossroads.* Translated by V. Green. New York: Seabury Press, 1975.

_____. *Faith in a Wintry Season.* Edited by Paul Imhof, Hubert Biallowons, and Harvey D. Egan. New York: Crossroad Publishing Company, 1990.

_____. *Foundations of Christian Faith.* Translated by William V. Dych. London: Darton Longman & Todd, 1978.

_____. *Hearers of the Word.* Revised by J. B. Metz. Translated by Ronald Walls. London: Sheed and Ward, 1969.

_____. *I Remember.* Translated by Harvey D. Egan. New York: Crossroad Publishing Company, 1985.

_____. *Spirit in the World.* Translated by Johannes B. Metz. London: Sheed and Ward, 1968.

_____. *Studies in Modern Theology.* London: Burns & Oates, 1965.

_____. *The Christian of the Future.* Translated by W. J. O'Hara. New York: Herder and Herder, 1967.

_____. *The Church after the Council.* Translated by Davis C. Herron and Rodelinde Albrecht. New York: Herder and Herder, 1966.

_____. *The Practice of Faith.* New York: Crossroad Publishing Company, 1983.

_____. *The Priesthood.* Translated by Edward Quinn. New York: Seabury Press, 1973.

_____. *The Religious Life Today.* New York: Seabury Press, 1975.

_____. *The Trinity.* Translated by Joseph Donceel. New York: Herder and Herder, 1970.

_____. *Theological Investigations.* 16 vols. Translated by David Bourke, Karl-H. and Boniface Kruger, Graham Harrison, Kevin Smyth, and Cornelius Ernst. New York: Seabury Press; London: Darton, Longman & Todd, 1961–77.

_____. *Words of Faith.* Edited by Alice Scherer. New York: Crossroad Publishing Company, 1987.

_____, and Karl-Heinz Weger. *Our Christian Faith.* Translated by Francis McDonagh. New York: Crossroad Publishing Company, 1981.

Rank, Otto. *Beyond Psychology.* New York: Dover Publications, 1941.

_____. *Psychology and the Soul.* Translated by William D. Turner. New York: A. S. Barnes & Company, 1950.

_____. *The Don Juan Legend.* Translated by David G. Winter. Princeton, N.J.: Princeton University Press, 1975.

_____. *The Double.* Translated by Harry Tucker, Jr. Chapel Hill, N.C.: University of North Carolina Press, 1971.

_____. *The Myth of the Birth of the Hero.* Translated by F. Robbins and Smith Ely Jelliffe. New York: Robert Brunner, 1952.

_____. *The Trauma of Birth.* New York: Robert Brunner, 1952.

_____. *Truth and Reality.* Translated by Jessie Taft. New York: Alfred A. Knopf, 1936.

_____. *Will Therapy.* Translated by Jessie Taft. New York: Alfred A. Knopf, 1964.

Ratzsch, Del. *Philosophy of Science.* Downers Grove, Ill.: InterVarsity Press, 1986.

Redfern, Martin. *Karl Rahner, SJ.* London: Sheed and Ward, 1972.

Reiff, Philip. *Freud: The Mind of the Moralist.* Chicago: University of Chicago Press, 1979.

_____. *The Triumph of the Therapeutic.* New York: Harper & Row, 1966.

Ricoeur, Paul. *Freud and Philosophy.* Translated by Denis Savage. New Haven, Conn.: Yale University Press, 1970.

Roazen, Paul. *Erik H. Erikson: The Power and Limits of a Vision.* New York: Free Press, 1976.

Roberts, Robert C. "Thinking Subjectively." *International Journal for Philosophy of Religion* 11 (1980).

Rogers, Carl R. "A Theory of Therapy, Personality, and Interpersonal Relationships, as Developed in the Client-Centered Framework." In *Psychology: A Study of a Science.* vol. 3. Edited by Sigmund Koch. New York: McGraw-Hill Book Company, 1959.

_____. *A Way of Being.* Boston: Houghton Mifflin Company, 1980.

_____. *Carl Rogers on Personal Power.* New York: Delacorte Press, 1977.

_____. *Client-Centered Therapy.* London: Constable & Company, 1951.

_____. *On Becoming a Person.* London: Constable & Company, 1961.

Rokeach, Milton. *The Open and Closed Mind.* New York: Basic Books, Inc., 1960.

Rowe, Trevor. *St. Augustine: Pastoral Theologian.* London: Epworth Press, 1974.

Rudnytsky, Peter A. *The Psychoanalytic Vocation: Rank, Winnicott and the Legacy of Freud.* New Haven, Conn.: Yale University Press, 1991.

Schaer, Hans. *Religion and the Cure of Souls in Jung's Psychology.* New York: Pantheon Books, 1950.

Schaff, Philip, ed. *A Select Library of the Nicene and Post-Nicene Fathers.* Grand Rapids: William B. Eerdmans Publishing Company, 1956.

Scharlemann, Robert P. *Reflection and Doubt in the Thought of Paul Tillich.* New Haven, Conn.: Yale University Press, 1969.

Sessions, William Lad. "Religious Faith and Rational Justification." *International Journal for Philosophy of Religion* 13 (1982).

Smith, David L. *A Handbook of Contemporary Theology.* Wheaton, Ill.: BridgePoint Books, 1992.

Smith, John E. *Jonathan Edwards: Puritan, Preacher, Philosopher.* Notre Dame, Ind.: University of Notre Dame Press, 1992.

Smith, Joel R. "Creation, Fall, and Theodicy in Paul Tillich's *Systematic Theology.*" In *Kairos and Logos: Studies in the Roots and Implications of Tillich's Theology.* Edited by John J. Carey. Atlanta: Mercer University Press, 1984.

Smith, M. B. "The Phenomenological Approach in Personality Theory: Some Critical Remarks." *Journal of Abnormal and Social Psychology* 45 (1950).

Sontag, Frederick. *A Kierkegaard Handbook.* Atlanta: John Knox Press, 1979.

Sproul, R. C. *The Psychology of Atheism.* Minneapolis: Bethany Fellowship, Inc., 1974.

Stagner, Ross. *A History of Psychological Theories.* New York: Macmillan Publishing Company, 1988.

Stendahl, Krister. *Paul among Jews and Gentiles.* London: SCM Press Ltd., 1977.

Stepansky, Paul E. *In Freud's Shadow: Adler in Context.* Hillsdale, N.J.: Analytic Press, 1983.

Stern, Kenneth. "Kierkegaard on Theistic Proof." *Religious Studies* 26.

Storr, Anthony. *The Integrity of the Personality.* Harmondsworth, Middlesex: Penguin Books, 1960.

Strupp, Hans H. "Clinical Psychology, Irrationalism, and the Erosion of Excellence." *American Psychologist* 31 (1976).

Sullivan, John Edward. *The Image of God.* Dubuque, Iowa: Priory Press, 1963.

Swinburne, Richard. *The Coherence of Theism.* Oxford: Clarendon Press, 1977.

_____. *The Existence of God.* Oxford: Clarendon Press, 1979.

_____. *Faith and Reason.* Oxford: Clarendon Press, 1981.

Szasz, Thomas. *The Myth of Mental Illness.* rev. ed. New York: Harper & Row, 1974.

Szent-Gyoergyi, Albert. "Drive in Living Matter to Perfect Itself." *Synthesis,* Spring 1974.

Tavard, George H. *Paul Tillich and the Christian Message.* London: Burns & Oates, 1962.

Taylor, Mark Kline. *Paul Tillich: Theologian of the Boundaries.* London: Collins, 1987.

TeSelle, Eugene. *Augustine the Theologian.* London: Burns & Oates, 1970.

Theissen, Gerd. *Psychological Aspects of Pauline Theology.* Translated by John P. Galvin. Edinburgh: T & T Clark, 1987.

Thomas, J. Heywood. *Paul Tillich—An Appraisal.* London: SCM Press Ltd., 1963.

Thompson, Ian E. *Being and Meaning: Paul Tillich's Theory of Meaning, Truth and Logic.* Edinburgh: Edinburgh University Press, 1981.

Thorne, Brian. *Carl Rogers.* London: SAGE Publications Ltd., 1992.

Thouless, Robert H. *An Introduction to the Psychology of Religion.* 3rd ed. Cambridge: Cambridge University Press, 1971.

Tillich, Paul. *Biblical Religion and the Search for Ultimate Reality.* London: James Nisbet & Co., 1955.

_____. *Dynamics of Faith.* New York: Harper & Row, 1957.

_____. *Love, Power, and Justice.* London: Oxford University Press, 1954.

_____. *Morality and Beyond.* New York: Harper Torchbooks, 1963.

_____. *Perspectives on 19th and 20th Century Protestant Theology.* Edited by Carl E. Braaten. New York: Harper & Row, 1967.

_____. *Systematic Theology.* 3 vols. London: SCM Press Ltd., 1951–63.

_____. *The Boundaries of Our Being.* London: Collins, 1966.

_____. *The Courage to Be.* New Haven, Conn.: Yale University Press, 1952.

_____. *The Eternal Now.* London: SCM Press Ltd., 1963.

_____. *The Protestant Era.* Translated by James Luther Adams. Chicago: University of Chicago Press, 1948; Phoenix Books, 1957.

_____. *The Religious Situation.* Translated by H. Richard Niebuhr. Meridian Books, 1956.

_____. *The Shaking of the Foundations.* London: SCM Press Ltd., 1949.

_____. *Theology of Culture.* Edited by Robert C. Kimball. New York: Oxford University Press, 1959.

Van Leeuwen, Mary Stewart. *The Person in Psychology.* Grand Rapids: William B. Eerdmans Publishing Company, 1985.

_____. *The Sorcerer's Apprentice: A Christian Looks at the Changing Face of Psychology.* Downers Grove, Ill.: InterVarsity Press, 1982.

Vitz, Paul C. *Psychology as Religion.* Grand Rapids: William B. Eerdmans Publishing Company, 1977.

_____. "The Use of Stories in Moral Development." *American Psychologist* 45:6 (June 1990).

von Franz, Marie-Louise. *C. G. Jung: His Myth in Our Time.* Translated by William H. Kennedy. New York: C. G. Jung Foundation for Analytical Psychology, 1975.

Vorgrimler, Herbert. *Karl Rahner: His Life, Thought and Works.* Translated by Edward Quinn. London: Burnes & Oates, 1965.

Walgrave, Jan Handrik. *Unfolding Revelation: The Nature of Doctrinal Development.* Philadelphia: Westminster Press, 1972.

Warfield, Benjamin B. *The Person and Work of Christ.* Philadelphia: Presbyterian and Reformed Publishing Company, 1950.

Weger, Karl-Heinz. *Karl Rahner: An Introduction to His Theology.* Translated by David Smith. New York: Seabury Press, 1980.

Westra, Helen Petter. "Jonathan Edwards and 'What Reason Teaches.'" *Journal of the Evangelical Theological Society* 34/4 (1991).

White, Victor. *God and the Unconscious.* Cleveland: World Publishing Company, 1952.

Wollheim, Richard, ed. *Freud: A Collection of Critical Essays.* Garden City, N.Y.: Anchor Books, 1974.

Wolman, Benjamin B. *Contemporary Theories and Systems in Psychology.* New York: Harper & Brothers, Publishers, 1960.

_____, ed. *International Encyclopedia of Psychiatry, Psychology, Psychoanalysis, and Neurology.* 12 vols. New York: Aesculapius Publishers, Inc., 1977.

Wolterstorff, Nicholas. *Reason within the Bounds of Religion.* Grand Rapids: William B. Eerdmans Publishing Company, 1976.

Wright, J. Eugene, Jr. *Erikson: Identity and Religion.* New York: Seabury Press, 1982.

Yarbrough, Stephen R., and John C. Adams. *Delightful Conviction: Jonathan Edwards and the Rhetoric of Conversion.* Westport, Conn.: Greenwood Press, 1993.

Zizioulas, Jean. *Being as Communion: Studies in Personhood and the Church.* Crestwood, N.Y.: St. Vladimir's Seminary Press, 1985.

ENDNOTES

Chapter 1

1. Frederick Copleston, *A History of Philosophy,* vol. 2: *Mediaeval Philosophy* (Westminster, Md.: Newman Press, 1960), 40.

2. Gerald Bonner, "The Spirituality of St. Augustine and Its Influence on Western Mysticism," in *God's Decree and Man's Destiny* (London: Variorum Reprints, 1987), 146.

3. John Neville Figgis, *The Political Aspects of S. Augustine's "City of God"* (London: Longmans, Green, and Company, 1921), 6–7.

4. John Edward Sullivan, *The Image of God* (Dubuque, Iowa: Priory Press, 1963), 4; Bonner, "The Spirituality," 150; "Vera lux illa est quae illuminat: The Christian Humanism of Augustine," in *God's Decree,* 19; Robert J. O'Connell, *St. Augustine's Early Theory of Man* (Cambridge, Mass.: Belknap Press, 1968).

5. Gerald Bonner, "Augustine's Doctrine of Man: Image of God and Sinner," in *God's Decree,* 497.

6. Idem, "The Spirituality," 157; "Christ, God and Man in the Thought of St. Augustine," in *God's Decree,* 291; "Augustine's Doctrine of Man," 512.

7. O'Connell, *Early Theory of Man,* 31–32, 121. Augustine did not repudiate his adaptation of the Platonic notion of participation to describe the image of God in man (Bonner, "The Spirituality," 157; "Christ, God and Man," 271–72; Augustine *De Trin.* 14. 8. 11). Most references to Augustine are from Philip Schaff, ed., *A Select Library of the Nicene and Post-Nicene Fathers* (Grand Rapids, Mich.: William B. Eerdmans Publishing Company, 1956). The rest are from John H. S. Burleigh, *Augustine: Earlier Writings* (Philadelphia: Westminster Press, 1953); *Confessions,* trans. R. S. Pine-Coffin (Harmondsworth, England: Penguin Books, 1961); *The City of God,* ed. Vernon J. Bourke, trans. Gerald G. Walsh, Demetrius B. Zema, Grace Monahan, and Daniel J. Honan (Garden City, N.Y.: Image Books, 1958).

8. Sullivan, *The Image of God,* ix.

9. Eugene TeSelle, *Augustine the Theologian* (London: Burns & Oates, 1970), 68; Bonner, "Christ, God and Man," 271, 293.

10. *De Gen. ad lit.* 6. 27. 38; cf. *Retr.* 2. 25. 2.; *De Trin.* 14. 2. 4; 14. 4. 6; Sullivan, *The Image of God,* 42–43; Bonner, "Augustine's Doctrine of Man," 504–7.

11. *De Trin.* 8–15; Sullivan, *The Image of God,* 84–162.

12. Sullivan, *The Image of God,* 143.

13. *De Trin.* 14. 16. 22.

14. John Burnaby, *Amor Dei* (London: Hodder & Stoughton, 1938), 135, 171; Augustine *In Ioh. Ev. tract.* 102. 5.

15. *De Trin.* 7. 3. 5. "Therefore He descended that we might ascend, and remaining in His nature was made a partaker of our nature, that we remaining in our nature might be made partakers of His Nature; but not simply thus; for His participation in our nature did not make Him worse, while participating in His nature makes us better" (*Ep.* 140. 4. 10).

16. *De pecc. mer. et rem.* 2. 9, 10.

17. Bonner, "The Spirituality," 154. In *De vera religione* 26. 49–27. 50, Augustine distinguishes seven stages from the old man of sin to the new man of righteousness.

18. *De fid. et sym.* 10. 24.

19. *De Trin.* 14. 17. 23.

20. Margaret Ruth Miles, *Augustine on the Body* (Missoula, Mont.: Scholars Press, 1979), 7, 85, 93, 97, 128. "Is not our absorbing love of life really the soul's love for its body, a love which will haunt it until that body is returned to it risen and glorious?" (*De Gen. ad lit.* 12. 35. 68).

21. TeSelle, *Augustine the Theologian,* 73.

22. *De lib. arb.* 1. 16. 35. "[T]he will which turns from the unchangeable and common good and turns to its own

23. Ibid., 3. 1. 2.

24. *Conf.* 1. 20. "This is what happens, O Fountain of life, when we abandon you, who are the one true Creator of all that ever was or is, and each of us proudly sets his heart on some one part of your creation instead of on the whole. So it is by the path of meekness and devotion that we must return to you" (*Conf.* 3. 8).

25. Herbert A. Deane, *The Political and Social Ideas of St. Augustine* (New York: Columbia University Press, 1963), 16.

26. Burnaby, *Amor Dei,* 185. (Italics his.)

27. Copleston, *Mediaeval Philosophy,* 85.

28. Deane, *Political and Social Ideas,* 16.

29. Burnaby, *Amor Dei,* 192.

30. "[T]he malice by which His so-called enemies oppose God is not a menace to Him, but merely bad for themselves—an evil because what is good in their nature is wounded. It is not their nature, but the wound in their nature, that is opposed to God—as evil is opposed to good" (*De civ. Dei* 12. 3).

31. Deane, *Political and Social Ideas,* 26–27.

32. Ibid., 28; Augustine *Ench.* 28–29; *De civ. Dei* 22. 30.

33. *Retr.* 1.9.6 (on *De libero arbitrio*).

34. Bonner, "Augustine's Doctrine of Man," 508; Sullivan, *The Image of God,* 53; Copleston, *Mediaeval Philosophy,* 83–84.

35. *Retr.* 1.9.4 (on *De libero arbitrio*); cf. *Ep.* 145. 3. 4; *Ep. ad Rom. inc. exp.* 44.

36. Deane, *Political and Social Ideas,* 20; Bonner, "The Christian Humanism of Augustine," 13.

37. *Retr.* 1.9.3 (on *De libero arbitrio*).

38. Oliver O'Donovan, *The Problem of Self-Love in St. Augustine* (New Haven: Yale University Press, 1980), 99; Burnaby, *Amor Dei,* 70–71.

39. Bonner, "Christ, God and Man," 280. "No one is likely to dispute the harshness of the Augustinian doctrine of Original Sin; but it must be recognised that it was from the notion of the coinherence of fallen humanity in Adam that Augustine derived his vision of the coinherence of redeemed humanity in the Body of Christ. Against the *massa peccati,* the lump of sin, Augustine sets the *corpus Christi*" (idem, "Augustine's Doctrine of Man," 502).

40. *Conf.* 7. 18.

41. *De lib. arb.* 2. 13. 36; *Sol.* 1. 15. 30.

42. In *De Utilitate Credendi* Augustine discusses the need for reliable authority so that the truth can be known (14. 30–16. 34). "In the *De Beata Vita* he says that no one is happy who does not possess what he strives to possess, so that the man who is seeking for truth but has not yet found it, cannot be said to be truly happy. Augustine himself sought for truth because he felt a need for it, and looking back on his development in the light of attainment, he interpreted this as a search for Christ and Christian wisdom, as the attraction of the divine beauty, and this experience he universalised" (Copleston, *Mediaeval Philosophy,* 51–52; cf. Burnaby, *Amor Dei,* 49).

43. *De Trin.* 12. 7. 12; Sullivan, *The Image of God,* 44–45, 51.

44. Sullivan, *The Image of God,* 62; Bonner, "The Spirituality," 149, 152.

45. Miles, *Augustine on the Body,* 128.

46. *In Ioh. Ev. tract.* 63. 1. "[F]aith hath already found Him, but hope still seeketh Him. But love hath both found Him through faith, and seeketh to have Him by sight, where He will then be found so as to satisfy us, and no longer to need our search" (*Enarr. in Psa.* 105. 3).

47. Burnaby, *Amor Dei,* 305.

48. Ibid., 16.

49. *In Ioh. Ev. tract.* 23. 6.

50. "Any man who has examined history and human nature will agree with me that there is no such thing as a human heart that does not crave for joy and peace" (*De civ. Dei* 19. 12).

51. Ibid., 12. 1. "Thus, the rational being, whether in the angelic spirit or in the human soul, is so constituted that it cannot be its own good, the source of its own happiness, but, if its changeable state is turned to the unchangeable good, it finds happiness; if it is turned away from it, it finds wretchedness" (*Ep.* 140. 23. 56).

52. *De civ. Dei* 18. 2.

53. *De ver. rel.* 21. 41.

54. *De civ. Dei* 19. 1–4.

55. Ibid., 19. 4; *De Trin.* 15. 4. 6.

56. *De civ. Dei* 19. 4.

57. *Conf.* 6. 6, 11.

58. *De civ. Dei* 19. 4. "So the soul defiles itself with unchaste love when it turns away from you and looks elsewhere for things which it cannot find pure and unsullied except by returning to you. All who desert you and set themselves up against you merely copy you in a perverse way; but by this very act of imitation they only show that you are the Creator of all nature and, consequently, that there is no place whatever where man may hide away from you" (*Conf.* 2. 6).

59. *Conf.* 6. 16. "What dangers threatened my soul when it rashly hoped that by abandoning you it would find something better! Whichever way it turned, on front or back or sides, it lay on a bed that was hard, for in you alone the soul can rest" (ibid.).

60. Burnaby, *Amor Dei,* 96–97.

61. *In I Ep. Ioh. tract.* 4. 6. Cf. *Enarr. in Psa.* 84. 3; 92. 1.

62. "Learn in the creature to love the Creator; and in the work Him who made it. Let not that which has been made by Him detain thine affections, so that thou shouldest lose Him by whom thou thyself wert made also. . . . But why dost thou love those things, except because they are beautiful? Can they be as beautiful as He by whom they were made? Thou admirest these things because thou seest not Him: but through those things which thou admirest, love Him whom thou seest not" (*Enarr. in Psa.* 40. 8; 80. 11).

63. *Conf.* 1. 1. Burnaby prefers the translation, "you made us to be toward you" to "you made us for yourself," because in his view the self-sufficient God does not seek or need human love (*Amor Dei,* 166).

64. *Conf.* 10. 22. "For in you our good abides and it has no blemish, since it is yourself. . . . our home is your eternity and it does not fall because we are away" (*Conf.* 4. 16). Cf. *Enarr. in Psa.* 56. 15–18; 73. 24; *De Trin.* 8. 3. 4.

65. *De civ. Dei* 22. 30. "For that is the one true and only happy life, in which, immortal and incorruptible in body and spirit, we may contemplate the joy of the Lord for ever. All other things are desired and are without impropriety prayed for, with a view to this one thing. For whoever has it shall have all that he wishes, nor can he possibly wish for anything with it which would be unbecoming. . . . For inasmuch as we cannot present it to our minds as it really is, we do not know it, but whatever image of it may be presented to our minds we reject, disown, and condemn. We know it is not that which we are seeking, although we do not yet know enough to be able to define what we seek. . . . For assuredly if it were utterly unknown it would not be desired; and on the other hand, if it were seen it would not have to be desired and sought for with groanings" (*Ep.* 130. 14. 27–15. 28).

66. *Sermo* 125. 11.

67. *De civ. Dei* 22. 30; 10. 3; *Conf.* 9. 10.

68. *Conf.* 4. 10. "Choose not to cleave to this aged world and to be unwilling to grow young in Christ, who saith to thee: The world is perishing, the world is growing old, the world is failing, has the laboured breathing of old age. Fear not, 'thy youth shall be renewed like an eagle's'" (*Sermo* 81. 8).

69. *De ver. rel.* 38. 70; cf. *De civ. Dei* 14. 4. There is an "intoxication which causes the world to forget you, its Creator, and to love the things you have created instead of loving you, because the world is drunk with the invisible

wine of its own perverted, earthbound will" (*Conf.* 2. 3). The will must be converted "from falling into temporal delights to the enjoyment of the eternal good" (*De lib. arb.* 3. 1. 3).

70. *De ver. rel.* 46. 86.

71. *Conf.* 10. 36.

72. *Enarr. in Psa.* 39. 11; 40. 7; 91. 7; 92. 1. "Nothing therefore is so hostile to hope as to look back, to place hope, that is, in those things which flit by and pass away. But we should place it in those things which are not yet given, which at some time will be given, and will never pass away. . . . For this cause doth God mingle bitternesses with the felicities of the world that another felicity may be sought, in whose sweetness there is no deceit" (*Sermo* 105. 5. 7; 7. 9).

73. *De doctr. Christ.* 1. 3. 3–4. 4; 1. 22. 20; Deane, *Political and Social Ideas,* 41, n. 11.

74. *De doctr. Christ.* 1. 35. 39. "In the earthly city, then, temporal goods are to be used with a view to the enjoyment of earthly peace, whereas, in the heavenly City, they are used with a view to the enjoyment of eternal peace" (*De civ. Dei* 19. 14; cf. 19. 17).

75. *De civ. Dei* 19. 10.

76. *Ep.* 140. 2. 3–3. 6; *Conf.* 4. 12.

77. *In Ioh. Ev. tract.* 40. 10; *Enarr. in Psa.* 144. 9; *De civ. Dei* 1. 8–9; 11. 25; *Sermo* 80. 7; Deane, *Political and Social Ideas,* 42–44.

78. The City of God, which contains the minority of the human race elected to salvation, cannot be identified with the visible Christian Church in this world. The true Jerusalem is the whole assembly of the saints, the invisible Church (Deane, *Political and Social Ideas,* 24, 28–29; Augustine *In Ioh. Ev. tract.* 115. 2). "For now we are pilgrims, we sigh, we groan" (*Enarr. in Psa.* 149. 3; cf. *In Ioh. Ev. tract.* 6. 2).

79. *De cat. rud.* 19. 31; *De civ. Dei* 18. 54; Deane, *The Political and Social Ideas,* 30, 34.

80. Etienne Gilson, "Foreword" to the Image Books edition of *The City of God,* 28. "[T]wo societies have issued from two kinds of love" (*De civ. Dei* 14. 28).

81. *De mend.* 10; Deane, *The Political and Social Ideas,* 44.

82. Copleston, *Mediaeval Philosophy,* 85; Deane, *Political and Social Ideas,* 40–41; Augustine *Enarr. in Psa.* 65. 2.

83. Burnaby, *Amor Dei,* 79, 312.

84. *De mor. eccl.* 48f; Burnaby, *Amor Dei,* 90–91.

85. O'Donovan, *The Problem of Self-Love,* 51–54, 57; Burnaby, *Amor Dei,* 116, 118.

86. O'Donovan, *The Problem of Self-Love,* 90–92; Augustine *De Trin.* 8. 8. 12; 14. 14. 18. "The self-love which is native to the human soul will become injurious to the self, will turn in effect to self-hatred, unless the image of God is restored by the transformation of this self-love into the love of Him in whose image the soul was made" (Burnaby, *Amor Dei,* 122).

87. O'Donovan, *The Problem of Self-Love,* 37, 39–40, 145. "Only of *perfect* self-love and *explicit* love of God can it be said, 'Herein you love yourself, by loving God'" (ibid., 147; cf. Burnaby, *Amor Dei,* 87, 123).

88. *Ep.* 155. 15; Burnaby, *Amor Dei,* 121.

89. "[Y]ou ought not to love even yourself for your own sake, but for His in whom your love finds its most worthy object . . ." (*De doctr. Christ.* 1. 22. 21). "Nature makes us egoists when she sets each of us upon the satisfaction of his own desires; individuality makes us egocentrists, because no man can jump out of his own skin or see the world with any eyes but his own. But the love of self that runs to the contempt of God is neither egoism nor egocentrism, but 'egotheism'—not selfishness but blasphemous rebellion" (Burnaby, *Amor Dei,* 121–22, 309).

90. O'Donovan, *The Problem of Self-Love,* 138, 156–58.

91. *De civ. Dei* 10. 3.

92. "Whoever, then, loves his neighbor aright, ought to urge upon him that he too should love God with his whole

heart, and soul, and mind" (*De doctr. Christ.* 1. 22. 21; 1. 29. 30; *Conf.* 4. 12; *De civ. Dei* 19. 14; O'Donovan, *The Problem of Self-Love*, 112).

93. Burnaby, *Amor Dei*, 306.

94. Ibid., 128; cf. 293.

95. *In Ioh. Ev. tract.* 67. 2.

96. Kenneth E. Kirk, *The Vision of God*, 2nd ed. (London: Longmans, Green and Co., 1932), 380; Frederick Copleston, *A History of Philosophy*, vol. 2: *Mediaeval Philosophy* (Westminster, Md.: Newman Press, 1960), 308–9, 312.

97. D. J. O'Connor, *Aquinas and Natural Law* (London: Macmillan & Co., 1967), 4; Copleston, *Mediaeval Philosophy*, 322–23, 424. "It is almost amusing . . . to watch how the saint turns the rather unprepossessing intellectualism of [Aristotle] into the vision of God, and makes a somewhat worldly-minded moralist the advocate of holiness" (M. C. D'Arcy, *Thomas Aquinas* [London: Ernest Benn Limited, 1930], 227).

98. Anton C. Pegis, *At the Origins of the Thomistic Notion of Man* (New York: Macmillan Company, 1963), 4, 20; O'Connor, *Aquinas and Natural Law*, 22; Copleston, *Mediaeval Philosophy*, 427.

99. Pegis, *The Thomistic Notion of Man*, 59.

100. Etienne Gilson, *The Christian Philosophy of St. Thomas Aquinas*, trans. L. K. Shook (London: Victor Gollancz Ltd., 1957), 375.

101. *Summa Theologica* (*ST*) 2–2. 85. 1. Quotations from the *Summa Theologica* are from the edition translated by Fathers of the English Dominican Province (London: Burns & Oates, 1947–48).

102. Copleston, *Mediaeval Philosophy*, 311; *ST* 1. 2. 1.

103. William B. Monahan, *The Psychology of St. Thomas Aquinas* (London: Ebenezer Baylis & Son Ltd., n.d.), 9–10, 120–23. "[M]an was created for a profounder and more intimate knowledge of God than he can attain by the exercise of his natural reason in this life, and so revelation was morally necessary in order that his mind might be raised to something higher than his reason can attain to in this life" (Copleston, *Mediaeval Philosophy*, 310; cf. 314–15, 320).

104. Pegis, *The Thomistic Notion of Man*, 33.

105. Maurice De Wulf, *The System of Thomas Aquinas* (New York: Dover Publications, Inc., 1959), 84.

106. Monahan, *The Psychology of St. Thomas Aquinas*, 66.

107. *ST* 1. 76. 1; Copleston, *Mediaeval Philosophy*, 375–76, 383–84, 425.

108. Pegis, *The Thomistic Notion of Man*, 40–42, 44.

109. Gilson, *The Christian Philosophy of St. Thomas Aquinas*, 189, 196; D'Arcy, *Thomas Aquinas*, 207.

110. *ST* 1. 75. 2.

111. Pegis, *The Thomistic Notion of Man*, 34; D'Arcy, *Thomas Aquinas*, 209–11.

112. M.-D. Chenu, *Nature, Man, and Society in the Twelfth Century*, trans. Jerome Taylor and Lester K. Little (Chicago: University of Chicago Press, 1968), 23–24, 70.

113. James E. O'Mahony, *The Desire of God* (London: Longmans, Green and Co., 1929), 19, 29. "As all sub-human forms of being are united in man, so his intellect is a connecting link with the purely spiritual intelligences" (Hans Meyer, *The Philosophy of St. Thomas Aquinas*, trans. Frederic Eckhoff [London: B. Herder Book Co., 1946], 212; cf. 216).

114. Monahan, *The Psychology of St. Thomas Aquinas*, 64; cf. 65. "The human mind is a curious combination of debility and audacity. Condemned to rise from humble origins, its ambition is directed towards a final unity of things" (O'Mahony, *The Desire of God*, 21; cf. 26).

115. *ST* 1. 78. 1; Monahan, *The Psychology of St. Thomas Aquinas*, 13, 74; Gilson, *The Christian Philosophy of St. Thomas Aquinas*, 201.

116. *ST* 1. 76. 3.

117. Monahan, *The Psychology of St. Thomas Aquinas*, 77, 250.

118. Kirk, *The Vision of God,* 384.

119. Ibid. "[T]he intellectual soul had to be endowed not only with the power of understanding, but also with the power of feeling. Now the action of the senses is not performed without a corporeal instrument. Therefore it behooved the intellectual soul to be united to a body fitted to be a convenient organ of sense" (*ST* 1. 76. 5).

120. *ST* 1. 5. 4.

121. O'Mahony, *The Desire of God,* 18, 90–93, 96. "A human soul, or any corporeal form, is a kind of incomplete perfection. But it is fitted for completion and feels the need and experiences the desire for it" (Gilson, *The Christian Philosophy of St. Thomas Aquinas,* 191).

122. *ST* 1. 6. 1.

123. Copleston, *Mediaeval Philosophy,* 425; O'Mahony, *The Desire of God,* 69–70.

124. O'Mahony, *The Desire of God,* xxiv; cf. 123, 136–37, 176–77, 183.

125. *ST* 1. 82. 4.

126. *ST* 1. 81. 2; 1. 78. 1; Meyer, *The Philosophy of St. Thomas Aquinas,* 164.

127. Gilson, *The Christian Philosophy of St. Thomas Aquinas,* 272; Monahan, *The Psychology of St. Thomas Aquinas,* 203; Meyer, *The Philosophy of St. Thomas Aquinas,* 192.

128. *ST* 1. 80. 2.

129. *Summa Contra Gentiles (SCG)* 3. 26. 8; *ST* 1. 83. 3; Gilson, *The Christian Philosophy of St. Thomas Aquinas,* 236–38. Quotations from book 3 of the *Summa Contra Gentiles* are from the edition translated by Vernon J. Bourke (Notre Dame, Ind.: University of Notre Dame Press, 1975).

130. *ST* 1–2. 8. 1; De Wulf, *The System of Thomas Aquinas,* 47; Monahan, *The Psychology of St. Thomas Aquinas,* 203–4; O'Connor, *Aquinas and Natural Law,* 18.

131. *ST* 1–2. 22. 3; Martin Grabmann, *Thomas Aquinas,* trans. Virgil Michel (New York: Longmans, Green and Co., 1928), 154; Meyer, *The Philosophy of St. Thomas Aquinas,* 167, 185; De Wulf, *The System of Thomas Aquinas,* 47, 51.

132. *ST* 1. 16. 1.

133. *ST* 1. 16. 4; Meyer, *The Philosophy of St. Thomas Aquinas,* 193–94.

134. *ST* 1–2. 31. 5; Gilson, *The Christian Philosophy of St. Thomas Aquinas,* 279.

135. *ST* 1–2. 4. 2; De Wulf, *The System of Thomas Aquinas,* 101–2; D'Arcy, *Thomas Aquinas,* 231–32.

136. D'Arcy, *Thomas Aquinas,* 227–29; Monahan, *The Psychology of St. Thomas Aquinas,* 244; Grabmann, *Thomas Aquinas,* 159.

137. *ST* 1–2. 3. 3; De Wulf, *The System of Thomas Aquinas,* 100–101.

138. Meyer, *The Philosophy of St. Thomas Aquinas,* 209, 384–85.

139. "[O]ne type of rational explanation is to be used for things which belong to the needs of the individual man, while a different one applies to the things that pertain to the needs of the group. In regard to things pertinent to the needs of the individual man, it is necessary to make provision for each person. Now, of this type are food and drink, and other goods having to do with the maintenance of the individual. Hence, each man must make use of food and drink. But, in the case of things that are necessary for the group, it is not necessary for the assignment to be given to each person in the group; indeed, this is not even possible. For it is clear that many things are needed by a group of men, such as food, drink, clothing, housing and the like, which cannot all be procured by one man. And so, different tasks must be given to different persons, just as different organs of the body are directed to different functions" (*SCG* 3. 136. 9; cf. 3. 128. 1; Gilson, *The Christian Philosophy of St. Thomas Aquinas,* 297).

140. *SCG* 3. 1. 2; 3. 3; 3. 16; *ST* 1. 5. 6; De Wulf, *The System of Thomas Aquinas,* 99.

141. *ST* 1–2. 1. 5.

142. *SCG* 3. 2. 3; 3. 17. 5; Monahan, *The Psychology of St. Thomas Aquinas,* 219, 221.

143. "[S]econdary objects of the appetite do not move the appetite, except as ordained to the first object of the appetite, which is the last end. . . . One need not always be thinking of the last end, whenever one desires or does

something: but the virtue of the first intention, which was in respect of the last end, remains in every desire directed to any object whatever, even though one's thoughts be not actually directed to the last end" (*ST* 1–2. 1. 6; cf. 1–2. 3. 1; Grabmann, *Thomas Aquinas*, 163–64).

144. *De Veritate* 14. 2–3. "Final and perfect happiness can consist in nothing else than the vision of the Divine Essence" (*ST* 1–2. 3. 8; cf. 1. 62. 1). "Through this consideration the error of the ancient natural philosophers is refuted; they claimed that all things come about as a result of material necessity, for they completely excluded final cause from things" (*SCG* 3. 2. 10; cf. Copleston, *Mediaeval Philosophy*, 316–18, 428–29; O'Mahony, *The Desire of God*, 171–75).

145. *ST* 1–2. 4. 5; 1–2. 3. 6; "[I]t is not possible for man's ultimate felicity to come in this life" (*SCG* 3. 48.1). "A certain participation of Happiness can be had in this life: but perfect and true Happiness cannot be had in this life. . . . Now the goods of the present life pass away; since life itself passes away, which we naturally desire to have, and would wish to hold abidingly, for man naturally shrinks from death. Wherefore it is impossible to have true Happiness in this life" (*ST* 1–2. 5. 3; cf. 1–2. 5. 5).

146. O'Mahony, *The Desire of God*, 149; cf. 34; *SCG* 3. 19–20; Meyer, *The Philosophy of St. Thomas Aquinas*, 201, 446, 512.

147. *SCG* 3. 39–40. "[N]othing finite can fully satisfy intellectual desire. This is shown from the fact that, whenever a finite object is presented, the intellect extends its interest to something more" (*SCG* 3. 50. 5).

148. *ST* 1–2. 4. 4; Copleston, *Mediaeval Philosophy*, 401–3.

149. *ST* 1–2. 2. 8.

150. *ST* 1–2. 1. 7.

151. *ST* 1–2. 2. 6; Monahan, *The Psychology of St. Thomas Aquinas*, 222.

152. *SCG* 3. 27–36; *ST* 1–2. 2. 1–8; Gilson, *The Christian Philosophy of St. Thomas Aquinas*, 352; Copleston, *Mediaeval Philosophy*, 398–400; Monahan, *The Psychology of St. Thomas Aquinas*, 223–25.

153. *SCG* 3. 27. 6.

154. *ST* 1–2. 73. 1.

155. *ST* 1. 26. 4.

156. *SCG* 3. 63.

157. *SCG* 3. 147. 7.

158. *SCG* 3. 121. 1–2; cf. 3. 129. 7; De Wulf, *The System of Thomas Aquinas*, 51; Monahan, *The Psychology of St. Thomas Aquinas*, 9; Gilson, *The Christian Philosophy of St. Thomas Aquinas*, 295; Kirk, *The Vision of God*, 384.

159. *SCG* 3. 126. 3.

160. *SCG* 3. 127. 1, 7. "[A] man must justly possess what he has; he must not set the end of his will in these things, and he must use them in a fitting way for his own and others' benefit" (*SCG* 3. 127. 7).

161. *SCG* 3. 37. 7.

162. *ST* 1–2. 4. 7–8.

163. Gilson, *The Christian Philosophy of St. Thomas Aquinas*, 355–56; Monahan, *The Psychology of St. Thomas Aquinas*, 223–25.

164. *ST* 1–2. 5. 8. "[A]ll desire happiness with one will. Now if this were not necessary, but contingent, there would at least be a few exceptions. Therefore the will desires something of necessity" (*ST* 1. 82. 1).

165. De Wulf, *The System of Thomas Aquinas*, 48; Monahan, *The Psychology of St. Thomas Aquinas*, 205–6; Copleston, *Mediaeval Philosophy*, 380.

166. "[M]an wills Happiness of necessity, nor can he will not to be happy, or to be unhappy. Now since choice is not of the end, but of the means, . . . it is not of the perfect good, which is Happiness, but of other particular goods. Therefore man chooses not of necessity, but freely" (*ST* 1–2. 13. 6; cf. 1. 82. 2; 1–2. 5. 8).

167. De Wulf, *The System of Thomas Aquinas*, 104–6; Monahan, *The Psychology of St. Thomas Aquinas*, 211; Copleston, *Mediaeval Philosophy*, 398.

168. O'Mahony, *The Desire of God,* 247.

169. Ibid., 248.

170. Gilson, *The Christian Philosophy of St. Thomas Aquinas,* 242–43; De Wulf, *The System of Thomas Aquinas,* 48–49; Copleston, *Mediaeval Philosophy,* 380–81; O'Mahony, *The Desire of God,* 169–70, 175, 199, 203, 205–6; Meyer, *The Philosophy of St. Thomas Aquinas,* 196.

171. *SCG* 3. 26. 12, 16; Jacques Maritain, *St. Thomas Aquinas,* trans. J. F. Scanlan (London: Sheed & Ward, 1931), 97; Gilson, *The Christian Philosophy of St. Thomas Aquinas,* 243; Meyer, *The Philosophy of St. Thomas Aquinas,* 386; Monahan, *The Psychology of St. Thomas Aquinas,* 226, 228; O'Mahony, *The Desire of God,* 36–38, 207–8, 211–12, 214, 229; D'Arcy, *Thomas Aquinas,* 235.

172. *SCG* 3. 25. 1–6; *ST* 1. 26. 2–3.

173. Maritain, *St. Thomas Aquinas,* 103.

174. Kirk, *The Vision of God,* 391–92; De Wulf, *The System of Thomas Aquinas,* 102–4; Michael J. Dodds, *The Unchanging God of Love* (Fribourg, Switzerland: Éditions Universitaires, 1986), 309–12.

175. R. Garrigou-Lagrange, *Christian Perfection and Contemplation,* trans. M. Timothea Doyle (St. Louis: B. Herder Book Co., 1946), 140–43; Maritain, *St. Thomas Aquinas,* 108. "[T]he intellect in itself and absolutely is higher and nobler than the will. But relatively and by comparison with something else, we find that the will is sometimes higher than the intellect, from the fact that the object of the will occurs in something higher than that in which occurs the object of the intellect" (*ST* 1. 82. 3).

176. Copleston, *Mediaeval Philosophy,* 382–83.

177. Chenu, *Nature, Man, and Society in the Twelfth Century,* 287.

178. *SCG* 3. 47, 55; O'Mahony, *The Desire of God,* xxi, 38; Copleston, *Mediaeval Philosophy,* 404.

179. *ST* 1. 12. 1; *SCG* 3. 54; O'Mahony, *The Desire of God,* xxiii, 143–44, 231–34, 238; Monahan, *The Psychology of St. Thomas Aquinas,* 125–28. "[T]he desire of the saints cannot be altogether frustrated. Now the common desire of the saints is to see God in His essence. . . . Now since the perfection of an intelligent being as such is the intelligible object, if in the most perfect operation of his intellect man does not attain to the vision of the Divine essence, but to something else, we shall be forced to conclude that something other than God is the object of man's happiness: and since the ultimate perfection of a thing consists in its being united to its principle, it follows that something other than God is the effective principle of man, which is absurd" (*ST* Suppl. 92. 1).

180. "[S]ince the natural appetite of everything comes to rest when the thing reaches its ultimate end, the natural appetite of an intellectual substance must come to rest completely when it sees the divine substance" (*SCG* 3. 59. 1; 3. 57). "Happiness is the attainment of the Perfect Good. Whoever, therefore, is capable of the Perfect Good can attain Happiness. Now, that man is capable of the Perfect Good, is proved both because his intellect can apprehend the universal and perfect good, and because his will can desire it. And therefore man can attain Happiness" (*ST* 1–2. 5. 1; 1–2. 3. 8).

181. O'Mahony, *The Desire of God,* 150; cf. 155, 159–66, 178–80.

182. *SCG* 3. 52. 7; 3. 53. 1; O'Mahony, *The Desire of God,* 43, 245–46.

183. *ST* 1. 12. 13; 1. 12. 2.

184. *SCG* 3. 57–58.

185. *SCG* 3. 51. 2; *ST* 1. 12. 4–10. "[T]he divine intellect sees the divine substance through itself, for the divine intellect is the divine essence itself whereby the substance of God is seen. . . . However, the created intellect sees the divine substance through the essence of God, as through something other than itself. Therefore, this vision cannot come to the created intellect except through God's action" (*SCG* 3. 52. 5; *ST* Suppl. 92. 1).

186. *SCG* 3. 61–62.

187. *ST* Suppl. 92. 2.

188. *SCG* 3. 149–53; Monahan, *The Psychology of St. Thomas Aquinas,* 53–54, 231–33; Meyer, *The Philosophy*

of St. Thomas Aquinas, 398. Aquinas adds that "it is reasonable to hold a man responsible if he does not turn toward God, even though he cannot do this without grace" (*SCG* 3. 159).

189. Maritain, *Moral Philosophy,* 74.

190. M. C. Tyler, in *A History of American Literature,* quoted in Iain H. Murray, *Jonathan Edwards: A New Biography* (Edinburgh: Banner of Truth Trust, 1987), 67 (cf. xvi–xvii); Perry Miller, in Jonathan Edwards, *Freedom of the Will,* ed. Paul Ramsey (New Haven: Yale University Press, 1957 [1754]), viii.

191. Paul Ramsey, in Edwards, *Freedom of the Will,* 8.

192. Murray, *Jonathan Edwards,* 104; Jonathan Edwards, *Memoirs,* in *The Works of Jonathan Edwards,* 2 vols. (Edinburgh: Banner of Truth Trust, 1974 [1834]), 1:xii–xiii. With the exception of *A Treatise on Religious Affections* and *Freedom of the Will,* all quotations from Edwards are from this two-volume edition and are designated by volume and page numbers (e.g., 2:597). Italics in these quotations will be deleted.

193. Edwards, *Memoirs,* 1:xiii–xiv, xxxiii.

194. Ibid., 1:xlvi–xlviii.

195. Idem, *Freedom of the Will,* 131; cf. *Memoirs,* 1:clxxxvii.

196. Murray, *Jonathan Edwards,* 68; cf. 454–66.

197. Edwards, *Some Thoughts Concerning the Present Revival of Religion in New England,* 1:381–83; *An Humble Attempt to Promote Explicit Agreement and Visible Union of God's People in Extraordinary Prayer,* 2:278–312. Tracing the success of redemption from the present time to the fall of Antichrist, Edwards states that "[t]he Spirit of God shall be gloriously poured out for the wonderful revival and propagation of religion" (*A History of the Work of Redemption,* 1:604–5).

198. Idem, *The Justice of God in the Damnation of Sinners,* 1:679; cf. *God's Sovereignty in the Salvation of Men,* 2:849–54.

199. Idem, *God Glorified in Man's Dependence,* 2:3–7.

200. Idem, *Remarks on Important Theological Controversies,* 2:525–43.

201. Paul Ramsey, in Edwards, *Freedom of the Will,* 3.

202. Edwards, *Freedom of the Will,* 20–23, 171–333.

203. "So now, learning is at a great height in the world, far beyond what it was in the age when Christ appeared; and now the world, by their learning and wisdom, do not know God; and they seem to wander in darkness, are miserably deluded, stumble and fall in matters of religion, as in midnight darkness. Trusting to their learning, they grope in the day-time as in the night. . . . They scorn to submit their reason to divine revelation, to believe any thing that is above their comprehension; and so being wise in their own eyes, they become fools" (idem, *History of Redemption,* 1:601).

204. Idem, *Miscellaneous Observations on Important Theological Subjects,* 2:479–87.

205. Murray, *Jonathan Edwards,* 429. Italics his.

206. Edwards, *The Great Christian Doctrine of Original Sin Defended,* 1:149.

207. Ibid., 1:213; cf. *Natural Man in a Dreadful Condition,* 2:817–29.

208. Idem, *History of Redemption,* 1:535.

209. Idem, *A Faithful Narrative of the Surprising Work of God in the Conversion of Many Hundred Souls,* 1:344–64; *Some Thoughts Concerning the Present Revival of Religion,* 1:365–430.

210. Idem, *God Makes Men Sensible of Their Misery Before He Reveals His Mercy and Love,* 2:836; *A Faithful Narrative,* 1:350–58.

211. Ibid., 2:830–38; *Sinners in the Hands of an Angry God,* 2:7–12; *Remarks on Important Theological Controversies,* 2:515–25; *Natural Man in a Dreadful Condition,* 2:817–29.

212. Idem, *Pressing into the Kingdom of God,* 1:659–63.

213. Idem, *Remarks on Important Theological Controversies,* 2:588.

214. Ibid., 2:590; *Justification by Faith Alone,* 1:623; *God Glorified in Man's Dependence,* 2:3–4.

215. Idem, *A Divine and Supernatural Light, Immediately Imparted to the Soul by the Spirit of God, Shown to Be Both a Scriptural and Rational Doctrine*, 2:14; cf. 2:16–17; *Remarks on Important Theological Controversies*, 2:593.

216. Idem, *A Treatise on Religious Affections* (Grand Rapids: Baker Book House, 1982 [1746]), 131, 138, 140, 162.

217. Idem, *Original Sin*, 1:215; *Sinners in the Hands of an Angry God*, 2:9. "Those who are truly converted, are new men, new creatures; they are sanctified throughout, in spirit, soul and body: old things are passed away, all things are become new; they have new dispositions, a new conversation, and a new practice; they walk in newness of life, and continue to do so to the end of life" (*Religious Affections*, 307–8).

218. Idem, *Religious Affections*, 351–55.

219. Murray, *Jonathan Edwards*, 151.

220. Edwards, *Remarks on Important Theological Controversies*, 2:596–98.

221. This is also the theme of *The Distinguishing Marks of a Work of the Spirit of God*, 2:257–77. The issue of perseverance in holiness also led to a controversy in Edwards's church in Northampton over the conditions for becoming a communicant (*An Humble Inquiry into the Rules of the Word of God, Concerning the Qualifications Requisite to a Complete Standing and Full Communion in the Visible Christian Church*, 1:431–84; *A Farewell Sermon Preached at the First Precinct at Northampton*, 1:cxcix).

222. Idem, *Religious Affections*, 5.

223. Idem, *Some Thoughts Concerning the Present Revival of Religion*, 1:371.

224. Idem, *Religious Affections*, 8.

225. Ibid., 12–13.

226. Ibid., 11, 14–15. "The Author of human nature has not only communicated affections to men, but has made them very much the spring of their actions. As the affections necessarily belong to human nature, so holy affections not only necessarily belong to true religion, but constitute a principal part of it" (ibid., 16–17; cf. 18).

227. Ibid., 16; cf. 19–40.

228. Ibid., 41–44.

229. Ibid., 50–125.

230. Ibid., 182.

231. Ibid., 182–92.

232. Ibid., 212–58.

233. Ibid., 192–211, 258–96.

234. Ibid., 311. "The true Christian perseveres in the way of universal obedience, through all the various trials by which he is exercised, to the end of life. . . . True saints may in some degree backslide, they may be foiled by particular temptations, and may fall even into great sins; but they never fall so as to grow weary of religion and the service of God, and habitually and finally to dislike and neglect it . . ." (ibid., 307).

235. Ibid., 339–44. Three years after writing *Religious Affections*, Edwards used the life of David Brainerd as a model for this position (*The Life and Diary of the Rev. David Brainerd*, 2:313–458).

236. Idem, *Religious Affections*, 166.

237. Idem, *The Nature of True Virtue*, 1:132, 135.

238. Idem, *Religious Affections*, 177.

239. Ibid., 167–81; *The Nature of True Virtue*, 1:130–35.

240. Idem, *Religious Affections*, 302. "The higher gracious affections are raised, the more is a spiritual appetite increased" (ibid., 296).

241. Idem, *Concerning the End for Which God Created the World*, 1:103; *The Justice of God*, 1:679.

242. Idem, *Religious Affections*, 46. "That which a man chooses for his god, he sets his heart mainly upon. . . . The gods which a natural man worships, instead of the God that made him, are himself and the world. He has withdrawn his esteem and honour from God, and proudly exalts himself" (*Men Naturally Are God's Enemies*, 2:133). Edwards

remarks that unbelievers are inconsistent in their wills. In some respects they want to come to Christ, but they are averse to do so. "They wish to have salvation from misery, but yet are averse to those things wherein salvation consists. . . . They do not like God as he is, and yet they would not like him if he were otherwise. . . . They do not like men that are holy, nor yet do they like men that are wicked. . . . They refuse to accept of heaven as it is; yet they would not like it if it were otherwise" (*Wicked Men Inconsistent with Themselves,* 2:919–21).

243. Idem, *The Christian Pilgrim,* 2:243.

244. Ibid., 2:244.

245. Idem, *Natural Men in a Dreadful Condition,* 2:820.

246. Idem, *The Peace which Christ Gives His True Followers,* 2:92.

247. Idem, *Ruth's Resolution,* 1:665–66; *Remarks on Important Theological Controversies,* 2:585.

248. Idem, *The Nature of True Virtue,* 1:127; *The Unreasonableness of Indetermination in Religion,* 2:60; *God the Best Portion of the Christian,* 2:104–6; *Religious Affections,* 343.

249. Idem, *Concerning the End for Which God Created the World,* 1:101.

250. Idem, *The Excellency of Christ,* 1:689.

251. Idem, *God Glorified in Man's Dependence,* 2:5; *History of Redemption,* 1:616–18; *The Church's Marriage to Her Sons, and to Her God,* 2:21, 29; *Miscellaneous Observations,* 2:618–41; *The Portion of the Righteous,* 2:888–901.

252. George E. Arbaugh and George B. Arbaugh, *Kierkegaard's Authorship* (London: George Allen & Unwin Ltd., 1968), 18.

253. Kierkegaard's M.A. thesis, *The Concept of Irony,* has been interpreted as a youthful Hegelian work, but it is more likely that this essay on irony is itself ironic in nature (Lee M. Capel, "Historical Introduction" to Søren Kierkegaard, *The Concept of Irony,* trans. Lee M. Capel [London: Collins, 1966], 14–15, 36; Arbaugh and Arbaugh, *Kierkegaard's Authorship,* 47).

254. Louis P. Pojman, *Kierkegaard as Philosopher* (Swindon, Wiltshire: Waterleaf Press, 1978), 3; James Collins, *The Mind of Kierkegaard* (Princeton, New Jersey: Princeton University Press, 1983), 98–136, 175–207.

255. Howard V. Hong and Edna H. Hong, ed. and trans., *Søren Kierkegaard's Journals and Papers,* 7 vols. (Bloomington, Ind.: Indiana University Press, 1978), 5324 (the serially ordered references in this edition will be cited rather than volume and page numbers); Walter Lowrie, *Kierkegaard* (London: Oxford University Press, 1938), 150.

256. Søren Kierkegaard, "A First and Last Declaration," in *Concluding Unscientific Postscript,* trans. David F. Swenson and Walter Lowrie (Princeton, N.J.: Princeton University Press, 1941); *The Point of View for My Work as an Author,* trans. Walter Lowrie (New York: Harper & Row, 1962), 5–6.

257. Louis P. Pojman, *The Logic of Subjectivity* (University, Alabama: University of Alabama Press, 1984), 89; Stephen Crites, "Introduction," to Søren Kierkegaard, *Crisis in the Life of an Actress,* trans. Stephen Crites (London: Collins, 1967), 42–43.

258. A profound religious experience during Holy Week, 1848 evidently made this more direct communication possible to Kierkegaard. "My whole nature is changed. My concealment and inclosing reserve are broken—I am free to speak" (*Journals,* 6131; Crites, "Introduction," to *Crisis,* 56; Walter Lowrie, "Preface" to Søren Kierkegaard, *Christian Discourses,* trans. Walter Lowrie [Princeton, N.J.: Princeton University Press, 1940], v, xi).

259. Pojman, *The Logic of Subjectivity,* 87–90; Paul L. Holmer, "Introduction" to Søren Kierkegaard, *Edifying Discourses,* ed. Paul L. Holmer, trans. David F. and Lillian Marvin Swenson (New York: Harper Torchbooks, 1958), x–xiii.

260. Alastair Hannay, *Kierkegaard* (London: Routledge & Kegan Paul, 1982), 7; Pojman, *The Logic of Subjectivity,* 1–2.

261. Søren Kierkegaard, *The Concept of Anxiety,* ed. and trans. Reidar Thomte and Albert B. Anderson (Princeton, N.J.: Princeton University Press, 1980), 81, 85. (Italics deleted in this and most other quotations.)

262. Idem, *The Sickness unto Death,* ed. and trans. Howard V. Hong and Edna H. Hong (Princeton, New Jersey: Princeton University Press, 1980), 13.

263. Idem, *The Concept of Anxiety,* 49; cf. 44. The idea of anxiety was a lifelong and pervasive concern in Kierkegaard's life. "Anxiety is the organ by which the subject appropriates sorrow and assimilates it. Anxiety is the energy of the movement by which sorrow bores its way into one's heart. But the movement is not swift like the thrust of a dart, it is successive; it is not once for all, but it is constantly continuing" (*Either/Or,* 2 vols., trans. David F. Swenson, Lillian Marvin Swenson, and Walter Lowrie [Princeton, N.J.: Princeton University Press, 1944, 1959], 1:152).

264. Idem, *Philosophical Fragments,* trans. David F. Swenson and Howard V. Hong (Princeton, New Jersey: Princeton University Press, 1936, 1962), 58. "Whoever has learned to be anxious in the right way has learned the ultimate. If a human being were a beast or an angel, he could not be in anxiety. Because he is a synthesis, he can be in anxiety; and the more profoundly he is in anxiety, the greater is the man—yet not in the sense usually understood, in which anxiety is about something external, about something outside a person, but in the sense that he himself produces the anxiety" (*The Concept of Anxiety,* 155).

265. Idem, *The Sickness unto Death,* 127; Regis Jolivet, *Introduction to Kierkegaard,* trans. W. H. Barber (London: Frederick Muller Ltd., 1950), 147–48.

266. Kierkegaard, *Postscript,* 474.

267. Idem, *The Sickness unto Death,* 77.

268. Ibid., 17–21; Arbaugh and Arbaugh, *Kierkegaard's Authorship,* 302; Jolivet, *Introduction to Kierkegaard,* 146–47, 158–64.

269. Kierkegaard, *The Sickness unto Death,* 82, 131; Arbaugh and Arbaugh, *Kierkegaard's Authorship,* 299–300.

270. Søren Kierkegaard, *Training in Christianity,* trans. Walter Lowrie (Princeton, New Jersey: Princeton University Press, 1941), 72; David F. Swenson, "Translator's Introduction," to *Philosophical Fragments,* xxxiii–xxxiv.

271. Kierkegaard, *Journals,* 4032.

272. However, Kierkegaard observed that "[m]ost men are characterized by a dialectic of indifference and live a life so far from the good (faith) that it is almost too spiritless to be called sin—indeed, almost too spiritless to be called despair" (*The Sickness unto Death,* 101; Edward John Carnell, *The Burden of Søren Kierkegaard* [Exeter, Devon: Paternoster Press, 1965], 78–80).

273. Søren Kierkegaard, *Stages on Life's Way,* trans. Walter Lowrie (Princeton, N.J.: Princeton University Press, 1940); Pojman, *The Logic of Subjectivity,* xi.

274. Kierkegaard, *Postscript,* 507. "[L]ife will soon teach one that there are many kinds of dialectics, that almost every passion has its own" (*Either/Or,* 1:157).

275. Idem, *Either/Or,* 2:215; *The Sickness unto Death,* 29–74. "One cannot despair at all without willing it, but to despair truly one must truly will it, but when one truly wills it one is truly beyond despair; when one has truly willed despair one has truly chosen that which despair chooses, i.e., oneself in one's eternal validity. The personality is tranquilized only in despair, not by necessity, for I never despair by necessity, but by freedom, and only thereby does one win the absolute. . . . It is a man's true salvation to despair" (*Either/Or,* 2:215, 225).

276. Idem, *Postscript,* 227–28.

277. Idem, *Either/Or,* 2:173; cf. 2:161–72, 179–82, 263.

278. Ibid., 2:151.

279. Ibid., 2:31, 140–41, 144, 151–55. Kierkegaard moved quickly from the aesthetic to the religious sphere, and at the time of writing *Either/Or* had decided to abandon his plans to marry Regina Olsen.

280. "Infinite resignation is the last stage before faith, so that anyone who has not made this movement does not have faith, for only in infinite resignation do I become conscious of my eternal validity, and only then can one speak of grasping existence by virtue of faith" (idem, *Fear and Trembling,* trans. Howard V. Hong and Edna H. Hong

[Princeton, N.J.: Princeton University Press, 1983], 46; T. H. Croxall, "Assessment," in Søren Kierkegaard, *Johannes Climacus or De omnibus dubitandum est,* trans. T. H. Croxall [London: Adam & Charles Black, 1958], 97; Jolivet, *Introduction to Kierkegaard,* 136–40).

281. Pojman, *The Logic of Subjectivity,* 7–8; Kierkegaard, *Postscript,* 448. In *The Concept of Irony,* Kierkegaard argues that "no authentic human life is possible without irony. He who does not understand irony and has no ear for its whisperings lacks *eo ipso* what might be called the absolute beginning of the personal life" (338–39).

282. Pojman, *The Logic of Subjectivity,* 8.

283. Kierkegaard, *Postscript,* 494.

284. Ibid., 495–97.

285. Ibid., 495, 498. "It is easier to become a Christian when I am not a Christian than to become a Christian when I am one" (ibid., 327).

286. Douglas V. Steere, "Introduction" to Søren Kierkegaard, *Works of Love,* trans. David F. Swenson and Lillian Marvin Swenson (London: Geoffrey Cumberlege, Oxford University Press, 1946), x; Walter Lowrie, "Introduction" to Kierkegaard, *Postscript,* xix–xx; Arbaugh and Arbaugh, *Kierkegaard's Authorship,* 29–31.

287. Kierkegaard, *Postscript,* 33. "[A]n eternal happiness is rooted in the infinite personal passionate interest, which the individual renounces in order to become objective, defrauded of his interest by the predominating objectivity" (ibid., 28).

288. Ibid., 54–55. "Passion and reflection are generally exclusive of one another" (ibid., 540; Crites, "Introduction" to *Crisis,* 26).

289. Kierkegaard, *Postscript,* 278, 173. "[O]nly the truth which edifies is truth for you" (*Either/Or,* 2:356).

290. Ibid., 116; "Remember Now Thy Creator in the Days of Thy Youth," in *Edifying Discourses,* 87–88.

291. Kierkegaard, *Postscript,* 182, 201.

292. Ibid., 25. "He makes it evident that in relation to Him there can be no question of any proofs, that a man does not come to Him by the help of proofs, that there is no direct transition to this thing of becoming a Christian, that at the most the proofs might serve to make a man attentive, so that once he has become attentive he may arrive at the point of deciding whether he will believe or be offended. For the proofs remain equivocal . . ." (*Training in Christianity,* 98).

293. Idem, *Philosophical Fragments,* 125, 130.

294. Idem, *Training in Christianity,* 28.

295. Idem, *Postscript,* 194–95.

296. Ibid., 188, 330; Neils Thulstrup, "Commentator's Introduction" to *Philosophical Fragments,* lxxxiii.

297. Idem, *Postscript,* 512. "Christianity is not a doctrine but an existential communication expressing an existential contradiction" (ibid., 339).

298. Ibid., 201.

299. Pojman, *The Logic of Subjectivity,* 77; Croxall, "Assessment," in Kierkegaard, *Johannes Climacus,* 84.

300. Kierkegaard, *Postscript,* 540.

301. Idem, *The Sickness unto Death,* 98–100.

302. Idem, *Judge for Yourselves!,* trans. Walter Lowrie (London: Oxford University Press, 1941), 118; *Postscript,* 189. "Faith is by no means partial to probability; to make such an assertion about Faith is to slander it" (*Philosophical Fragments,* 118).

303. Idem, *Postscript,* 383–85. "For without risk there is no faith, and the greater the risk the greater the faith; the more objective security the less inwardness (for inwardness is precisely subjectivity), and the less objective security the more profound the possible inwardness" (ibid., 188; Pojman, *The Logic of Subjectivity,* 80, 82–83).

304. Kierkegaard, *Postscript,* 90; Arbaugh and Arbaugh, *Kierkegaard's Authorship,* 406; Pojman, *Kierkegaard as Philosopher,* 22.

305. Kierkegaard, *Johannes Climacus,* 152.

306. Idem, *The Sickness unto Death*, 129–31.

307. Idem, *Philosophical Fragments*, 81.

308. "[M]an receives the condition in the Moment, the same condition which, since it is requisite for the understanding of the eternal Truth, is *eo ipso* an eternal condition" (ibid., 77; cf. 21–23, 26, 30, 79).

309. Pojman, *Religious Belief and the Will*, 11–12, 71–74, 92, 99.

310. Kierkegaard, *Training in Christianity*, 67–68; *Philosophical Fragments*, 85, 128.

311 ·Idem, *Repetition*, trans. Howard V. Hong and Edna H. Hong (Princeton, New Jersey: Princeton University Press, 1983).

312. Carnell, *The Burden of Søren Kierkegaard*, 148; Kierkegaard, *Works of Love*, 201; "The Expectation of Faith," in *Edifying Discourses*, 10–27.

313. Kierkegaard, "Man's Need of God Constitutes His Highest Perfection," in *Edifying Discourses*, 141.

314. Ibid., 136, 145. "[T]he Christian knows that a sense of the need of God is man's perfection. Thus the Christian is once for all aware of God and is saved from the presumption which might be called ungodly awareness" ("The Anxieties of the Heathen," in *Christian Discourses*, 67). "To need God is man's highest perfection. . . . If man did not have absolute need of God he could not (1) know himself—self-knowledge, (2) be immortal. . . . Man's highest achievement is to let God be able to help him" (*Journals*, 53–54).

315. Idem, "Man's Need of God," 150–51. "Christianly it is not at all right to stress that all mankind needs Christianity and then to prove it and demonstrate it. The Christian stress is: *I* need Christianity" (*Journals*, 2028).

316. Idem, "Man's Need of God," 170.

317. Ibid., 175.

318. Idem, *Training in Christianity*, 81–82; *Journals*, 1137, 1414. "Only when a person has become so unhappy or has penetrated the wretchedness of this existence so deeply that he must truly say: For me life has no value—only then can he make a bid for Christianity. And then life can get its highest value" (*Journals*, 1152).

319. Idem, "Thoughts Which Wound from Behind—for Edification," in *Christian Discourses*, 250. "God's kingdom only can be sought when it is sought first; he who does not seek God's kingdom first does not seek it at all" ("The Lilies of the Fields and the Birds of the Air," in *Christian Discourses*, 331).

320. Idem, "The Anxieties of the Heathen," in *Christian Discourses*, 37, 47–49.

321. Idem, *Postscript*, 351.

322. Idem, *Purity of Heart Is to Will One Thing*, trans. Douglas V. Steere (New York: Harper Torchbooks, 1958).

323. Ibid., 69, 72; *Postscript*, 352; Hannay, *Kierkegaard*, 218–23.

324. Kierkegaard, *Postscript*, 367. "Christianity in no wise seeks . . . to destroy sensuousness, for it teaches that it is only in the resurrection that none shall be taken in marriage nor given in marriage. But it also calls to mind the man who had no time to attend the great marriage feast because he was holding his own" (*The Concept of Irony*, 305, note).

325. Idem, "Joyful Notes in the Strife of Suffering," in *Christian Discourses*, 105; Arbaugh and Arbaugh, *Kierkegaard's Authorship*, 33, 36, 352. The individual "does not mediate between the absolute *telos* and finite ends. In his immediacy the individual is rooted in the finite. But when resignation has convinced itself that he has acquired the absolute direction toward the absolute *telos*, all is changed, and the roots have been severed" (Kierkegaard, *Postscript*, 367).

326. Idem, "Man's Need of God," 175.

327. Idem, *Works of Love*, 22; Hannay, *Kierkegaard*, 215.

328. Kierkegaard, "Joyful Notes," 146; cf. 142.

329. Idem, *Journals*, 1365; *Postscript*, 350; Pojman, *The Logic of Subjectivity*, 17–21.

330. "Deep within every human being there still lives the anxiety over the possibility of being alone in the world, forgotten by God, overlooked among the millions and millions in this enormous household. One keeps this anxiety at a distance by looking at the many round about who are related to him as kin and friends, but the anxiety is still

there, nevertheless, and one hardly dares think of how he would feel if all this were taken away" (Kierkegaard, *Journals,* 100).

331 Idem, *Postscript,* 346.

332. Idem, "The Expectation of an Eternal Happiness," in *Edifying Discourses,* 117; cf. 112–26.

333. Idem, *Postscript,* 19–20; Carnell, *The Burden of Søren Kierkegaard,* 166.

334. Søren Kierkegaard, *Attack upon "Christendom,"* trans. Walter Lowrie (Princeton, N.J.: Princeton University Press, 1944, 1968), 247. "[W]hen the individual is secure in his God-relationship and suffers only outwardly, then this is not religious suffering. . . . for suffering is precisely the expression for the God-relationship, that is, the religious suffering, which signalizes the God-relationship and the fact that the individual has not arrived at happiness by emancipating himself from a religious relationship to an absolute *telos*. . . . If I take the uncertainty away—in order to get a still greater certainty—then I do not get a believer in his humility, in fear and trembling, but I get an aesthetic coxcomb, a devil of a fellow, who wishes, speaking loosely, to fraternize with God, but who, speaking precisely, stands in no relationship to God whatever" (*Postscript,* 405, 407).

335. Idem, *Attack upon "Christendom,"* 271; cf. 168–69, 287–88.

336. Idem, "Joyful Notes," 103–10; *Training in Christianity,* 196. "So when retributive justice, either here on earth or hereafter at the Day of Judgement, seeks the place where I a sinner stand with all my guilt—it does not find me, I no longer stand in that place, I have left it, Another stands in my place, Another who entirely puts Himself in my place. For this I thank Thee, Lord Jesus Christ" ("Three Discourses at the Communion on Fridays," in *Christian Discourses,* 369).

337. Idem, *Attack upon "Christendom,"* 197; cf. 29, 32, 166; *Postscript,* 423–24.

338. Idem, *Judge for Yourselves!* 202.

339. Idem, *For Self-Examination,* trans. Walter Lowrie (London: Oxford University Press, 1941), 42; *Judge for Yourselves!* 199; *Journals,* 1497.

340. Idem, *Judge for Yourselves!* 131; cf. 113–57; *For Self-Examination,* 106; *Attack upon "Christendom,"* 172.

341. Idem, "The Anxieties of the Heathen," 86. "And the love which loves God is the most beneficial bond, which by keeping a man wholly in God's service saves him from anxieties. This love unifies a man, it makes him eternally in agreement with himself and with the Master who is one; and it unifies a man in likeness to God" (ibid.; cf. *Works of Love,* 17).

342. Idem, "Thoughts Which Wound from Behind," 197. "Woe to the presumptuous man who would make bold to love God without needing Him! . . . Thou shalt not presume to love God for God's sake; thou shalt eternally understand that thy life's welfare eternally depends upon this, and for this reason thou shalt love Him" (ibid.).

343. Idem, *Philosophical Fragments,* 48; *Works of Love,* 15.

344. Idem, *Works of Love,* 125; cf. 8–9, 33, 56, 116.

345. Idem, "Love Shall Cover a Multitude of Sins," in *Edifying Discourses,* 50–51.

346. Idem, *Works of Love,* 5–6.

347. Paul Tillich, *Perspectives on 19th and 20th Century Protestant Theology,* ed. Carl E. Braaten (New York: Harper & Row, 1967), 91; J. Heywood Thomas, *Paul Tillich—an Appraisal* (London: SCM Press Ltd., 1963), 176.

348. Alexander J. McKelway, *The Systematic Theology of Paul Tillich* (London: Lutterworth Press, 1964), 18–20, 23.

349. Paul Tillich, *Systematic Theology,* 3 vols. (London: SCM Press Ltd., 1951–63), 2:53–54. Tillich, however, regarded Freud's analysis of human libido as "adequate for man only in his existential predicament but not in his essential nature" (ibid., 2:54).

350. Ibid., 2:52.

351. Ibid.

352. Ibid., 2:54; *Love, Power, and Justice* (London: Oxford University Press, 1954), 29–30, 116–17.

353. Idem, *Love, Power, and Justice,* 117.

354. Idem, *The Courage to Be* (New Haven: Yale University Press, 1952), 41.

355. Idem, *Systematic Theology,* 2:34.

356. Ibid., 1:193–94.

357. "The decisive event which underlies the search for meaning and the despair of it in the 20th century is the loss of God in the 19th century" (idem, *The Courage to Be,* 142).

358. Ibid., 52.

359. Ibid., 56.

360. Ibid., 74–75. There are also pathological or neurotic forms of these three anxieties that produce an unrealistic security, certitude, and perfection (ibid., 75–77; cf. 64–69).

361. Idem, "The Right to Hope," in Mark Kline Taylor, *Paul Tillich: Theologian of the Boundaries* (London: Collins, 1987), 325; "The Good that I will, I do not," in *The Eternal Now* (London: SCM Press Ltd., 1963), 38.

362. Idem, *Systematic Theology,* 3:30–31.

363. Ibid., 3:32.

364. Idem, *The Courage to Be,* 87.

365. Idem, *The Protestant Era,* trans. James Luther Adams (Chicago: University of Chicago Press, 1948; Phoenix Books, 1957), 187.

366. Charles W. Kegley and Robert W. Bretall, eds., *The Theology of Paul Tillich* (New York: Macmillan Company, 1952), 123.

367. Paul Tillich, *Theology of Culture,* ed. Robert C. Kimball (New York: Oxford University Press, 1959), 43–44, 46; *The Religious Situation,* trans. H. Richard Niebuhr (Meridian Books, 1956 [1932]), 52.

368. Idem, *Perspectives on 19th and 20th Century Protestant Theology,* 237–38; "Author's Introduction," in *The Protestant Era,* xvi.

369. Idem, *The Religious Situation,* 20.

370. Ibid., 101; Roger L. Shinn, "Tillich as Interpreter and Disturber of Contemporary Civilization," in James Luther Adams, Wilhelm Pauck, and Roger Lincoln Shinn, eds., *The Thought of Paul Tillich* (San Francisco: Harper & Row, 1985), 52.

371. Tillich, "Author's Introduction," in *The Protestant Era,* xv; *Perspectives on 19th and 20th Century Protestant Theology,* 238.

372. Idem, *The Protestant Era,* 56–57; cf. xii.

373. Idem, "Man and Earth," in *The Eternal Now,* 59–60; cf. 64.

374. Idem, *Dynamics of Faith* (New York: Harper & Row, 1957), 41–42, 45. Symbols are good when they point unambiguously to the transcendent, but they become false "when they are regarded as possessing an intrinsic meaning or when they claim absolute value for themselves" (*The Religious Situation,* 12).

375. Robert P. Scharlemann, *Reflection and Doubt in the Thought of Paul Tillich* (New Haven, Connecticut: Yale University Press, 1969), 45.

376. Tillich, *Theology of Culture,* 22, 26–27.

377. Idem, *Biblical Religion and the Search for Ultimate Reality* (London: James Nisbet & Co., 1955), 27. Although for Tillich, God as *a* being is transcended by God as Being-itself, the Ground of Being is nevertheless the Ground of personal being. "[O]ur encounter with the God who is a person includes the encounter with the God who is the ground of everything personal and as such not *a* person" (ibid., 83).

378. Idem, *Systematic Theology,* 2:19–44.

379. McKelway, *The Systematic Theology of Paul Tillich,* 26–27, 65, 146–50. In volume 1 of *Systematic Theology,* Tillich gives an essentialist account of human life as grounded in the divine being, followed by an existential analysis of the human situation in volume 2.

380. Tillich, *Systematic Theology,* 2:29–36.

381. Ibid., 2:44.

382. Idem, *Theology of Culture*, 123.

383. "Destructive conflict and tragedy in human life come from sin, not from finitude; yet it is finitude that makes sin possible. This is the point at which the doctrine of Creation and the doctrine of the Fall join; and this is the point at which one must either accept Tillich's account as doing justice to the mystery of human existence, or reject it as unintelligible" (Kegley and Bretall, *The Theology of Paul Tillich*, 125–26; McKelway, *The Systematic Theology of Paul Tillich*, 29, 31).

384. Thomas, *Paul Tillich—an Appraisal*, 132.

385. Paul Tillich, "You Are Accepted," in *The Shaking of the Foundations* (London: SCM Press Ltd., 1949), 154–55.

386. Idem, *Biblical Religion*, 55.

387. Idem, "The Good that I will, I do not," 45.

388. Idem, *Systematic Theology*, 2:75.

389. Idem, "What Is Wrong with the 'Dialectic' Theology?" in Taylor, *Paul Tillich: Theologian of the Boundaries*, 113.

390. Idem, *Theology of Culture*, 125.

391. Idem, "We Live in Two Orders," in *The Shaking of the Foundations*, 22–23.

392. Idem, *Systematic Theology*, 3:97.

393. Idem, *Biblical Religion*, 55; William Pauck, "To Be or Not to Be: Tillich on the Meaning of Life," in Adams, Pauck, and Shinn, *The Thought of Paul Tillich*, 42.

394. Paul Tillich, "Our Ultimate Concern," in *The Boundaries of Our Being* (London: Collins, 1966), 268; cf. 264–70.

395. Ibid., 269.

396. Idem, *Dynamics of Faith*, 1–2.

397. Idem, *The Religious Situation*, 108. "[T]he question of what a basic need is cannot be answered with assurance. But the problem comes into the open if, after the satisfaction of basic needs, new needs are endlessly engendered and satisfied and—in a dynamic economy—engendered in order to be satisfied" (*Systematic Theology*, 3:73–74).

398. Idem, "The Meaning of Joy," in *The Boundaries of Our Being*, 259–60.

399. Idem, "Our Ultimate Concern," 264, 269–70.

400. Idem, "The Paradox of the Beatitudes," in *The Shaking of the Foundations*, 27.

401. Idem, *Biblical Religion*, 72.

402. Ibid., 59; Scharlemann, *Reflection and Doubt in the Thought of Paul Tillich*, 71–72.

403. Tillich, *Systematic Theology*, 2:78–79.

404. Idem, "You Are Accepted," 155–56.

405. Idem, *Systematic Theology*, 2:79.

406. Idem, *Theology of Culture*, 142–43.

407. Idem, *The Protestant Era*, xvii, 209; James Luther Adams, *Paul Tillich's Philosophy of Culture, Science, and Religion* (New York: Harper & Row, 1965), 60. "[O]ne cannot command the courage to be and one cannot gain it by obeying a command. Religiously speaking, it is a matter of grace" (Tillich, *The Courage to Be*, 84–85).

408. Paul Tillich, *Morality and Beyond* (New York, Harper Torchbooks, 1963), 62.

409. Idem, *Theology of Culture*, 68; Ann Belford Ulanov, "The Anxiety of Being," in Adams, Pauck, and Shinn, *The Thought of Paul Tillich*, 125.

410. Tillich, *The Protestant Era*, xvii; Adams, *Paul Tillich's Philosophy of Culture, Science, and Religion*, 42.

411. Tillich, *Theology of Culture*, 40. "[F]aith is the state of being *grasped* by the transcendent unity of unambiguous life—it embodies love as the state of being *taken into* that transcendent unity" (*Systematic Theology*, 3:129).

412. Idem, *Dynamics of Faith*, 6, 35, 38, 40; *Biblical Religion*, 51–53.

413. Idem, "You Are Accepted," 162; *The Courage to Be,* 182–90; *Theology of Culture,* 144.

414. Idem, "To Whom Much Is Forgiven . . ." in *The Boundaries of Our Being,* 160; *Theology of Culture,* 211.

415. Idem, *Theology of Culture,* 68. "Accepting that one is accepted is the paradox of salvation without which there would be no salvation but only despair" (*Systematic Theology,* 2:179).

416. Idem, *The Courage to Be,* 3–4; cf. 155–78.

417. Idem, *Dynamics of Faith,* 17–18; *The Courage to Be,* 78–79; "The Right to Hope," 327–31.

418. Idem, *Biblical Religion,* 55–56.

419. Idem, *Theology of Culture,* 213; cf. 211; *Systematic Theology,* 2:119, 125; Ian E. Thompson, *Being and Meaning: Paul Tillich's Theory of Meaning, Truth and Logic* (Edinburgh: Edinburgh University Press, 1981), 17.

420. Idem, *Systematic Theology,* 2:177.

421. Idem, *The Protestant Era,* 93; *Theology of Culture,* 212; *Morality and Beyond,* 64.

422. McKelway, *The Systematic Theology of Paul Tillich,* 23, 25, 159.

423. Langdon Gilkey, "The New Being and Christology," in Adams, Pauck, and Shinn, *The Thought of Paul Tillich,* 319–21; cf. 307–10.

424. Tillich, *Systematic Theology,* 2:121; *The Protestant Era,* 112.

425. Idem, *Systematic Theology,* 3:107, 112.

426. Ibid., 3:108–9, 401–2; *Love, Power, and Justice,* 116.

427. "It is not an exaggeration to say that today man experiences his present situation in terms of disruption, conflict, self-destruction, meaninglessness, and despair in all realms of life. . . . The question arising out of this experience . . . is the question of a reality in which the self-estrangement of our existence is overcome, a reality of reconciliation and reunion, of creativity, meaning, and hope. We shall call such a reality the 'New Being'" (idem, *Systematic Theology,* 1:49; cf. 3:260–61, 358; "The Riddle of Inequality," in *The Eternal Now,* 36; Ulanov, "The Anxiety of Being," 126).

428. Tillich, *Theology of Culture,* 212; "The Right to Hope," 331. "The *appetitus* of every being to fulfil itself through union with other beings is universal and underlies the *eros* as well as the *philia* quality of love" (*Love, Power, and Justice,* 33).

429. Idem, "Loneliness and Solitude," in *The Eternal Now,* 17.

430. Karl Rahner, *The Practice of Faith* (New York: Crossroad Publishing Company, 1983), ix–xii; idem, *Words of Faith,* ed. Alice Scherer (New York: Crossroad Publishing Company, 1987), viii; "Translator's Foreword" to Karl Rahner, *I Remember,* trans. Harvey D. Egan (New York: Crossroad Publishing Company, 1985), 1–2, 5, 76.

431. Johannes B. Metz, "Foreword" to Karl Rahner, *Spirit in the World,* trans. Johannes B. Metz (London: Sheed and Ward, 1968 [1939]), xvii–xviii; Karl-Heinz Weger, *Karl Rahner: An Introduction to His Theology,* trans. David Smith (New York: Seabury Press, 1980), 14–16; Rahner, *I Remember,* 3.

432. Rahner, *Spirit in the World,* 202.

433. Ibid., 69; cf. xlii–xliii, 42, 68, 239; idem, *Hearers of the Word,* rev. J. B. Metz, trans. Ronald Walls (London: Sheed and Ward, 1969 [1941]), 59.

434. Rahner, *Hearers of the Word,* 143.

435. Ibid., 53; *Spirit in the World,* 240.

436. Idem, *Hearers of the Word,* 63–66; *Spirit in the World,* xvi, xliii–xliv, liii.

437. Idem, *Hearers of the Word,* 64; idem, *Foundations of Christian Faith,* trans. William V. Dych (London: Darton Longman & Todd, 1978), 20–21, 33. "Thus in its pre-apprehension, the spirit already and always possesses in every act being in its totality, and seeks to fill up the formal emptiness of the being given in the pre-apprehension through the object of every individual act" (*Spirit in the World,* 283).

438. Idem, *Spirit in the World,* 282.

439. Johannes B. Metz, "Foreword" to Rahner, *Spirit in the World,* xvi, quoting a lecture given by Rahner in Chicago in 1966.

440. Rahner, *Foundations of Christian Faith*, 34–35.

441. Idem, *Theological Investigations (TI)*, vol. VII: *Further Theology of the Spiritual Life 1*, trans. David Bourke (New York: Seabury Press, 1977), 278.

442. Idem, *TI*, vol. VIII: *Further Theology of the Spiritual Life 2*, trans. David Bourke (New York: Seabury Press, 1977), 191.

443. Idem, *TI*, vol. III: *The Theology of the Spiritual Life*, trans. Karl-H. and Boniface Kruger (London: Darton, Longman & Todd, 1967), 31.

444. Idem, *Spirit in the World*, 296; *Hearers of the Word*, 66; *Foundations of Christian Faith*, 34.

445. Idem, *Spirit in the World*, 406–7.

446. Idem, *Hearers of the Word*, 106–8; *Foundations of Christian Faith*, 32.

447. Idem, *TI*, vol. II: *Man in the Church*, trans. Karl-H. Kruger (London: Darton, Longman & Todd, 1963), 94; cf. 91–96.

448. Idem, *TI*, vol. IX: *Writings of 1965–67 1*, trans. Graham Harrison (London: Darton, Longman & Todd, n.d.), 122; *The Practice of Faith*, 68.

449. Idem, *The Practice of Faith*, 7.

450. Idem, *Foundations of Christian Faith*, 39; *TI*, III:388–89.

451. Idem, *TI*, vol. VI: *Concerning Vatican Council II*, trans. Karl-H. and Boniface Kruger (London: Darton, Longman & Todd, 1969), 78; *TI*, vol. XIII: *Theology, Anthropology, Christology*, trans. David Bourke (New York: Seabury Press, 1975), 163; *Christian at the Crossroads*, trans. V. Green (New York: Seabury Press, 1975), 18, 23; Paul Imhof and Hubert Biallowons, eds., *Karl Rahner in Dialogue*, trans. Harvey D. Egan (New York: Crossroad Publishing Company, 1986), 147; *Words of Faith*, 8.

452. "There are after all two unsurpassable words and realities which consequently converge: there is man—the infinite question—and there is the infinite Mystery—the infinite and absolute answer by remaining a mystery: there is man and God" (idem, *TI*, vol. V: *Later Writings*, trans. Karl-H. Kruger [London: Darton, Longman & Todd, 1966], 14).

453. Idem, *The Trinity*, trans. Joseph Donceel (New York: Herder and Herder, 1970), 46–47; *Faith in a Wintry Season*, ed. Paul Imhof, Hubert Biallowons, and Harvey D. Egan (New York: Crossroad Publishing Company, 1990), 23; *The Religious Life Today* (New York: Seabury Press, 1975), 4.

454. Idem, *The Trinity*, 43; *Belief Today*, trans. M. H. Heela, Ray and Rosaleen Okendon, and William Whitman (New York: Sheed and Ward, 1965, 1967), 69; *TI*, VIII:241–46.

455. Idem, *Studies in Modern Theology* (London: Burns & Oates, 1965), 62; *Hearers of the Word*, 15; *Spirit in the World*, xliii–xliv.

456. Idem, *Foundations of Christian Faith*, 52, 57.

457. Ibid., 12, 128; *TI*, V:38–39.

458. Idem, *Foundations of Christian Faith*, 120; *Karl Rahner in Dialogue*, 141; *The Religious Life Today*, 75.

459. Idem, *TI*, vol. IV: *More Recent Writings*, trans. Kevin Smyth (London: Darton, Longman & Todd, 1974 [1966]), 183–84.

460. Idem, *TI*, vol. I: *God, Christ, Mary and Grace*, trans. Cornelius Ernst (London: Darton, Longman & Todd, 1974 [1961]), 178; *Words of Faith*, 3.

461. Idem, *Spirit in the World*, xlv; *The Religious Life Today*, 42, 47; *TI*, VIII:230–31.

462. Idem, *The Christian of the Future*, trans. W. J. O'Hara (New York: Herder and Herder, 1967), 86–87.

463. Idem, *The Practice of Faith*, 86–90, 135, 276; *TI*, III:130; VIII:234.

464. Idem, *The Practice of Faith*, 133–34.

465. Ibid., 255; *Foundations of Christian Faith*, 125; *Words of Faith*, 25–26; *TI*, V:12.

466. Idem, *Faith in a Wintry Season*, 2, 27; *The Practice of Faith*, 68.

467. Idem, *TI*, vol. XI: *Confrontations 1*, trans. David Bourke (London: Darton, Longman & Todd, 1974), 174–75.

468. Idem, *The Practice of Faith*, 82, 135; *The Religious Life Today*, 48–49.

469. Karl Rahner and Karl-Heinz Weger, *Our Christian Faith*, trans. Francis McDonagh (New York: Crossroad Publishing Company, 1981), 25; Martin Redfern, *Karl Rahner, SJ* (London: Sheed and Ward, 1972), 25; Rahner, *The Practice of Faith*, 43.

470. Rahner, *Words of Faith*, 15; *Belief Today*, 108; *Studies in Modern Theology*, 409–10; *TI*, V:20; VII:166–67.

471. Idem, *The Religious Life Today*, 57.

472. Ibid., 5; *Spirit in the World*, 408; *TI*, V:46.

473. Idem, *The Practice of Faith*, 160; *TI*, VIII:13, 15, 218.

474. Idem, *TI*, VII:271–72. "[T]he incarnation of God is the uniquely supreme case of the actualisation of man's nature in general" (ibid., VI:393).

475. Ibid., II:244–45; VIII:221; IX:167; *Words of Faith*, 91–92.

476. Idem, *TI*, VIII:226, 239.

477. Ibid., VIII:236; IX:124; *The Practice of Faith*, 9.

478. Idem, *TI*, V:191; *Words of Faith*, 89; *Christian at the Crossroads*, 26; *The Practice of Faith*, 61.

479. Idem, *Words of Faith*, 86; *The Religious Life Today*, 45; *TI*, VIII:14.

480. Idem, *TI*, II:278–79; III:134–35; VIII:39; *The Practice of Faith*, 299; *Foundations of Christian Faith*, 409.

481. Idem, *Christian at the Crossroads*, 73, 75.

482. Idem, *TI*, IX:122–23; XIII:149–51; *Foundations of Christian Faith*, 91–93, 123; *The Practice of Faith*, 268.

483. Idem, *TI*, II:96; V:97–98; IX:126.

484. Ibid., V:97.

485. Rahner and Weger, *Our Christian Faith*, 123; Rahner, *Foundations of Christian Faith*, 146–47; *Studies in Modern Theology*, 419.

486. Idem, *TI*, II:35–36, 82–83; *Studies in Modern Theology*, 53. The church is "the community of those who hope, those who are waiting, of pilgrims who still seek their own homeland, of those who understand and master their present in terms of the future" (*TI*, VI:297).

487. Idem, *Studies in Modern Theology*, 203–4.

488. Idem, *Foundations of Christian Faith*, 322; *The Christian of the Future*, 82.

489. Idem, *The Religious Life Today*, 32.

490. Idem, *TI*, V:118.

491. Ibid., II:44–45; VI:390–91.

492. Ibid., II:76–77, 84–86.

493. Ibid., II:45; *Words of Faith*, 76.

494. Idem, *TI*, V:122–23; VIII:121; *The Practice of Faith*, 8, 11; *The Church after the Council*, trans. Davis C. Herron and Rodelinde Albrecht (New York: Herder and Herder, 1966), 61–62.

495. Idem, *TI*, V:128; IX:145–64; *Foundations of Christian Faith*, 401; *Karl Rahner in Dialogue*, 184.

496. Idem, *Words of Faith*, 76–79.

497. Idem, *Foundations of Christian Faith*, 309; *TI*, VIII:16–17.

498. Idem, *TI*, VIII:18, 20.

499. Idem, *The Practice of Faith*, 136.

500. Ibid.; *The Church after the Council*, 25; *The Practice of Faith*, 142; *TI*, VI:231–49. In response to criticism concerning his integration of love for God and neighbor, Rahner notes that he never disputed that at least theoretically, God's love is more important than love of neighbor (*Faith in a Wintry Season*, 26).

501. Idem, *Words of Faith*, 38, 50–51.

502. Idem, *The Practice of Faith*, 15, 238.

503. Ibid., 170; *Words of Faith*, 55–56.

504. Idem, *Foundations of Christian Faith*, 322–23.

505. Idem, *The Religious Life Today,* 29–30.

506. Ibid., 6; *Foundations of Christian Faith,* 322–23; *TI,* II:239–40.

507. Idem, *TI,* V:7–8; vol. X: *Writings of 1965–67 2,* trans. David Bourke (New York: Seabury Press, 1977), 365.

508. Idem, *The Practice of Faith,* 296–97.

509. Ibid., 251–52, 297; *TI,* V:8.

510. Idem, *Foundations of Christian Faith,* 403–4; *The Religious Life Today,* 8–10. "A Christian is a person who believes that in the very brief course of his existence he really makes an ultimate and radical and irreversible decision in a matter which really concerns his ultimate and radical happiness, or his permanent and eternal loss" (*Foundations of Christian Faith,* 403).

511. Idem, *TI,* XIII:176–78; *The Religious Life Today,* 78.

512. Idem, *TI,* VI:60–62, 144; X:251; XIII:183; *Foundations of Christian Faith,* 277–78, 405; *The Priesthood,* trans. Edward Quinn (New York: Seabury Press, 1973), 5–6. "An act of hope in one's resurrection is something which takes place in every person by transcendental necessity either in the mode of free acceptance or of free rejection. For every person wants to survive in some final and definitive sense and experiences this claim in his acts of freedom and responsibility, whether he is able to make this implication of the exercise of his freedom thematic or not, and whether he accepts it in faith or rejects it in despair" (*Foundations of Christian Faith,* 268).

513. Idem, *The Practice of Faith,* 248.

514. Ibid., 298; cf. 6–7, 248, 264–65; *TI,* VI:152; *Foundations of Christian Faith,* 209; Rahner and Weger, *Our Christian Faith,* 164; Imhof and Biallowons, *Karl Rahner in Dialogue,* 351.

Chapter 2

1. Murray, *Jonathan Edwards,* xix.

2. Edwards, *The Preciousness of Time,* 2:236; *Natural Men in a Dreadful Condition,* 2:828–29; *God's Sovereignty in the Salvation of Men,* 2:854; *Religious Affections,* 126–29.

3. Kierkegaard, *Philosophical Fragments,* 130; *Postscript,* 31.

4. Pojman, *The Logic of Subjectivity,* 145.

5. Joel R. Smith, "Creation, Fall, and Theodicy in Paul Tillich's *Systematic Theology,*" in John J. Carey, ed. *Kairos and Logos: Studies in the Roots and Implications of Tillich's Theology* (Atlanta: Mercer University Press, 1984), 164.

6. Tillich, *Systematic Theology,* 2:145.

7. Rahner, *TI,* V:131–33; VI:394–98; ibid., vol. XII: *Confrontations 2,* trans. David Bourke (London: Darton, Longman & Todd, 1974), 161–78.

8. Idem, *Karl Rahner in Dialogue,* 350; *The Church after the Council,* 64; *TI,* V:11.

9. Idem, *TI,* VI:394–98; *Foundations of Christian Faith,* 402.

Part 2

1. Salvatore R. Maddi, *Personality Theories: A Comparative Analysis,* 4th ed. (Homewood, Ill.: Dorsey Press, 1980); cf. Calvin S. Hall and Gardner Lindzey, *Theories of Personality,* 3rd ed. (New York: John Wiley & Sons, 1978).

2. Ego psychology (represented by Erikson) can be regarded as a modification or even a departure from Freudianism in that it theorizes that the ego did not arise from the id and thus has a sphere of conflict-free autonomy. The object-relations position (e.g., Melanie Klein, Heinz Hartmann, Otto Kernberg) can be viewed as a variant on the psychosocial conflict model (Maddi, *Personality Theories,* 50–65; Jay R. Greenberg and Stephen A. Mitchell, *Object Relations in Psychoanalytic Theory* [Cambridge, Mass.: Harvard University Press, 1983]).

3. Maddi, *Personality Theories,* 88.

4. Representatives include George A. Kelley, Leon Festinger, and David C. McClelland.

5. Donald W. Fiske and Salvadore R. Maddi represent this version.

6. It is for this reason that no attempt will be made to discuss need differences between men and women.

7. Maddi, *Personality Theories,* 13–17.

8. Although Henry A. Murray developed an elaborate typology of needs, his position (a Freudian variation) is not developed in this thesis, because his discussion of needs concerns the peripheral level of the personality; the many needs he lists are largely learned and involve concrete goals and actions (ibid., 43–47, 307–17; Hall and Lindzey, *Theories of Personality,* 205–40).

9. James F. T. Bugental, *Challenges of Humanistic Psychology* (New York: McGraw-Hill, 1967), 130.

Chapter 4

1. *Introductory Lectures on Psychoanalysis,* 1:46–47. With the exception of *The Question of Lay Analysis, On Dreams, Beyond the Pleasure Principle, Three Essays on the Theory of Sexuality, The Ego and the Id,* "The Unconscious," "Some Elementary Lessons in Psychoanalysis," "Instincts and Their Vicissitudes," "Formulations on the Two Principles of Mental Functioning," "Repression," "Neurosis and Psychosis," and "The Loss of Reality in Neurosis and Psychosis," all references are from Sigmund Freud, 15 vols. *The Pelican Freud Library,* gen. eds. Angela Richards and Albert Dickson, trans. ed. James Strachey (Harmondsworth, Middlesex: Penguin Books, 1973–86). The other references are from Sigmund Freud, *The Essentials of Psycho-Analysis,* ed. Anna Freud, trans. James Strachey (Harmondsworth, England: Penguin Books, 1986).

2. "The Resistances to Psychoanalysis," 15:272.

3. *An Outline of Psychoanalysis,* 15:430.

4. "Some Elementary Lessons in Psychoanalysis," 186.

5. *New Introductory Lectures on Psychoanalysis,* 2:105–6.

6. Ibid., 2:106.

7. "The Unconscious," 159–60.

8. *Beyond the Pleasure Principle,* 219.

9. *The Ego and the Id,* 447.

10. *An Outline of Psychoanalysis,* 15:377; *New Introductory Lectures,* 2:109.

11. *The Ego and the Id,* 461–62.

12. "The Unconscious," 143.

13. *The Ego and the Id,* 440–44; *An Outline of Psychoanalysis,* 15:390–94. "But none of this implies that the quality of being conscious has lost its importance for us. It remains the one light which illuminates our path and leads us through the darkness of mental life" ("Some Elementary Lessons in Psychoanalysis," 189).

14. *An Outline of Psychoanalysis,* 15:394–96.

15. *Civilization and Its Discontents,* 12:263.

16. Ibid., 12:264–65, 271.

17. *Beyond the Pleasure Principle,* 220.

18. *An Outline of Psychoanalysis,* 15:377.

19. "Formulations on Two Principles of Mental Functioning," 510, 514; *New Introductory Lectures,* 2:108; *Beyond the Pleasure Principle,* 221.

20. *New Introductory Lectures,* 2:89–91.

21. Ibid., 2:96; *An Outline of Psychoanalysis,* 15:442; *The Ego and the Id,* 455–59.

22. *New Introductory Lectures,* 2:94; *Moses and Monotheism,* 363–64, 367.

23. *The Ego and the Id,* 474.

24. Ibid., 469. "What has belonged to the lowest part of the mental life of each of us is changed, through the formation of the ideal, into what is highest in the human mind by our scale of values. . . . the ego ideal answers to everything that is expected of the higher nature of man" (ibid., 459).

25. *New Introductory Lectures,* 2:110–11; *The Ego and the Id,* 476.

26. *An Outline of Psychoanalysis,* 15:379; "The Unconscious," 151.

27. "Instincts and Their Vicissitudes," 201–2; *New Introductory Lectures*, 2:128–29.

28. "Instincts and their Vicissitudes," 202.

29. Along similar lines, Freud contrasted ego-love and object-love: "[T]he development of the individual seems to us to be a product of the interaction between two urges, the urge towards happiness, which we usually call 'egoistic,' and the urge towards union with others in the community, which we call 'altruistic'" (*Civilization and Its Discontents*, 12:334).

30. "Instincts and Their Vicissitudes," 204.

31. *An Outline of Psychoanalysis*, 15:379.

32. Ibid., 15:379–80; *Beyond the Pleasure Principle*, 250–55, 265. Because of this instinct to return to the inanimate state, Freud noted that "the aim of all life is death" (*Beyond the Pleasure Principle*, 246).

33. *The Ego and the Id*, 464–68. Freud introduced this instinct in his theorizing after World War I and during the time of his struggle with cancer.

34. "Towards the two classes of instincts the ego's attitude is not impartial. Through its work of identification and sublimation it gives the death instincts in the id assistance in gaining control over the libido, but in so doing it runs the risk of becoming the object of the death instincts and of itself perishing. In order to be able to help in this way it has had itself to become filled with libido; it thus itself becomes the representative of Eros and thenceforward desires to live and to be loved" (ibid., 476). "The dangerous death instincts are dealt with in the individual in various ways: in part they are rendered harmless by being fused with erotic components, in part they are diverted towards the external world in the form of aggression, while to a large extent they undoubtedly continue their internal work unhindered" (ibid., 474).

35. *Totem and Taboo*, 13:159.

36. "Thoughts for the Times on War and Death," 12:69. In view of the id, people are more immoral than they believe, but in view of the superego, they are more moral than they know (*The Ego and the Id*, 472).

37. Ibid., 12:68.

38. *New Introductory Lectures*, 2:137.

39. *Why War?* 12:359.

40. *Beyond the Pleasure Principle*, 249. "I have no faith . . . in the existence of any such internal instinct and I cannot see how this benevolent illusion is to be preserved. The present development of human beings requires, as it seems to me, no different explanation from that of animals. What appears in a minority of human individuals as an untiring impulsion towards further perfection can easily be understood as a result of the instinctual repression upon which is based all that is most precious in human civilizations" (ibid.).

41. Identification also refers to the phenomenon of internalizing and modeling the characteristics of other people in order to enhance the satisfaction of instinctual needs. This kind of identification is the "earliest expression of an emotional tie with another person" (*Group Psychology and the Analysis of the Ego*, 12:134), but it is normally ambivalent.

42. *The Ego and the Id*, 476–77; *New Introductory Lectures*, 2:117.

43. *New Introductory Lectures*, 2:126.

44. "Instincts and Their Vicissitudes," 205–11. In his *New Introductory Lectures*, Freud observed that "anxiety makes repression and not, as we used to think, the other way round, and . . . the instinctual situation which is feared goes back ultimately to an external situation of danger" (2:121).

45. "The Unconscious," 153–56; "Repression," 527–33. "When an instinctual trend undergoes repression, its libidinal elements are turned into symptoms, and its aggressive components into a sense of guilt" (*Civilization and Its Discontents*, 12:332). The "return of the repressed" in symbolic form is, for Freud, a significant factor in the dynamic of dreams. Sleep inactivates the censor that limits access to the unconscious and enables the mind to engage in the primary process of wishful thinking. But due to the reduction of repression, this attempt at wish-fulfillment is not always successful: "While the sleeper is obliged to dream, because the relaxation of repression at night allows the

upward pressure of the traumatic fixation to become active, there is a failure in the functioning of his dream-work, which would like to transform the memory-traces of the traumatic event into the fulfillment of a wish" (*New Introductory Lectures*, 2:59; cf. *Introductory Lectures*, 1:111–278; *An Outline of Psychoanalysis*, 15:397–404). The phenomena that Freud called parapraxes (e.g., slips of the tongue, forgetting) arise from a psychical mechanism that is similar to that of dreams (*On Dreams*, 113, 117; *Introductory Lectures*, 1:50–108).

46. *Totem and Taboo*, 13:84.

47. *The Future of an Illusion*, 12:187.

48. *Introductory Lectures*, 1:362–82; *An Outline of Psychoanalysis*, 15:382–86.

49. *New Introductory Lectures*, 2:131–34.

50. *Beyond the Pleasure Principle*, 230; *New Introductory Lectures*, 2:145–69.

51. "Formulations on the Two Principles of Mental Functioning," 515. "A human being remains to some extent narcissistic even after he has found external objects for his libido. The cathexes of objects which he effects are as it were emanations of the libido that still remains in his ego and can be drawn back into it once more" (*Totem and Taboo*, 13:147).

52. *Totem and Taboo*, 13:222; "'Civilized' Sexual Morality and Modern Nervous Illness," 12:42–43. "[T]he fact which is characteristic of the neurosis is the preponderance of the sexual over the social instinctual elements. . . . Neuroses are asocial structures; they endeavour to achieve by private means what is effected in society by collective effort" (*Totem and Taboo*, 13:130).

53. *Group Psychology*, 12:178. "[N]eurosis is the result of a conflict between the ego and its id, whereas psychosis is the analogous outcome of a similar disturbance in the relations between the ego and the external world" ("Neurosis and Psychosis," 563–66; "The Loss of Reality in Neurosis and Psychosis," 570–72).

54. *The Question of Lay Analysis*, 58–59.

55. *New Introductory Lectures*, 2:112.

56. Ibid.

57. "Postscript" to *The Question of Lay Analysis*, 71; *The Ego and the Id*, 476.

58. This difference of interpretation is evident in these contrasting statements: "[I]t is the task and the goal of psycho-analytic work to enlarge the domain of conscious thinking, to fill gaps in it, to uncover and dissolve resistances against permitting psychic contents to gain consciousness. It is a triumph for every analyst when he succeeds in making unconscious processes conscious" (Anna Freud, "Introduction" to "The Concept of the Unconscious" in *The Essentials of Psycho-Analysis*, 129). "[T]he notion of replacing id with ego is not very likely to mean making unconscious things conscious. . . . The most accurate description of the goal of psychoanalysis, if the position is to have logical consistency, is the substitution, for defenses that heavily distort truth, of defenses that constitute less of a distortion" (Maddi, *Personality Theories*, 38–39).

59. *An Outline of Psychoanalysis*, 15:406–7.

60. Ibid., 15:408–16; *On Dreams*, 83–84; *Introductory Lectures*, 1:482–500. "We serve the patient in various functions, as an authority and a substitute for his parents, as a teacher and educator; and we have done the best for him if, as analysts, we raise the mental processes in his ego to a normal level, transform what has become unconscious and repressed into preconscious material and thus return it once more to the possession of his ego" (*An Outline of Psychoanalysis*, 15:415).

61. "'Civilized' Sexual Morality and Modern Nervous Illness," 12:54.

62. *Civilization and Its Discontents*, 12:284; "Thoughts for the Times on War and Death," 12:69.

63. *Civilization and Its Discontents*, 12:327; cf. 12:274–75, 280, 315–22, 329; *The Future of an Illusion*, 12:190. "Civilized man has exchanged a portion of his possibilities of happiness for a portion of security" (*Civilization and Its Discontents*, 12:306). Because of the evolution of a communal superego, Freud draws an analogy between the process of civilization and the libidinal development of the individual (ibid., 12:286, 335).

64. "'Civilized' Sexual Morality and Modern Nervous Illness," 12:38–49.

65. *The Future of an Illusion,* 12:194.

66. Ibid., 12:185; *Civilization and Its Discontents,* 12:302–3, 309–14.

67. "Thoughts for the Times on War and Death," 12:70, 72; cf. 12:66–67. "[War] strips us of the later accretions of civilization, and lays bare the primal man in each of us" (ibid., 12:88).

68. *Totem and Taboo,* 13:134. Freud draws a comparison between these phases in the development of a view of the universe and the stages of an individual's libidinal development (ibid., 13:146–48).

69. Ibid., 13:56–70, 79–82.

70. Ibid., 13:104–5.

71. *The Future of an Illusion,* 12:196–98, 201–2.

72. *Totem and Taboo,* 13:150; *The Future of an Illusion,* 12:226. "[I]f the totem animal is the father, then the two principal ordinances of totemism, the two taboo prohibitions which constitute its core—not to kill the totem and not to have sexual relations with a woman of the same totem—coincide in their content with the two crimes of Oedipus, who killed his father and married his mother, as well as with the two primal wishes of children, the insufficient repression or the re-awakening of which forms the nucleus of perhaps every psychoneurosis. . . . Totemic religion arose from the filial sense of guilt, in an attempt to allay that feeling and to appease the father by deferred obedience to him. All later religions are seen to be attempts at solving the same problem. . . . God is nothing other than an exalted father. . . . while the totem may be the *first* form of father-surrogate, the god will be a later one, in which the father has regained his human shape. . . . In the Christian myth the original sin was one against God the Father" (*Totem and Taboo,* 13:192, 206, 209–10, 216). Thus, Freud traces the Eucharist back to the totem meal (ibid., 13:217, 220). In *Moses and Monotheism,* Freud constructs a scenario in which the forgotten memory-trace of the killing of the primal father-figure was awakened in the murder of an Egyptian Moses who communicated the monotheism of Akhenaten to the Jews. A second (Midianite) Moses brought in the religion of Yahweh but legend soldered the two figures and religions together. After a period of latency, the first religion of monotheism emerged victorious. In this construction, Freud saw analogy with the psychopathology of trauma, repression, latency, and defensive reactions against the partial return of the repressed. According to him, Christianity took this a step further by exorcizing humanity's sense of guilt through the idea of redemption.

73. *The Future of an Illusion,* 12:204.

74. *Civilization and Its Discontents,* 12:262–63.

75. Ibid., 12:269, 273; *The Future of an Illusion,* 12:212–13, 215; "Obsessive Actions and Religious Practices," 13:31–40.

76. *The Future of an Illusion,* 12:207–11, 214, 220–21, 231–33.

77. *New Introductory Lectures,* 2:193–211.

78. Ibid., 2:218–19. "We believe that it is possible for scientific work to gain some knowledge about the reality of the world, by means of which we can increase our power and in accordance with which we can arrange our life" (*The Future of an Illusion,* 12:239).

79. Erik H. Erikson, *Identity: Youth and Crisis* (New York: W. W. Norton & Company, 1968), 50.

80. Ibid., 46; *Identity and the Life Cycle* (New York: W. W. Norton & Company, 1959), 17–18.

81. *Identity: Youth and Crisis,* 73–74; *Identity and the Life Cycle,* 162.

82. *Identity and the Life Cycle,* 49.

83. *Childhood and Society,* 2nd ed. (New York: W. W. Norton & Company, 1963), 34–37, 46.

84. *Identity: Youth and Crisis,* 23. "In recent years we have come to the conclusion that a neurosis is psycho- and somatic, psycho- and social, and interpersonal" (*Childhood and Society,* 23).

85. *Identity and the Life Cycle,* 49–50.

86. Ibid., 50.

87. Ibid. "In general, the concept of the ego was first delineated by previous definitions of its better-known opposites, the biological id and the sociological 'masses': the ego, the individual center of organized experience and

reasonable planning, stood endangered by both the anarchy of the primeval instincts and the lawlessness of the group spirit" (ibid., 18–19).

88. *Identity: Youth and Crisis,* 50, 53–54; *Childhood and Society,* 240–41.

89. *Childhood and Society,* 15–16.

90. Ibid., 154. Erikson's study of the Sioux Indians illustrates the problem of cultural pathology generated by the transplanting of a civilization into a radically different cultural system (ibid., 131, 154–56, 164). Among the Sioux, "the very expression of what was once considered to be efficient and aristocratic behavior—such as the disregard for property and the refusal to compete—only leads to an alignment with the lowest strata of our society" (ibid., 156).

91. Ibid., 35, 42; *Identity: Youth and Crisis,* 72.

92. *Identity: Youth and Crisis,* 64, 67–68. "Except in cases of stark disorganization of thought, we can assume that what we call the synthesizing function of the ego will tend to associate what 'belongs together,' be the associated items ever so remote in history, separate in space, and contradictory in legal terms" (*Insight and Responsibility* [New York: W. W. Norton & Company, 1964], 58).

93. *Insight and Responsibility,* 146–47 (italics deleted); *Identity: Youth and Crisis,* 217–19; *Childhood and Society,* 193.

94. *Identity: Youth and Crisis,* 50; cf. *Identity and the Life Cycle,* 22.

95. *Identity: Youth and Crisis,* 49, 208–11.

96. Ibid., 220; cf. 219–24.

97. Ibid., 92; *Identity and the Life Cycle,* 53.

98. *Childhood and Society,* 246; *Identity and the Life Cycle,* 7; *Insight and Responsibility,* 114.

99. *Identity: Youth and Crisis,* 16, 95–96; *Identity and the Life Cycle,* 57.

100. *Identity and the Life Cycle,* 125 (italics deleted). Identity formation has both a self-aspect and an ego-aspect (ibid., 161).

101. *Identity: Youth and Crisis,* 104–5; *Identity and the Life Cycle,* 177–78.

102. *Childhood and Society,* 72–80, 247–51; *Identity: Youth and Crisis,* 96–107.

103. *Childhood and Society,* 250.

104. Ibid., 80–85, 251–54; *Identity: Youth and Crisis,* 107–14.

105. *Childhood and Society,* 254. "A general ability, indeed, a violent need, develops to alternate withholding and expelling at will and, in general, to keep tightly and to throw away whatever is held" (*Identity: Youth and Crisis,* 107).

106. *Identity: Youth and Crisis,* 113.

107. *Childhood and Society,* 85–92, 255–58; *Identity: Youth and Crisis,* 115–22.

108. *Childhood and Society,* 92–97, 258–61; *Identity: Youth and Crisis,* 122–28.

109. "It is immediately obvious that for the vast majority of men, in all times, this has been not only the beginning but also the limitation of their identity; or better: the majority of men have always consolidated their identity needs around their technical and occupational capacities" (*Identity: Youth and Crisis,* 127).

110. *Childhood and Society,* 261–63; *Identity: Youth and Crisis,* 128–35.

111. *Childhood and Society,* 261; *Identity: Youth and Crisis,* 128.

112. *Childhood and Society,* 263–66; *Identity: Youth and Crisis,* 135–38.

113. *Identity: Youth and Crisis,* 135.

114. *Childhood and Society,* 266–68; *Identity: Youth and Crisis,* 138–39.

115. *Childhood and Society,* 268–69; *Identity: Youth and Crisis,* 139–41.

116. *Identity: Youth and Crisis,* 140.

117. *Childhood and Society,* 269–74; *Identity and the Life Cycle,* 150–78. Since Erikson's primary concern is with the development of identity, the vertical and the horizontal cells in the diagram at stage five (adolescence) are filled in, but the other noncrisis cells are not.

118. "While the end of adolescence . . . is the stage of an overt identity crisis, identity formation neither begins nor ends with adolescence; it is a lifelong development largely unconscious to the individual and to his society. Its roots go back all the way to the first self-recognition: in the baby's earliest exchange of smiles there is something of a self-realization coupled with a mutual recognition. . . . A child, in the multiplicity of successive and tentative identifications, thus begins early to build up expectations of what it will be like to be older and what it will feel like to have been younger—expectations which become part of an identity as they are, step by step, verified in decisive experiences of psychosocial 'fittedness'" (*Identity and the Life Cycle*, 122–23, italics his).

119. Ibid., 128 (italics deleted).

120. Ibid., 165; *Childhood and Society*, 80.

121. *Identity and the Life Cycle*, 52–53.

122. *Identity: Youth and Crisis*, 141.

123. *Insight and Responsibility*, 231; *Identity and the Life Cycle*, 65.

124. *Identity: Youth and Crisis*, 83.

125. Ibid., 84.

126. Ibid., 106. "All religions have in common the periodical childlike surrender to a Provider or providers who dispense earthly fortune as well as spiritual health; some demonstration of man's smallness by way of reduced posture and humble gesture; the admission in prayer and song of misdeeds, of misthoughts, and of evil intentions; fervent appeal for inner unification by divine guidance; and finally the insight that individual trust must become a common faith, individual mistrust a commonly formulated evil" (*Childhood and Society*, 250; cf. *Identity and the Life Cycle*, 66–67).

127. *Identity: Youth and Crisis*, 106. "Each society and each age must find the institutionalized form of reverence which derives vitality from its world-image—from predestination to indeterminacy" (*Childhood and Society*, 251).

128. *Insight and Responsibility*, 153.

129. Ibid., 127; *Childhood and Society*, 251. "Whosoever says he has religion must derive a faith from it which is transmitted to infants in the form of basic trust; whosoever claims that he does not need religion must derive such basic faith from elsewhere" (*Identity and the Life Cycle*, 67).

130. *Identity: Youth and Crisis*, 259.

131. *Identity and the Life Cycle*, 109.

132. Ibid.

133. Ibid., 94; *Identity: Youth and Crisis*, 87–89, 159–63. "The emerging identity bridges the stages of childhood when the bodily self and the parental images are given their cultural connotations; and it bridges the stage of young adulthood, when a variety of social roles become available and, in fact, increasingly coercive" (*Childhood and Society*, 235).

134. *Identity: Youth and Crisis*, 22–23.

135. *Childhood and Society*, 413. In contemporary industrialized society, there is also a danger of creating a "mass-produced mask of individuality" instead of individualism (ibid., 295).

136. Ibid., 412.

137. *Identity: Youth and Crisis*, 40–41, 165; *Childhood and Society*, 412.

138. *Identity: Youth and Crisis*, 27, 35; *Insight and Responsibility*, 65.

139. *Insight and Responsibility*, 94–96; *Identity and the Life Cycle*, 175.

140. *Identity: Youth and Crisis*, 80–81; *Insight and Responsibility*, 92–93.

141. *Identity: Youth and Crisis*, 42.

142. Erikson also speaks of the basic virtues that must be formed in the course of the human life cycle to direct people through the seasons of life. In a healthy psychosocial context, the virtues of hope, will, purpose, and competence are developed in childhood; the virtue of fidelity is generated in adolescence; and the central virtues formed in adulthood are love, care, and wisdom (*Insight and Responsibility*, 115–34).

143. *Identity: Youth and Crisis,* 74; *Identity and the Life Cycle,* 50, 104.

144. *Identity and the Life Cycle,* 104.

145. *Insight and Responsibility,* 89; *Identity: Youth and Crisis,* 140–41.

146. Peter Homans, *Jung in Context* (Chicago: University of Chicago Press, 1979), 5–22. Homans contextualizes Jung's thought by analyzing the personal dimensions that contributed to its development and identifies four phases in the formative years of 1900–1918 during which Jung went through a process of identity diffusion and reconstruction, especially with regard to his relationship to Freud (ibid., 43–91). Homans contends that all the major ideas in Jung's mature thought can be traced to this process and that noncontextual approaches that overlook these psychobiographical dynamics cannot give an adequate account of the complexities and nuances of Jungian theory.

147. Ibid., 17.

148. C. G. Jung, *The Structure and Dynamics of the Psyche,* trans. R. F. C. Hull, 2nd ed., vol. 8 of *The Collected Works of C. G. Jung,* 20 vols., ed. William McGuire (London: Routledge & Kegan Paul, 1969), 19.

149. Maddi, *Personality Theories,* 67–68; Homans, *Jung in Context,* 14–15.

150. C. G. Jung, *Psychological Types,* trans. H. G. Baynes and R. F. C. Hull, vol. 6 of *The Collected Works,* 483.

151. Idem, *Psychological Reflections: An Anthology of His Writings 1905–1961,* ed. Jolande Jacobi (London: Routledge & Kegan Paul, 1971; Ark Paperbacks, 1986), 15; *Modern Man in Search of a Soul,* (London: Routledge & Kegan Paul, 1933; Ark Paperbacks, 1984), 20.

152. Idem, *Psychological Reflections,* 248.

153. Idem, *Modern Man in Search of a Soul,* 20–21.

154. Ibid., 5, 18.

155. Idem, *The Structure and Dynamics of the Psyche,* 253. Jung recognizes other dream functions such as reaction and anticipation but stresses that the contents of the unconscious are compensatory and therefore relative to consciousness (ibid., 252–60).

156. Idem, *Modern Man in Search of a Soul,* 30, 75.

157. Idem, *Psychological Reflections,* 38–39.

158. Idem, *The Structure and Dynamics of the Psyche,* 158; *The Archetypes and the Collective Unconscious,* trans. R. F. C. Hull, vol. 9 of The Collected Works, 42–43.

159. Idem, *The Archetypes and the Collective Unconscious,* 44.

160. Idem, *The Structure and Dynamics of the Psyche,* 218.

161. Ibid., 115–20.

162. Ibid., 206–7.

163. Idem, *Psychological Reflections,* 33, 42; *The Structure and Dynamics of the Psyche,* 158.

164. Idem, *The Structure and Dynamics of the Psyche,* 342.

165. Jung uses the terms *instinct* and *spirit* to stand for "powerful forces whose nature we do not know" (*Modern Man in Search of a Soul,* 136–37).

166. Ibid., 18–30.

167. Ibid., 18.

168. Idem, *Modern Man in Search of a Soul,* 20.

169. Maddi, *Personality Theories,* 78–80. "We psychologists have learned, through long and painful experience, that you deprive a man of his best resource when you help him to get rid of his complexes. You can only help him to become sufficiently aware of them and to start a conscious conflict within himself" (Jung, *Psychological Reflections,* 217).

170. Jung, *The Structure and Dynamics of the Psyche,* 39.

171. Idem, *Psychological Reflections,* 308.

172. Jung also stresses the importance of a balance between the pull of the collective consciousness and the collective unconscious. For subjective consciousness to avoid the identification with the collective consciousness that

produces a mass psyche, it must recognize the shadow of collective consciousness as well as the existence and the importance of the archetypes (idem, *The Structure and Dynamics of the Psyche,* 219–21).

173. Idem, *The Archetypes and the Collective Unconscious,* 288.

174. Ibid., 164, 187; *The Structure and Dynamics of the Psyche,* 223–26.

175. Idem, *The Archetypes and the Collective Unconscious,* 275; *Psychological Reflections,* 306.

176. Idem, *The Structure and Dynamics of the Psyche,* 72–73. "Man needs difficulties; they are necessary for health. What concerns us here is only an excessive amount of them" (ibid., 73).

177. Idem, *Modern Man in Search of a Soul,* 56; cf. 35–62; *Psychological Reflections,* 89.

178. Idem, *Psychological Reflections,* 27, 35, 147, 316.

179. Idem, *The Archetypes and the Collective Unconscious,* 289; *The Structure and Dynamics of the Psyche,* 73–74; *Memories, Dreams, Reflections,* ed. Aniela Jaffé, trans. Richard and Clara Winston, rev. ed. (New York: Vintage Books, 1963), 334–35.

180. Idem, *Psychological Reflections,* 357. "We have to learn to think in antinomies, constantly bearing in mind that every truth turns into an antinomy if it is thought out to the end" (ibid., 189).

181. Ibid., 152–72, 310.

182. Homans, *Jung in Context,* 143; cf. 135–50, 174–80.

183. Jung, *Psychological Reflections,* 146, 237. "Civilized life today demands concentrated, directed conscious functioning, and this entails the risk of a considerable dissociation from the unconscious. The further we are able to remove ourselves from the unconscious through directed functioning, the more readily a powerful counter-position can build up in the unconscious, and when this breaks out it may have disagreeable consequences" (idem, *The Structure and Dynamics of the Psyche,* 71).

184. Idem, *Psychological Reflections,* 224–28. "Individual self-reflection, return of the individual to the ground of human nature, to his own deepest being with its individual and social destiny—here is the beginning of a cure for that blindness which reigns at the present hour" (ibid., 230).

185. Idem, *The Structure and Dynamics of the Psyche,* 59–60. "[The] shift of the locus of meaning and order from the social to the personal, psychological sphere is the central conceptual leitmotiv that runs throughout Jung's personal life and his system of thought, unifying the two, and it constitutes both the positive achievement and the major limitation of his work" (Homans, *Jung in Context,* 208; cf. 178–79, 196–200, 209). Homans observes that Jung applied the core process of individuation to three major areas: psychoanalysis, the problem of modernity, and religion (ibid., 24, 98–107, 154–55).

186. C. G. Jung, *Symbols of Transformation,* trans. R. F. C. Hull, vol. 5 of *The Collected Works.*

187. Raymond Hostie, *Religion and the Psychology of C. G. Jung* (New York: Sheed and Ward, 1957); William Johnson, *The Search for Transcendence* (New York: Harper & Row, 1974); H. L. Philp, *Jung and the Problem of Evil* (London: Rockliff, 1958).

188. David Cox, *Jung and Saint Paul* (New York: Association Press, 1959); Morton T. Kelsey, *Christo-Psychology* (London: Darton, Longman & Todd, 1982); Hans Schaer, *Religion and the Cure of Souls in Jung's Psychology* (New York: Pantheon Books, 1950); Victor White, *God and the Unconscious* (Cleveland: World Publishing Company, 1952). W. Harold Grant, Magdala Thompson, and Thomas E. Clarke write, "Where Jung spoke of individuation, Jesus spoke of love. Both were thinking of the fullness of living to which we are all called. Both saw this vocation in terms of likeness to God" (*From Image to Likeness* [New York: Paulist Press, 1983], 179; cf. 180–85).

189. C. G. Jung, *Answer to Job,* trans. R. F. C. Hull (London: Ark Paperbacks, 1954, 1984), 28, 35, 53, 74, 93, 111; Homans, *Jung in Context,* 64–65.

190. C. G. Jung, *The Undiscovered Self,* trans. R. F. C. Hull (New York: Mentor Books, 1958), 48–49; cf. 84–85. "This is not to say that Christianity is finished. I am, on the contrary, convinced that it is not Christianity, but our conception and interpretation of it, that has become antiquated in face of the present world situation. The Christian symbol is a living thing that carries in itself the seeds of further development" (ibid., 74–75).

191. Idem, *Psychology and Religion: West and East,* trans. R. F. C. Hull, vol. 11 of *The Collected Works,* 81–96; *Psychological Types,* 53; Homans, *Jung in Context,* 131, 153, 183–91.

192. Jung, *The Undiscovered Self,* 102; *Psychological Reflections,* 337–38. "One should not be deterred by the rather silly objection that nobody knows whether these old universal ideas—God, immortality, freedom of the will, and so on—are 'true' or not. Truth is the wrong criterion here. One can only ask whether they are helpful or not, whether man is better off and feels his life more complete, more meaningful and more satisfactory with or without them" (*Psychological Reflections,* 326).

193. Idem, *Memories, Dreams, Reflections,* 336–38.

194. Idem, *Psychological Reflections,* 340.

195. Idem, *Memories, Dreams, Reflections,* 302; *Modern Man in Search of a Soul,* 203–7, 213; *The Structure and Dynamics of the Psyche,* 342.

196. Idem, *The Structure and Dynamics of the Psyche,* 409; *Modern Man in Search of a Soul,* 137.

197. C. G. Jung, et al., *Man and His Symbols* (Garden City, N.Y.: Doubleday & Company, 1964), 93–95.

198. Ibid., 101.

199. Jung, *Psychological Reflections,* 96, 336. "Since the only salutary powers visible in the world today are the great psychotherapeutic systems which we call the religions, and from which we expect the soul's salvation, it is quite natural that many people should make the justifiable and often successful attempt to find a niche for themselves in one of the existing creeds and to acquire a deeper insight into the meaning of the traditional saving verities" (ibid., 358).

200. Idem, *The Undiscovered Self,* 107–12, 116–17.

201. Idem, *Answer to Job,* 175–78. "The religious need longs for wholeness, and therefore lays hold of the images of wholeness offered by the unconscious, which, independently of our conscious mind, rise up from the depths of our psychic nature" (ibid., 178).

202. Idem, *Psychological Reflections,* 252.

203. "Hemmed round by rationalistic walls, we are cut off from the eternity of nature" (idem, *The Structure and Dynamics of the Psyche,* 380–81; *Psychological Reflections,* 314).

204. Idem, *Memories, Dreams, Reflections,* 358–59; cf. *Psychological Reflections,* 281–85.

205. Idem, *The Archetypes and the Collective Unconscious,* 12–15; *Psychological Reflections,* 344.

206. Idem, *Modern Man in Search of a Soul,* 264.

207. Ibid., 224, 277–80; *The Structure and Dynamics of the Psyche,* 402, 408; *Psychological Reflections,* 257.

208. David G. Winter, "Introduction" to Otto Rank, *The Don Juan Legend,* trans. David G. Winter (Princeton: Princeton University Press, 1975 [1922]), 3–16.

209. Otto Rank, *The Myth of the Birth of the Hero,* trans. F. Robbins and Smith Ely Jelliffe (New York: Robert Brunner, 1952 [1909]), 6.

210. Ibid., 61–69, 82, 91–93.

211. Idem, *The Double,* trans. Harry Tucker Jr. (Chapel Hill, N.C.: University of North Carolina Press, 1971 [1914]), 7, 12.

212. Ibid., 69–70; idem, *Beyond Psychology* (New York: Dover Publications, 1941 [1939]), 62–101.

213. Idem, *The Double,* 7, 12, 21, 33, 35, 42, 48, 69–70, 74–77.

214. Idem, *The Don Juan Legend,* 41, 56. Rank interpreted the Stone Guest in Mozart's *Don Giovanni* as an expression of guilt and paternal punishment (ibid., 77–80).

215. Winter, "Introduction," 30–32.

216. Otto Rank, *The Trauma of Birth* (New York: Robert Brunner, 1952 [1924]), xiii, xv, 54, 211.

217. Ibid., 194–95.

218. Ibid., 17 (italics deleted).

219. Ibid., 199.

220. Ibid., 23, 34–35, 38, 69–71, 88, 183.

221. Ibid., 28, 74–83, 106–11.

222. Ibid., 199. ". . . virtually the whole creation of civilization has only resulted from man's libidinal over-estimation of the maternal primal object and from its elimination through the primal repression" (ibid., 189).

223. Ibid., 43, 85–86, 92–99, 103–5, 173–77.

224. Ibid., 60–61, 73, 113–17, 126, 128–29, 131–32, 136–37.

225. Ibid., 210.

226. Ibid., 5 (italics deleted).

227. Ibid., 4–7, 11, 205, 207, 213–16.

228. Rank appears to sympathize with Freud's remark that after treatment, the cured neurotic often shows only ordinary unhappiness, where he previously had neurotic unhappiness (ibid., 200–201).

229. S. Ferenczi and Otto Rank, *The Development of Psycho-Analysis,* trans. Caroline Newton (Madison, Conn.: International Universities Press, 1986 [1924]), 54. "Psychoanalysis thus allows the patient to relive . . . the original infantile libidinal situation with a partial satisfaction under the condition of consciously giving up its unadjusted realization" (ibid., 19).

230. Ibid., 6–8, 19–22, 48, 67–68.

231. Ibid., 9–16, 45, 62.

232. Otto Rank, *Will Therapy,* trans. Jessie Taft (New York: Alfred A. Knopf, 1964 [1929, 1931]), vii–x.

233. Ibid., 35–36.

234. Ibid., 6, 26, 28–34, 37–41, 110.

235. Ibid., 21–22.

236. Ibid., 106–110. By this time, Rank rejected the Freudian interpretation of the Oedipus complex as a misleading projection of infantile content into the adult situation (ibid., 50–52).

237. Idem, *Truth and Reality,* trans. Jessie Taft (New York: Alfred A. Knopf, 1936 [1929]), 13.

238. Ibid., 42.

239. Ibid., 89; *Will Therapy,* 109, 113; *Beyond Psychology,* 28, 30–31.

240. Rank, *Beyond Psychology,* 49.

241. Idem, *Will Therapy,* 108, 119–24, 134.

242. Arthur Janov, *The Primal Scream* (New York: Delta Books, 1970).

243. Idem, *Truth and Reality,* 47.

244. Idem, *Will Therapy,* 101.

245. Ibid., 111–12; *Beyond Personality,* 50, 53.

246. Idem, *Will Therapy,* 44–45; *Psychology and the Soul,* trans. William D. Turner (New York: A. S. Barnes & Company, 1950 [1931]), 169, 171–77, 180–81, 194–95.

247. Idem, *Beyond Psychology,* 34, 46–48, 278; *Will Therapy,* 24–25.

248. Idem, *Will Therapy,* 8–9; *Truth and Reality,* 27–29, 31–33; *Psychology and the Soul,* 162–65.

249. Idem, *Truth and Reality,* 38; *Will Therapy,* 11.

250. Idem, *Psychology and the Soul,* 190; *Beyond Psychology,* 48.

251. Rank argues that "the man who suffers from pedagogical, social and ethical repression of will, must again learn to will. . . . the patient should make himself what he is, should will it and do it himself, without force or justification and without need to shift the responsibility for it" (*Truth and Reality,* 41).

252. Idem, *Will Therapy,* 146. However, this separation from reality is "only a seeming one" since the neurotic is "bound up in a kind of magic unity with the wholeness of life around him much more than the adjusted type who can be satisfied with the role of a part within the whole" (ibid., 147).

253. Ibid., 58, 72–74, 81–84.

254. Idem, *Truth and Reality,* 90.

255. Idem, *Will Therapy*, 154–55. According to Rank, the main body of neurotics are those who have "outgrown" the Jewish-Christian morality (*Truth and Reality*, 43, 45).

256. Idem, *Will Therapy*, 95, 146.

257. Ibid., 130–31, 133.

258. Rank differentiates "two fundamental types of artist, as there are also two great groups of neurotics, sometimes called the Dionysian and the Apollonic, and again the romantic and the classic" (ibid., 163).

259. Ibid., 127–28, 135, 141; *Truth and Reality*, 90; *The Trauma of Birth*, 190.

260. Idem, *Beyond Psychology*, 76.

261. In *The Don Juan Legend*, Rank observes that this is doomed to failure if the artist's work becomes popular because it becomes the new ego ideal of the masses (24, 122–23).

262. Idem, *Will Therapy*, 99–100.

263. Idem, *Psychology and the Soul*, 192; *The Trauma of Birth*, 212–13.

264. Idem, *Will Therapy*, 160. "The average man has reality consciousness more strongly developed, the creative type will consciousness, the neurotic individual self-consciousness. Reality consciousness comes from adaptation of will, the creative phantasy consciousness from will affirmation, the neurotic self consciousness from will denial" (*Truth and Reality*, 86).

265. Idem, *Will Therapy*, 86–88.

266. Ibid., 199; *Truth and Reality*, 16; *Psychology and the Soul*, 193.

267. Idem, *Truth and Reality*, 24–25.

268. Ibid., 8–10, 18, 68–69, 108–110, 113; *Beyond Psychology*, 11–14.

269. Idem, *Will Therapy*, 48–49, 62–65, 71; *Beyond Psychology*, 267, 269.

270. Idem, *Will Therapy*, 195; cf. 64, 67–68; *Truth and Reality*, 162–63; *Beyond Psychology*, 51.

271. "The patient must learn to live, to live with his split, his conflict, his ambivalence, which no therapy can take away, for if it could, it would take with it the actual spring of life. The more truly the ambivalence is accepted the more life and possibilities of life will the human being have and be able to use" (idem, *Will Therapy*, 206; cf. 4, 13, 15–17, 19, 32, 56).

272. Ibid., 14, 182–83, 190, 206.

273. Idem, *Truth and Reality*, 167, 169–70, 173–75, 181, 190.

274. Ibid., 54, 58, 60–61, 192–93; *Psychology and the Soul*, 183, 185; *Will Therapy*, 133.

275. Idem, *Truth and Reality*, 191–92.

276. Ibid., 117, 119, 131, 135–36, 138–41, 144, 156, 191–92.

277. Ibid., 83–86; *Will Therapy*, 96; *Beyond Psychology*, 15.

278. Idem, *Will Therapy*, 173.

279. Idem, *Truth and Reality*, 76–77.

280. Ibid., 6–7.

281. Idem, *Beyond Psychology*, 15, 20–23, 27, 291.

282. Ibid., 194.

283. Ibid., 290; cf. 195–97.

284. Ibid., 40–41; *Psychology and the Soul*, 148–49.

285. Idem, *Beyond Psychology*, 62; cf. 59–60, 64–65.

286. Ibid., 55, 87, 233; *Psychology and the Soul*, 13–14, 16, 21, 25, 27–28, 30, 38, 142–43; *The Double*, 84–86.

287. Idem, *Psychology and the Soul*, 31; cf. 86–87.

288. Ibid., 11–12, 84.

289. "The soul may not exist, and, like belief in immortality, it may prove to be man's greatest illusion; nevertheless it must picture not only the objects, but the content, of psychology, whose objects are not things or facts but ideas

and ideologies. And, like our entire human reality, which includes scientific psychology, these same ideologies are products of spiritual belief" (ibid., 191–92; cf. 31–32, 90; 193).

290. Idem, *Beyond Psychology,* 16 (italics his).

Chapter 5

1. Maddi, *Personality Theories,* 100.

2. Abraham H. Maslow, *Toward a Psychology of Being,* 2nd ed. (New York: Van Nostrand Reinhold Company, 1968), 16.

3. Idem, *Motivation and Personality,* 3rd ed. (New York: Harper & Row, 1987), 3, 211–38.

4. Idem, *Psychology of Being,* 216–18.

5. Jacob Bronowski, *Science and Human Values* (New York: Harper & Row, 1956).

6. Maslow, *Motivation and Personality,* 183, 186, 188–93.

7. Ibid., 59–60, 116, 149.

8. Idem, *Psychology of Being,* 3–4.

9. Hall and Lindzey, *Theories of Personality,* 268.

10. Maslow, *Motivation and Personality,* 47–55, 82–91.

11. Ibid., 6, 28.

12. Idem, *Psychology of Being,* 21–23.

13. Idem, *Motivation and Personality,* 30.

14. Ibid., 76–78, 118.

15. Ibid., 42–45.

16. Ibid., 7–10.

17. Ibid., 15–22.

18. Ibid., 7, 17–18, 56–59.

19. Ibid., 26.

20. Ibid., 28.

21. Idem, *Psychology of Being,* 25.

22. Idem, *Motivation and Personality,* 57–59.

23. Maddi, *Personality Theories,* 104.

24. Maslow, *Motivation and Personality,* 23–25.

25. Idem, *Psychology of Being,* 83; *The Farther Reaches of Human Nature* (New York: Viking Press, 1971), 308–9.

26. Idem, *Psychology of Being,* 15, 214.

27. Ibid., 26; *Motivation and Personality,* 128–49.

28. Idem, *Motivation and Personality,* 156; *Psychology of Being,* vi, 97.

29. Idem, *Psychology of Being,* 27–42.

30. Ibid., 73; *Eupsychian Management* (Homewood, Ill.: Richard D. Irwin, Inc. and The Dorsey Press, 1965), 119–21.

31. Ibid., 74–96, 104–14.

32. John A. Clippinger, "Toward a Human Psychology of Personality," in Malony, *Current Perspectives in the Psychology of Religion,* 317.

33. Maslow, *Psychology of Being,* 115–23.

34. Ibid., vi, 160.

35. James R. Scroggs and William G. T. Douglas, "Issues in the Psychology of Religious Conversion," in Malony, *Current Perspectives in the Psychology of Religion,* 261.

36. Maddi, *Personality Theories,* 100–101.

37. Maslow, *Motivation and Personality*, 5, 11–12, 62–68.

38. Ibid., 6, 28–29, 89.

39. When deficiency needs are gratified, they are no longer behavioral motivators (ibid., 30).

40. Ibid., 91, 117.

41. Ibid., 60.

42. Idem, *Psychology of Being*, 45–56, 163, 204–5; *The Farther Reaches*, 37.

43. Idem, *Psychology of Being*, 163, 204.

44. Maslow, *Psychology of Being*, iii.

45. Ibid., iii–iv.

46. Ibid., 206, iv; cf. Hall, "A Conversation with Abraham H. Maslow," 65.

47. Maslow, *Psychology of Being*, 210.

48. Ibid., 4–5, 10, 149–53, 167–75.

49. Carl R. Rogers, *A Way of Being* (Boston: Houghton Mifflin Company, 1980), 49.

50. Idem, *On Becoming a Person* (London: Constable & Company, 1961), ix; Maddi, *Personality Theories*, 86.

51. Carl R. Rogers, *Client-Centered Therapy* (London: Constable & Company, 1951), 15, 17; *On Becoming a Person*, 10–13.

52. Idem, *Client-Centered Therapy*, 440.

53. Idem, "A Theory of Therapy, Personality, and Interpersonal Relationships, as Developed in the Client-Centered Framework," in *Psychology: A Study of a Science*, ed. Sigmund Koch, vol. 3 (New York: McGraw-Hill Book Company, 1959), 191–92.

54. Rogers, *On Becoming a Person*, 226.

55. Idem, *Client-Centered Therapy*, 132–42; "A Theory of Therapy," 244–51; *On Becoming a Person*, 225–70.

56. Idem, "A Theory of Therapy," 184–256. Rogers has called this "the most rigorously stated theory of the process of *change* in personality and behavior that has yet been produced" but adds that it is also the most thoroughly ignored of anything he has written (*A Way of Being*, 59–60).

57. Idem, *Client-Centered Therapy*, 8; *On Becoming a Person*, 268–69.

58. Idem, *A Way of Being*, 58.

59. Idem, *Client-Centered Therapy*, 7 n. 1.

60. Idem, *A Way of Being*, 115.

61. Idem, *On Becoming a Person*, 61.

62. Ibid., 16–17, 51.

63. Ibid., 52–53, 62.

64. Idem, *Client-Centered Therapy*, 21.

65. Idem, *On Becoming a Person*, 53–56; *Client-Centered Therapy*, 29–30, 35, 45.

66. Idem, *On Becoming a Person*, 18–19.

67. Idem, *Client-Centered Therapy*, 30, 223–25.

68. Ibid., 199–203, 208–9, 218.

69. Idem, *On Becoming a Person*, 18–19, 22.

70. Idem, "A Theory of Therapy," 216.

71. Ibid., *Client-Centered Therapy*, 191–95.

72. Idem, *On Becoming a Person*, 128–58.

73. Ibid., 64–66, 76–105, 167–75; *Client-Centered Therapy*, 69–77, 108, 135–48; "A Theory of Therapy," 218–19.

74. Idem, *On Becoming a Person*, 91.

75. Ibid., 105.

76. Ibid., 26, 184; "A Theory of Therapy," 248.

77. Idem, *On Becoming a Person*, 26–27, 177–78, 194–95.

78. Ibid., 108, 110–14, 164–66.

79. Ibid., 22; *A Way of Being,* 118.

80. Idem, *On Becoming a Person,* 23–24.

81. Idem, *Client-Centered Therapy,* 157.

82. Ibid., 195; *On Becoming a Person,* 60.

83. Idem, *Client-Centered Therapy,* 196.

84. Idem, *A Way of Being,* 134.

85. Ibid., 119; Kurt Goldstein, *Human Nature in the Light of Psychopathology* (Cambridge, Mass.: Harvard University Press, 1947); Andras Angyal, *Foundations for a Science of Personality* (New York: Commonwealth Fund, 1941); *Neurosis and Treatment* (New York: John Wiley & Sons, 1965); Maslow, *Motivation and Personality.*

86. Rogers, *On Becoming a Person,* 35.

87. Idem, *Client-Centered Therapy,* 483–532; "A Theory of Therapy," 192–240.

88. Idem, "A Theory of Therapy," 222.

89. Idem, *Client-Centered Therapy,* 491–92.

90. Idem, "A Theory of Therapy," 200.

91. Idem, *A Way of Being,* 127.

92. Ibid., 123.

93. Idem, "A Theory of Therapy," 223–24.

94. Ibid., 224.

95. Idem, *Client-Centered Therapy,* 524.

96. Idem, *Carl Rogers on Personal Power* (New York: Delacorte Press, 1977), 244–45.

97. Idem, "A Theory of Therapy," 224–30; *Client-Centered Therapy,* 498–520.

98. Idem, *Client-Centered Therapy,* 532.

99. Idem, *On Becoming a Person,* 188–89.

100. Ibid., 115–24, 187–91; "A Theory of Therapy," 234–35.

101. Idem, *On Becoming a Person,* 122, 185–87, 195–96.

102. Ibid., 27.

103. Ibid., 194. When a person is functioning fully, "there are no barriers, no inhibitions, which prevent the full experiencing of whatever is organismically present" (*A Way of Being,* 128).

104. Idem, *A Way of Being,* 67.

105. Idem, "A Theory of Therapy," 235–40.

106. Idem, *A Way of Being,* 115–16, 139; *On Becoming a Person,* 37–38.

107. Idem, *Client-Centered Therapy,* 235–478; "A Theory of Therapy," 241–43; *On Becoming a Person,* 315–36, 348–59.

108. Idem, *A Way of Being,* ix. (Italics his.)

109. Ibid., 56. (Italics his.)

110. Ibid., 106.

111. What Szent-Gyoergyi terms "syntropy" in contrast to entropy. In this perspective, the universe is always building and creating as well as deteriorating (Albert Szent-Gyoergyi, "Drive in Living Matter to Perfect Itself," *Synthesis,* Spring 1974: 12–24).

112. Rogers, *A Way of Being,* 41–42.

113. Ibid., 96–108.

114. Ibid., 129–33, 253–56, 343–45. In 1979 he modified his view on death because of his experiences with a medium and his wife Helen before and after her death (ibid., 90–92).

115. Ibid., 347–52.

116. Alfred Adler, *The Individual Psychology of Alfred Adler,* ed. Heinz L. Ansbacher and Rowena R. Ansbacher (New York: Basic Books, 1956; Harper Torchbooks, 1964), 4–9.

117. Although these personality theorists are often called "neo-Freudians," it has been suggested that they would more aptly be named "neo-Adlerians" (ibid., 16–17).

118. Because of his phenomenological approach, Adler also developed propositions that were similar to those later articulated by Abraham Maslow and Carl Rogers.

119. Idem, *Individual Psychology,* 372.

120. Ibid., 376–82; Calvin S. Hall and Gardner Lindzey, *Introduction to Theories of Personality* (New York: John Wiley & Sons, 1985), 153.

121. Alfred Adler, *Understanding Human Nature,* trans. W. Béran Wolfe (Greenwich, Conn.: Fawcett Publications, 1927, 1954), 103–22; *Individual Psychology,* 45–52.

122. Maddi, *Personality Theories,* 111; Hall and Lindzey, *Introduction to Theories of Personality,* 163.

123. Adler, *Understanding Human Nature,* 32.

124. Idem, *What Life Should Mean to You,* trans. Alan Porter (New York: Perigree Books, 1958 [1931]), 8.

125. Idem, *Understanding Human Nature,* 35–37.

126. Idem, *Individual Psychology,* 39–40.

127. Idem, *Understanding Human Nature,* 62.

128. Idem, *What Life Should Mean to You,* 127.

129. Idem, *Understanding Human Nature,* 67.

130. Idem, *What Life Should Mean to You,* 71.

131. Idem, *Individual Psychology,* 77–88.

132. Hall and Lindzey, *Theories of Personality,* 161.

133. Adler, *Individual Psychology,* 92.

134. Ibid., 97–100.

135. Ibid., 107.

136. Ibid., 93.

137. Idem, *Understanding Human Nature,* 28–31. "The most important determinants of the structure of the soul life are generated in the earliest days of childhood. . . . One can determine how a child stands in relation to life a few months after his birth" (ibid., 17, 45).

138. Idem, *Individual Psychology,* 206.

139. Ibid., 178.

140. Ibid., 191.

141. Ibid., 208.

142. Idem, *What Life Should Mean to You,* 96–97.

143. Idem, *Understanding Human Nature,* 20.

144. Idem, *Individual Psychology,* 207. This is reflected in differing degrees of activity and in the variety of types and temperments that are manifested in human behavior (ibid., 163–71; *Understanding Human Nature,* 147–48).

145. Idem, *What Life Should Mean to You,* 29.

146. "All our strivings are directed towards a position in which a feeling of security has been achieved, a feeling that all the difficulties of life have been overcome and that we have emerged finally, in relation to the whole situation around us, safe and victorious" (ibid., 27). "The psychic life is a complex of aggressive and security-finding activities whose final purpose is to guarantee the continued existence on this earth of the human organism, and to enable him to securely accomplish his development" (*Understanding Human Nature,* 28).

147. Idem, *What Life Should Mean to You,* 61, 176.

148. Ibid., 12–13, 34, 58. Adler claimed that the first memory reveals the individual's fundamental view of life, "his first satisfactory crystallization of his attitude" (ibid., 19, 75).

149. Idem, *Individual Psychology*, 189.

150. "Just as all [the individual's] previous expressions were coherent with his interpretation of life, so now, if he is able to correct the mistake, his new expressions will be coherent with his new interpretation" (idem, *What Life Should Mean to You*, 34; cf. 63–64).

151. Idem, *Individual Psychology*, 190; *What Life Should Mean to You*, 13.

152. Idem, *What Life Should Mean to You*, 58; *Understanding Human Nature*, 92, 135–36. "There are certain ideas which one cannot hold too openly, both for the sake of others and for the sake of oneself" (*Understanding Human Nature*, 90).

153. Idem, *Individual Psychology*, 191.

154. Idem, *What Life Should Mean to You*, 4.

155. Ibid., 95, 98, 100–103; *Individual Psychology*, 89, 233, 360.

156. Idem, *What Life Should Mean to You*, 3.

157. Idem, *Understanding Human Nature*, 49–58, 84, 99. "Man utilizes only what and how his goal demands. Therefore the process of perception can be comprehended only when one has gained a picture of the hidden goal of a person and has understood everything in him as influenced by this goal. . . . Perceptions are not strictly identical with reality, for man is able to transform his contact with the external world according to the demands of his uniqueness" (*Individual Psychology*, 210; cf. 213–14).

158. Idem, *What Life Should Mean to You*, 73–74.

159. Idem, *Understanding Human Nature*, 102.

160. Maddi, *Personality Theories*, 112.

161. Adler, *What Life Should Mean to You*, 8, 11.

162. Idem, *Individual Psychology*, 155.

163. Ibid., 153; *What Life Should Mean to You*, 9, 247–48.

164. Idem, *What Life Should Mean to You*, 120–26.

165. Ibid., 5–8, 241, 262.

166. Ibid., 14–19; *Individual Psychology*, 366–70.

167. Idem, *Individual Psychology*, 239–59.

168. Ibid., 159.

169. Ibid., 156.

170. Ibid., 263–79; *Understanding Human Nature*, 155–59, 176–84, 224.

171. Idem, *Individual Psychology*, 219.

172. Ibid., 326–32; *Understanding Human Nature*, 19, 22.

173. Idem, *Individual Psychology*, 335.

174. Ibid., 197, 199, 397; *Understanding Human Nature*, 140.

175. Idem, *Individual Psychology*, 336–43.

176. Ibid., 399–459.

177. Erich Fromm, *The Fear of Freedom* (London: Ark Paperbacks, 1984 [1942]), 118.

178. *The Heart of Man* (London: Routledge & Kegan Paul, 1964), 120. (Italics deleted.)

179. Ibid., 116–17.

180. *The Sane Society* (London: Routledge & Kegan Paul, 1956), 25.

181. *The Heart of Man*, 117–20.

182. *The Sane Society*, 25. (Italics deleted.)

183. *The Anatomy of Human Destructiveness* (New York: Holt, Rinehart and Winston, 1973), 226.

184. *Man for Himself* (London: Ark Paperbacks, 1986 [1949]), 46; *The Sane Society*, 28.

185. *The Fear of Freedom*, 246–47, 250.

186. *To Have or to Be?* (London: Abacus Classic Library, 1979 [1976]), 14.

187. *The Fear of Freedom,* 13–14.

188. Ibid., 15.

189. *The Sane Society,* 30.

190. Ibid., 32–33; *The Anatomy of Human Destructiveness,* 233–34.

191. *The Sane Society,* 35–36.

192. Ibid., 39; *The Anatomy of Human Destructiveness,* 232–33; *The Art of Loving* (London: Unwin Books, 1962 [1957]), 29–33.

193. *The Sane Society,* 37–38; *The Art of Loving,* 41.

194. *The Sane Society,* 61–63.

195. *To Have or to Be?* 134–35. (Italics deleted.)

196. *Man for Himself,* 46–47.

197. *The Sane Society,* 64.

198. *To Have or to Be?* 137–38; *The Anatomy of Human Destructiveness,* 230–32.

199. *The Anatomy of Human Destructiveness,* 235–37.

200. Ibid., 237–42.

201. Ibid., 251–52.

202. Ibid., 253.

203. *The Fear of Freedom,* 120–21.

204. Ibid., 115–16.

205. Ibid., 116; *The Art of Loving,* 15–20.

206. *The Fear of Freedom,* 29–40.

207. Ibid., 53–88.

208. Ibid., 66, 74.

209. Ibid., 89–221.

210. Ibid., 91.

211. *Man for Himself,* 54–82; *The Crisis of Psychoanalysis* (New York: Holt, Rinehart and Winston, 1970), 78; Hall and Lindzey, *Introduction to Theories of Personality,* 169–70.

212. *Man for Himself,* 112–17.

213. Ibid., 83–84.

214. Ibid., x.

215. *The Art of Loving,* 9.

216. Ibid., 11–12, 78–84. Fromm discusses the disintegration of love in Western capitalistic society and describes several forms of pseudo-love (idolatrous love, sentimental love, projective mechanisms); ibid., 62–74.

217. Ibid., 20–28; *Man for Himself,* 98–101.

218. *The Art of Loving,* 45–47.

219. Ibid., 75.

220. *Man for Himself,* 102–6.

221. Ibid., 26–28, 37–53, 103.

222. Ibid., 109–12.

223. *The Sane Society,* 29.

224. *Man for Himself,* 40–42, 91.

225. *To Have or to Be?* 87, 126–27.

226. *Man for Himself,* 44–45. (Italics deleted.)

227. Ibid., 20, 233–37.

228. Ibid., ix.

229. Ibid., viii, 5, 34–37.

230. Ibid., 12–13.

231. Ibid., 21–33.

232. Ibid., 18. (Italics deleted.)

233. Ibid., 19–20, 50, 248–50.

234. *To Have or to Be?* 121–25. In Fromm's interpretation of the garden of Eden myth, acting against the command of authority, committing a sin, was in its positive human aspect the first act of freedom (*The Fear of Freedom*, 27–28).

235. *Man for Himself,* 157.

236. Ibid., 159.

237. Conversely, "The less productively one lives, the weaker becomes one's conscience; the paradoxical—and tragic—situation of man is that his conscience is weakest when he needs it most" (ibid., 160).

238. *Psychoanalysis and Religion* (London: Victor Gollancz, 1951), 29.

239. *Man for Himself,* 197–209.

240. Ibid., 201.

241. *The Dogma of Christ* (London: Routledge & Kegan Paul, 1963 [1930]), 12.

242. Ibid., 11; *Psychoanalysis and Religion,* 11–12, 42–43.

243. *The Dogma of Christ,* 30. In his discussion of the adoptionist character of early Christology, Fromm wrote: "The belief that a man is elevated to a god was an expression of the unconscious impulse of hostility to the father that was present in these masses. . . . a still deeper regression . . . finds expression in the Homoousian dogma: the fatherly God, whose pardon is to be obtained only through one's own suffering, is transformed into the mother full of grace who nourishes the child, shelters it in her womb, and thus provides pardon. Described psychologically, the change taking place here is the change from an attitude hostile to the father, to an attitude passively and masochistically docile, and finally to that of the infant loved by its mother. If this development took place in an individual, it would indicate a psychic illness. It takes place over a period of centuries, however, and affects not the entire psychic structure of individuals but only a segment common to all; it is an expression not of pathological disturbance but, rather, of adjustment to the given social situation" (ibid., 37, 69; Fromm wrote this essay in 1930 when he was a strict Freudian).

244. *Psychoanalysis and Religion,* 17.

245. Ibid., 44.

246. Ibid., 44–45.

247. Ibid., 49–56.

248. Ibid., 82, 91–92, 97–98.

249. *The Art of Loving,* 87–91.

250. *Man for Himself,* 210–30.

251. *The Anatomy of Human Destructiveness,* 437–38.

252. *To Have or to Be?* 18–19, 133.

253. Ibid., 19.

254. Ibid., 165–68.

255. *The Fear of Freedom,* 119.

256. *To Have or to Be?* 172, 174; *The Fear of Freedom,* 253.

257. *To Have or to Be?* 170–97; *The Fear of Freedom,* 234–35, 238; *The Art of Loving,* 92–95.

Chapter 6

1. *Group Psychology,* 12:172.

2. *Three Essays on the Theory of Sexuality,* 280.

3. Erik H. Erikson, *Toys and Reasons* (New York: W. W. Norton & Company, 1977); *Gandhi's Truth: On the Origins of Militant Non-violence* (New York: W. W. Norton & Company, 1969).

4. Maslow, *Psychology of Being*, 48. (Italics his.)

5. M. H. Hall, "A Conversation with Abraham H. Maslow," *Psychology Today* (July 1968): 35.

6. Maddi, *Personality Theories*, 103.

7. Abraham H. Maslow, "Self-Actualizing and Beyond," in *Theories of Personality: Primary Sources and Research*, ed. G. Lindzey, C. S. Hall, and M. Manosevitz, 2nd ed. (New York: John Wiley & Sons, 1973), 250–52.

8. Hall and Lindzey, *Theories of Personality*, 303–5; M. B. Smith, "The Phenomenological Approach in Personality Theory: Some Critical Remarks," *Journal of Abnormal and Social Psychology* 45 (1950): 516–22.

9. Hans H. Strupp, "Clinical Psychology, Irrationalism, and the Erosion of Excellence," *American Psychologist* 31 (1976): 561–71.

10. Maddi, *Personality Theories*, 92.

11. Rogers, *On Becoming a Person*, 123.

12. Adler, *Individual Psychology*, 460–61.

13. Ibid., 463; *What Life Should Mean to You*, 11–12.

Chapter 7

1. Henri F. Ellenberger, *The Discovery of the Unconscious* (New York: Basic Books, Inc., 1970).

2. Jung, *Modern Man in Search of a Soul*, 132–42; *The Structure and Dynamics of the Psyche*, 19; *Memories, Dreams, Reflections*, 146–69; Homans, *Jung in Context*, 94–95, 166–71.

3. Freud, *On the History of the Psychoanalytic Movement*, 15:110–22; *New Introductory Lectures*, 2:172–81, 188.

4. Jung, *Modern Man in Search of a Soul*, 50–53, 65–67; Rank, *Psychology and the Soul*, 9, 89.

5. Rank, *Will Therapy*, 6.

6. Ernest Becker, *The Denial of Death* (New York: The Free Press, 1973); Norman O. Brown, *Life Against Death: The Psychoanalytical Meaning of History* (New York: Viking Books, 1959); Maslow, *Motivation and Personality*, 110. This approach "has been able to keep the roundness and soberness of the master without the errors, extreme formulations, and dogma of strict Freudianism" with its "nineteenth-century reductionism, instinctivism, and biologism" (Becker, *The Denial of Death*, 30, 62).

7. Fromm, *The Fear of Freedom*, 117, 129.

8. Rank, *Truth and Reality*, 13.

9. Freud, *Beyond the Pleasure Principle*, 219, 221; *The Ego and the Id*, 447; "Formulations on Two Principles of Mental Functioning," 510, 514; *New Introductory Lectures*, 2:108.

10. Jung, *Modern Man in Search of a Soul*, 20; *Psychological Reflections*, 217; *The Structure and Dynamics of the Psyche*, 219–21.

11. Rank, *Will Therapy*, 108, 119–24, 133–34; *Truth and Reality*, 54, 58, 60–61, 192–93; *Psychology and the Soul*, 183, 185.

12. Rogers, *On Becoming a Person*, 27, 122, 185–87, 195–96.

13. In *Psychoanalysis and Faith: Dialogues with the Reverend Oskar Pfister* (New York: Basic Books, 1963), 61–62, Freud stated, "I have found little that is 'good' about human beings on the whole. In my experience most of them are trash. . . . If we are to talk of ethics, I subscribe to a high ideal from which most of the human beings I have come across depart most lamentably." Jung added, "All that gush about man's innate goodness, which had addled so many brains after the dogma of original sin was no longer understood, was blown to the winds by Freud, and the little that remains will, let us hope, be driven out for good and all by the barbarism of the twentieth century" (*Psychological Reflections*, 277; *Modern Man in Search of a Soul*, 46–47).

14. Maslow, *Toward a Psychology of Being*, 16; Rogers, *On Becoming a Person*, 91; "A Theory of Therapy," 248.

15. Rogers, *A Way of Being*, 106.

16. Fromm, *The Heart of Man*, 120; *The Sane Society*, 125; Ernest Becker, *The Birth and Death of Meaning* (London: Collier Macmillan Publishers, 1971), 164–79.

Chapter 8

1. "[I]t is unwise and inadvisable for theologians, apologists or anyone else to build upon a foundation so liable to change or rejection as psychoanalytic theory" (Malcolm Jeeves, "Christian Belief, Experience and Practice in the Light of Expanding Psychological Knowledge," in Jeeves, *Behavioural Sciences: A Christian Perspective,* 19; Gordon W. Allport, *The Person in Psychology* [Boston: Beacon Press, 1968], 141–54; Thomas C. Oden, *Kerygma and Counseling* [San Francisco: Harper & Row, 1978]).

2. "[T]he best existential analysis of the human condition leads directly into the problems of God and faith, which is exactly what Kierkegaard had argued" (Becker, *The Denial of Death,* 68).

3. Don S. Browning, *Religious Thought and the Modern Psychologies* (Philadelphia: Fortress Press, 1987), 161.

4. Tillich, *The Courage to Be*; Mary Jo Meadow and Richard D. Kahoe, *Psychology of Religion* (New York: Harper & Row, 1984), 5.

5. Ann Belford Ulanov, "The Anxiety of Being," in Adams, Pauck, and Shinn, *The Thought of Paul Tillich,* 122; cf. Sister Eileen Dolores Hughes, "The Christian Perspective on Individuation: Psychological and Spiritual Helps for the Journey to Wholeness," *The Journal of Pastoral Counseling* 22 (1987): 24–31.

6. Neil Pembroke, "God in the Life-Cycle: An Integration of Karl Rahner's Theology of Anonymous Faith and Erik Erikson's Psychology of Identity," *Journal of Psychology and Christianity* 9:1 (Spring 1990): 70–78.

7. Lawrence Kohlberg, "Moral Stages and Moralization: The Cognitive-Developmental Approach," in Thomas Lickona, ed., *Moral Development and Behavior* (New York: Holt, Rinehart and Winston, 1976), 31–53; Kohlberg, "Implications of Moral Stages for Adult Education," *Religious Education* 72 (1977): 183–201; Jane Loevinger, *Ego Development* (San Francisco: Jossey-Bass, 1976); James W. Fowler, *Stages of Faith: The Psychology of Human Development and the Quest for Meaning* (New York: Harper & Row, 1981); James W. Fowler, *Stages of Faith and Religious Development: Implications for Church, Education, and Society* (New York: Crossroad, 1991); Meadow and Kahoe, *Psychology of Religion,* 50–61, 324–25, 398, 415; Peter Homans, ed., *Childhood and Selfhood* (Cranbury, N.J.: Associated University Presses, Inc., 1978). Some, however, have challenged these parallels (e.g., Paul C. Vitz, "The Use of Stories in Moral Development," *American Psychologist* 45:6 [June 1990]:709–20).

8. Van Leeuwen, *The Person in Psychology,* 223–29.

9. Maslow, *Motivation and Personality,* 92–107.

10. In his criticisms of the one-sidedness of Freudian and Adlerian theories that are based upon drives and overlook the spiritual needs or aspirations, Jung concluded that certain religious convictions not founded on reason are a necessity of life for many persons (*Modern Man in Search of a Soul,* 224, 259, 261, 264, 266, 277–80).

11. Viktor E. Frankl, from "Address before the Third Annual Meeting of the Academy of Religion and Mental Health, 1962," in Frank T. Severin, ed., *Discovering Man in Psychology: A Humanistic Approach* (New York: McGraw-Hill Book Company, 1973), 132–33.

12. Meyer, *The Philosophy of St. Thomas Aquinas,* 210; Peter Homans, ed., *The Dialogue Between Psychology and Theology* (Chicago: University of Chicago Press, 1968).

13. Tillich, *Theology of Culture,* 120–23; Peter Homans, *Theology after Freud* (Indianapolis: Bobbs-Merrill Company, Inc., 1970), 66–90.

14. Tillich, *Theology of Culture,* 143.

15. Idem, *Love, Power, and Justice,* 29–30, 116–17.

16. Idem, *Systematic Theology,* 2:53–54.

17. Rahner, *TI,* VIII:191; *Karl Rahner in Dialogue,* 222.

18. Idem, *TI,* II:278–79; XIII:135.

19. Browning, *Religious Thought and the Modern Psychologies*; Vitz, *Psychology as Religion*; Becker, *The Denial of Death*; Becker, *Escape from Evil* (New York: Free Press, 1975); Richard W. Coan, *Hero, Artist, Sage, or Saint?* (New York: Columbia University Press, 1977); Christopher Lasch, *The Culture of Narcissism* (New York: W. W. Norton & Company, 1979); Thomas Szasz, *The Myth of Mental Illness,* rev. ed. (New York: Harper & Row, 1974);

Malcolm Jeeves, *Psychology and Christianity* (Downers Grove, Ill.: InterVarsity Press, 1976); David Myers, *The Human Puzzle* (San Francisco: Harper & Row, 1978); Ronald L. Kotenskey, *Psychology from a Christian Perspective* (Nashville: Abingdon, 1980); Martin L. Gross, *The Psychological Society* (New York: Random House, 1978); William Kirk Kilpatrick, *Psychological Seduction* (Nashville: Thomas Nelson Publishers, 1983); Kilpatrick, *The Emperor's New Clothes* (Westchester, Ill.: Crossway Books, 1985); Van Leeuwen, *The Person in Psychology*; Van Leeuwen, *The Sorcerer's Apprentice: A Christian Looks at the Changing Face of Psychology* (Downers Grove, Ill.: InterVarsity Press, 1982); Martin and Deidre Bobgan, *The Psychological Way/The Spiritual Way* (Minneapolis: Bethany Fellowship, 1979); MacKay, *Human Science and Human Dignity*; MacKay, *Brains, Machines and Persons* (Grand Rapids: William B. Eerdmans Publishing Company, 1980).

20. Browning, *Religious Thought and the Modern Psychologies*, 35–40.

21. Paul Ricoeur, *Freud and Philosophy*, trans. Denis Savage (New Haven: Yale University Press, 1970).

22. Browning, *Religious Thought and the Modern Psychologies*, 41–44.

23. Ibid., 30, 47–52; Philip Reiff, *Freud: The Mind of the Moralist* (Chicago: University of Chicago Press, 1979); idem, *The Triumph of the Therapeutic* (New York: Harper & Row, 1966). Nevertheless, the content of Freud's ethical requirements coincided with the Mosaic decalogue, though he thought he could substantiate them on a rational rather than a religious basis (Hans Küng, *Freud and the Problem of God*, trans. Edward Quinn [New Haven: Yale University Press, 1979], 87).

24. Erikson, *Identity and the Life Cycle*, 9, 66–67.

25. Idem, *Identity: Youth and Crisis*, 70.

26. Ibid., 293–94; *Childhood and Society*, 417–18.

27. Idem, *Insight and Responsibility*, 157, 221–28; *Identity: Youth and Crisis*, 140–41.

28. Jung, *Psychology and Religion: West and East*, 81–96.

29. Browning, *Religious Thought and the Modern Psychologies*, 182.

30. Rogers, *On Becoming a Person*, 22–24; *A Way of Being*, 118; *Client-Centered Therapy*, 157.

31. "A glance at the careers of the most prominent humanistic psychologists shows an almost invariable progression from subjectivist principles to an embrace with Eastern and immanentist modes of thought" (Kilpatrick, *The Emperor's New Clothes*, 47).

32. Fromm, *Man for Himself*, 5, 12–13, 21–37.

33. Anthony Storr, *The Integrity of the Personality* (Harmondsworth, Middlesex: Penguin Books, 1960), 12, 15. "Amongst historians, as in other fields, the blindest of all the blind are those who are unable to examine their own presuppositions, and blithely imagine therefore that they do not possess any" (Herbert Butterfield, *Christianity and History* [New York: Charles Scribner's Sons, 1949], 46).

34. Paul C. Vitz, "Secular Personality Theories: A Critical Analysis," in *Man and Mind: A Christian Theory of Personality*, ed. Thomas J. Burke (Hillsdale, Mich.: Hillsdale College Press, 1987), 75.

35. Idem, "A Covenant Theory of Personality: A Theoretical Introduction," in *The Christian Vision: Man in Society*, ed. Lynne Morris (Hillsdale, Mich.: Hillsdale College Press, 1984), 77–79.

36. James R. Scroggs and William G. T. Douglas, "Issues in the Psychology of Religious Conversion," in *Current Perspectives in the Psychology of Religion*, ed. H. Newton Malony (Grand Rapids: William B. Eerdmans Publishing Company, 1977), 262.

37. Arthur F. Holmes, *Faith Seeks Understanding* (Grand Rapids: William B. Eerdmans Publishing Company, 1971); idem, *Contours of a World View* (Grand Rapids: William B. Eerdmans Publishing Company, 1983); J. P. Moreland, *Christianity and the Nature of Science* (Grand Rapids: Baker Book House, 1989). When psychology is elevated into a complete explanation of reality, methodological nontheism has been transformed into ideological nontheism.

38. Küng, *Freud and the Problem of God*, 80.

39. Mircea Eliade, *Myths, Dreams, and Mysteries,* trans. Philip Mairet (New York: Harper & Row, 1960), 23–26; Ian Barbour, *Myths, Models and Paradigms* (London: SCM Press, 1974), 49.

40. Becker, *The Denial of Death,* 276; Tillich, *Systematic Theology,* 1:130–31.

41. "We are living in a world in which depth-psychology is discovering in man abysses which, on the one hand, it seeks to control, not through an appeal to the rational freedom of the subject, but through psychotechnics conceived in terms of natural science and, on the other hand, undertakes to resolve man into the anonymous forces of his biological and social origin" (Rahner, *The Practice of Faith,* 29–30).

42. Many aspects of human behavior contain elements of projection, but this does not mean that the objects of projection do not exist. Similarly, children's attitudes to their fathers may influence their view of God, but this has no bearing on God's existence or character (Küng, *Freud and the Problem of God,* 77–78).

43. Robert H. Thouless, *An Introduction to the Psychology of Religion,* 3rd ed. (Cambridge: Cambridge University Press, 1971), 74–76; Meadow and Kahoe, *Psychology of Religion,* 7–11. Freud derived his theory of culture and religion from his general theory of psychology, and this in turn was generalized from his clinical treatment of neurosis.

44. Erikson, *Insight and Responsibility,* 153–55; *Identity: Youth and Crisis,* 82–84.

45. Rank, *Beyond Psychology,* 142; cf. 102–4, 147, 159–67, 181, 224, 235, 240; *Psychology and the Soul,* 73–79, 92, 153–54.

46. Fromm, *The Fear of Freedom,* 82, 86–87; *Man for Himself,* 197–209; *The Dogma of Christ,* 12; *Psychoanalysis and Religion,* 17, 44–56, 82–98.

47. Susan Budd, *Sociologists and Religion* (London: Collier Macmillan Publishers, 1973), 42–43; Jerry H. Gill, *Faith in Dialogue* (Waco, Tex.: Jarrell [Word Books], 1985), 51–55.

48. Homans, *Jung in Context,* 8–9, 194. Theissen, *Psychological Aspects of Pauline Theology,* 11–28.

49. R. C. Sproul, *The Psychology of Atheism* (Minneapolis: Bethany Fellowship, Inc., 1974), 48–50. The Freudian argument that religious belief evolved from an infantile need for a universal father figure overlooks the fact that belief in God, especially as a father, is not a part of the most primitive religions (Ralph W. Clark, "The Evidential Value of Religious Experiences," *International Journal for Philosophy of Religion* 16 [1984]:200).

50. Becker, *The Denial of Death,* 11–12, 190–91, 200–204, 275.

51. Rahner, *The Practice of Faith,* 40.

52. Idem, *Foundations of Christian Faith,* 404.

53. Rudolf Otto, *The Idea of the Holy,* trans. John W. Harvey, 2nd ed. (Oxford: Oxford University Press, 1950 [1917]).

54. Edwards, *Men Naturally Are God's Enemies,* 2:130–41.

55. Sproul, *The Psychology of Atheism,* 56–155; Thouless, *An Introduction to the Psychology of Religion,* 75–76; C. Stephen Evans, *Philosophy of Religion: Thinking about Faith* (Downers Grove, Ill.: InterVarsity Press, 1985), 130. "Religion is explained away in the cognitive realm as being derived from psychological or sociological forces and is considered as illusion or ideology, while in the aesthetic realm, religious symbols are replaced by finite objects in the different naturalistic styles, especially in critical naturalism and some types of non-objective art. . . . Within large sections of contemporary mankind, this reductive way of profanizing religion, reduction by annihilation, is tremendously successful. . . . Religion can be secularized and finally dissolved into secular forms only because it has the ambiguity of self-transcendence" (Tillich, *Systematic Theology,* 3:101).

56. Rahner, *TI,* VII:12; Gill, *Faith in Dialogue,* 53–55; C. Stephen Evans, *Preserving the Person* (Downers Grove, Ill.: InterVarsity Press, 1977), 42, 78.

57. Prominent titles in this vast literature include Norman Geisler, *Christian Apologetics* (Grand Rapids: Baker Book House, 1976); Peter Kreeft, *Fundamentals of the Faith* (San Francisco: Ignatius Press, 1988); J. P. Moreland, *Scaling the Secular City* (Grand Rapids: Baker Book House, 1987); Alvin Plantinga, *God and Other Minds* (Ithaca, N.Y.: Cornell University Press, 1967); Plantinga, *The Nature of Necessity* (Oxford: Clarendon Press, 1974); *God, Freedom, and Evil* (Grand Rapids: William B. Eerdmans Publishing Company, 1974); Richard Swinburne, *The*

Coherence of Theism (Oxford: Clarendon Press, 1977); Swinburne, *The Existence of God* (Oxford: Clarendon Press, 1979).

58. Gordon W. Allport, *The Individual and His Religion* (New York: Macmillan Company, 1950), 18, 83, 160; Evans, *Philosophy of Religion,* 164–71.

59. Michael Polanyi, *Personal Knowledge* (Chicago: University of Chicago Press, 1962), vii, 17; Louis P. Pojman, *Religious Belief and the Will* (London: Routledge & Kegan Paul, 1986), 86.

60. Robert Audi and William J. Wainwright, eds., *Rationality, Religious Belief, and Moral Commitment* (Ithaca, N.Y.: Cornell University Press, 1986), 10.

61. Thouless, *An Introduction to the Psychology of Religion,* 17–18; Meadow and Kahoe, *Psychology of Religion,* 10; Pojman, *Religious Belief and the Will,* 183–87; John A. Clippinger, "Toward a Human Psychology of Personality," in Malony, *Current Perspectives in the Psychology of Religion,* 312; Gary Gutting, *Religious Belief and Religious Skepticism* (Notre Dame, Ind.: University of Notre Dame Press, 1982), 141–76.

62. Michael Polanyi, *The Tacit Dimension* (Garden City, N.Y.: Anchor Books, 1966); Milton Rokeach, *The Open and Closed Mind* (New York: Basic Books, Inc., 1960).

63. Evans, *Preserving the Person,* 141; Richard Swinburne, *Faith and Reason* (Oxford: Clarendon Press, 1981); Alvin Plantinga and Nicholas Wolterstorff, eds., *Faith and Rationality: Reason and Belief in God* (Notre Dame, Ind.: University of Notre Dame Press, 1983).

64. Pojman, *Religious Belief and the Will,* 198–200, 209–10.

65. J. Kellenberger, "Three Models of Faith," *International Journal for Philosophy of Religion* 12 (1981): 218–31.

66. Gutting, *Religious Belief and Religious Skepticism,* 106–8; Robert C. Roberts, "Thinking Subjectively," *International Journal for Philosophy of Religion* 11 (1980): 83–86, 91.

67. Michael Argyle and Benjamin Beit-Hallahmi, *The Social Psychology of Religion* (London: Routledge & Kegan Paul, 1975), 26, 77–79, 99–100, 124–30, 179–207; Thouless, *An Introduction to the Psychology of Religion,* 15–17.

68. Walter Houston Clark, *The Psychology of Religion* (New York: Macmillan Company, 1958), 387–408; Allport, *The Individual and His Religion,* 9–10; Meadow and Kahoe, *Psychology of Religion,* 40–43, 97–102; Malony, *Current Perspectives in the Psychology of Religion,* 173–87, 201–23, 246, 262; Thouless, *An Introduction to the Psychology of Religion,* 20–25, 58–63.

69. H. Newton Malony, "N=1 Methodology in the Psychology of Religion," in Malony, *Current Perspectives in the Psychology of Religion,* 352–67.

70. Nicholas Wolterstorff, *Reason within the Bounds of Religion* (Grand Rapids: William B. Eerdmans Publishing Company, 1976), 11–16, 62–66; Evans, *Philosophy of Religion,* 58–78, 139, 161–63.

71. Pojman, *Religious Belief and the Will,* 197–98; 246; Gill, *Faith in Dialogue,* 101–2.

72. Norman Malcolm, "Anselm's Ontological Arguments," in *The Existence of God,* ed. John Hick (New York: Macmillan Company, 1964), 67; Pojman, *Religious Belief and the Will,* 153.

73. Philosophers have distinguished two general types of justification for religious beliefs. If there is sufficient reason for thinking that belief in a proposition or in a person will have beneficial consequences for the believer, one has utilitarian justification for the belief (e.g., Pascal's Wager). If there is sufficient reason for thinking that a belief is true, one has evidential justification for the belief. Some philosophers argue that the satisfaction of human needs through religious belief has utilitarian but not evidential justification (Diogenes Allen, *The Reasonableness of Faith* [Washington: Corpus Books, 1968]; "Motives, Rationales, and Religious Beliefs," *American Philosophical Quarterly* 3 [1966]: 111–27; William Lad Sessions, "Religious Faith and Rational Justification," *International Journal for Philosophy of Religion* 13 [1982]: 143–56). Others contend that there is evidential justification for religious beliefs based on the satisfaction of human needs (C. Stephen Evans, *Subjectivity and Religious Belief* [Washington: University Press of America, 1982]; Paul Helm, *The Varieties of Belief* [London: George Allen and Unwin, 1973];

Robert Holyer, "Human Needs and the Justification of Religious Belief," *International Journal for Philosophy of Religion* 17 [1985]: 29–40). The position taken here is that satisfaction of needs in the lives of believers provides subjective evidence for their beliefs.

74. Thouless, *An Introduction to the Psychology of Religion*, 146–47; Gutting, *Religious Belief and Religious Skepticism*, 110–11.

75. Rahner, *TI*, XI: 174–75. (Italics his.)

76. Jürgen Moltmann, *Theology of Hope* (London: SCM Press, Ltd, 1967), 91, 337–38.

77. A. R. Peacocke, *Creation and the World of Science* (Oxford: Clarendon Press, 1979), 164, 329–37; Richard Dawkins, *The Selfish Gene* (Oxford: Oxford University Press, 1976); Dawkins, *The Blind Watchmaker* (Harlow, Essex: Longman Scientific & Technical, 1986); David L. Edwards, *A Reason to Hope* (London: Collins, 1978), 201; Don Cupitt, *The Worlds of Science and Religion* (London: Sheldon Press, 1976), 107.

78. This argument must deal with the problem of circularity in defining the needs of humans in such a way that Christian theism will meet them. In Western culture, affected as it is by Christianity, fulfillment is thought of in terms of developing active potentialities and deepening personal relationships. But a self-emptying ideology with little emphasis on personal relationships is characteristic of forms of Eastern religion. On the other hand, one can argue that very few people in Eastern societies live as though relational disinterest is desirable.

79. C. S. Lewis, *The Pilgrim's Regress* (Grand Rapids: William B. Eerdmans Publishing Company, 1933, 1958), 10; Lewis, *Mere Christianity* (New York: Macmillan Publishing Co., 1943, 1945, 1952), 118–21; Peter Kreeft, *Heaven: The Heart's Deepest Longing* (San Francisco: Ignatius Press, 1989), 201–32.

80. Kreeft, *Heaven: The Heart's Deepest Longing*, 201–2. (Italics his.)

81. Robert Merrihew Adams, "The Problem of Total Devotion," in Audi and Wainwright, *Rationality, Religious Belief, and Moral Commitment*, 173.

82. Drawing on the philosophical distinction between the autonomous individual and the person who exists in covenant and connection with others (e.g., Jacques Maritain, *The Person and the Common Good* [Notre Dame, Ind.: Notre Dame Press, 1966]), Vitz asserts that due to Rogers's psychological agenda, his book, *On Becoming a Person* would more aptly be titled, *On Becoming an Individual* ("A Covenant Theory of Personality," 95–96).

83. Kilpatrick, *The Emperor's New Clothes*, 148–51. If self-esteem or self-actualization is perceived as one's deepest need, it would be more appropriate for one to turn to Rogers and Maslow than to the New Testament. Humanistic psychology focuses on self-worth *coram homnibus* (before humans); the New Testament deals with the issue of moral worth *coram Deo* (before God); cf. Michael Scott Horton, ed., *Power Religion* (Chicago: Moody Press, 1992), 245–61.

84. Fromm, *Man for Himself*, 119–40.

85. Maslow, *Motivation and Personality*, 156.

86. C. S. Lewis, *The Four Loves* (New York: Harcourt Brace Jovanovich, Inc., 1960).

87. *Agape* and *eros* are not entirely separate, Nygren and Bultmann; instead, divine love completes the human loves (Reinhold Niebuhr, *The Nature and Destiny of Man*, 2 vols. [New York: Charles Scribner's Sons, 1941], 2:84; Anders Nygren, *Agape and Eros* [Philadelphia: Westminster Press, 1953]; M. C. D'Arcy, *The Mind and Heart of Love* [New York: Henry Holt and Company, 1947]; Browning, *Religious Thought and the Modern Psychologies*, 57).

88. Maritain, *Moral Philosophy*, 78–79.

89. Rahner, *The Practice of Faith*, 135.

90. Bernard of Clairvaux, *The Love of God*, ed. James M. Houston (Portland, Ore.: Multnomah Press, 1983), 154–60.

91. In a discussion on Kierkegaard, Becker writes, "The self must be destroyed, brought down to nothing, in order for self-transcendence to begin. Then the self can begin to relate itself to powers beyond itself. It has to thrash around in its finitude, it has to 'die,' in order to question that finitude, in order to see beyond it . . . to infinitude, to absolute transcendence, to the Ultimate Power of Creation which made finite creatures" (*The Denial of Death*, 89).

92. "[I]f we consider the unblushing promises of reward and the staggering nature of the rewards promised in the Gospels, it would seem that Our Lord finds our desires, not too strong, but too weak. We are half-hearted creatures, fooling about with drink and sex and ambition when infinite joy is offered us, like an ignorant child who wants to go on making mud pies in a slum because he cannot imagine what is meant by the offer of a holiday at the sea. We are far too easily pleased" (C. S. Lewis, "The Weight of Glory," in *The Weight of Glory and Other Addresses* [Grand Rapids: William B. Eerdmans Publishing Company, 1949], 1–2).

93. Rahner, *The Religious Life Today,* 48–49.

94. Stendahl argues that "the introspective conscience reached its theological climax and explosion in the Reformation, and its secular climax and explosion in Sigmund Freud" (*Paul Among Jews and Gentiles,* 16–17).

95. Alistair I. McFadyen, *The Call to Personhood* (Cambridge: Cambridge University Press, 1990), 17–66; Lesslie Newbigin, *The Other Side of 1984* (Geneva: World Council of Churches, 1983), 56–57. "We are all equal in our basic need for survival; this is the need we share with the animals. But to be human means to need other things—respect, honor, love. These needs, social rather than merely biological, call precisely for differentiation rather than for equality. . . . It is only within a shared community of mutual respect, honor, and love freely given that needs are acknowledged as the ground for claims of right" (Lesslie Newbigin, *Foolishness to the Greeks* [London: SPCK, 1986], 120–21).

96. Vitz, *Psychology as Religion,* 91–105; Vitz, "A Covenant Theory of Personality," 93; Storr, *The Integrity of the Personality,* 31–37, 44, 145; Mark P. Cosgrove, *Psychology Gone Awry* (Leicester: InterVarsity Press, 1979), 123–37.

97. Gordon Stanley, "Sensitization Techniques and Interpersonal Relations," in Jeeves, *Behavioural Sciences: A Christian Perspetive,* 200; Browning, *Religious Thought and the Modern Psychologies,* 140–59.

98. Lawrence J. Crabb, Jr., *Basic Principles of Biblical Counseling* (Grand Rapids: Zondervan Publishing House, 1975); *Effective Biblical Counseling* (Grand Rapids: Zondervan Publishing House, 1977).

99. David Brown, *The Divine Trinity* (London: Duckworth, 1985), 16–18.

100. Del Ratzsch, *Philosophy of Science* (Downers Grove, Ill.: InterVarsity Press, 1986), 100–104; Moreland, *Christianity and the Nature of Science,* 103–38.

101. Browning, *Religious Thought and the Modern Psychologies,* 137.

102. Tillich, *The Religious Situation,* 140.

103. Evans, *Preserving the Person,* 110–12, 150–51; Jeeves, "Christian Belief, Experience and Practice in the Light of Expanding Psychological Knowledge," 27–30; David G. Myers and Malcolm A. Jeeves, *Psychology through the Eyes of Faith* (San Francisco: Harper & Row, 1987), 5–10.

104. Gill, *Faith in Dialogue,* 116–19.

105. Peter L. Berger, *The Sacred Canopy* (Garden City, N.Y.: Anchor Books, 1967); Berger, *A Rumor of Angels* (Garden City, N.Y.: Doubleday & Company, 1969); Martin E. Marty, *The Modern Schism* (London: SCM Press, 1969); Os Guiness, *The Gravedigger File* (Downers Grove, Ill.: InterVarsity Press, 1983).

106. Cupitt, *The Worlds of Science and Religion,* 105–6; Hanbury Brown, *The Wisdom of Science* (Cambridge: Cambridge University Press, 1986), 143–77.

107. Walker Percy, *Lost in the Cosmos* (New York: Washington Square Press, 1983), 166; cf. 165, 246–48. Peacocke argues that much of the implausibility to the modern mind of traditional Christian formulations "arises not from any basic inadequacy in their analysis of man's predicament . . . but through the traditional static images not really relating at all to the world of dynamic process that the sciences now show it to be. . . . We have had to learn that God is not in the gaps in the nexus of events but is somehow in the whole process" (*Creation and the World of Science,* 48, 1–4–6, 132, 203, 210).

108. "Without self-transcendence the demand of humanist fulfillment becomes a law and falls under the ambiguities of the law. Humanism itself leads to the question of culture transcending itself" (Tillich, *Systematic Theology,* 3:86).

109. Browning, *Religious Thought and the Modern Psychologies,* 117–25; Kilpatrick, *Psychological Seduction,* 144–60.

110. W. D. Hudson, ed., *The Is-Ought Question* (London: Macmillan, 1969); Jonathan Glover, *What Sort of People Should There Be?* (Oxford: Oxford University Press, 1984), 174–81; Brown, *The Wisdom of Science,* 133–35; Peacocke, *Creation and the World of Science,* 176.

111. These include "the basic beliefs that life has a meaning; that history has a progressive pattern; that within that pattern every human person is very precious; that the State exists to serve that person; that freedom is necessary for the person's fulfillment; that interpersonal love rather than force ought to, and will, prevail ultimately" (Edwards, *A Reason to Hope,* 182).

112. Allen E. Bergin, "Psychotherapy and Religious Values," *Journal of Consulting and Clinical Psychology* 48 (1980): 100; Tillich, *Systematic Theology,* 3:271.

113. Meadow and Kahoe, *Psychology of Religion,* 12–15.

114. Becker, *The Denial of Death,* 190.

115. Ibid., 190–91.

116. E. L. Mascall, *The Christian Universe* (New York: Morehouse-Barlow Co., 1966), 34–35.

117. Pieper, *On Hope,* 49–50; Moltmann, *Theology of Hope,* 32, 69, 92.

118. Becker, *The Denial of Death,* 264–74. The terror of death can be repressed, but it cannot be eliminated; "a full apprehension of man's condition would drive him insane. . . . everything that man does in his symbolic world is an attempt to deny and overcome his grotesque fate" (ibid., 27).

119. Ibid., 193–94. (Italics his.)

120. C. Stephen Evans, *Existentialism: The Philosophy of Despair and the Quest for Hope* (Grand Rapids: Zondervan Publishing House, 1984), 90–95.

121. Clifton Fadiman, ed. *The Little, Brown Book of Anecdotes* (Boston: Little, Brown and Company, 1985), 295–96. It is arguable that this ironic observation by Woody Allen reveals a deeper grasp of existential angst than many of these psychologists: "More than any other time in history, mankind faces a crossroads. One path leads to despair and utter hopelessness. The other to total extinction. Let us pray we have the wisdom to choose correctly."

122. Becker, *The Denial of Death,* 107–24, 284–85.

123. "Those who hope in Christ can no longer put up with reality as it is, but begin to suffer under it, to contradict it. Peace with God means conflict with the world, for the goad of the promised future stabs inexorably into the flesh of every unfulfilled present" (Moltmann, *Theology of Hope,* 21).

124. "We can believe . . . that the joy of heaven is not solitary, and that heavenly beatitude is accompanied by the vision which the blessed have of one another's joy, and that it is embellished with eternal friendships" (Gilson, *The Christian Philosophy of St. Thomas Aquinas,* 356; Meyer, *The Philosophy of St. Thomas Aquinas,* 200, 443–45).

125. Becker, *The Denial of Death,* 173–75, 196.

Appendix

1. Compare Gerd Theissen's warning against this kind of exegesis in *Psychological Aspects of Pauline Theology,* trans. John P. Galvin (Edinburgh: T & T Clark, 1987), 1–2.

2. The first quest was chronicled and concluded by Schweitzer, and the second or "New Quest" flourished in the 1950s and 1960s (N. T. Wright, "The Vindication of the Son of Man," Oxford-Bonn Seminar, 1988, 1; Stephen Neill and Tom Wright, *The Interpretation of the New Testament, 1861–1986,* 2nd ed. [Oxford: Oxford University Press, 1988], 379–403).

3. B. F. Meyer, *The Aims of Jesus* (London: SCM Press Ltd., 1979); E. P. Sanders, *Jesus and Judaism* (London: SCM Press Ltd., 1985); Gerd Theissen, *The Shadow of the Galilean,* trans. John Bowden (London: SCM Press Ltd., 1987); Marcus J. Borg, *Conflict, Holiness & Politics in the Teachings of Jesus* (New York: Edwin Mellen Press, 1984).

4. "Jesus was not just a moralist whose teachings had some political implications; he was not primarily a teacher

of spirituality whose public ministry unfortunately was seen in a political light; he was not just a sacrificial lamb preparing for his immolation, or a God-Man whose divine status calls us to disregard his humanity. Jesus was, in his divinely mandated (i.e. promised, anointed, messianic) prophethood, priesthood, and kingship, the bearer of a new possibility of human, social, and therefore political relationships" (John H. Yoder, *The Politics of Jesus* [Grand Rapids: William B. Eerdmans Publishing Company, 1972], 62–63).

5. Theissen, *The Shadow of the Galilean,* 95.

6. G. B. Caird, *Jesus and the Jewish Nation* (London: Athlone Press, 1965), 11.

7. Borg, *Conflict, Holiness & Politics,* 123, 199; Wright, "The Vindication of the Son of Man," 10.

8. N. T. Wright, "Jesus, Israel and the Cross," in K. M. Richards, ed., *Proceedings of the SBL* (Atlanta: Scholastic Press, 1985), 90.

9. Norman Perrin argues that the tension between present and future in Jesus' teaching on the kingdom of God is "a tension between that which began as God manifested himself as King in the ministry of Jesus, and that which he will consummate in a manner and at a time of his choosing. But the teaching of Jesus gives us no guidance as to this manner and this time; rather it directs attention to what will be involved in the consummation: judgment, the vindication of Jesus himself, the establishment of the values of God, and the enjoyment of all the blessings to be associated with a perfect relationship with God" (*The Kingdom of God in the Teaching of Jesus* [London: SCM Press Ltd., 1963], 198–99).

10. Caird, *Jesus and the Jewish Nation,* 16–17; N. T. Wright, "'Constraints' and the Jesus of History," *Scottish Journal of Theology* 39 (1986): 201.

11. Yoder, *The Politics of Jesus,* 191; Borg, *Conflict, Holiness & Politics,* 256, 260.

12. Yoder, *The Politics of Jesus,* 113.

13. Caird, *Jesus and the Jewish Nation,* 19.

14. Borg, *Conflict, Holiness & Politics,* 247, 249–50; Gerd Theissen, *Sociology of Early Palestinian Christianity* (Philadelphia: Fortress Press, 1978), 104–105. "[N]othing but the thoroughgoing change of heart which Jesus demanded and made possible could in the end keep the nation out of disastrous conflict with Rome" (Caird, *Jesus and the Jewish Nation,* 22).

15. Matthew (Matt.) 6:19–34; Luke 12:22–34. All Scripture quotations are from the *Revised Standard Version of the Bible* (New York: Thomas Nelson & Sons, 1946, 1952).

16. Matt. 7:7–11; Luke 11:9–13.

17. Matt. 6:8.

18. Matt. 6:11–13; Luke 11:3–4.

19. Matt. 12:28.

20. Stephen Neill, *Jesus through Many Eyes* (Philadelphia: Fortress Press, 1976), 85.

21. Matt. 14:13–21; Mark 6:31–44; Luke 9:11–17; Matt. 15:32–38; Mark 8:1–9.

22. Mark 12:41–44; Luke 21:1–4.

23. Luke 4:18–19.

24. Matt. 11:2–6; Luke 7:20–23.

25. Matt. 4:23–24; 8:1–17; 12:22–28; 14:34–36; 15:30–31; Mark 1:21–34; 2:1–12; 5:24–34; 6:53–56; 7:31–37; 8:22–26; Luke 4:31–41; 5:12–15, 17–26; 7:1–10; 8:26–39, 43–48; 11:14–20.

26. Mark 5:35–43; Luke 7:11–17; 8:41–42,49–56.

27. Matt. 9:36; Benjamin B. Warfield, *The Person and Work of Christ* (Philadelphia: Presbyterian and Reformed Publishing Company, 1950), 98–99.

28. Matt. 9:1–8; Luke 5:17–26.

29. Matt. 4:1–11; Luke 4:1–12; Matt. 4:19; Mark 1:17; Luke 5:10.

30. Luke 12:13–21.

31. Luke 16:19–31; Matt. 19:16–26; Mark 10:17–27; Luke 18:18–27.

32. Matt. 6:24; Luke 16:13.

33. E.g., Matt. 5:21–32; Borg, *Conflict, Holiness & Politics,* 238.

34. Mark 7:14–23; Matt. 12:33–37; 15:11, 17–20.

35. Matt. 9:10–13; Mark 2:15–17; Luke 5:29–32.

36. Luke 18:9–14.

37. Luke 7:36–50.

38. Matt. 1:21.

39. Howard Marshall, *Luke: Historian and Theologian* (Grand Rapids: Zondervan Publishing House, 1971), 19, quoted in Neill, *Jesus through Many Eyes,* 133 n. 17.

40. Luke 19:10; Matt. 20:28; 26:26–28; Mark 10:45; 14:22–25; Luke 22:19–20.

41. Matt. 23:4; Mark 3:1–6; Matt. 11:28–30.

42. Matt. 3:2; 4:17; Mark 1:4,14–15.

43. Luke 7:36–50; 18:9–14; Matt. 11:20–24; Luke 13:1–5; 10:13–15; 11:29–32.

44. Luke 20:17–18; Matt. 7:13.

45. Matt. 22:1–14; Luke 14:15–24; Matt. 7:24–27; Luke 6:47–49.

46. Matt. 13:3–23; Mark 4:3–20; Luke 8:5–15.

47. Matt. 11:25–27; 16:17; Luke 10:21–24; 19:42.

48. Luke 18:17.

49. Matt. 9:36; 18:20; 28:20.

50. Matt. 8:18–22; Luke 9:57–62; 14:26–33.

51. Matt. 10:39; 16:24–26; Mark 8:34–37.

52. Luke 20:45–47.

53. Matt. 10:37.

54. Matt. 8:18–22; Luke 9:57–62.

55. Matt. 5:6; Luke 12:16–21.

56. Matt. 13:44–46.

57. Luke 10:42.

58. Matt. 6:33; cf. 6:19–34; Luke 12:22–34.

59. Matt. 24:45–25:30; Mark 13:33–37; Luke 12:35–48.

60. Borg, *Conflict, Holiness & Politics,* 245.

61. Matt. 6:1–6,16–18.

62. E.g., Matt. 14:28–33.

63. Matt. 6:19–21; Luke 18:28–30; cf. Luke 10:20.

64. Matt. 22:36–40; Mark 12:28–34; Luke 10:25–28.

65. Luke 6:27–28,31; Matt. 5:43–44; 7:12.

66. Matt. 18:21–35; 5:23–24; Mark 11:25–26.

67. Matt. 25:35–45; 18:1–4; 20:20–28; Mark 10:35–45; Luke 9:46–48; 22:24–27.

68. Luke 4:18–19; 7:20–23.

69. Matt. 9:1–8; Luke 5:17–26.

70. John 6:27.

71. John 6:35, 50–51.

72. John 4:9–14; 7:37–39; 4:31–34.

73. John 9:1–7, 35–39.

74. John 4:48–54; 5:20, 36, 44–47.

75. John 11:25–26; 8:51; 5:25–29.

76. John 3:3–8; 6:63.

77. John 3:18–19, 36; 5:25–29.

78. John 1:12, 29; 3:16–17.

79. John 8:12, 34, 51; 9:39–41; 12:46.

80. John 5:24; 8:31–36.

81. John 6:35, 48. Just as his food was to do the will of his Father (John 4:34), so Jesus by accomplishing this will became the nourishment of those who partake of him (John 6:50–58).

82. John 8:12; 9:5; 12:36, 46.

83. John 10:1–18, 25–29.

84. John 1:4; 5:25–29; 8:51; 10:10; 11:25–26.

85. John 15:1–8.

86. John 20:31; 21:24.

87. John 6:35–65.

88. John 1:12.

89. John 4:10–29, 39–42; cf. 11:27.

90. John 3:16, 36; 5:24, 38, 40; 6:29, 36, 40, 47, 64; 8:24; 12:48; 14:11; 20:29.

91. John 14:1–3, 16–20, 27; 15:15; 16:13–15, 22–24, 27, 33; 17:3, 12.

92. John 13:34–35; 14:15, 21; 15:9–12, 17.

93. John 17:21–26.

94. Acts 17:24–31.

95. Acts 3:2–16; 5:12–16; 8:7, 13; 9:33–42; 14:3, 8–10; 16:16–18; 19:11–12; 28:8–9.

96. Acts 2:44–46; 4:34–35; 6:1–4; 11:27–30; 20:33–35.

97. Acts 5:40–41; 20:22–24; 21:10–13.

98. Acts 2:21, 47; 4:11–12; 13:22–39; 16:30–31; 26:22–23.

99. Acts 2:36–40; 3:17–19; 5:42; 7:51–53; 8:34–37; 10:1–4, 22–48; 13:40–41, 46–48; 16:30–31; 17:2–3; 18:5–6, 28; 26:17–18, 20; 28:23–28.

100. W. D. Davies, *Paul and Rabbinic Judaism* (London: S.P.C.K., 1948) was particularly important in setting the stage for later developments in this area.

101. E.g., Krister Stendahl, *Paul among Jews and Gentiles* (London: SCM Press Ltd., 1977).

102. "Seek ye first the original meanings—and all these things shall be yours as well" (ibid., 36).

103. Herman Ridderbos, *Paul: An Outline of His Theology,* trans. John Richard De Witt (Grand Rapids: William B. Eerdmans Publishing Company, 1975), 51–52.

104. Acts 9:1–22.

105. Seyoon Kim, *The Origin of Paul's Gospel,* 2nd rev. ed. (Tübingen: J. C. B. Mohr, 1984), 136 (italics deleted); cf. 104, 329.

106. Acts 9:15.

107. Yoder, *The Politics of Jesus,* 220.

108. Stendahl, for example, argues that Romans 1–8 was written as a preface to Romans 9–11, "in which Paul argues that since justification is by faith it is equally possible for both Jews and Gentiles to come to Christ. In that preface he does not deal with the question of how man is to be saved—be it by works or law or by something else" (Stendahl, *Paul among Jews and Gentiles,* 29; cf. 1–4, 26–27).

109. Neill and Wright, *The Interpretation of the New Testament,* 362; Robert Banks, *Paul's Idea of Community* (Grand Rapids: William B. Eerdmans Publishing Company, 1980), 13–32.

110. Wayne A. Meeks, *The First Urban Christians* (New Haven: Yale University Press, 1983), 73; Gerd Theissen, *The Social Setting of Pauline Christianity,* ed. and trans. John H. Schütz (Philadelphia: Fortress Press, 1982); Abraham J. Malherbe, *Social Aspects of Early Christianity,* 2nd ed. (Philadelphia: Fortress Press, 1983).

111. Meeks, *The First Urban Christians,* 183–84; Theissen, *The Social Setting of Pauline Christianity,* 106; Malherbe, *Social Aspects of Early Christianity,* 71, 84.

112. Gal. 3:28.

113. 1 Cor. 12:12–13; Eph 4:4–7.

114. Ridderbos, *Paul: An Outline of His Theology,* 63–64; Yoder, *The Politics of Jesus,* 217–18.

115. Stendahl, *Paul among Jews and Gentiles,* 16.

116. Ridderbos, *Paul: An Outline of His Theology,* 63.

117. N. T. Wright, *The Epistles of Paul to the Colossians and to Philemon* (Grand Rapids: William B. Eerdmans Publishing Company, 1986), 40.

118. Yoder, *The Politics of Jesus,* 218–19 n. 2.

119. Neill, *Jesus through Many Eyes,* 72.

120. 1 Cor. 12:9, 28, 30; cf. Phil. 2:25–30.

121. Rom. 12:7–8, 13; 1 Cor. 16:1–2; 2 Cor. 11:8–9; 1 Tim. 5:5–11, 17–18.

122. 2 Cor. 8:1–15; 9:1–15.

123. Phil. 4:14–19.

124. Phil. 4:11–13; 1 Thess. 5:16–18.

125. 1 Cor. 4:11–13.

126. 2 Cor. 4:7–15; 11:23–28; 12:9–10. "Therefore I endure everything for the sake of the elect, that they also may obtain the salvation in Christ Jesus with its eternal glory" (2 Tim. 2:10).

127. 2 Cor. 4:17.

128. 2 Cor. 4:18–5:8.

129. Rom. 8:18; 1 Cor. 3:13–14; 15:35–56; 2 Cor. 5:9–10. "But whatever gain I had, I counted as loss for the sake of Christ. Indeed I count everything as loss because of the surpassing worth of knowing Christ Jesus my Lord. For his sake I have suffered the loss of all things, and count them as refuse, in order that I may gain Christ" (Phil. 3:7–8; cf. 3:9–21).

130. 2 Cor. 6:10; Eph. 1:3.

131. 1 Tim. 6:8.

132. 1 Tim. 6:7, 17–19.

133. "For no human being will be justified in his sight by works of the law, since through the law comes knowledge of sin" (Rom. 3:20).

134. Eph. 2:1–3; Col. 2:13.

135. Rom. 5:10; 8:7–8; Eph. 2:11–13; Col. 1:21.

136. "For our sake he made him to be sin who knew no sin, so that in him we might become the righteousness of God" (2 Cor. 5:21). "... when the goodness and loving kindness of God our Savior appeared, he saved us, not because of deeds done by us in righteousness, but in virtue of his own mercy, by the washing of regeneration and renewal in the Holy Spirit, which he poured out upon us richly through Jesus Christ our Savior, so that we might be justified by his grace and become heirs in hope of eternal life" (Titus 3:4–7).

137. Rom 5:6–8; 1 Tim 2:5–6. "To believe is to see that God in Christ has moved toward the sinner before the sinner began to move toward God, to know oneself to be accepted in him without regard to any question of virtue or of compensation for the wrong done. Such knowledge must result in a deep and permanent sense of indebtedness and of gratitude for the immensity of the favor conferred. Great harm has been done by interpretations of the doctrine of justification that present it as an almost mechanical transaction unrelated to the dark and personal realities of the situation" (Neill, *Jesus through Many Eyes,* 60).

138. Rom. 8:21; 2 Cor. 5:17. Neill, *Jesus through Many Eyes,* 52.

139. E. P. Sanders, *Paul and Palestinian Judaism* (London: SCM Press Ltd., 1977), 443–44. Paul "did not *start* from man's need, but from God's deed" (ibid., 444).

140. Ibid., 446.

141. "When Gentiles who have not the law do by nature what the law requires, they are a law to themselves, even though they do not have the law. They show that what the law requires is written on their hearts, while their conscience also bears witness and their conflicting thoughts accuse or perhaps excuse them on that day when, according to my gospel, God judges the secrets of men by Christ Jesus" (Rom. 2:14–16).

142. Rom. 1:16–17; 3:21–5:21; 10:9–10; Gal. 2:16; 3:1–14, 23–29; Eph. 2:4–10; 2 Thess. 2:13–14; 1 Tim. 1:15.

143. 1 Cor. 1:9; Wright, *The Epistles of Paul to the Colossians and to Philemon,* 29.

144. "While we were living in the flesh, our sinful passions, aroused by the law, were at work in our members to bear fruit for death" (Rom. 7:5; cf. 8:6–7).

145. Sanders, *Paul and Palestinian Judaism,* 497.

146. 1 Cor. 6:11; Gal. 2:20; Col. 1:20–22; 2 Tim. 1:9–10.

147. Rom. 6:12–19; 8:9–17; Gal. 5:13–25.

148. 2 Cor. 5:17–20; Gal. 1:4; Col. 1:13–14.

149. Ridderbos, *Paul: An Outline of His Theology,* 162–65, 205.

150. 2 Cor. 4:17. "I consider that the sufferings of this present time are not worth comparing with the glory that is to be revealed to us" (Rom. 8:18).

151. 2 Thess. 2:16; 1 Tim. 1:1.

152. Gal. 5:5; 1 Thess. 1:10.

153. 1 Thess. 5:23–24; 2 Tim. 1:12.

154. 1 Cor. 15:13–58; 1 Thess. 4:13–18. "Therefore, my beloved brethren, be steadfast, immovable, always abounding in the work of the Lord, knowing that in the Lord your labor is not in vain" (1 Cor. 15:58).

155. Rom. 8:1.

156. "What no eye has seen, nor ear heard, nor the heart of man conceived, what God has prepared for those who love him" (1 Cor. 2:9; cf. 3:10–15; 2 Cor. 5:9–10; 1 Thess. 2:19–20; 2 Tim. 4:7–8).

157. 1 Thess. 4:3.

158. Rom. 6:1–8:17; 12:1–2; 13:11–14; 1 Cor. 2:12–3:3; 2 Cor. 7:1; Gal. 5:16–25; Eph. 4:22–24; 6:10–18; Phil. 1:9–11; Col. 2:6–7; 3:5 ,8–10; 1 Thess. 4:1–7; 5:23; 2 Thess. 3:5; Titus 2:11–14.

159. Wright, *The Epistles of Paul to the Colossians and to Philemon,* 27.

160. "Such is the confidence that we have through Christ toward God. Not that we are competent of ourselves to claim anything as coming from us; our competence is from God" (2 Cor. 3:4–5).

161. "I have been crucified with Christ; it is no longer I who live, but Christ who lives in me; and the life I now live in the flesh I live by faith in the Son of God, who loved me and gave himself for me" (Gal. 2:20). "I can do all things in him who strengthens me" (Phil. 4:13; cf. 1 Cor. 4:7–8; 2 Cor. 3:17–18; 4:7–14; 5:14–17; Gal. 4:4–7; 6:14; Eph. 1:3–23; 3:14–19; Phil. 1:21; 4:6–7, 19; Col. 1:9, 13–14; 3:1–4). "We are not to be content to gaze upon him or to admire him: we must become imitators of him, until we are metamorphosed into the same image" (Warfield, *The Person and Work of Christ,* 143).

162. Rom. 12:4–21; 13:8–10; 14:13, 19; 15:1–8; 1 Cor. 1:10; 10:24, 33; 12:4–13:13; 2 Cor. 13:11; Gal. 5:13–14; 6:2, 10; Eph. 4:1–16, 25–32; 5:1–2; Phil. 2:1–4, 19–24; Col. 3:12–14; 1 Thess. 4:9–12; 5:11–15; 1 Tim. 2:1; Philem. 5–7.

163. James 1:9–10.

164. Heb. 10:34.

165. 1 Pet. 4:12–13.

166. 1 Pet. 5:6–7. "And after you have suffered a little while, the God of all grace, who has called you to his eternal glory in Christ, will himself restore, establish, and strengthen you" (1 Pet. 5:10).

167. Heb. 9:27; 10:30–31; 1 Pet. 4:6; Rev. 5:9.

168. "In this the love of God was made manifest among us, that God sent his only Son into the world, so that we

might live through him. In this is love, not that we loved God but that he loved us and sent his Son to be the expiation for our sins" (1 John 4:9–10).

169. Heb. 7:25.

170. Heb. 5:9; 9:14; 1 Pet. 2:24–25. Cf. Heb. 2:3–4; 7:26–27; 9:11–15, 28.

171. Heb. 2:14–18; 4:14–16; 1 John 5:1. Warfield, *The Person and Work of Christ*, 143–44.

172. 1 Pet. 2:9–10; 1 John 3:1; 5:4–5, 11–13. "To him who loves us and has freed us from our sins by his blood and made us a kingdom, priests to his God and Father" (Rev. 1:5–6).

173. Jude 24.

174. "By his great mercy we have been born anew to a living hope through the resurrection of Jesus Christ from the dead, and to an inheritance which is imperishable, undefiled, and unfading, kept in heaven for you, who by God's power are guarded through faith for a salvation ready to be revealed in the last time. . . . Without having seen him you love him; though you do not now see him you believe in him and rejoice with unutterable and exalted joy. As the outcome of your faith you obtain the salvation of your souls" (1 Pet. 1:3–5, 8–9).

175. Heb. 6:11–20; 7:19. "Let us hold fast the confession of our hope without wavering, for he who promised is faithful" (Heb. 10:23).

176. "Beloved, we are God's children now; it does not yet appear what we shall be, but we know that when he appears we shall be like him, for we shall see him as he is. And every one who thus hopes in him purifies himself as he is pure" (1 John 3:2–3; cf. 2 Pet. 3:11–13). "Therefore gird up your minds, be sober, set your hope fully upon the grace that is coming to you at the revelation of Jesus Christ" (1 Pet. 1:13).

177. "These all died in faith, not having received what was promised, but having seen it and greeted it from afar, and having acknowledged that they were strangers and exiles on the earth. . . . they desire a better country, that is, a heavenly one. . . . For here we have no lasting city, but we seek the city which is to come" (Heb. 11:13, 16; 13:14; cf. 11:1, 6, 39–40; James 1:12; 1 Pet. 5:4).

178. Rev. 7:16–17; 21:3–4; 22:3–5.

179. 2 Pet. 1:3–11. "And now, little children, abide in him, so that when he appears we may have confidence and not shrink from him in shame at his coming. If you know that he is righteous, you may be sure that every one who does right is born of him" (1 John 2:28–29).

180. Heb. 5:12–6:1; James 4:7–8; 1 Pet. 1:14–16; 2:1–2.

181. "Let us hold fast the confession of our hope without wavering, for he who promised is faithful; and let us consider how to stir up one another to love and good works. . . . Do not neglect to do good and to share what you have, for such sacrifices are pleasing to God. . . . Having purified your souls by your obedience to the truth for a sincere love of the brethren, love one another earnestly from the heart. . . . Above all hold unfailing your love for one another, since love covers a multitude of sins. Practice hospitality ungrudgingly to one another. . . . Beloved, let us love one another; for love is of God, and he who loves is born of God and knows God" (Heb. 10:23–24; 13:16; 1 Pet. 1:22; 4:8–9; 1 John 4:7; cf. Heb. 3:13; 10:25; 13:1–3; James 1:27; 2:1–9, 14–17; 1 Pet. 3:8–9; 1 John 2:9–11; 3:11, 16–19, 23; 4:11–12, 20–21; 2 John 5–6).

182. James 4:14.

183. James 3:9.

184. Mary Stewart Van Leeuwen, *The Person in Psychology* (Grand Rapids: William B. Eerdmans Publishing Company, 1985), 48; cf. 46–56.

185. Donald M. MacKay, *Human Science and Human Dignity* (Downers Grove, Ill.: InterVarsity Press, 1979), 114–17.

186. Rom. 5:1–2.

187. 1 John 4:10–11. Wright refers to the "double truth of God's attitude towards sinful human beings. As sinners, they need to die to sin; as human beings made in God's image, they need to have their true humanity reaffirmed and recreated in the resurrection" (*The Epistles of Paul to the Colossians and to Philemon*, 117).

188. Jacques Maritain, *Moral Philosophy* (London: Geoffrey Bles, 1964), 76–77. "The moral heroism to which we are in truth called [in Christianity] is attained neither by the athleticism of mystical concentration, after the Hindu manner, which claims to draw us into inner solitude in the absolute, nor by the athleticism of virtue, after the manner of the Stoics, which pretends to render us incapable of sin. It is attained through the force of another who descends into us and fills us with His plenitude, and by a love for Him which even in the depths of our weakness removes all obstacles to His love. . . . The Christian saint is not a superman formed by human agency, a Hercules of moral virtue like the Stoic sage; he is a friend of God who draws his life from supernatural charity and is formed by the divine hand, and who throws human weakness open to the divine plenitude descending into him. The vainglory of Man is dethroned, and humility, wherein lives the force of God, is exalted" (ibid., 74, 84).

189. John Cole, "Holy Trinity a Light amidst Darkness," *The Times,* 5 May 1988.

190. Jean Zizioulas, *Being as Communion: Studies in Personhood and the Church* (Crestwood, N.Y.: St. Vladimir's Seminary Press, 1985), 17, 49–54, 56, 64. "The goal of salvation is that the personal life which is realized in God should also be realized on the level of human existence. Consequently salvation is identified with the realization of personhood in man" (ibid., 50). Cf. Robert L. Pavelsky, "The Commandment of Love and the Christian Clinical Psychologist," in *Current Perspectives in the Psychology of Religion,* ed. H. Newton Malony (Grand Rapids: William B. Eerdmans Publishing Company, 1977), 414–18; Stanley Hauerwas, *A Community of Character: Toward a Constructive Christian Social Ethic* (Notre Dame, Ind.: University of Notre Dame Press, 1981).

191. "Identification with Christ should result in a focus away from the egoecentric concern with that 'self which we truly are' to a Christocentric emphasis on that which we can become in Christ (Galatians 2:20). Such an identification can form the basis for deep and meaningful relationships with others who have had a similar experience" (Gordon Stanley, "Sensitization Techniques and Interpersonal Relations," in *Behavioural Sciences: A Christian Perspetive,* ed. Malcolm A. Jeeves [Leicester: Inter-Varsity Press, 1984], 200).

192. E. W. Kemp, ed., *Man: Fallen and Free* (Hodder & Stoughton, 1969), 145.

193. Zizioulas, *Being as Communion,* 15, 105–8.

194. John Macmurray, *Persons in Relation* (London: Faber and Faber Limited, 1961), 211. "We need one another to be ourselves. This complete and unlimited dependence of each of us upon the others is the central and crucial fact of personal existence. Individual independence is an illusion; and the independent individual, the isolated self, is a nonentity" (ibid.; cf. 27).

195. 2 Cor. 5:17; Philem. 2:1–4; Zizioulas, *Being as Communion,* 64; Macmurray, *Persons in Relation,* 157–59. ". . . the realisation that all men are one man in Christ, the new Adam, that our life is with our brother, and that it is in the intense realisation of the unity of all men that we shall discover the true uniqueness of our own personal being" (Kemp, *Man: Fallen and Free,* 151).

196. Matt. 16:25.

197. 1 Cor. 13; Col. 3:1–4, 12–17.

198. 1 Cor. 15:19, 32.

199. Rom. 6:511; Philem. 3:20–21.

200. Col. 3:3–4.

201. Col. 1:27. Wright, *The Epistles of Paul to the Colossians and to Philemon,* 132–33.

202. Josef Pieper, *On Hope* (San Francisco: Ignatius Press, 1986), 40; cf. 34–35, 42–43.

203. Kemp, *Man: Fallen and Free,* 105–7, 109, 128–30.

204. Rev 4–5; 21–22; Maritain, *Moral Philosophy,* 75–76, 80, 83.